Advertising the Self in Renaissance France

THE EARLY MODERN EXCHANGE

Series Editors
Gary Ferguson, University of Virginia; Meredith K. Ray, University of Delaware

Series Editorial Board
Frederick A. de Armas, University of Chicago; Valeria Finucci, Duke University; Barbara Fuchs, UCLA; Nicholas Hammond, University of Cambridge; Kathleen P. Long, Cornell University; Elissa B. Weaver, Emerita, University of Chicago

The Early Modern Exchange publishes studies of European literature and culture (c. 1450–1700) exploring connections across intellectual, geographical, social, and cultural boundaries: transnational, transregional engagements; networks and processes for the development and dissemination of knowledges and practices; gendered and sexual roles and hierarchies and the effects of their transgression; relations between different ethnic or religious groups; travel and migration; textual circulation/s. The series welcomes critical approaches to multiple disciplines (e.g., literature and law, philosophy, science, medicine, music, etc.) and objects (e.g., print and material culture, the visual arts, architecture), the reexamination of historiographical categories (such as medieval, early modern, modern), and the investigation of resonances across broad temporal spans.

Titles in the Series
Involuntary Confessions of the Flesh in Early Modern France, Nora Martin Peterson
The Enemy in Italian Renaissance Epic: Images of Hostility from Dante to Tasso, Andrea Moudarres
Advertising the Self in Renaissance France: Lemaire, Marot, and Rabelais, Scott Francis

Advertising the Self in Renaissance France

Lemaire, Marot, and Rabelais

Scott Francis

UNIVERSITY OF DELAWARE PRESS
Newark
Distributed by the University of Virginia Press

University of Delaware Press
© 2019 by Scott Francis
All rights reserved
Printed in the United States of America on acid-free paper

First published 2019
1 3 5 7 9 8 6 4 2

Library of Congress Cataloging-in-Publication Data is available for this title.

Cover art: Étienne Dolet's printer's mark, title page of Claude Baduel, *Cl. Baduelli oratio funebris in Floretae Sarrasiae habita*, Lyon: Étienne Dolet, 1542. (FC5 B1449 5420, f. A1r, Kislak Center for Special Collections, Rare Books, and Manuscripts, University of Pennsylvania)

À mes treschers frères et sœurs, tous enfants d'Apollon,
et tous bons pantagruélistes

Contents

Acknowledgments ix
List of Abbreviations xi
Author's Note xiii

Introduction 1

Part I. "Ung petit tableau de mon industrie": Jean Lemaire de Belges and Gratitude for Historiography

1. The Judgment of the Reader in the *Illustrations de Gaule et singularitez de Troye* 19
2. Lemaire's Genius in the *Concorde des deux langages* 53

Part II. Clément Marot, or Proteus in Print

3. "Quel bien par rime on a": Authorial and Printerly Personae in the *Adolescence clementine* 81
4. "Je n'en donne ung festu, pourveu qu'ayons son livre": The *Suite* and the 1538 *Œuvres* 112

Part III. The Cure Is the Disease: Self-Fashioning and Charlatanism in François Rabelais's Prologues

5. The Prophylactic Prologues of *Pantagruel* and *Gargantua* 139
6. Rabelais, Doctor of Iatrosophism 167

Afterword: The Triumph of Advertising		185
Appendix: Marot Editions and Their Contents		189
Notes		197
Bibliography		233
Index		257

Acknowledgments

The point of departure for this book was my doctoral dissertation, "Authorial Personae, Ideal Readers, and Advertising for the Book in Lemaire, Marot, and Rabelais," which I defended at Princeton in May 2012. My thanks to François Rigolot, Sarah Kay, François Cornilliat, and Kevin and Marina Brownlee for their invaluable advice in researching and writing the dissertation, and in reworking it into a book. My thanks as well to my colleagues in the French section of the Department of Romance Languages for playing Mercury to my Amant Vert (or if you prefer, Pantagruel to my Panurge) during my first years at Penn.

I could not have undertaken this project without the generous assistance of the Georges Lurcy Charitable and Educational Trust, whose fellowship afforded me the opportunity to do primary research in Europe in 2009–10. I would like to thank the staff of the Bibliothèque nationale de France, the École Normale Supérieure, the Bibliothèque Municipale d'Orléans, the British Library, the Folger Shakespeare Library, Princeton University Library, Rutgers University Library, the Rosenbach Museum and Library, and the University of Pennsylvania's Kislak Center for Special Collections, Rare Books, and Manuscripts for their assistance and, where relevant, for the permission to use images from their collections.

Chapter 6 appeared in an earlier form as "La publicité iatrosophiste de Rabelais: *Captatio benevolentiae* et *persona* de l'auteur" in *L'Année Rabelaisienne* 1 (Paris: Classiques Garnier, 2017): 183–202. I am grateful to Classiques Garnier for their permission to reuse this material. I am equally grateful to the University of California Press and to Jim Frame for the permission to use Donald M. Frame's *The Complete Works of François Rabelais* in Chapters 5–6.

Last, but not least, I'd like to thank all my *seiziémiste* friends and colleagues for the intellectual stimulation, kind words, and convivial company with which they've provided me since I entered the field. And of course, I'd like to thank my parents, Keith and Patricia Francis, without whom none of this would have been possible.

Abbreviations

BHR	*Bibliothèque d'humanisme et Renaissance*
BNF	Bibliothèque nationale de France
CL	*Cinquiesme Livre*
ENS	École Normale Supérieure, Paris
ER	*Études Rabelaisiennes*
G	*Gargantua*
LCL	*Loeb Classical Library*
NRB	Stephen Rawles and Michael Screech, *A New Rabelais Bibliography*, ER 20 (Geneva: Droz, 1987)
OC	Clément Marot, *Œuvres complètes*, ed. François Rigolot, vols. 1–2 (Paris Garnier, 2007–9)
OPC	Clément Marot, *Œuvres poétiques complètes*, ed. Gérard Defaux, vols. 1–2 (ParisBordas, 1990–93)
P	*Pantagruel*
QL	*Quart Livre*
Recueil-*Epistre*	Jean Lemaire de Belges, *Epistre du Roy a Hector de Troye, et aucunes aultres oeuvres assez dignes de veoir*
TL	*Tiers Livre*

Author's Note

In citing sixteenth-century editions of Lemaire, Marot, and Rabelais, I have respected the original orthography and accentuation, with two exceptions. In keeping with modern usage, I have resolved abbreviations ("et" for "&," "devant" for "devãt," etc.) and distinguished between "i" and "j" and "u" and "v." For the sake of clarity, I have also added modernized punctuation and capitalization where appropriate. Unless otherwise noted, all translations are my own.

Advertising the Self in Renaissance France

Introduction

THE PROLOGUE TO the 1546 *Tiers Livre* details François Rabelais's concern that his book, a peculiar blend of philosophical inquiry and often-crude comedy, will not be to his readers' liking. The French Lucian, so called by his adversaries for his supposed irreligion, relates his anxiety with an anecdote from his Samosatan namesake, "To One Who Said, 'You're a Prometheus in Words,'" in which Lucian wonders whether the compliment for his originality is backhanded.[1] Prometheus's fashioning of humans from clay was original, and so too are Lucian's lectures in that they combine philosophical dialogue with humor, but originality is not necessarily a good thing. On the contrary, something novel, but ugly, as Prometheus's men turned out to be once beset by the evils released from Pandora's box, deserves to be destroyed. Ptolemy, Alexander the Great's general and ruler of Egypt from 323 to 283 BCE, learned this lesson the hard way when he tried to win over his Egyptian subjects by showing them two marvels he had won from his conquests, a black Bactrian camel and a slave who was white on one side of his body and black on the other. Far from being impressed, Ptolemy's subjects were frightened and offended by the camel, and either amused by or appalled at the slave.[2] Like Lucian, Rabelais worries that his book will backfire on him in the same way that Ptolemy's display backfired: "Cestuy exemple me faict entre espoir et craincte varier, doubtant que pour contentement propensé, je rencontre ce que je abhorre: mon thesaur soit charbons: pour Venus adviegne Barbet le chien: en lieu de les servir, je les fasche: en lieu de les esbaudir, je les offense: en lieu de leurs complaire, je desplaise." [This example makes me oscillate between hope and fear, afraid that in place of anticipated contentment I encounter what I abhor, my treasure proves to be lumps of coal, instead of Venus, I come up with Whiskers the dog, instead of serving them I offend them, instead of pleasing them I displease.]³

Rabelais evokes the broad possibilities and daunting risks for those who distribute their books in print. The printing press, capable of producing books faster and in greater number than copyists working by hand, brought with it the hope of reaching and winning over more readers than previously possible. It also brought the fear that these readers, whose proclivities, priorities, and manners of reading and interpreting the author could not ascertain as readily as those of a specific dedicatee or courtly milieu, would react less favorably than the author would hope. Having one's works printed was potentially a very profitable venture, less in terms of direct remuneration from sales—writers typically saw little, if anything, of this revenue—than in terms of prestige and the ability to attract patrons, but it also meant exposing oneself to piracy, unauthorized appropriation, and misinterpretation. If the Renaissance and the transition from manuscript to print culture marked the birth of the modern author whose death Roland Barthes notoriously proclaimed, this birth was accompanied by a sense of losing control over one's work.⁴ Instead of striking gold, an author may end up with a lump of coal in keeping with the Erasmian adage "Thesaurus carbones erant" ["The treasure consisted of coals"].⁵ It is akin to playing at games of chance, as Rabelais suggests in his allusion to knucklebones: "Venus" is the highest possible score for any given throw, whereas "Whiskers the dog" is the lowest. To use analogous terms from craps, by publishing the *Tiers Livre*, Rabelais hopes to roll boxcars, but risks rolling snake eyes.

If printing was risky business for authors, it was no less risky for printers or booksellers. In 1538, eight years before the first printing of the *Tiers Livre*, the Lyonnais printer/bookseller François Juste—whose shop brought out the *princeps* edition of Rabelais's *Gargantua* (1534/5)—appended a letter to Jacques Colin's translation of Castiglione's *Corteggiano*, edited by Étienne Dolet. In this letter, addressed to Jean du Peyrat, the king's Lieutenant General in Lyon, Juste gives a dramatic account of how the book came to be.⁶ Claiming that several of his friends and acquaintances have long been clamoring for a translation of Castiglione, Juste tells of the considerable lengths to which he has gone in convincing the reluctant Colin to hand over his translation for printing, "Ce que je n'ay peu facilement sans en desbourcer gros deniers, et oultre ce user des prieres et requestes de mes bons seigneurs et amys envers celluy, qui pour riens ne le vouloit laisser aller hors de sa main: ou, comme il disoit, le conservoit entier des calumnies envieuses" [Which I wasn't able to do without spending a fortune, and beyond that, relying on the prayers and requests my good lords and friends made of that man, who didn't want to let go of it for anything; he said he was keeping it safe from jealous slander].[7] Colin seems to share Rabelais's fear of unfavorable reception, and would rather not risk exposing his work to this sort of blame.

However, Juste learns that he has been beaten to the punch not once, but twice, as Colin's translation has already been printed, first in Paris, and then in Lyon.[8] Worse still, these editions contain faulty translations, not due to any mistakes on Colin's part, but to the carelessness of their printers. At this point, Juste launches into a diatribe on how a few bad apples are spoiling the entire printerly barrel:

> Et pource ja long temps a nous autres imprimeurs, par l'avarice d'aulcuns meuz plustost du gaing que de l'honneur, qui doibt estre et veritablement est le plus asseure et permanent loyer de bien faire, en sommes en tresmauvaise reputation: de manière que si n'estoit qu'on ne se peult bonnement passer de noz ouvrages, seroient laisses en noz boutiques les livres pour estre ronges des teignes, et soris.

> [And this is why we other printers have long had a nasty reputation, thanks to the greed of some who are driven more by profit than by honor, which should be and truly is the surest and most permanent reward for doing good. It's such a problem that if it weren't the case that people can't rightly do without our works, the books would be left in our shops to be gnawed at by moths and mice.][9]

Printers/booksellers' prospects hinged upon their reputation for accuracy and craftsmanship. It is no surprise, then, that Juste refers to the books he and his colleagues printed and sold as "noz ouvrages"; they were as much their work as that of the authors who wrote them. While they derived greater monetary gain from their sale than the authors did, they were also likelier to incur a direct loss if the books failed to sell, which is why Juste concludes his diatribe with the mercantile nightmare of his wares being left to rot and get devoured by vermin. Printers also ran an equal or greater risk than authors did of experiencing reprisals for faulty, controversial, or heretical works, and in many cases, they were more recognizable and easier for both readers and the authorities to track down than writers were.[10]

Especially in its earlier years, printing was a very expensive venture from a material standpoint alone, to say nothing of the cost of labor and transportation. To give an idea of how expensive it could be to print a book, Rudolf Hirsch, based on his study of paper prices in Frankfurt from 1401 to 1536, estimates that for a 250-page book (*in folio*) produced in a fairly limited run of one hundred copies, the paper alone would have cost almost as much as six tons of wheat did in the late fifteenth century.[11] While paper quality and format size tended to decrease as the sixteenth century progressed, resulting in books that were cheaper to produce and more affordable, a work of literature or history was still a considerable purchase for all but the wealthiest of buyers. According to Natalie Zemon Davis, in the 1540s, a history of France could cost as much as a day's wages for a journeyman.[12] Given that such works were so expensive, most printers, in France as elsewhere in Europe, focused on books or printed materials for which there was a known and steady demand, such as liturgical manuals or ephemera required by municipal or ecclesiastical authorities. Vernacular literary works accounted for a small fraction of their production, and they were more likely to favor texts inherited from the past that were still popular, like prose adaptations of *chansons de geste* or romances, than vernacular works by new authors, especially in the first quarter of the sixteenth century.[13] If they were willing to print a work by an unestablished author, it was a calculated risk.[14]

As for Colin's translation of Castiglione, Juste is fortunate enough to have had a clientele who "can't rightly do without" what he had to sell. His letter points at a way to make printing and selling books less aleatory, to load the dice, as it were: either produce something that readers want, or convince potential readers that they should want what you're printing. Where demand is smaller and reception less certain, authors and printers try to put readers in a favorable frame of mind and convince them of the utility, or even the necessity, of a given literary work. Of course, they cannot compel readers to fall in line, and one could characterize the history of reception as a struggle between the attempted imposition of authority and the reader's irrepressible freedom, as Roger Chartier does.[15] Nevertheless, the uncertainty of success did not deter authors and printers in the Renaissance from using the persuasive techniques at their disposal, and it for this reason that print culture marks the birth of modern advertising.

Advertising: A Rhetorical Approach to the Problem of Supply and Demand

Scholars have put advertising in dialogue with literature on multiple occasions, but they have overwhelmingly focused on the nineteenth and early twentieth centuries.[16] A small few have taken this approach to premodern works, as Andrew Cowell does in his account of wine crying in two medieval French plays, the *Jeu de Saint Nicolas* and *Courtois d'Arras*.[17] Intuitively, this discrepancy would seem to make sense. Is it even possible to speak of premodern advertising without falling into the trap of anachronism or robbing advertising of its historical specificity? Is Elizabeth Eisenstein right to describe printed books as inventions uniquely capable of advertising for themselves?[18]

To answer these questions, we must first understand what is meant by the term "advertising." Etymologically, it derives from the Latin *adverto*, which means "to turn toward," "to direct," or "to steer," and can be used to convey either physical motion or attention and consideration.[19] In this most basic sense, "advertising" is something that draws attention for one purpose or another, much like its French cognate *avertissement*. In a commercial context, this kind of "advertising" is not specific to any historical period, and things like tavern signs or *si quis* (the ancestor of the classified ad) could be called premodern advertising.[20] In this vein, Eisenstein points out that the term "avertissement" originates in the colophons of books copied in the medieval scriptoria of the Low Countries during holy days, and was used to indicate that these books were not for sale.[21] However, these forms of advertisement are more informative than persuasive, and the same may be said of early advertisements in the book trade, which, much like the *si quis*, predominantly indicated at which shop or stall a certain book could be purchased.[22]

Consequently, cultural critics who attempt to trace the history of advertising make a point of distinguishing between advertising in the general sense and advertising in the modern sense of the term. Raymond Williams defines advertising as "an institutionalized system of commercial information and persuasion" that was born with the mass production of goods in the Industrial Revolution and developed fully with the rise of monopoly capitalism between 1880 and 1930.[23] Mass production inevitably creates situations where supply vastly outpaces demand, and advertising addresses this gap by creating demand for a product and turning potential consumers into actual consumers.

Yet, if Juste's letter is any indication, sixteenth-century printers were not unfamiliar with gaps between supply and demand and the dangers they pose for business, which would suggest that premodern commerce had no less a need for advertising than its modern equivalent does. Indeed, Williams's own account casts doubt on the rigidity of his definitions, as he claims that as early as the eighteenth century, sophisticated advertising techniques were used to sell goods such as pills, soaps, hats, and sensational literature. He even admits that there is an "obvious continuity between the methods used to sell pills and washballs in the eighteenth century and the methods used in the twentieth century to sell anything from a drink to a political party." What distinguishes advertising before 1914 from advertising after 1914, he claims, is its "comparative crudeness," which should be "immediately evident" to all those who look at it.[24] At least as far as printed editions are concerned, the persuasive games that play out between author, printer/bookseller, and reader are anything but crude, even if they first arose prior to industrialization and modern mass media. Of course, I do not claim that there are no differences between persuasive techniques from different eras with different technologies or between techniques designed to sell different goods or services. I do contend that advertising is a useful concept for understanding how early modern printed books were conceived of and presented to the reader, because the ways in which advertising represents the producer and the consumer closely resemble the ways in which early modern books represent the author, the editor, the printer, and the reader.

Prestige Advertising, *Captatio Benevolentiae*, and the Authorial or Printerly Persona

In *The Language of Advertising*, Torben Vestergaard and Kim Schrøder refer to a concept they call "prestige advertising" or "goodwill advertising," which does not advertise a product or service so much as a positive image of its producers or of the care and expertise that go into making it. In this regard, prestige advertising is quite similar to what is meant by the term "publicity" in English, though French more fully conveys the proximity of advertising to publicity by using one word (*publicité*) to denote both. The image created by prestige advertising addresses concerns over the incompatibility, real or perceived, between mass production and quality by portraying the product as artisanal, and allays distrust of the profit motive by portraying the producer as charitable toward the consumer.[25] For example, beer commercials often stress the pride and craftsmanship that go into brewing, spotlighting brewmasters and other workers or recalling the beer's origins so as to suggest that their methods have changed little since the days of yore.

Prestige advertising and publicity are not radically new innovations of twentieth-century marketing, however. They are simply modern permutations of persuasive techniques dating back at least to the formal treatises of classical rhetoric. Insofar as their purpose is to pave the way for favorable reception, prestige advertising and publicity are tantamount to rhetorical *captatio benevolentiae* ["securing good will"]. In the same way that modern producers have recourse to modern advertising techniques in their effort to put forth a positive image of themselves, early modern authors, printers, editors, and booksellers had recourse to rhetorical techniques for fashioning a public persona.

Classical rhetorical treatises, such as those of Aristotle, Cicero, and Quintilian, who had been "rediscovered" by Poggio Bracciolini at St. Gallen in 1416, were well known and widely available, and were printed and reprinted numerous times beginning in the late fifteenth century.[26] The evangelical humanism of the Reformation also sought to restore classical rhetoric to prominence and to reconcile it with Pauline Christianity, as attested to by Philip Melanchthon's *Institutiones Rhetoricae* (1521). Vernacular translations and adaptations such as Pierre Fabri's *Le grand et vrai art de pleine rhétorique* (1521), whose first part closely follows the *Rhetorica ad Herennium* dubiously attributed to Cicero, were also common. Sixteenth-century authors and printers versed in the Classics thus had access to a set of references on how to put one's audience in a propitious state of mind for reception. As Fabri describes it, *captatio* "n'est aultre chose que d'appareiller les courages des auditeurs a croire ou a faire ce que on veult, et soy mettre en leur grace" [is nothing other than preparing listeners' hearts to believe or do what one wishes, and getting in their good graces].[27] A closer look at some of the most prominent rhetorical treatises reveals how they portray public speaking as a continual process of image adjustment, which, according to Aristotle's *Rhetoric*, is one of the most effective means of persuasion.[28]

The *Rhetorica ad Herennium* situates *captatio benevolentiae* within the canon of *inventio*, as it entails finding the best way to make an initial appeal to listeners. It specifies that orators should aim to make listeners not only well-disposed (*"benivolus"*) toward them and toward their cause, but also attentive (*"adtentus"*) and receptive (*"docilis"*), which is more properly rendered as "teachable" or "willing to learn," as it derives from the verb *doceo* ["to teach"].[29] Attentiveness and willingness to learn may be inspired by promising to speak of something important and useful to the audience, whereas good will may be assured by praising oneself or one's audience and blaming one's opponents.[30] Orators must shape themselves, or rather the way in which their listeners perceive them, according to the latter's opinions and preferences: "Semper oratorum eloquentiae moderatrix fuit auditorum prudentia. Omnes enim qui probari volunt voluntatem eorum qui audiunt intuentur ad eamque et ad eorum arbitrium et nutum totos se fingunt et accommodant" [The eloquence of orators has always been controlled by the good sense of the audience, since all who desire to win approval have regard to the goodwill of their auditors, and shape and adapt themselves completely according to this and to their opinion and approval].[31] The orator is a creature of perception tailored to the audience's desires, and is as much an actor as a speaker. Through *captatio*, the orator puts on a persona in the Latin sense of an actor's mask, a meaning also conveyed by the Middle French terms *personne* and *personnage*. These are, in fact, the very terms that the *Rhetorica ad Herennium* and Fabri use to describe how orators should present themselves to their audience.[32]

The persona is of the utmost importance to reception, as it is the means by which the audience forms an idea of the speaker's intentions and motivations. According to Aristotle, the most important element of a favorable persona is nobility of character, which consists of magnanimity, generosity, and concern with the needs of others rather than one's own needs.[33] If orators adopt such personae before their audiences, authors, printers, and booksellers also adopt them in the text and paratext of printed books in hopes of training their readers to desire a book that they have not personally commissioned. The persona is prestige advertising for authors, printers, booksellers, and editors: it is the guise in which they appear before buyers and readers as benevolent and conscientious producers of an object of commerce.

As with any form of commerce, an exchange between bookseller and book buyer, as well as an exchange between author and reader, depends upon the integrity of those involved in the exchange.[34] The authorial persona provides a sense of this integrity by reassuring readers of the author's good intentions in writing a book and in having it printed and sold, and the printerly persona reassures readers that the producers of the physical volume are more dedicated to their craft and to the advancement of knowledge than to the pursuit of profit, which they are willing to sacrifice if need be. This is the case in Juste's letter, in which he portrays himself as willing to part with "gros deniers" [a large amount of money] to preserve "l'honneur et diligence mienne, et de ceulx, des presses desquelz yssent plus propres, et nets ouvrages" [my honor and diligence and that of others, whose presses put out even more correct and neat works].[35] Authorial and printerly personae also stress the artisanal qualities of the printed book so as to allay misgivings about the inaccuracies and human error inherent in all but the most painstaking printing jobs. In discussing Erasmus's representation of Aldus Manutius in the adage "Festina lente," Leah Chang contends that the Dutch humanist puts forth "a fiction of good printing, in which the ideal printer is elevated above the economic concerns of the market and imbued with the values that the scholar holds."[36] Of course, a printer concerned with the humanist restitution of *bonae litterae* [the texts and wisdom of classical antiquity] at the expense of profit (much like how Juste presents himself) is a rarity, if not an outright fantasy. Regardless, authorial and printerly personae are designed to perpetuate this sort of myth by stressing meticulous craftsmanship and an overriding concern for the reader's entertainment and edification, and by appearing to be exactly what the reader wants or needs.

The single biggest variable that sets print apart from oratory, though, is the fact that it has to deal with an unknown reader and all the uncertainty that reader entails.[37] *Captatio* is predicated on the immediacy of oratory and the speaker's knowledge of who is in the audience and how they are disposed before the speech even begins. Classical rhetoric thus provides a useful set of commonplaces and stylistic guidelines for addressing large assemblies in public forums or for pleading a case in court, but indicates no explicit rules for addressing a disparate group of people not united by fixity of place or perhaps even time.[38] How, then, can personae be tailored to the desires of an unknown reader? Part of the answer lies in the fact that the structure of the printed book corresponds to, and is often explicitly modeled on, rhetoric. In particular, the role of the prologue or *exordium* in a speech is filled by the paratext, notably the title pages and prefaces that saw a dramatic rise in prevalence during the Renaissance—a "preface boom," as Philippe Desan puts it.[39] The increasingly clear separation of paratext and text during this period, as well as the heavy emphasis on front matter, marked a departure from manuscript culture in that where scribal colophons came last, printers put the promotion of themselves and the authors they printed at the front of their volumes.[40] Paratext even served a very practical commercial purpose in the Renaissance: at the time, books were typically sold unbound and uncut, so instead of judging books by their covers, buyers could judge them by their title pages. The paratext is a space where seller-buyer and author-reader relationships are elaborated at the same time, and often in the same terms.[41]

Still, if authors or printers could make ready use of the paratext to advertise through their personae, this does not fully explain how they dealt with the problem of not knowing their readership as intimately as skilled orators know their audiences. After all, the goal of most every author (and of many printers) is not just to have their works be bought, but also to have them be read, and to be read how they wanted the works to be read, if for no other reason than because, at least in the sixteenth century, misprision could have severe consequences for texts of a political or religious nature. To deal with this unknown, authors and printers try to turn the unknown reader into the kind of reader they would prefer. This is what Susan Suleiman calls the rhetorical strain of reception theory, which describes forms of communication where the sender attempts to govern the receiver's behavior by compelling the receiver to follow certain instructions or inhabit a certain role; the critic's task is to determine how the rhetorical strategies of a given work invite this identification.[42] Suleiman's choice of the term "rhetorical" is quite apt, as classical rhetoric is not only concerned with influencing the audience's behavior, but also with inviting the audience to conform to an ideal of the orator's design, and if rhetorical skill "provides the meeting ground between text and reader," as William Kennedy puts it, it aims to ensure that this ground is of the producer's choosing.[43] In terms of printed books in the Renaissance, these concerns are borne out in what I will refer to as the "ideal reader," an image posited by the text and paratext and made accessible to the reader through the philosophical discourse of self-fashioning.

Fashioning the Ideal Reader

The term "ideal reader" has been used by a number of writers and theorists to mean a range of different things, and has often been met with skepticism.[44] For Wolfgang Iser, a chief theorist of the Constance School along with H. R. Jauss, it is a deliberately vague concept that can be summoned to answer nearly any interpretative quandary: a reader capable of exhausting all the meaning in a text or of reading a book in exactly the way its author intends.[45] In place of this imaginary construct, Iser posits what he calls the "implied reader," who fills in the indeterminate gaps in a text's structure and completes the work of art. The implied reader, while still hypothetical and not to be confused with real, historical readers, is more textually verifiable than the ideal reader as defined by Iser, and is not plagued by the latter's claims to omniscience, finality, or intentionality.[46]

When we approach reception theory from a rhetorical perspective, though, the ideal reader seems less like an imaginary criterion for how to read than a very real attempt on the part of the author to control reception in keeping with Suleiman's definition of rhetorical reception theory. One way to control reception is to hold up an idealized image of the reader that may be attained by reading and receiving the book in a certain way. In fact, the ideal reader as a model for reception may be traced to *captatio*, which describes an ideal audience to which the orator should make the real audience conform. An ideal listener would be attentive, well-disposed, and willing to learn right from the start, and the orator could dispense entirely with *captatio* if addressing such an ideal listener, which is why, for Aristotle, the strategies of *captatio* are a necessary concession designed to bring reality closer to the ideal.[47] In the same way, a book's indications of how it should be read are meant to bring real readers closer to the book's ideal reader. In the words of Guy Demerson, writers, like orators, prefer to deal only with prejudices favorable to their cause.[48]

In this sense, the ideal reader is a paragon toward which the real reader is encouraged to strive, much like Lowry Nelson's conceptualized "optimum reader," whose responses are written into the literary work itself and become normative for any individual performance. This "optimum reader" is capable of influencing how the real reader reads or prepares to read a book, as readers are given the task of being or of making themselves optimum.[49] Wayne Booth ties this identification to the distinction between the author and the implied author, the persona the author adopts in the text. The reader is asked to interact with this persona by becoming the kind of reader that will complement it: "The author creates, in short, an image of himself and another image of his reader; he makes his reader, as he makes his second self, and the most successful reading is one in which the created selves, author and reader, can find complete agreement."[50] In this respect, individual authors, and indeed individual texts, each have their own ideal reader that best suits their purposes.

If authors and printers cannot tailor a book to the desires of an unknown reader, then they can use ideal readers to teach real readers what and how to read. In the Renaissance, this persuasive technique was grounded in self-fashioning. Stemming from texts now regarded as quintessential expressions of Renaissance humanism, such as Erasmus's *On the Education of Children* or Pico's *Oration on the Dignity of Man*, self-fashioning is commonly taken to be an expression of faith in man's limitless potential for improvement, often through the educational projects so near and dear to humanists. More accurately, famous formulations such as Erasmus's "homines non nascuntur, sed finguntur" [men are not born, but made] or Pico's metaphor of man as chameleon portray the human being as indeterminate, and as Michel Jeanneret explains, the fact that humanistic self-fashioning is predicated on the lack of a definite human nature means that man's malleability carries both great potential and great risk.[51] This makes it an effective means of persuasion, especially for authors and printers, who readily advertise the positive effects of their own books and the negative effects of their competitors on self-fashioning. In fact, self-fashioning and rhetoric go hand in hand, as Stephen Greenblatt points out, in that rhetoric "implied that human character itself could be similarly fashioned, with an eye to audience and effect."[52]

As it so happens, self-fashioning is also one of the pillars of modern advertising, which itself posits human nature as indeterminate and in need of proper molding. However, whereas Renaissance thinkers tend to hold up a Christian humanist education as the proper basis on which to fashion oneself, advertising instead endows the product with this transformative power. As John Berger puts it, advertising "is never a celebration of a pleasure-in-itself . . . but is always about the future buyer. It offers him an image of himself made glamorous by the product or opportunity it is trying to sell."[53] The product is not the goal, but rather something that supposedly will help the consumer attain the idealized image of himself or herself presented in the ad. For example, a commercial for body spray isn't selling body spray, but the ability of body spray to bring out one's unique masculine allure that women will presumably find irresistible. This is why Vestergaard and Schrøder compare the role of the product to that of the adjuvant, or helper, in A.-J. Greimas's actantial model of narrative; the product is like a kind fairy godmother that helps us on our quest to become our ideal selves.[54]

The notion that we can come closer to an idealized version of ourselves directly connects modern consumerist culture to Renaissance humanism. As such, it should not come as a surprise that in his discussion of advertising as the "liberté précaire" [precarious freedom] to distinguish oneself based on the products one purchases, Jean Baudrillard calls it a "nouvel humanisme" [new humanism].[55] Judith Williamson defines advertising in similar terms, though she compares it to Sartrean existentialism rather than to humanism: "We are both product and consumer; we consume, buy the product, yet we *are* the product. Thus our lives become our own creations, through *buying*; an identikit of different images of ourselves, created by different products."[56]

Through the lens of authorial or printerly personae and ideal readership, we can see the printed editions of the Renaissance as the birthplace of modern advertising. They mark the first widespread use of prestige advertising and self-fashioning to address the difficulties posed by mass production, and they ultimately represent the book's producers and consumers in a way that would not be unfamiliar to anyone subjected to the barrage of commercials that is an inevitable aspect of life in contemporary society. To speak of advertising in print culture is therefore not a mere anachronistic comparison made for the convenience of the modern mind. Rather, historical and philological approaches to authorship, readership, and print culture can teach us about how advertising functions, and vice versa. To understand print culture or modern advertising, we must grasp how they advertise the self: the benevolent, yet fictional self that is the authorial or printerly persona, and the ideal self promised to the compliant reader or consumer.

Authorial Personae and Ideal Readers in Lemaire, Marot, and Rabelais

Advertising the Self in Renaissance France examines case studies of how authorial or printerly personae and ideal readers are crafted in sixteenth-century printed editions of French vernacular literary works by three authors: Jean Lemaire de Belges, Clément Marot, and François Rabelais. These authors were selected not only for their prominent place in the French Renaissance literary canon and for the fact that a filiation exists between them, but also because each of their particularly rich publication histories brings to light a different aspect of how personae and ideal readers can be used to advertise for a book and for its correct reading. Each of the three authors approached this enterprise with a distinct background and distinct aims, each was heavily invested in elaborating a certain authorial persona (or personae) and in convincing readers why their work, or a certain edition of their work, was important or useful, and each posited ideal readership according to his own aims and purposes.

Part One (Chapters 1–2) centers on Jean Lemaire de Belges (1473–c. 1524), the most prominent member of the generation of French-speaking poets referred to by scholars as the *Rhétoriqueurs*.[57] Lemaire spans the threshold between the Middle Ages and Renaissance and between the manuscript and print eras: he was one of the first *Rhétoriqueurs* to embrace the possibilities offered by print to disseminate a favorable authorial persona and to ensure that his works were received as he intended. While I focus on the years 1511–1513, which were marked by the publication of Lemaire's mythico-historical magnum opus, the *Illustrations de Gaule et singularitez de Troye*, and of what is now his most-studied work, the *Concorde des deux langages*, I also consider the printed afterlife of these works up to 1549.

Lemaire published the *Illustrations* at the height of the conflict between Louis XII and Pope Julius II not long after he left the service of Margaret of Austria, daughter of Holy Roman Emperor Maximilian I, to become Anne of Brittany's historiographer. He was also concerned with the growing influence of Italian letters in France, particularly the increasing vogue for Petrarchism and the presence of Italian historians like Michele Riccio at the French court. He wanted to reassure his royal patrons and the reading public of his loyalty to France, and to convince readers that they should prefer French history like the *Illustrations* to the Italian poetry that was becoming more and more popular among the literate public. To address these concerns, he appropriated the mythological framework of the Trojan War and the Judgment of Paris to represent his own work as a writer of history and to fashion an ideal readership favorable to his enterprise. Essentially, he associated Italy and Italian poetry with Venus, the life of pleasure, and effeminacy, and French history like the *Illustrations* with Pallas, the contemplative life, and masculinity, presenting himself and his work as belonging entirely to Pallas and encouraging the reader to make his or her own Judgment of Paris not only by reading the *Illustrations*, but also by approaching them as an authoritative text to be read allegorically. The publication history of the *Illustrations* and their accompanying pieces serves as an example of how the authorial persona and ideal readership can function in the context of political and cultural conflict, as well as of how masculinity can be used to advertise books and modes of reading.

Part Two (Chapters 3–4) focuses on Francis I's royal poet, Clément Marot (1496–1544), whose publication history is so prodigious that Gérard Defaux has called him the most popular French poet aside from Victor Hugo.[58] Marot's poetic corpus is notoriously perplexing and variegated, a blend of humorous accounts of his own misfortunes and financial difficulties, bawdy celebrations of sex, and sincere devotional poetry, including Psalm translations that would be sung by French-speaking Protestants for centuries. He also became one of the most vocal proponents of an author's right to exercise control over the publication of his works, only to see dozens of unauthorized editions of his works spring up like so many weeds in his carefully tended poetic garden. Marot's seemingly paradoxical nature has prompted François Rigolot to describe the poet, in keeping with Pico, as a chameleon who cannot be made to stay the same color.[59] Nevertheless, scholarly understanding of the man and his work has been heavily influenced by Defaux, who produced what is still regarded as the definitive critical edition of Marot's works in 1990–1993. Defaux sees Marot as a committed evangelical who used the printing press to disseminate his message, and he tries to pigeonhole as many aspects of Marot's complicated publication history into this persona as possible. However, scholars have recently returned in earnest to Marot's thorny publication history, which has forced us to reconsider Defaux's version of the poet. Rigolot's 2009 edition of Marot's complete works breaks with precedent by starting with the 1532 *Adolescence clementine* and indicating which works were added over time to create the *Suite de l'Adolescence,* the 1538 *Œuvres,* and subsequent editions, giving a clear sense of the extent to which Marot's printed works were in a continual state of flux and evolution. Additionally, Guillaume Berthon's

L'Intention du poète: Clément Marot "autheur" debunks a number of Defaux's assumptions, as will Berthon's forthcoming and sorely needed new bibliography of Marot. In keeping with these developments, I refuse to force Marot into a given mold, and instead show that his publication history is itself a series of attempts to impose a fixed meaning upon a vast and varied body of work through the manipulation of the author's persona.

Given Marot's centrality to the development of authorial self-consciousness in the Renaissance, scholars have tended to focus on his attempts to assert control over the printing and distribution of his works, and hence on his authorized editions.[60] I examine both authorized and unauthorized editions of Marot's collected poetic works from the 1532 *Adolescence clementine*, the first authorized collection, to the monumental 1538 *Œuvres*. In both authorized and unauthorized editions—the latter of which comprise the vast majority of Marot's publication record—Marot's editors and printers promote their own personae and establish a connivance with the reader. Marot's persona is a product of the choices made by different printers and editors, especially with regard to the order in which they placed his works and the evolution (or lack thereof) this order implies. By giving equal weight to authorized and unauthorized editions, we can see that Marot was a product not only of how he chose to represent himself, but also of how printers chose to advertise him and his oeuvre to their readership.[61]

Part Three (Chapters 5–6) turns to François Rabelais (c. 1483–1553), every bit as chameleonic a figure as Marot, and the most well-documented French Renaissance writer alongside Michel de Montaigne and Pierre de Ronsard. Rabelais's prologues, in particular, have long been the site of lively scholarly debates on how to interpret Rabelais's persona or that of his narrator, Alcofrybas Nasier, as well as the promises they make and the instructions they give to the reader. I do not claim to have resolved so rich and complicated an issue, but in the context of advertising books and modes of reading, I show how Rabelais drew on rhetoric, medicine, and farce to encourage the reader to take a critical distance from ideal readership and promises of self-fashioning. In the paratexts of each of the five entries in the *Geste Pantagruéline*, he calls attention to the way in which promising a transformative experience to the reader invents a problem so as to offer a solution to it, instilling in readers a sense of lack and inspiring the thirst etymologically connected with Pantagruel's name in what Romain Menini calls "tantaltération."[62] This approach not only reveals the profound irony of Rabelais's prologues, but also sets Rabelais apart as an author who practices advertising in order to call it into question.

Part I

"Ung petit tableau de mon industrie"

*Jean Lemaire de Belges and
Gratitude for Historiography*

On peut comme l'argent trafiquer la louange. [As with money, one can traffic in praise.]
—Joachim Du Bellay, *Les Regrets*, 152

CHAPTER I

The Judgment of the Reader in the *Illustrations de Gaule et singularitez de Troye*

JEAN LEMAIRE DE BELGES has long enjoyed a privileged status among the poets of his generation, as critics have tended to see an anticipation of Renaissance evangelical humanism in his engagement with classical authors and scathing denunciation of ecclesiastical abuse, often pointing to the fact that Rabelais and Marot both acknowledge his influence. Even Henri Guy, the Third Republic critic whose sweeping disdain for the *Rhétoriqueurs* is manifest, calls Lemaire their corypheus.[1] Where Lemaire truly stands apart from his peers, though, is with respect to how he crafts the relationship between writer and reader. How that relationship is altered by print is a question that critics have tended to approach from the perspective of the poet/patron relationship, and with good reason. In the early years of the Italian Wars (1494–1559), patrons on all sides relied on writers to justify their policies to the public, a process made easier by printing. Writers' literary power thus became inextricably linked with the political power of their protectors, so as they used print culture to shape how others would perceive their current or potential patrons, they learned to promote their own identity and authority.[2] Lemaire himself was no stranger to producing works in verse and prose meant to justify his patrons' policies: the *Concorde du genre humain* praises Margaret of Austria, the Duchess of Savoy and regent of the Netherlands, for her role in negotiating the League of Cambrai against Venice in December 1508; the *Légende des Vénitiens* praises France's participation in the ensuing war; and the *Traicté de la différence des schismes et des conciles de l'Eglise* defends the Council of Pisa, convened by Louis XII in May 1511 with the aim of deposing his nemesis, Pope Julius II.

What is perhaps less obvious than Lemaire's eagerness to participate in these propaganda campaigns is how he justified his participation by insisting on his capacity as a writer of history. Michael Sherman underscores this metadiscursive element in Lemaire by showing how the *Légende des Vénitiens* makes a case for the importance of historiographers in explaining and publicizing the actions of kings to the world outside the court.[3] Reflection on historiography is a common trait across the different generations of *Rhétoriqueurs*, especially Georges Chastelain and Jean Molinet, who preceded Lemaire as *indiciaire* at the Burgundian court, a position that comprised the duties of chronicler, poet, advisor, and delegate. In a 1508 letter to Charles Le Clerc, Lemaire reflects upon the etymology of the title, equating it with "demonstrator" and asserting that an *indiciaire*'s duty is not only to record events, but also to discern their significance for the past, present, and future, which makes the position so demanding that it may only be given to someone who most convincingly proves the power of his wit ["au mieulx monstrant la force de son engin"].[4] An *indiciaire* must therefore attest to his own abilities as he recounts and interprets historical events: the writing of history necessarily entails self-representation.

The conventions of print, especially of the paratext, facilitate this sort of self-representation, uniting a vast and varied body of work through the presence of the author.[5] Lemaire was the first of the *Rhétoriqueurs* to take full advantage of this possibility, and an examination of his publication history reveals one of the key differences between manuscript and print culture: in manuscripts, writers make their work apparent to the reader through formal virtuosity, whereas in print, they do so through paratextual discourse.[6] Yet, authorial self-representation is only half the story in Lemaire's printed works. The other half is the way in which Lemaire constructs his readers and guides their reception, and scholars dealing with this aspect have tended to ground it in his relationship with patrons like Margaret of Austria or Anne of Brittany, or with other prominent readers like Claude of France or the future Charles V. While Lemaire does address these specific readers, he also envisions a broader public to which he tailors both his own image as an author and the reader's image. In Cynthia Brown's words, Lemaire realized that "he had to sell 'himself'—his genius or his vision—as a way of selling his work, that he had to satisfy a public (and not simply a patron) by guiding its reading."[7]

This interdependence between Lemaire's and the reader's image comes to the fore in Lemaire's magnum opus, the *Illustrations de Gaule et singularitez de Troye*, a three-part historical treatise that details how European rulers descended from Noah through Hercules of Libya and the House of Troy. Most modern scholars have preferred to focus on Lemaire's poetry or polemics rather than on a work as ponderous and plodding as the *Illustrations* often are, especially Book Three with its dry Merovingian genealogy, but they were by far the most influential and well known of Lemaire's works in the first half of the sixteenth century. Even the Pléiade, usually so disdainful of previous generations of French poets, saw in the *Illustrations* a welcome contribution to the illustration of the French language: Jacques Peletier du Mans and Joachim du Bellay praised them, while Pierre de Ronsard drew on them for the *Franciade*. No fewer than nineteen editions of the *Illustrations* were published between 1511 and 1549, though their fortunes declined sharply in the second half of the century after Lemaire's works were put on the Index in 1549 on account of their pro-conciliar stance.

Part of the *Illustrations'* success may be attributed to the felicity with which Lemaire advertises his own use of first (prose) and second (verse) rhetoric and their salubrious effects on the reader. All three books of the *Illustrations* are strewn with examples of orations and the effects they produce in their listeners for good or for ill, so much so that the *Illustrations* are an account of rhetoric and its efficacy as much as of the genealogy of Europe's ruling houses.[8] This is most readily apparent in Book One's account of the Judgment of Paris. After insisting upon Paris's freedom to forge his own path despite his youth and Venereal disposition, Lemaire shows how Venus clouds the young prince's judgment with a display of rhetorical virtuosity. In so doing, he invites readers to identify with Paris and realize that in order to avoid repeating the prince's mistake, they must embrace the historical truth and exemplarity that only a writer like him can provide, a service for which they should display gratitude through favorable reception and eagerness for further works by him. In a word, Lemaire uses the Judgment of Paris to advertise for the *Illustrations* and his work as a historiographer.

As Tom Conley has shown in his analysis of the *Illustrations'* paratext, Lemaire is an effect of his own writing, and it falls to readers to decipher this creative personality who will accompany them as they read.[9] I would add that readers are meant not only to discern Lemaire's personality, or rather his persona, but also to realize how this persona and the writing for which it is responsible can help them fashion themselves for the better. This interaction between authorial persona and ideal readership defines the paratext of the *Illustrations* and the role of such accompanying works as the *Épîtres de l'Amant*

Vert, included at the conclusion of Book One, and the *Epistre du Roy a Hector de Troye, et aucunes aultres oeuvres assez dignes de veoir* (or "recueil-*Epistre*" for short), a collection containing Lemaire's most commented-upon work, the *Concorde des deux langages*. It is is crucial that the *Illustrations* be read alongside these works, as they were meant to be published and bound together in what is now called a composite volume, or *Sammelband*. In fact, between 1524 and 1549, Ambroise Girault was the only printer who did not combine these works into a single edition.[10] Even more importantly, these works advertise for the *Illustrations* by situating them in the political and cultural landscape of France and Burgundy in the early 1510s.

Between the publication of Book One of the *Illustrations* in May 1511 and the publication of Book Three and the recueil-*Epistre* in July–August 1513, France's fortunes in the Italian Wars went from bad to worse. The Council of Pisa, convoked with a mind to deposing Julius II, met with such opposition from the city that it had to be moved to Milan, where attendance was poor. Not to be outdone, the Warrior Pope formed the so-called Holy League with Spain, England, Venice, and the Swiss cantons against France in November 1511. The French army lost one of its most charismatic and effective generals, Louis XII's nephew Gaston of Foix, in a pyrrhic victory at Ravenna on Easter Sunday, 1512, and was subsequently driven out of Italy. In late 1512, the Spanish took Navarre and Emperor Maximilian I committed to the Holy League, leaving James IV of Scotland as France's lone ally. The death of Julius II on February 21, 1513 brought little relief to Louis, as the new pope, Leo X (Giovanni di Lorenzo de' Medici), had little love for the French, who had helped oust his family from power in Florence, and initially showed every sign of continuing Julius's policies.[11] Meanwhile, Henry VIII's invasion of France from the north got underway in June 1513, and the English army laid siege to the French stronghold at Thérouanne in July, eventually taking it in August, while at the same time, a force of twenty thousand Swiss pikemen laid siege to Dijon. In short, it is no exaggeration to describe the period from 1511 to 1513 as a time of unremitting crisis for France and especially for Louis, and it was against this bleak political backdrop that the *Illustrations* and recueil-*Epistre* were printed.

The publication history of the *Illustrations* reflects Lemaire's own precarious political situation and his literary response to the Gallican crisis. By the time Book One was published, Lemaire had already left Margaret of Austria's service for Anne of Brittany's, as reflected in the gradual substitution of Louis's and Anne's arms for Margaret's in editions of the *Illustrations*. In his new job, Lemaire found himself obliged to defend the interests of a king whose aggressive foreign policy he had previously denounced in the *Chroniques annales* composed for Margaret. As tempting as it may be for modern scholars to chalk Lemaire's shift in allegiance up to opportunism or resentment toward his former patron, it should be remembered that Lemaire's overarching vision was one of European political unity, a vision that informs the *Illustrations* themselves. By showing the common descent of European rulers, especially those of France and the Holy Roman Empire, referred to as "France occidentale" and "France orientale" respectively in Book Three, Lemaire calls upon the European states to unite against the Ottoman Empire and reclaim Troy from its Turkish usurpers.[12]

The need for a crusade against the Turk is an *idée fixe* of Lemaire's, not to mention a commonplace of European political discourse in the Renaissance, that he hammers home time and time again, even promising to devote a fourth volume of *Illustrations* to proving the illegitimacy of the Ottomans' claim to Asia Minor. It also underpins the *Légende des Vénitiens*, in which he accuses Venice of preferring engagement in lucrative trade with the Ottomans to lending its redoubtable navy to the fight against them. Crusade even serves as the basis for Lemaire's criticism of Julius II in the *Traicté des schismes et des conciles*, which contrasts Julius with Urban II, whose exhortation at the Council of Clermont (November 18–28, 1095) achieved unity of purpose among his listeners and provided the impetus for the First Crusade: "Tout le peuple assistent commença à s'écriier tout à une voix, comme se ce eust esté ung cop de tonnoire, 'Dieu le veult'" [All the people in attendance began to cry out "Deus vult" in unison, as if in a thunderclap].[13] Julius, however, prefers to defraud Louis XII of his rightful claims in Italy by fomenting war between France and its neighbors. The spiritual leader of Christendom works against the interests of his own religion, while even Muslim princes like Shah Ismail I of Persia or the Mamluk sultan Qansou Ghoury make war on the Ottomans and conclude treaties with the French. It is on account of this failing that Lemaire supports Louis's call to reform the Church at the Council of Pisa.

The *Illustrations* and their accompanying published works oppose Roman political machinations, but they also express concern over what Lemaire sees as the undue influence of Italian letters in France. On multiple occasions, he holds up the *Illustrations* as a remedy for historical misconceptions perpetrated by Italians. While Lemaire draws extensively on Italian authors such as Boccaccio, Pius II, and, unfortunately for his claims to veracity, Annius of Viterbo, Pierre Jodogne has shown that he was far from the Italophile that Georges Doutrepont believed him to be.[14] At the close of Book Two's account of the Trojan War, Lemaire juxtaposes his "œuvre laborieuse et bien digeree" [laborious and properly-disposed work] to the "erreur inveteree" [deep-seated error] of Guido delle Colonne's *Historia destructionis Troiae* and its followers.¹⁵ In Book Three, he complains that although Italians think themselves the masters of history, they only abuse themselves and others by seeking to obscure the nobility of the Gallic nation. He points specifically to "Michel de Rys" [Michele Riccio], a counselor of Louis XII (2:3.272), pitting his own work as a historiographer against the Italian author of what was regarded as the definitive medieval adaptation of Dictys Cretensis's *Ephemeris belli Troiani* and Dares Phrygius's *De excidio Troiae*, as well as against an Italian contemporary at the French court. In publishing the *Illustrations* and the recueil-*Epistre*, Lemaire aims to counteract the pernicious effects of this Italian historiography, but he is equally concerned with Italian poetry.

An active participant in the intellectual life of Lyon, Lemaire was well aware of the influence that Tuscan poetry was exerting on the city as early as the 1500s and 1510s. His close associates in what could be called the "Académie de Fourvière," such as Jean Perréal, Symphorien Champier, and Humbert Fournier, were no exception to that influence: Fournier in particular aspired to ape Petrarch and sang sonnets in Tuscan. In this vein, Mireille Huchon has argued that when Lemaire describes the Temple of Venus in the *Concorde des deux langages* as a place where "D'Amours servir ung chascun s'estude" [everyone applies himself to serving Love], he is, in fact, describing his own Lyonnais milieu.¹⁶ However, in the context of the *Illustrations* and Lemaire's literary agenda, the Temple of Venus is not a celebration of the vogue for Tuscan love poetry in Lyon, but an indictment of it. As François Cornilliat has demonstrated, the *Concorde* is meant to reveal the limitations of the Italian tradition, to prove that love poetry is inferior to history, and to convince French writers fascinated with their transalpine neighbors to reconsider their choice of subject.¹⁷

The recueil-*Epistre* and the *Illustrations*, then, are Lemaire's attempt to recondition the priorities of his readers in the intellectual milieu of Lyon, the city in which the *Illustrations* were first printed. Through the central episode of the Judgment of Paris, Lemaire crafts his ideal readership and his authorial persona around self-fashioning so as to make the *Illustrations* appear to be the only acceptable choice of reading material. By showing through the examples of Paris in the *Illustrations* and the French youth in the *Concorde* the disastrous effects that choosing Venus, or by extension the Italianate love poetry associated with her, can have on self-fashioning, Lemaire creates a need for the kind of historiography that only he can provide.

The *Illustrations* as Mirror for Princes and Masculinity

In the prologue of Book One of the *Illustrations*, Mercury details the circumstances of the book's composition to its dedicatee, Margaret of Austria. The fleet-footed messenger of the gods structures the book's purpose around the Judgment of Paris, offering Paris's virtuous youth under the tutelage of Pallas as a mirror for the education of the young Archduke Charles, the future Charles V. When Charles reaches maturity, Mercury, who presided over the Judgment of Paris, will, in turn, preside over the Judgment of Charles: he will present the young prince with a golden apple representing his free will, and have him choose between Pallas, Venus, and Juno, who represent Prudence, Pleasure, and Power, respectively. Given that Charles is wise, Mercury is certain that he will choose "the best and fairest" from among them, though he does not specify which of the goddesses this might be (1:1.6–7).

In styling the *Illustrations* as a mirror for princes, Lemaire centers them upon self-fashioning. Readers who occupy or who will occupy positions of power are encouraged to see themselves in Paris, and ultimately to choose a better path to follow than the Trojan prince does. However, Charles is not the only reader with a judgment to make: the book is also intended for "tous nobles et clers entendemens de l'un et de l'autre sexe, qui sont de la bende Mercurienne, et ayment la lecture des bonnes choses" (1:1.5) [all noble and bright minds of both sexes who are in the company of Mercury and who love reading good things]. In this capacity, the *Illustrations* contain a moral dimension concerned with the behavior of men and women, a dimension that has not gone unnoticed by critics. For example, Judy Kem has devoted considerable attention to Lemaire's moral lessons for female readers based on Paris's two wives: women are encouraged to emulate the chaste and faithful Oenone and to define themselves against the licentious Helen, a duality also seen in Lemaire's distinction, borrowed from Marsilio Ficino's *Commentary on Plato's Symposium*, between the earthly Venus of lust and procreation and the heavenly Venus of the mind, chaste desire, and lawful marriage.[18]

As far as Lemaire's male readership is concerned, the full effect of the *Illustrations*' moral dimension must be understood in the context of masculine self-fashioning during the reign of Louis XII. Discussions of masculinity among the French royalty and nobility have tended to take Francis I as a point of departure, focusing on the king's efforts to transform turbulent lords into faithful courtiers through a cultural campaign meant to mitigate their potentially dangerous masculinity.[19] Francis's reign is seen as a departure from his predecessor's with respect to culture's role as a determining factor in masculinity; according to Gilbert Gadoffre, Louis XII's reign was characterized by an "obsessive" fear of feminization through learning.[20] While Gadoffre no doubt overstates the case, the contrast he draws between Francis I and Louis XII might account for the way in which Lemaire promotes the usefulness of his *Illustrations* to male readers. Far from presenting them as a means of reining in unbridled masculinity, he stresses how their historical exemplarity strengthens masculinity and counteracts feminizing influences.

As is especially apparent in his treatment of the Judgment of Paris, Lemaire's account of rhetorical efficacy in the *Illustrations* is largely one of how the wrong kind of rhetoric can sway men like Paris toward "effeminate" behavior. Lemaire's Judgment of Paris posits the male reader as free to make himself, but in need of a product that will help him make himself into an ideal ruler or simply an ideal man. That product is properly motivated rhetoric: the Judgment of Paris is a choice of what rhetoric to heed, or more to the point, of what to read and how to read it. As such, the *Illustrations* typify what David LaGuardia calls intertextual masculinity, "a continuous reflection upon the relation of texts to other texts, and a constant consideration of what it meant to *be* a man, and to *read* as a man within the social context that was defined by those texts."[21]

Paris's birth and youth reveal him to be of a sanguine temperament, which, according to humoral theory inherited from Aristotle, Hippocrates, and Galen, predisposes him to amorous pursuits. Even in Hecuba's prophetic dream signifying that her child will bring about the ruin of Troy, she gives birth to a burning, bloodstained torch that incinerates the city, an image that suggests that Paris's passion, connoted by the torch, a traditional attribute of Cupid, and complexion, connoted by the blood, will be to blame: the destruction of the city and the slaughter of its inhabitants are directly tied to Paris's Venereal disposition (1:1.124). Fittingly, Hecuba's old lady-in-waiting judges that Paris is "mieux taillé de servir une fois la Deesse Venus en matiere d'amours, que le Dieu Mars au fait de ses batailles, ne de faire la guerre si avant, que jusque à destruire ce beau Royaume" (1:1.130) [better suited to serving the goddess Venus in matters of love one day than to serving the god Mars in his battles, or to waging war to such an extent that he destroys this fair kingdom]. Needless to say, the course of events reveals the irony of her pronouncement.

The prominence of Paris's complexion in these prophecies conveys a sense of inevitability and necessity, as if Troy's destruction were written in Paris's humoral imbalance. In the Judgment of Paris itself, Venus argues that since Paris was born under the influence of her planet, her young judge cannot escape his fate, and must follow the morning star's radiant beauty and desirable fecundity (1:1.247). However, Venus's argument is meant to raise the reader's suspicions, as Paris's sanguine complexion does not exclusively predispose him to erotic love. It also makes him especially capable of fashioning himself under the guidance of proper instruction: "Et pource qu'il estoit sanguin, ingénieux et bien complexionné, tout ce qu'il veoit faire aux autres il l'apprenoit de leger" (1:1.134) [And because he was sanguine, quick-witted, and well-complexioned, he easily learned everything he saw others do]. Paris is quite capable of imitating virtuous examples when he lives under the tutelage of Pallas, a point that Lemaire, speaking through Mercury, stresses in the prologue of Book Two: "[T]ant et si longuement, comme Paris meit son estude à contempler la beauté de Pallas, il fut vertueux et bien moriginé" (2:2.2) [(A)s long as Paris applied himself to the contemplation of Pallas's beauty, he was virtuous and well-behaved]. While "bien moriginé" usually means "well-behaved" or "of sound morals," it also carries the sense of "well-fashioned" or "well-raised."[22] The term calls attention to Paris's indeterminate nature and the positive influence exerted upon him by Pallas before the Judgment, during which Pallas declares his nature to be "flexible à toute docilité" (1:1.237) [pliant to every kind of willingness to learn].

Lemaire also insists repeatedly on Paris's free will as alluded to in the prologue. He follows Fulgentius's *Mythologies*, one of his primary sources, in his interpretation of the Judgment as the choice between the active life, the contemplative life, and the life of pleasure.[23] He then equates Paris giving the golden apple to Venus with giving his mind over to pleasure, while Jupiter's refusal to intervene represents God's refusal to remove free will from man. For his part, the youthful Paris is a fitting judge for the contest in his capacity as "celuy qui n'avoit encores nulle façon de vivre determinee, et neantmoins estoit capable de toutes les trois dessusdites" [one who did not yet have a set way of life, and who was still capable of all three], an interpretation Lemaire reinforces with a reference to the philosopher Niceta's interpretation of the Judgment in the *Clementine Recognitions* (1:1.273–74). Paris's sanguine disposition does not absolve him of responsibility, as it does not override his free will. Consequently, Archduke Charles and anonymous male readers are every bit as free as Paris when faced with their own choice, which is why Lemaire does not say which way of life Charles will choose. Yet, Lemaire's selective appropriation of Fulgentius and Boccaccio's *Genealogy of the Pagan Gods* makes it clear just what he believes the correct choice to be.

For Fulgentius, the active life is the pursuit of wealth or power, and while it is preferable to the life of pleasure and the pursuit of carnal delights, it is still inferior to the contemplative life and the pursuit of wisdom. Boccaccio does not condemn the active life as openly as Fulgentius does, but he agrees with his predecessor's interpretation and points to Aristotle as a philosophical source for the choice between three kinds of life.[24] Lemaire, for his part, dedicates the *Illustrations* to noble patronesses who must choose the active life by virtue of their station. As such, he does not aim at creating a sweeping distinction between two kinds of life, but at synthesizing a single method of ruling correctly in which the active and contemplative lives work in concert, in keeping with the project of providing a mirror for princes. Pallas and Juno represent prudence and power respectively, rather than the contemplative and active lives, and Lemaire's description of both goddesses' accoutrements reveals just how necessary prudence is to power.

In keeping with Fulgentius, Lemaire insists on Juno as the embodiment of wealth, enumerating the costly fabrics, precious metals, and rare jewels that constitute her outfit, which is "riche et pompeux oultre mesure, pour denoter qu'elle est Deesse de toute richesse et opulence" (1:1.232) [rich and magnificent beyond measure, to show that she is the goddess of all wealth and opulence]. Though he does not denounce the pursuit of wealth in as clear terms as does Fulgentius, Lemaire hints at the excessiveness of Juno's pomp by describing it as "oultre mesure" [beyond measure]. He goes on to explain that Juno's chariot and the many colors of her attendant Iris (the rainbow) denote the fact that Fortune, "combien qu'elle soit aornee pour un temps, de grand resplendeur, et speciosité, neantmoins elle est legerement fugitive, et tost anichilee" [though she be adorned for a while with great splendor and beauty, is nevertheless quick to fly away, and soon reduced to nothing]. Margaret Ehrhart claims that Lemaire's Juno represents a life of inner and outer nobility, but the interpretation assigned to the many-colored Iris implies that Juno represents outer nobility alone, the signs and trappings of power that are unstable and impermanent insofar as they are subject to the mutable Fortune of Boethius's *Consolation of Philosophy*, whose influence remained considerable in the French Middle Ages and Renaissance.[25] To choose Juno would be to choose to pursue power and wealth as their own ends without cultivating the qualities needed to endure the slings and arrows of outrageous fortune, and while a prince who makes such a choice may enjoy the fruits of his station "for a while," he will learn sooner or later that his good fortune is "quick to fly away, and soon reduced to nothing." A mirror for princes, on the other hand, is meant to show a future ruler how to maintain control in the face of adverse fortune, the "mesprisement asseuré de tous cas fortuits" [reassured disdain for all contingencies] that Pallas promises Paris, and that, incidentally, serves as the guiding principle for Machiavelli in *The Prince* (1:1.237–39). What distinguishes Lemaire from previous *Rhétoriqueurs*, then, is the way in which he accepts and accounts for historical contingency, which ultimately informs his preference for history over poetry.[26]

To this end, Lemaire insists that Pallas's gifts are necessary to successful rule in peace, signified by the goddess's sacred olive branch, and in war undertaken to preserve peace. The prudence of Pallas allows a prince like Charles to approach wealth, power, and even pleasure in the correct frame of mind. The trappings of Juno and Venus will ultimately betray a prince who does not have recourse to prudence, without whose aid "les sceptres des Princes sont facilement brisez, leurs couronnes demolies, et leurs affaires obombrez d'ignavité, seuffrent detriment irreparable, ne leurs delices voluptueux ne sont point asseurez de placide oisiveté" (1:1.239) [the scepters of princes are easily broken, their crowns destroyed, and their affairs obscured by indolence; they suffer irreparable harm, and their pleasurable delights are not safe from placid idleness]. Pallas is the correct choice for Charles if he wishes to fashion himself into an ideal ruler, and she is also the correct choice for readers who wish to fashion themselves into ideal men: for Lemaire, masculinity is every bit as contingent as power.

Pallas is the patron deity not only of prudence, but also of "fortitude," and her attributes are those of "l'homme prudent." In Pallas, prudence and masculinity go hand-in-hand, as indicated by her winged arms and heels, which signify that "Prudence est diligente à toute œuvre vertueuse" [Prudence is diligent in every virtuous work], a play on the etymological connection between "vertueuse" and *vir* [man/male] that presents Pallas as a *virago*, a goddess who is virtuous because of her male qualities (1:1.236–37). Fittingly, when Pallas alludes to Lemaire's professed purpose for the *Illustrations* by inviting Paris to look into the mirror of her celestial beauty, she begins by exhorting him to lade the vessel of his soul with "liqueur prudente et vertueuse," and concludes by alluding to her parthenogenetic birth from Jupiter's head "sans coadiutoire de sexe feminin" (1:1.238–40) [with no help from the female sex]. Pallas's virtue is uncontaminated by the effeminacy to which Paris eventually succumbs.

In contrast, Lemaire continually insists upon the enervating and feminizing effects of the voluptuous life represented by Venus. In her admonition to Paris before he pronounces his judgment, Juno warns of the consequences of choosing Venus's way of life:

> Congnois aussi d'autre part la meschance et vilité des autres encores plus mesprisables, qui n'ensuivent sinon le delit corporel et la doctrine

Epicurienne pleine de contemnement et nonchaloir de vertu. Et sont
rempliz de luxurieuse immundicité, bannis de conversation honneste,
et tous enclins à corruption, rapine et homicide. Lesquelz tous vivans
sont enseveliz en ordure mortelle, et detestable. Leurs forces enervees,
leur pouvoir debilité, leur vigueur effeminee, et leur renom denigré de
toute obscure viciosité. (1:1.235)

[Know also the wickedness and baseness of others even more worthy
of disdain, who follow nothing but bodily delight and the teachings
of Epicurus, which are full of contempt for and indifference toward
virtue. They are filled with luxurious impurity, unwelcome in honest
company, and inclined toward corruption, ravishment, and murder.
They are buried alive in deathly, detestable filth, their strength sapped,
their power debilitated, their vigor made womanly, and their reputation besmirched with every sort of dark depravity.]

Ignoring the virtue that both Juno and Pallas claim as their own leads directly to a loss of masculine vigor, a state of non-manhood sullied by vice. In keeping with this warning, Paris becomes in the course of Book Two the very sort of ravisher and murderer that Juno describes, while at the same time giving himself over to "lasciveté et mignotise effeminee" [lasciviousness and effeminate daintiness]:

Si laissa ses vertus palladiennes, qu'il avoit eu en jeunesse, et ne luy
chalut du haut emprendre de Juno. Il se desaccoustuma de la chasse et
du noble travail dont il avoit esté paravant en recommandation louable,
enervant toute la force de sa puissance corporelle, et animosité hautaine, en oisiveté vénérienne, en reduisant tout son sens et son entente,
sans plus, à complaire à celle, qui sera cause de destruire luy et les siens.
(2:2.128)

[And so, he gave up Pallas's virtues with which he had been endowed
in his youth, and Juno's lofty undertakings no longer interested him,
either. He fell out of practice at hunting and the noble work for which
he had previously been commended, enervating all of his bodily might
and proud hardiness with Venereal idleness, focusing his mind and
understanding entirely on pleasing the woman who would bring about
his and his family's demise.]

By stressing that Paris had previously lived under the tutelage of Pallas, Lemaire calls attention to the virgin goddess's masculinizing influence even on a person born under the influence of Venus, as well as to the ease with which choosing a life of pleasure can lead to effeminacy and ruin. The implication is that had Paris chosen more wisely, he would have turned out differently, a point Lemaire drives home by comparing the Trojan prince to Hector. Before he abducts Helen from Sparta and becomes emasculated, Paris is Hector's equal, as he proves by besting his brother at wrestling upon returning to Troy for the first time (1:1.316–20). The fact that someone who "souloit estre égal en force et en vertu à son frère Hector, le plus rude chevalier du monde" [used to be equal in force and virtue to his brother Hector, the strongest knight in the world] could become "si treseffeminé et si appaillardy, qu'il n'ha plus vigueur ne courage" [so very effeminate and debauched that he has no vigor or courage left] is, in Lemaire's assessment, an example "bien à noter pour tous gentilzhommes modernes" [worth noting for all modern gentlemen] (2:2.168). The latter should be aware that their masculinity would also be at risk if they chose pleasure over prudence.

While Lemaire makes it clear that Pallas is the necessary choice for sovereigns and their male subjects, whose masculinity is determined by the choices they make, he also emphasizes the role that rhetoric and writing can play in influencing this choice, a role most fully revealed through the juxtaposition of Mercury with Pallas and Venus. Boccaccio is the principal source for Lemaire's description of Mercury's appearance, as he and Lemaire focus on three of Mercury's attributes: his winged hat (*petasus*), his winged sandals, and the caduceus.[27] The *petasus*, or "Galere" (*galerum*), signifies that eloquence makes for a strong defense against one's enemies, which Boccaccio equates with *captatio benevolentiae* (1:1.204). Lemaire adds a detail not found in Boccaccio: the hat is decorated with "belles plumes," making the link with writerly activity all the more explicit. Mercury's winged heels are equated with "la grande velocité de la parole, qui va legerement en diverses regions loingtaines" [the great swiftness of speech, which travels quickly to different distant regions]. Finally, the caduceus and the snakes entwined around it are equated with prudence, which reinforces the notion that eloquence is a valid form of defense, as prudence and fair speech ("beau parler") can put even clever opponents to rest in the same way that Mercury defeats the watchful Argus. Prudence also anticipates the affiliation between Mercury and Pallas borne out by Lemaire's description of the virgin goddess's attributes.

The similarities between Pallas and Mercury suggest that prudence and eloquence serve similar purposes, and that readers must exercise prudence not only in their conduct, but in their choice of writers. Just like Mercury's cap, Pallas's aegis and shield reveal that eloquence serves as a stout defense against one's enemies (1:1.236–37). Lemaire also gives Pallas winged arms and heels, a singular attribute not mentioned by either Fulgentius or Boccaccio that strengthens the connection between Pallas and Mercury, as does the description of her lance, whose considerable length shows that a wise person's speech can strike from afar. Perhaps most tellingly, the list of Pallas's soldiers is comprised of a number of qualities proper to a writer of history, including "Eloquence non vaine" [eloquence that is not frivolous], "Cognoissance historiale," [knowledge of history], and "Inquisition de verité" [seeking the truth] (1:1.238–39).

Although Mercury and Pallas can potentially serve the same purpose, Mercury and the eloquence he represents are morally indeterminate, "neutre et indifferente, bonne avec les benivoles, mauvaise avec les malivoles" (1:1.249) [neutral and indifferent, good for the good, and bad for the wicked]. Lemaire's use of the term "indifferente" classifies rhetoric as one of the *adiaphora*, the "indifferent matters" of Cynic and Stoic philosophy whose righteousness or sinfulness depend on how they are approached and used, and that later occupied a central place in theological arguments for Christian liberty during the Reformation.[28] In the *Illustrations*, Venus's mastery of rhetoric underscores this ambiguity, as she proves to be the most skilled at swaying her judge to action, appealing to his emotions and even turning her opponents' strategies against them by borrowing the extended ship metaphor first employed by Juno and Pallas. The same language may be used for ends that are diametrically opposed in terms of morality, and the eloquence so closely associated with Pallas may also be put to use by Venus, resulting in the eventual ruin of Paris and of Troy: "L'eloquence artificielle de dame Venus, ses paroles delicates, et sa douce persuasion causerent telle efficace et telle emotion au coeur du jeune adolescent Paris, que encores en pourra il maudire les rhetoriques couleurs, qui luy seront retorquees en douleurs" (1:1.249) [Lady Venus's artful eloquence, delicate words, and sweet persuasion inspired such an effect and such emotion in young Paris's heart that there would yet come a time when he would curse the rhetorical colors that would come back to give him grief]. The moral ambiguity of Venus's skill as a rhetorician is conveyed by the term "artificielle," which means both "skillful" and "cunning," and sure enough, she succeeds in moving Paris and stirring his emotions. Moreover, in using a figure of speech in the pun (paronomasia) on "rhetoriques couleurs" and "retorquees en douleurs" that Venus herself employs in promising Paris "mellifluence sans male influence," Lemaire conveys both that Venus is using rhetoric for ill ends and that the very same rhetoric may be used to teach a valuable lesson.[29] If Lemaire paints as seductive a picture of Venus as possible, it is to make readers aware of their own vulnerability to this seduction, and hence of the need for rhetoric intended to strengthen and edify.

It is with this aim in mind that Lemaire calls attention to the potentially corrupting influence of second rhetoric through the presence of the Sirens at Peleus and Thetis's wedding. Lemaire's description of them contains elements highly reminiscent of Mercury. They have the same power to enchant and put to sleep as Mercury's "beau parler," and their "figures de musique"— a turn of phrase that underscores Lemaire's approximation of music with second rhetoric—have just such a soporific effect on the Olympians (1:1.218–19). If Mercury shows how powerful a defense second rhetoric can be, then the Sirens reveal that it is also an enchantment that can lure the unsuspecting to their doom.

Furthermore, enchantment associates second rhetoric and ornamentation with an Italian cultural context in the *Illustrations*, and in this vein, Jodogne has equated the naked children on the fringes of Venus's clothing with *putti*.[30] In fact, this association is present from the beginning of Book One, which details how Ham, Noah's degenerate son, usurps the rule of Italy, corrupting its youth with "tous vices et infametez" [all sorts of vices and disgraceful behaviors], including usury, theft, murder, and poisoning (1:1.32, 41–42). Usury and poisoning are vices that were stereotypically attributed to Italians in the Renaissance, but what is most significant in this etiological myth is the depiction of Ham as an enchanter who casts his "charme" upon Noah's "parties viriles," rendering him impotent (1:1.24). Lemaire plays here upon the etymology of *charme*, hinting at its Latin equivalent, *carmen* ("poem" or "song"). This "charme" has the same emasculating effect on Noah as Paris's choice of the life of pleasure does on him, and inspires in the Italian youth the same vices to which Paris eventually succumbs.

Lemaire would have the reader believe that poetry has served Venus from time immemorial in Italy, but not in French-speaking Europe. Ham's corruption of the Italian youth stands in stark contrast to Lemaire's account of Bardus, the fifth king of Gaul who first introduced poetry and rhetoric to his people: "Et introduisit une secte de Poëtes et rhetoriciens, lesquelz furent nommez Bardes, qui chantoient melodieusement leurs rhythmes, avec instrumens, en louant les uns et blasmant les autres" (1:1.70) [And he introduced a sect of poets and orators called bards who sang their rhymes melodiously and accompanied them with instruments, praising some and blaming others].

In Gaul, both first and second rhetoric revolved in their epideictic capacity around exemplarity through praise and blame, and in this respect, Gallic rhetoric has always served the ends of Pallas. The Judgment of Paris thus extends to the choice of what to read, with Lemaire promoting his own work in the face of the rising influence of Italian sources in his literary milieu of Lyon.

The Judgment of Paris places the onus on Lemaire's readers to fashion themselves as rulers and as men through reading, and consequently, the authorial persona that Lemaire creates for himself in the paratext of the *Illustrations* and in its accompanying works is also structured around the Judgment of Paris. This persona allies Lemaire with both Mercury's eloquence and Pallas's prudence in such a way as to reassure readers that Lemaire's books contain the kind of rhetoric that will truly benefit them. To return to the question of why Mercury does not explicitly state what choice Charles makes, it is because the very book that raises the question is itself the answer. To choose Pallas is to choose prudence and eloquence used for proper ends, and by reading the *Illustrations*, Lemaire's readers choose wisely.

Pallas in the Paratext of the *Illustrations*

The *princeps* edition of Book One of the *Illustrations* was printed in Lyon by Étienne Baland, most likely in early May 1511, and sold by Baland and Jean Richier.[31] Directly below its title is the first paratextual contribution of the Dominican preacher Petrus Lavinius (Pierre de La Vigne), a Latin distich addressed to the reader: "Ingeniosa legas Marii monumenta Joannis. / Gallorum regum que sit origo docent" [You should read the ingenious chronicles of Jean Lemaire. / They teach the origin of the Gallic kings]. The distich introduces the book as a historical work meant to instruct and as a literary work that will stand the test of time, as the plural "monumenta" means "annals" or "chronicles" but also connotes the Horatian "exegi monumentum."[32] It is the first instance of what I would call the vocabulary of genius that underpins Lemaire's persona, and that becomes central to the *Concorde des deux langages*. Lemaire's constitution (*ingenium*) is perfectly suited to the kind of historical work that would come to occupy a permanent place in the consciousness of the French-speaking nations, and the term "Gaul" indicates the project of fostering unity between France, Burgundy, and the Low Countries by bringing their common ancestry to light.

Below the distich is Lemaire's coat of arms (fig. 1), which reflects the reorientation of his project, originally called the *Singularitez de Troye et de Turcquie*, toward the Gallic myth, as well as the work that went into producing the

Figure 1. Lemaire's coat of arms, title page of Book One of the Illustrations. *(BnF Rés. La² 4 [f. A1r]; reprinted with permission of the Bibliothèque nationale de France)*

Illustrations. The arms are comprised of a trophy occupying the center with a hand holding a wreath extending from the top of it, and a banner above it that reads, "Si non utile est quod facimus, stulta est gloria" ["If what we accomplish is not useful, our glory is foolish"]. Below the trophy is Lemaire's motto, "De peu assez" [Of little, enough], to its left is a rooster with a banner that reads "Gallis aeternum decus" ["Everlasting glory to the Gauls"], and to its right is a beehive surrounded by a swarm of bees upon which a parrot perches, with a banner reading "Favus distillans labia mea" ["Honey dripping from my lips"]. If we are to understand this coat of arms as a defining aspect of Lemaire's authorial persona, an "author portrait," to borrow Deborah McGrady's phrase, produced by both the author himself and members of his audience, then we must consider this paratextual portrait in relation to the text that it frames and the choice with which the text presents the reader.[33]

"Si non utile est quod facimus, stulta est gloria" first appeared at the end of the 1509 edition of the *Concorde du genre humain*, directly preceded by Lemaire's signature, "Jo. Marianus, apis belga, subdyaconus, fecit" ["By Jean Lemaire, Belgian bee and subdeacon"].[34] It is a quotation from Phaedrus's fable "Arbores in deorum tutela" ["Trees under the Protection of the Gods"]:

> Olim, quas vellent esse in tutela sua,
> divi legerunt arbores. quercus Jovi,
> at myrtus Veneri placuit, Phoebo laurea,
> pinus Cybebae, populus celsa Herculi.
> Minerva admirans quare sterilis sumerent
> interrogavit. Causam dixit Juppiter:
> "Honorem fructu ne videamur vendere."
> "At mehercules narrabit quod quis volverit,
> oliva nobis propter fructum est gratior."
> tum sic deorum genitor atque hominum sator:
> "O nata, merito sapiens dicere omnibus.
> *nisi utile est quod facimus, stulta est gloria."*
> Nihil agere quod non prosit fabella admonet.[35]

[Long ago, the gods chose the trees that they wanted to be under their protection. Jupiter picked the oak, Venus the myrtle, Apollo the laurel, Cybele the pine, and Hercules the tall poplar. Minerva, marveling at this, asked them why they were choosing trees that bore no fruit. Jupiter told her why: "So that we do not seem to be selling honor in exchange for fruit." "By Hercules, people will say whatever they want to say, but I find the olive tree more pleasing on account of its fruit." Then, the father of the gods and the progenitor of men said: "Daughter, everyone says you're wise for a good reason. *If what we accomplish is not useful, our glory is foolish.*" This fable instructs us to do nothing which is not profitable.]

The irony of Phaedrus's fable is that it is the virgin goddess Minerva who vouches for fruit-bearing trees and adopts the olive as her own. Even more striking than the fable's humorous irony, though, is the fact that it justifies Phaedrus's *Fables* themselves. Just as trees that bear no fruit are useless, so too are any endeavors, including literary ones, that are enjoyable without being profitable, but the *Fables* avoid this fate, as they instruct the reader through the content of the fables and the morals appended to them. In adopting a citation of this fable as a motto, Lemaire insists upon the utility of the *Illustrations* and the entirety of his work in the same way that Lavinius's distich does. By implication, Lemaire also adopts Minerva as his patron goddess, and she will continue to be associated with the image of his work from the *Illustrations* to the *Concorde des deux langages*. Pallas is equally present in the wreath above the trophy, which scholars have typically assumed to be laurels. Yet, the intertext of Phaedrus suggests that it is actually a crown of Minerva's olive similar to the one awarded to the young, virtuous Paris after he routs the Skepsian cattle thieves (1:1.162–63). Lemaire's persona serves as a reminder of what Paris could have been had he heeded the *Illustrations*' advice.

The modern Gauls, for whose benefit the *Illustrations* were written, are referenced by the rooster (*gallus*) and the phrase "Gallis aeternum decus," which reinforces the Horatian intertext of Lavinius's distich; as Adrian Armstrong explains, it could be read as "an everlasting source of glory to the Gauls."[36] The rooster, herald of the new day, was also traditionally associated with Mercury, who narrates the prologues of the three books of the *Illustrations*. The *gallus* even echoes Mercury's "Galere," a connection made even clearer on the engraving representing Anne of Brittany as Juno in the paratext of Book Three (fig. 2). In the upper-right corner, Mercury watches over the presentation of a manuscript to Anne, holding his caduceus with a rooster perched atop his *petasus*, a notable difference from the painting in the manuscript of Book Three upon which the engraving is based. In the latter, Mercury has his winged hat and sandals as well as his caduceus, but there is no rooster.[37] Through this addition, the printed book is made more explicitly Gallic than the manuscript in keeping with Lemaire's effort to publicize his loyalty to France, and Mercury is united with Pallas in Lemaire's arms and in the engraving of Anne as Juno so as to prove that Lemaire's eloquence is closer to Bardus's than to Ham's.

The remaining elements of the coat of arms pertain to Lemaire's eloquence and its cultural ends. The bees, perhaps a nod to the "apis belga" of the *Concorde du genre humain*, represent Lemaire's scholarly labors as an *acteur*, or

Figure 2. Engraving of Anne of Brittany as Juno from the Tiers Livre des Illustrations. (BNF Rés. La² 4, f. a1v; reprinted with permission of the Bibliothèque nationale de France)

diligent gatherer (*ago*) of material, a point driven home by the inclusion of a list of authors cited in each of the three books. The hive also conveys Lemaire's allegiance to the French crown, as the hive was a commonly used image of the ideal, harmonious monarchical state since antiquity, of which Louis XII made prominent use.[38] The adoption of this image in Lemaire's coat of arms reinforces Lemaire's willingness to serve the monarchy and hints at his ability to sting its enemies with such polemical tracts as the *Légende des Vénitiens* or the *Traicté des schismes et des conciles*.

Lavinius's remaining paratextual contributions, which begin on the verso of the title page, further underscore Lemaire's historical contribution to Gallic cultural supremacy. The first of these is a letter in Latin to François de Rohan, the Archbishop of Lyon, which specifically targets learned readers:

> Historia siquidem Gallica (ut Troianam omittam) patrio sermone hactenus edita, ita corrupta et mendosa extiterat, ut illustrissima Gallorum gentis origo plerosque viros etiam doctos variis scriptorum figmentis delusos lateret, et galli praeclarissimi generis antiquitate philosophiae multarumque aliarum disciplinarum et literarum, quibus nunc utuntur Graeci, inventione fraudarentur, ab externis gentibus probris insectarentur, barbari denique et ignari, ab his qui a Gallis et disciplinas et disciplinarum elementa acceperant, vocarentur. (4:1.433–34)

> [If any histories of Gaul (to say nothing of histories of Troy) have come out in our nation's tongue, they have proven incorrect and faulty, so much so that the most illustrious origin of the Gallic race remains hidden to most men, even learned ones, as they have been deceived by various inventions of writers, defrauded of the ancientness of the most excellent Gallic lineage, the invention of philosophy and many other disciplines and letters (for which the Greeks are now given credit), harried by shameful foreign peoples, and called barbaric and ignorant by those who received their learning and even the rudiments of learning from the Gauls.]

The *Illustrations* have restored to the French-speaking peoples their rightful claim to cultural supremacy, a task that no other work has been able to accomplish thus far. What distinguishes the *Illustrations* from other works of history, according to Lavinius, is that it tells the truth; he uses the noun *veritas* or the superlative adjective *verissimus* three times throughout the letter.

Lavinius advertises for the *Illustrations* by demonstrating that readers, even those learned readers who think themselves better-informed than others, must have access to truth to become fully aware of the superiority of the Gauls to the Greeks and Romans.

Indeed, the use of the term "barbari" calls to mind the Italian Wars and the competing claims to cultural supremacy that accompanied the constant and bloody fighting. Following a tradition that began with Petrarch, Italian writers like Francesco Guicciardini were united in their tendency to draw a contrast between the civilized, humane Italians and the brutal, barbaric French invaders.[39] The *Illustrations*, Lavinius explains, redress the grievous application of the term "barbari" to the French-speaking peoples by proving that it was in fact the Greeks and Romans who inherited learning from the Gauls, not vice versa. Fittingly, the simile that Lavinius applies to the *Illustrations* in his quatrain to Lemaire following the epistle is a military one:

> Bellica magnanimi lituo resonante per orbem
> Ut galli vastum signa tulere duces,
> Sic tua quaesitos variis authoribus ortus
> Veridicis gallos, undique scripta ferent.
> (4:1.435)

[Just as the noble leaders of the Gauls gave the signal to break camp with a clarion call resonating through the wide world, so do your writings bring tidings everywhere of the true origins of the Gauls that you have sought out in various authorities.]

The military vocabulary of the quatrain presents the publication of Lemaire's book as a contribution to the Italian Wars: the expansion of France into Italy is mirrored by the diffusion of the *Illustrations* "per orbem" through printing.

It should also be noted that Lavinius's epistle describes Lemaire's publication of the *Illustrations* not as a commercial venture or a sale, but rather as a gift to the nation: "Eas Gallorum praeclaras illustrationes, pro nostre gentis ornamento editas nobis legendas Marius noster dedit" (4:1.434) [Our Lemaire gave us an edition of his most excellent Illustrations of the Gauls to read for the distinction of our race].[40] In keeping with the logic of prestige advertising, Lemaire appears benevolent or even charitable toward his readership, as if he had written the *Illustrations* for the sole purpose of their edification. This notion of the gift recurs in Lavinius's final contribution to the paratext, a longer poem in praise of Lemaire and his work. It reinforces the martial overtones of the quatrain by virtue of its dactylic hexameter, the meter of epic. It also summarizes the contents of the first book, instructs the reader on how to receive it, situates Lemaire's account of the Judgment of Paris within a moralizing framework, and recalls Lemaire's coat of arms:

> Memorat quam sit damnosa voluptas
> Judicio: Voluit demens praeferre pudori
> Qui vitium; spernens foelicia dona Minervae,
> Ac Junonis opes, Veneris fugienda sequutus.
> (4:1.436–37)

[It tells of how harmful pleasure was to judgment: how a senseless man was willing to put vice before propriety, spurning the fruitful gifts of Minerva and the riches of Juno, and pursued the gifts of Venus, which are to be avoided.][41]

Paris's decision to grant Venus the apple is not only a choice of vice over propriety, but also a rejection of the very same fruitfulness alluded to in Lemaire's coat of arms and its citation of Phaedrus. Lavinius's poem connects the reader's reception of the Judgment of Paris in the *Illustrations* with the persona of Lemaire, an anti-Paris who chooses Pallas over Venus by writing truthful history.

The prologue of Book One continues to ground Lemaire's self-referentiality in his account of the Judgment of Paris through the figure of Mercury. Mercury's salutation to Margaret of Austria recalls the title page's insistence on Lemaire's eloquence and diligence, as the deity introduces himself as the "Dieu d'eloquence, ingeniosité et bonne invention" (1:1.3) [god of eloquence, ingeniousness, and good invention]. As the patron deity of eloquence and "bonne invention" (*inventio*), Mercury governs Lemaire's rhetorical activity, and the affinity between Mercury and Lemaire is made even clearer by the fact that the deity is also the patron god of "ingeniosité," which echoes the "ingeniosa monumenta" of Lavinius's distich. The Mercury of this prologue is the neutral Mercury that presides over the Judgment of Paris, as Lemaire cleverly chooses between the accounts of Mercury in Fulgentius and Boccaccio, opting to privilege the latter. For Fulgentius, Mercury is the god of commerce, middlemen, and thieves, whereas Boccaccio, though he acknowledges that there are many different conceptions of Mercury, opts for the one that depicts him as the divine messenger and god of eloquence.[42] By placing the *Illustrations* under the tutelage of that Mercury, Lemaire avoids presenting the book as an object of commerce, a good to be haggled over and ultimately sold for profit. Like Lavinius's epistle does, the Mercury of the prologue reveals Lemaire to be motivated not by gain, but by a calling to perform a necessary service for the public good.

The writing of the *Illustrations*, a task on which Lemaire claims to have spent more than a decade, is depicted as a choice of intellectual labor over pleasure through the parallel that Mercury draws between Aeneas, who restores Troy by founding Rome, and Lemaire, who restores Troy by revealing to the Gauls that they are its rightful heirs. This parallel is suggested by the opening quotation, taken from Book One of the *Aeneid:* "Quis genus Iliadum, quis Troiae nesciat urbem," followed by a deliberately amplified translation: "Qui ne congnoit le noble sang de Troye, / Et la cité, qui des Grecs fut la proye?" (1:1.3) [Who does not know of the noble line of Troy, or of the city that fell prey to the Greeks?].[43] By mentioning the Greeks, Mercury harkens back to Lavinius's epistle and its claim that the Greeks have usurped the Gauls the same way they overthrew Troy. Lemaire's quest thus mirrors Aeneas's, and the fact that it is Dido who pronounces the aforementioned lines in the *Aeneid* suggests that Mercury intervenes with Lemaire in the same way that he convinced the uxorious Aeneas to stop helping rebuild Carthage and get back to finding the spot on which to found his city.[44] After all, it was Mercury who first encouraged Lemaire to write the *Illustrations:* "Je stimulay et enhardis l'entendement du tien tresadonné serviteur voluntaire, Secretaire, Indiciaire et Historiographe Jean le Maire de Belges, environ l'an XXVII. de son aage, qui fut l'an de grace Mil cinq cens, à ce qu'il osast entreprendre ce labeur" (1:1.4) [I stimulated and emboldened the understanding of your most devoted and willing servant, secretary, *indiciaire*, and historiographer, Jean Lemaire de Belges, when he was around twenty-seven years of age in the year of our Lord 1500, so that he would dare to undertake this labor].[45] Lemaire, like Aeneas, chooses hard-won glory over pleasure by dedicating himself to the *Illustrations* for the better part of a decade. In this sense, his choice to write the *Illustrations* constitutes his own Judgment of Paris.

By the same token, those who read the *Illustrations* also choose Pallas over Venus insofar as they choose a source of eloquence that will properly guide them with historical truth and exemplarity. Indeed, Lemaire concludes Book One by asking his "nobles lecteurs benivoles" [noble, benevolent readers] to judge "combien il y ha peu avoir de peine, et d'industrie, d'avoir recueilli et assorty tant de matieres diverses, et de tant d'Acteurs autentiques pour les faire servir tout à un propos" (1:1.342–43) [just how much toil and hard work it was to collect and organize so many different matters and approved authorities in order to make them all serve a single purpose]. He then appends a quotation of Lucretius's well-known apian simile: "Floriferis ut apes in saltibus omnia libant, / Omnia nos itidem decerpsimus aurea dicta" [As bees in the flowery glades sip all the sweets, so we likewise feed on all your golden words].[46] In Lucretius, these lines praise the very same Epicurus denounced by Juno in her admonition to Paris, but in this context, they become a model for how readers should receive the *Illustrations* in which they feed freely on Lemaire's rhetorical flourishes ("flores"). By appreciating his golden words ("aurea dicta"), they effectively award the apple to him, and hence to Pallas.

The framework of the Judgment of Paris thus serves to elicit the reader's gratitude, a recurring theme in Lemaire's correspondence and printed works. For example, in an oft-cited letter to Margaret of Austria dating from November 20 and 25, 1510, Lemaire expresses his dismay at Margaret's disapproval for the alabaster he has sourced for the tomb of her dead husband, Philibert of Savoy, at Brou. He complains that his efforts go unappreciated and unrewarded, and in keeping with the proverbial saying, "ma fortune est telle que je bas tousjours les buissons et ung autre prent les oisillons" [my fortune is such that I always beat the bushes and somebody else catches the birds]. He uses the same expression in a letter to Margaret's secretary, Louis Barangier, written one year later, right around the time he passed into Anne of Brittany's service.[47] This need for recognition is equally palpable in Lemaire's paratexts, which contain an entire discourse on gratitude written as early as the *Concorde du genre humain*. Its paratext contains a liminary epistle to Mercurin de Gattinaire in which Lemaire explains how the fact that even wild animals show gratitude to their benefactors should move the hearts of men so that the vice of ingratitude does not prevail among them.[48] Lemaire, for his part, proves his own gratitude toward Gattinaire by dedicating the work to him. Over the three volumes of the *Illustrations*, he increasingly holds up gratitude as the ideal mode of reception for his own work.

In the "Excuse de l'acteur" addressed to readers at the end of Book One, the reader's debt of gratitude is tied to favorable reception of the author's work. Lemaire, explaining why only one volume of the *Illustrations* has been printed thus far, states that, in addition to needing more time to correct and augment the next two volumes, he will wait for proof that "les petites forces de son industrie auront impetré faveur, recueil et grace devant les yeux de voz magnificences et benignitez, et de toutes la chose publique de Gaule" (1:1.349) [the meager strength of his industry has obtained favor, welcome, and grace in the eyes of Your Magnificences and Graces, and of the entire nation of Gaul]. In addressing the entirety of his readership with an honorific usually reserved for royalty ("voz magnificences"), Lemaire suggests that they, like the young Archduke Charles, are capable of displaying the generosity and gratitude expected of an ideal ruler. In other words, readers may fashion themselves not only by reading the book, but also by receiving it in the manner described at the conclusion of Book Two: "qu'ilz ne prennent les choses sinon en bonne part, et excusent les fautes par benevolence" (2:2.244–45) [they should only take things in good part, and excuse the mistakes out of benevolence].

In the paratext of Book Three, gratitude comes even more prominently to the fore. On the title page, readers are encouraged to receive the book as graciously as they have the previous volumes, and to ensure that other readers do the same: "Lecteurs et auditeurs benivolentz, prenez le bien en gré et le gardez d'injure et d'oultraige comme vous avez fait les autres precedentz de vostre bonne grace. Et l'acteur vous en prie, affin qu'il congnoisse que la nation Françoise ne soit point ingrate de ses petiz labeurs, pour lesquels mettre au net il a beaucoup veillé et traveillé" (2:3.247–48n1) [Benevolent readers and listeners, take the good you see here thankfully and protect it from injury and abuse as you have the previous ones out of your good grace. The author asks that you do this so that he may know the French nation is not ungrateful for his small labors, the perfecting of which has cost him a lot of sleep and work]. Gratitude is also the theme of Lemaire's liminary epistle to Guillaume Cretin, which attributes Adam and Eve's original sin to their ingratitude toward God's gift of eternal life. Given the "ruyne pecheresse dont sont maculez tous les filz d'Adam" [sinful ruin with which all the sons of Adam are stained], ingratitude is the reader's default state, and readers may only rise above this fallen condition by displaying gratitude.[49]

Perhaps the strongest testimony to the coherence of Lemaire's paratextual advertising strategies may be seen in how posthumous editions adopt them.[50] In particular, two later editions involve significant changes to the paratext, but changes that create very much the same authorial persona as the *princeps* editions do. The 1531 Galliot du Pré edition, exceptional in that it contains only the *Illustrations* and not the *Épîtres de l'Amant Vert*, suppresses Lavinius's paratext in favor of an anonymous preface "aux lecteurs" and a dedication of the work to Francis I. It is conceivable that Lemaire wrote a dedication to Francis in an attempt to secure the new king's patronage after the death of Louis XII on January 1, 1515, but the significant lapse of time between Francis's accession and the publication of this edition, not to mention the fact that Lemaire's motto, "De peu assez," does not appear in either the preface or the dedication, makes his authorship of the pieces dubious at best. However, if the author is not Lemaire, whoever it is does display a level of familiarity with previous editions of Lemaire, and employs the same strategies for presenting the author and his work to the reader.

The dedication claims that reading ancient histories of the deeds of chivalrous and valiant men of ages past nourishes and enlarges the hearts of noblemen and courtiers, spurring them on to lofty undertakings. This exemplarity is especially meant to incite the young to "vouloir ensuivir semblables faictz qu'ilz oyent reciter en esperance d'avoir icelluy honneur qu'on faisoit à leurs predecesseurs" [desire to imitate the same deeds they hear recounted in hope of being honored like their predecessors]. The author of the dedication then urges those who wish to avoid idleness to read "ce present oeuvre de grand fruict et utilité" [the present work, of great profit and usefulness].[51] Though Lemaire's arms and the Phaedrus quotation are absent, the emphasis on utility and on exemplarity as a corrective to youthful dissolution remains. Moreover, the dedication to Francis I is remarkably similar to the paratext of Book Three, as "Lemaire" asks that Francis receive his "petit labeur en aussi bonne part comme de tout mon cueur, et en toute humblesse et subjection je le vous presente, intitule et dedie" [small labor in good part, just as I, with all my heart and in all humility and subjection, present it, entitle it, and dedicate it to you], encouraging the king to base his reception of the work on the intentions of its author.[52]

The shared edition of Lemaire's works published in Paris in 1548 preserves the original paratext, but adds three epigraphs by François Barat, a poet from Argenton.[53] The first, addressed to Barat's uncle Pierre de Vaulx, is in Latin, and appears after the recueil-*Epistre*. It resembles Lavinius's epigraphs in that it stresses the didactic value of the *Illustrations*:

>Antiquum genus, et gentis primordia Gallae
>Certior haec Marii perdocet historia.
>Nosse igitur nostrorum res qui curat avorum,
>Hanc legat, haec Gallum Gallica scripta juvent.

[Lemaire's history teaches more thoroughly and surely of the ancient lineage and origins of the Gallic race. Therefore, whoever cares to know about the matters of our forefathers should read it, and may this Gallic work be of aid to a Gaul.][54]

The second and third epigraphs, addressed to the "lecteur françoys" and Jean Baron, respectively, appear at the end of the volume after the *Temple d'Honneur et de Vertus*. Both stress the exhortation to virtue that the volume may impart, as the French reader is encouraged to "deschasser ce qui ame et corps blesse / Oysiveté, de vertu la foiblesse" [chase away what wounds body and soul: / Idleness, the weakness of virtue] by reading the *Illustrations*. Barat also extols the volume's corrective virtues to Baron:

> ... sachant que tu verse[s]
> (Où de vertu honneur à homme est quiz)
> A lire autheurs à ton esprit requiz,
> Qui evader faict mainte chose adverse.
>
> [... knowing that you spend your time
> (where men seek honor through virtue)
> Reading the authors your mind seeks out,
> Which allows you to avoid many adverse things.][55]

Of course, not all printers were faithful to Lemaire's vision, especially after his death. Two particularly salient examples of this are the 1535 *Triumphe de l'Amant Vert* published by Denis Janot, which groups the *Épîtres de l'Amant Vert* with courtly love poems of Charles d'Orléans and others, and the last edition of Lemaire published until the nineteenth century, the 1549 *Illustrations* published by Jean de Tournes that Elise Rajchenbach-Teller characterizes as the first attempt to produce Lemaire's complete works, as well as an appropriation of Lemaire as a father of French letters for the purposes of an editorial enterprise that sought to place Lyon and Lyonnais printers at the center of French vernacular literature.[56] Yet, given that such appropriations were the norm rather than the exception in the sixteenth century, what might account for the relative consistency of Lemaire's authorial persona throughout his publication history? The fact is that those who edited or produced paratextual material for posthumous editions of Lemaire were themselves readers of earlier editions, and the manner in which they presented Lemaire and the *Illustrations* to their readers is evidence of how they themselves read the *Illustrations* and interpreted Lemaire's persona. Their rendering of it is a testament to just how effectively it is constructed and conveyed in its original editions.

When we consider Lemaire's persona as advertising for the *Illustrations* and their reception, it also changes how we consider the inclusion of the *Épîtres de l'Amant Vert* after the conclusion of Book One. At first glance, the *Illustrations* and the *Épîtres* seem rather incongruous: a highly ambitious mythico-historical tome that claims to provide a definitive account of European genealogy and cultural heritage gives way to a humorous imitation of

Ovid's *Heroides* and the vernacular poetic tradition of letters from abandoned lovers. The two *Épîtres* are narrated by Margaret of Austria's pet parrot, the titular Amant Vert, whom she abandons at Pont d'Ain after departing to meet with her father. In the first epistle, the parrot grows despondent and resolves to commit suicide by throwing himself into the jaws of a hungry mastiff. In the second epistle, a descent into the underworld in the style of Book Six of the *Aeneid* or Dante's *Inferno*, the spirit of the Amant Vert is met by Mercury, who guides him through Hell and then leads him to the Elysian Fields, where he is welcomed by another parrot, the Esprit Vermeil, often taken to be a double of Jean Molinet.

The delightful and often bold humor of the *Épîtres*, which at one point describe how the Amant Vert has witnessed Margaret *in flagrante delicto* with her successive husbands, accounts for their warm reception both today and in their own time, when they reflected and perhaps even encouraged a vogue for pet parrots and parakeets among the French royalty.[57] Conventional logic dictates that the *Épîtres*, which had previously circulated in manuscripts, would simply have been added to the *Illustrations* to spice them up and attract interest. Yet, the fact that they did not appear in print independently of the *Illustrations* until 1535 would seem to suggest that the two works form a cohesive unit, and that modern scholarship, which tends to consider the *Épîtres* in isolation, would benefit from considering them as a complementary piece to the *Illustrations*.

What connects the *Illustrations* and the *Épîtres* is Lemaire's persona, as implied by the parrot in Lemaire's coat of arms. Scholars have also pointed out the obvious parallels between the Amant Vert and the historical Lemaire, though they have drawn varying conclusions from them.[58] When we regard the Amant Vert as an extension of Lemaire's authorial persona in the *Illustrations*, however, it becomes apparent that the parrot's narrative mirrors less the historical Lemaire than the authorial persona of Lemaire as depicted in Mercury's prologue to Book One. In their manuscript form, the *Épîtres de l'Amant Vert* are a clever take on a literary convention written for the amusement of specific patrons, but in the context of the printed *Illustrations*, they are a testament to Lemaire's choice of Pallas.

"Soubz ce noir marbre gist l'Amant Vert": The *Épîtres de l'Amant Vert* and Lemaire's Historical Turn

The *Épîtres* are preceded by a dedicatory letter to the royal painter of Louis XII, Jean Perréal, Lemaire's longtime friend and advocate, in which Lemaire requests that Perréal read the two epistles to Queen Anne on his behalf, since she had enjoyed the first epistle so much.[59] The queen's enjoyment, moreover, prompts Lemaire to conclude that it would be neither unseemly nor unpleasant for his readers if he printed the epistles along with the *Illustrations*. As McGrady has noted, Anne and Perréal act as ideal readers in terms of how they receive and disseminate the work, filling a role into which the book's general readership is consequently encouraged to step.[60] Yet, the dedication also encourages the reader to approach the *Épîtres* as a narrative of Lemaire's career. The salutation establishes this parallel by introducing the author as "Jan Le Maire de Belges, treshumble disciple et loingtain imitateur des meilleurs indiciaires et historiographes" [Jean Lemaire de Belges, most humble disciple and far-removed imitator of the best *indiciaires* and historiographers]. The fact that Lemaire is introduced as an "imitateur" of the greatest *indiciaires* and historiographers associates the image of the parrot with Lemaire's historical work, and suggests that the ensuing parrot poems confirm that Lemaire is up to the task he has undertaken.

The *Épîtres* call into question the relative worth of history and love poetry, the latter of which is tied to the Amant Vert's despair and death in the description of his song as "ung couteau mortellement trenchant" (8.90) [a knife that makes a mortal cut]. The Amant Vert also calls to mind the Venus of the *Illustrations* through his amorous nature, and especially through his appearance: the "vert gay" of his plumage directly recalls Venus's petticoat, itself "d'un verd gay" (1:1.241), and his tomb, as he envisions it, will be sacred to Venus (7.79, 11.211). Moreover, a shepherdess's description of the parrot to passers-by as "[e]spris d'amours en ung cueur juvenil" [taken with love in his young heart] invites a comparison of the Amant Vert with the young Paris of the *Illustrations*, as does her ensuing explanation that he lost his lady thanks to "Fortune rebelle" (12.232, 237). In an excursus during the account of Paris's life as a shepherd in Book One, Lemaire points to Paris as an example of the unrestrained power of "Fortune la diverse" [mutable Fortune], who makes Paris spend his youth in obscurity only to restore him to his rightful place so that he can bring about the fall of Troy (1:1.241).

If the Amant Vert is a young lover, then his tomb would seem to express the limitations of love poetry. There is, of course, a distinct parallel between the "Lame en vers" [tombstone with verses] and the very epistle that describes it and concludes with the Amant Vert's epitaph ("L'Amant Vert").[61] However, the epitaph emphasizes the confinement of the tomb and the parrot's servitude: "Soubz ce tumbel, qui est ung dur conclave, / Git l'Amant Vert et le tresnoble esclave" (17.377–78) [Beneath this tomb, a hard enclosure, / Lies the

Amant Vert and the most noble slave]. The tomb, and by extension, the first epistle and the tradition it represents become as much a formal and thematic prison ("conclave") as a physical one, and the description of the Amant Vert as an "esclave" reflects not only the commonplace of the lover as the lady's *serviteur*, but also the more disconcerting notion of enslavement to love as seen, for example, in Petrarch's *Trionfi*.

The first epistle thus invites the reader to see the Amant Vert's fate as an expression of Lemaire's dissatisfaction with love poetry. It also foreshadows the shift in the Amant Vert's character trajectory from the first to the second epistle through a resemblance between the tomb and the description of Lemaire as an "imitateur" in the liminary epistle. The Amant Vert demands to be buried not at Pont d'Ain, but in a proper tomb, as such was the honor conferred upon another bird in Ancient Rome. He refers to an anecdote in Pliny about how a raven was so esteemed that when a cobbler killed it, he was put to death and the bird was given an elaborate funeral (11.202–4).[62] What made this raven so special was that it could talk, and each morning, it would perch on the rostrum facing the Forum and salute Tiberius, Germanicus, and Drusus Caesar, and the Roman people as they passed. This raven, in other words, was an avian orator capable of addressing both powerful political figures and the general populace, not unlike what Lemaire claims to do in the *Illustrations*. The Amant Vert, in desiring the same funeral proceedings as those of the orator-raven, imitates it in the same way that Lemaire imitates historical authorities like Pliny.

Lemaire's imitation also figures in an oft-neglected component of the paratext that appears after the end of the first epistle and before the start of the second. It is composed of a quatrain addressed by Madame (Margaret) to the author, and a Latin passage on the tradition of poems lamenting dead parrots. The quatrain and the Latin passage are present in every sixteenth-century edition of the *Illustrations* except for the 1531 Galliot du Pré edition and the 1549 Du Moulin edition, which contains only the quatrain. Though the attribution of the quatrain to Marguerite is not contested, the authorship of the Latin passage is unclear, and it may be for this reason that most critics do not discuss it; Jean Frappier's edition of the *Épîtres* does not even reproduce it. In the quatrain, Margaret's praise is directed less at Lemaire himself or the first epistle in particular than it is more generally at the fruits of his labors as a writer:

> Ton escriptoire a si bonne practicque
> Que, si m'en crois, sera bien estimée.

> Parquoy concludz: Ensuyz sa Rhetoricque,
> Car tu scez bien que par moy est aymée.
> (51n43)

[Your writing desk is put to such good use
That it will be highly esteemed, believe me.
That is why I conclude that you should follow its rhetoric,
For you know well that I love it.][63]

It is Lemaire's "escriptoire" (a synecdoche that calls to mind an image of Lemaire hard at work on the *Illustrations*) that will win him esteem and that Margaret loves, and the use of the verb "ensuivre" recalls the proximity of Lemaire to the Amant Vert as an imitator; "ensuivre" not only means "to follow" or "to act accordingly with," but also "to imitate."

The Latin passage following Margaret's quatrain relates how Statius imitated Ovid's poem about a dead parrot: "Psitacum Corinne mortuum deflevit Ovidius. Statius Papinius Atedii Melioris psitacum mortuum ita ornat, ut non tantum cum Ovidio contendere quam eum precessisse videatur" [Ovid lamented the death of Corinna's parrot, and Statius Papinius honored the death of Atedius Melior's parrot so that he would seem not so much to compete with Ovid as to surpass him].[64] Ovid's *Amores* and Statius's *Silvae* are intertexts for the first epistle in terms of both content and structure; notably, Ovid's lamentation of Corinna's parrot concludes with an epitaph similar to that of the first epistle. Yvonne LeBlanc has claimed that this passage reduces the majestic scale of the *Amores* and *Silvae* to the "humble level of the animal kingdom," which amounts to a self-effacing gesture on the part of Lemaire.[65] Ovid's and Statius's parrot poems are quite deliberately humorous to begin with, though, and if they are written in the heightened style proper to elegy, it is precisely to underscore the humor of lamenting a dead parrot as if it were a person of note. In fact, Statius, in his salutation to Atedius Melior, compares his "leves libellos" [trifling items] on Melior's tree and parrot to epigrams.[66] Far from reducing the scale of these poems, the passage inscribes them within the tradition of *translatio studii*, implying that just as Statius imitated and surpassed Ovid, so too does Lemaire imitate and surpass both Roman poets.[67]

The explanatory passage is followed by a selection from Statius's poem that serves as a reminder of the Amant Vert's emulation of Pliny's orator-raven:

> Psitace, dux volucrum domini facunda voluptas,
> Humane solers imitator psitace lingue,

> Quis tua tam subito preclusit munera fato?
> Psitacus ille plage viridis regnator Eoe
> Ille salutator regum nomenque loquutus
> Cesareum etc.⁶⁸

[Parrot, chief of birds, your master's eloquent delight, Parrot, skilled mimic of human tongue: who cut short your murmurs by so sudden a fate? Parrot, green sovereign of the eastern clime, saluter of kings that spoke Caesar's name.]

Like Pliny's raven, Melior's parrot can speak Caesar's name. The Amant Vert, in turn, displays the very same ability at the beginning of the first epistle, addressing Margaret as "fille à Cesar" (5.2). This Latin paratext, then, ultimately confirms the Amant Vert's death and burial as a turn away from love poetry and toward rhetoric in the service of sovereigns. The narrative of the two epistles, which recount the parrot's despair, planned demise and interment, and finally the journey of his spirit through Hell and the Elysian Fields, confirms this abandonment of love poetry for rhetoric based on truth.

In the second epistle, the parrot/poet bids farewell to his former self and to his former poetic inclinations, undergoing a process of purification that resonates distinctly with Mercury's intervention in Lemaire's career. Sure enough, it is Mercury, playing his traditional role as the usher of dead souls to the afterlife, who takes the Amant Vert's soul under his wing the very instant it leaves the parrot's body. Having left his devotion to Venus dead and buried with his physical body, the Amant Vert, like Lemaire, turns toward Pallas and spiritual pursuits in his ascent to the Elysian Fields.

Mercury, having shown the Amant Vert through Hell, brings him before Minos for judgment. Minos, in keeping with the earlier description of the parrot's soul as "tout innocent et vierge," judges him to be worthy of the Elysian Fields on the basis of his innocence and virginity (20.60, 27.261–62). Mercury then guides him there through a "voye estroitte, / Forte à monter, tresdifficille et droite" [narrow path, / hard to climb, very difficult and straight] that closely resembles the commonplace of the virtuous path as a straight and narrow one (*per angusta ad augusta*) and Hesiod's account of the Mountain of Virtue (27.276–78).⁶⁹ When they reach the entrance to the Fields, they pass through a gate made of transparent horn reminiscent of those in the *Odyssey* and the *Aeneid*, where it is explained that there are two sets of gates, one of ivory and the other of horn, through which dreams pass into our world. Dreams that exit through the ivory gates are false visions, whereas dreams that exit through the gates of horn are true (27.291–92).[70] The Amant Vert moves not only toward the straight and narrow path after his death, but toward truth and transparency, much as Lemaire does by devoting himself to a project intended to reveal the truth behind the origins of the Gauls.

If the *Épîtres* reinforce the narrative of Lemaire's career as one of devotion to historical truth and the imitation of *auctoritates* (authorities), then the recueil-*Epistre* confirms this narrative by grounding it all the more firmly in the cultural context of the Italian Wars. In this context, the cornerstone of the collection, the *Concorde des deux langages*, reads as an extension of the Judgment of Paris. Like the Amant Vert, the *acteur* of the *Concorde* turns away from Venus and toward Pallas, all while showing his French readers the stakes of their choice between the Italian poetry associated with the Temple of Venus and the French historical exemplarity associated with the Temple of Minerva. Readers are thus encouraged to associate the *acteur* of the *Concorde* with Lemaire's persona as seen in the paratext of the *Illustrations*.

CHAPTER 2

Lemaire's Genius in the *Concorde des deux langages*

Jean Lemaire de Belges's recueil-*Epistre* was first printed in August 1513 in Paris by Geoffroy de Marnef.[1] It is composed of five pieces: the "Epistre du Roy à Hector de Troye" [Epistle from the King to Hector of Troy], the "24 coupletz de la valitude et convalescence de la Royne" [Twenty-four couplets on the Queen's health and convalescence], an epitaph of Gaston de Foix, the *Concorde des deux langages*, and Guillaume Cretin's "Plaincte sur le trespas de messire Guillaume de Byssipat" [Lament on the death of My Lord Guillaume de Bissipat]. A letter from Lemaire to François Le Rouge, Queen Anne's Master of Requests, is appended to the end of the volume. The collection is defined by the Italian Wars, the explicit subject of the "Epistre du Roy," Gaston's epitaph, and Cretin's "Plaincte," and the implicit subject of the *Concorde*; the "Epistre du Roy," in particular, is highly critical of Julius II. However, the context of these pieces, all composed prior to 1513 and circulated at court, raises two questions about the publication of the recueil-*Epistre*: given that the collection discussed dated events and a pope who had been dead for six months, why would it have been published when it was, and what role was it meant to serve?

Cynthia Brown, focusing on the "Epistre du Roy," suggests that it was not published until after Julius's death because it makes the controversial gesture of placing criticism of the pope directly in the king's mouth.[2] To be sure, contemporary polemical works critical of Julius, such as Pierre Gringore's *Jeu du Prince des Sotz et Mere Sotte*, tend to represent the Most Christian King as a victim rather than as an aggressor, and a work in which Louis excoriates the pope might have made his case seem all the more like a costly personal quarrel in the eyes of an already wary public. Yet, this risk only explains why the recueil-*Epistre* was not printed sooner. It does not explain what its purpose might be, other than to publish more of Lemaire's works. Why are these works "dignes de veoir" [worth seeing] as the collection's title claims?

The letter to Le Rouge gives a sense of how the recueil-*Epistre* fits within the body of Lemaire's printed works. It states that the collection is meant to accompany the third book of the "*Illustrations de France*," Lemaire having been persuaded to include it by some of his close friends.[3] Lemaire refers to the *Illustrations* not by their usual title of the *Illustrations de Gaule*, but as the *Illustrations de France*, abandoning the deliberately ambiguous term "Gaul" to clear up any remaining doubts about his loyalties, much as he does in dedicating Book Three to the French Cretin. The recueil-*Epistre* is published as a companion piece to the *Illustrations*, and its contents promote a distinctly French military, political, and cultural agenda. Adrian Armstrong, noting the prominence of this "propagandist context," argues that it attenuates the authorial self-consciousness of the "Epistre du Roy" and the *Concorde* that figures so prominently in the manuscript versions of these poems.[4] In light of Lemaire's authorial self-representation in the *Illustrations*, however, the context of the Italian Wars actually heightens the self-conscious features of the recueil-*Epistre*, as the collection confirms the essential role that historiographers play in a time of crisis like the one France was experiencing in 1513.

The "Epistre du Roy" was originally a reply to an epistle from Hector to Louis XII by the royal chronicler Jean d'Auton.[5] In Brown's assessment, its realistic development of Hector's role as addressee detracts from the polemical tone of the work, and it was composed more to entertain Louis and the court than to win public support for the king's policies. At the same time, though, she acknowledges that the letter's focus on historical veracity, disposition, and elocution represents "the concerns of an historiographer more than those of a royal correspondent."[6] Seen in this light, the "Epistre du Roy" as a companion piece to the *Illustrations* defends both royal policies and the usefulness of history.

The epistle reiterates Lemaire's consistent criticism of Julius II as ungrateful toward the French for their help in reclaiming Church lands, and as an impediment to the Crusade that would reclaim the Holy Land and Ancient Troy from the Turks (35.104–5; 42–43.333–38; 43.352).[7] At the same time, it stresses the role of "vraye histoire" in drumming up support for the crown in both theory and practice (35.116). Even the fact that Louis addresses Hector as his ancestor articulates with the *translatio* at the heart of the *Illustrations*, certain episodes of which, such as Francus founding Sycamber, are recounted in the "Epistre du Roy" (46–47.425–70).⁸ More to the point, the epistle stresses the exemplarity of Hector as a leader and warrior defending his land against invasion, which justifies the shift in Louis's military campaign from offensive to defensive and portrays it not as an invasion of Italy, but as a defense of France's rightful possessions: "Et que tu es droit exemple aux bons princes / Pour bien garder royaulmes et provinces." (34.88–92) [And you are a proper example for good princes / Of how to protect kingdoms and provinces]. Hector's exemplarity is equally a point of emphasis in Book Three of the *Illustrations*, which directly attributes the success of Francus and all his descendants (including the kings of France) to the chivalric example set by Hector, whose "hauts faits memorables" [lofty, memorable deeds] Andromache encourages Francus to imitate (2:3.279–82).

The "Epistre du Roy" and its companion pieces advertise for the *Illustrations* and their author, as they provide a set of exempla, both good and bad, in order to define virtue and exhort readers to conform to this definition.⁹ This is, in fact, the theme of two brief poems by Lemaire that were included in a presentation manuscript with other poems centered on the Italian Wars and the value of history, the ballad "A la louenge des princes et princesses qui ayment la science historialle" [In praise of princes and princesses who cherish the knowledge of history] and the brief "Histoire, que faiz-tu?" [History, what is it that you do?].¹⁰ The ballad stresses the moral capacity of history, without which virtue and vice would be indistinguishable. We are once again confronted with the ambiguous morality of rhetoric, which is why Lemaire stresses that historical truth can sway readers' emotions as effectively as Venus sways Paris's emotions in the *Illustrations*:

> Histoire noble est ainsi certes comme
> Ung droit maillet, qui les pervers assomme,
> Et rend les bons mieulx luysans que la flamme.
> C'est ung brandon, qui nobles cueurs enflamme
> Pour acquerir le riche dyadesme
> Dont la clarté s'espart en maint royaume,
> Resplendissant trop plus que nulle gemme.
> (11–12.27–33)

> [Surely, noble history is akin to
> A straight hammer that strikes the twisted

And makes the good glow brighter than flame.
It is a torch that sets noble hearts afire
To acquire the rich diadem
Whose splendor spreads in many a kingdom,
Glittering so much more than any gem.]

Historical exemplarity, here compared to the torch commonly associated with Venereal passion and with Hecuba's prophetic dream about the birth of Paris, can counteract *eros* with an equally strong force, the desire for everlasting glory. It fashions those who heed it in the way that a smith's hammer can straighten and refine metal, and the value of what history thereby provides is closer to Pallas's virtue than to Juno's *gloria mundi*, as emphasized by the ballad's refrain, "Glittering so much more than any gem." To obtain such riches, one must read and cherish history, a point also stressed in "Histoire, que faiz-tu," which reveals that history "fay les bons ensuivre" [allows the good to be imitated] and that its virtue may be found "en maint volume et livre" [in many a volume and book] (13.1–4).

Presenting historical exemplarity as the key to self-fashioning creates a need for Lemaire's book and puts the reader in a favorable frame of mind for its reception, in keeping with the goal of rendering an audience willing to be taught (*docilis*) through rhetorical *captatio benevolentiae*. History answers the question "Qui te peut poursuivir?" [Who can pursue you?] with "Qui bien se laisse instruire" [Those who suffer to be taught] (13.13–14). As in the *Illustrations*, ideal readership in the recueil-*Epistre* is self-fashioning through the reading of history, and like the paratext of the *Illustrations*, the remaining pieces of the collection portray Lemaire as a purveyor of historical exemplarity and truth at a moment when France and French readers were in desperate need of both.

The collection's second piece, the "24 coupletz de la valitude et convalescence de la Royne," calls attention to the work performed by a historiographer in properly interpreting events. The poem is a dialogue in which France and Brittany pray to God to save Anne from her grave illness in March 1512. The twenty-four couplets are followed by a prose section in which the *acteur* recounts how Louis, seeing that the prayers of France and Brittany have gone unanswered, intervenes with God in his capacity as the Most Christian King, "au moyen duquel il a achevé maintes haultes besoignes et evité maintz grandz perilz et infortunes dressez à lui et à son peuple" (63) [by means of which he has performed many great works and has avoided many great dangers and calamities set against him and his people]. His intervention proves efficacious, implying that his power to intercede with God on behalf of his people will lead to France's triumph against Julius and the Holy League.[11]

Yet, the political and military situation could hardly have seemed more desperate than it did in the summer of 1513. This is precisely why the French nation would have needed a historiographer like Lemaire, who, in keeping with the meaning of the term *indiciaire*, could correctly interpret and demonstrate the truth behind historical events that might mislead the uninitiated: God's actions and graces must be written about and their memory must be preserved, "affin qu'on congnoisse cy après par exemples certains, ou plustost histoires approuvées, de combien les puissances supercelestes et ultramondaines sont plus familieres et enclines au secours de la sacrée couronne et majesté treschrestienne que ne sont les choses terrestres et visibles" (63–64) [so that hereafter it may be known through certain examples, or rather confirmed histories, how the heavenly and otherworldly powers are much more friendly toward and inclined to help the sacred crown and most Christian majesty than earthly, visible things are]. The pronoun "on" suggests that history is capable of teaching this lesson to everyone who needs to learn it. Even though the vast majority of "earthly, visible things" in the summer of 1513 suggested that Louis's expansionist policy had pushed France to the brink of collapse, Lemaire is able to point to Anne's near-death experience and Louis's apparently successful intervention on her behalf to reassure readers that, in spite of appearances, God is still on the side of the Most Christian King. In so doing, he simultaneously points to his own unique ability to provide this reassurance as a historiographer capable of discerning "the heavenly and otherworldly powers" at work in events.

Gaston de Foix's epitaph, the third piece in the recueil-*Epistre*, recounts the Duke of Nemours's last words as he lay dying on the battlefield at Ravenna. It serves as a reminder not only of Gaston's valor, but also of Lemaire's ability to point to true examples for a vernacular audience in his capacity as *indiciaire* and as the "truchemant" [interpreter] mentioned in the *Épîtres de l'Amant Vert*. According to the epigraph's title, it has been "Translaté de latin en françois par Jan le Maire, secretaire et indiciaire de la Royne, et rendu le françois correspondant au nombre des syllabes du latin" (69) [translated from Latin into French by Jean Lemaire, secretary and *indiciaire* of the Queen, and the French made to correspond to the number of syllables in the Latin]. The Latin original, if indeed there ever was one, has not been located, but the resulting French version is in alexandrines.

The alexandrine was commonly used in inscriptions and epitaphs at the time, especially by Burgundian poets, closely approximated the Latin elegiac couplet, and, of course, had strong ties to French national identity.¹² The alexandrine is also the verse used for the Temple of Minerva in the *Concorde des deux langages*, which alludes to its derivation from the *Roman d'Alexandre*, described by the *acteur* as "les prouesses du roi Alexandre le grant" [the valiant acts of king Alexander the Great].¹³ The description of the romance as a chronicle of Alexander's "prouesses" emphasizes Alexander's exemplarity, which is akin to that of Hector in the "Epistre du Roy." Moreover, the name "alexandrine" recalls the virtuous Paris while under Pallas's tutelage before the Judgment, who was given the title of Alexander, meaning "homme aydant" [bulwark of men], after routing the Skepsians (1:1.163). As such, it is interesting to consider with Nicole Hochner the possibility that Lemaire's epitaph of Gaston denounces the absurdity of the bloody Italian Wars, which would amount to a return to the stance Lemaire adopted under Burgundian patronage, but the introduction of the alexandrine underscores Gaston's Frenchness as well as his heroism, which corresponds more closely to those pieces that celebrate the deceased Duke as the epitome of military genius and boldness.¹⁴

Lemaire's choice of the alexandrine is further elucidated by the *Pronosticque historial de la felicite future de l'an mil cincq cens et douze*, an as yet unedited work that, to my knowledge, only survives in a manuscript held by the Rosenbach Museum and Library in Philadelphia.¹⁵ It is a brief numerological treatise on the number twelve presented, fittingly enough, on New Year's Day, 1512, to Anne of Brittany, herself the queen consort of Louis, twelfth of that name. The manuscript opens with an illustration of a star with twelve points and the word "Bona" [good things] in three concentric circles at its center, followed by a Latin quatrain that reiterates the three "Bona" in wishing the most deserving Queen Anne a happy and prosperous 1512 (fig. 3). The treatise goes on to extol the virtues of the number twelve in all imaginable domains, from the economic to the celestial, so as to reassure Anne that good things are in store for 1512, a prognostication that seems amusingly sanguine in hindsight. Predictive accuracy aside, Lemaire's remarks in the treatise connect the number twelve to the *Illustrations* and its project for a unified French Europe: "Xii. provinces en Asie la Mineur, qu'on dit maintenant Turcquie, possedoit le Roy Priam, pere d'Hector de Troye. Xii. pers ou Royaume de France establit l'empereur Charlemagne. En douze ans que regna, Alexandre le Grand, il se fit monarque de tout le monde, et a xii. de ses princes il distribua sa monarchie" [King Priam, father of Hector of Troy, held twelve provinces in Asia Minor, now called Turkey. Emperor Charlemagne established twelve peers for the Kingdom of France. Alexander the Great, in the twelve years that he reigned,

Figure 3. Illustration of twelve-pointed star from the Pronosticque historial de la felicite future de l'an mil cincq cens et douze. *(Rosenbach Museum and Library ms. 232/11 [f. 1v])*

made himself ruler of the entire world, and he divided this monarchy among twelve of his princes].[16] The number twelve thus connotes France's Trojan heritage and its military prowess; Lemaire also points out that Louis XII won his decisive victory over the Venetians at Agnadello in 1509, the twelfth year of his reign. It is hardly surprising, then, that Lemaire would have opted for the alexandrine in Gaston's epitaph, as it is the perfect meter both formally and numerologically with which to convey historical exemplarity and elevate Gaston to the same exemplary status as Hector, Alexander, and the virtuous, masculine Paris, not to mention Louis XII, and as we will see, Lemaire turns once again to the alexandrine at the decisive moment of the *Concorde des deux langages*.

Much like Gaston's epitaph, the final poem of the collection, Cretin's "Plaincte sur le trespas de messire Guillaume de Byssipat," laments the death of a prominent man killed during the siege of Bologna in 1512. While Cretin is not directly named as its author, he is identified by the inclusion of his motto, "Mieulx que pis" [Better than worse]. Why would an allographic work have been added to a collection otherwise constructed around an authorial persona specific to Lemaire? Part of Lemaire's motivation may have been to make the recueil-*Epistre* appear more specifically French. As he explains in the letter to Le Rouge, by having the collection published, he intends to show how the French language is enriched and exalted by Cretin, who has done as much for it as Johannes Ockhegem has done for music (71).[17] Even so, Cretin's "Plaincte" is not the most obvious choice for the collection at first glance: although its circumstances connect it with the Italian Wars, it is not overtly propagandistic or even political. Rather, it seems to be a condemnation of war in general along the lines of Jean Molinet's *Temple de Mars* or Erasmus's *Querela pacis*, as Cretin, saddened and embittered by the loss of his friend, laments the senseless bloodshed of war "quoy que on ayt la victoire" [even in victory].[18] Cretin's stance on war seems to run counter to Lemaire's pro-Louis propaganda, implying that not even victory is worth the loss of men like Guillaume de Bissipat. However, in the context of the collection, the "Plaincte" and its lamentations of war read as a criticism less of Louis XII's aggression and its bloody consequences than of a war fomented by the belligerent pope lambasted in the "Epistre du Roy."

Bissipat also closely resembles Lemaire's authorial persona. In describing the deceased Bissipat, Cretin stresses first of all that he was a gifted writer skilled in Greek, Latin, and especially French (76.89–92). The ensuing dream vision, in which the *acteur* visits Parnassus and witnesses the nine Muses arguing in rondeaus for Bissipat's apotheosis, further emphasizes his knowledge and skill as a writer. Calliope, the muse of epic, even praises Bissipat's "vertu et grace palladine" [virtue and grace worthy of Pallas] (88.446). In this sense, Bissipat serves as a double for Lemaire: by showing just how much France loses with the death of such a gifted writer, Cretin's "Plaincte" makes readers even more grateful for the continued services of Lemaire, who shares Bissipat's traits as well as those of Cretin's *acteur*. The latter draws attention to his own work within the dream vision, presenting himself as a scribe or a secretary and insisting on the accuracy and clarity of his transcription (82.287–89). By holding up Cretin as the prince of French poets and including a piece by Cretin in which the *acteur* behaves very much like the perfect "truchemant" that is Lemaire, the recueil-*Epistre* stakes the claim that precision and accuracy are tantamount to excellence, and that Lemaire and his *Illustrations* embody this excellence every bit as much as Cretin does.

If the components of the recueil-*Epistre* illustrate France's need for historical exemplarity and Lemaire's ability to provide it, how does the enigmatic *Concorde des deux langages* fit into it? As Brown has suggested, it directs the focus of the reader toward the literary text itself, as well as toward Lemaire's own endeavors.[19] It revisits the Judgment of Paris and its consequences for both Lemaire's authorial persona and Lemaire's readers. Critics have been sharply divided over how to interpret the *Concorde*, disagreeing over the seeming disparity between its prologue and its content, and over whether Lemaire privileges either the Temple of Venus or the Temple of Minerva, or regards the two as complementary. François Cornilliat separates these critical accounts into three strains: moralizing readings like his own, which support the text's official preference of Minerva over Venus; synthetic readings, which support the concord of Venus and Minerva; and estheticizing readings, which attempt to flesh out a preference for Venus over Minerva on formal grounds.[20] When the *Concorde* is considered as a part of the recueil-*Epistre* and as a complement to the *Illustrations*, it becomes clear that this context encourages a moralizing reading, as the moral lessons Lemaire draws from the Judgment of Paris are key to understanding how Lemaire's readers and Lemaire's *acteur* are represented in the *Concorde*.

The *Concorde*'s *acteur* undergoes an evolution not unlike that of the Amant Vert, initially thronging with a crowd of French youth to worship at the Temple of Venus, only to be rebuffed, whereupon he turns toward the Temple of Minerva and becomes the authorial persona depicted in the paratext of the *Illustrations*. This is not to suggest that the *Concorde* may be taken as an autobiographical conversion narrative, as Paul Imbs claims.[21] On the contrary, the *Concorde* is revealed to be a hypothetical exercise in its prologue, which concludes with a perfect conditional: "Or commenceray je ce labeur, comme se autrefois je eusse esté curieux de frequenter le temple de Venus, et que maintenant je cerche le chemin de celuy de Mynerve, la belle et vertueuse deësse, à qui ce present est consacré, desirant qu'elle le reçoyve pour agrëable" (6) [Now I will begin this task, as if I had been eager to frequent the Temple of Venus in the past, and were now searching for the path to the Temple of Minerva, the fair and virtuous goddess to whom this offering is dedicated in the hope that she might find it to her liking]. The *Concorde* is not the farewell to love poetry it is sometimes thought to be, as Lemaire does not claim to have ever espoused it. Rather, he writes *as if* he had once been eager to choose Venus over Minerva. In other words, the Temple of Venus does not reflect the historical Lemaire's literary evolution, but rather makes the Temple of Minerva, which so clearly resonates with Lemaire's authorial persona, appear even more salutary by way of opposition.[22] Not unlike a sixteenth-century *It's a Wonderful Life*, the *Concorde* makes readers all the more grateful for Lemaire's production by showing them what could have happened had he chosen to follow a different path and reassuring them that he will stay on his chosen path, given the proper recompense for his efforts.

Malus Genius: The Parasitic *Rhétoriqueur* and His Willing Victims

The prologue of the *Concorde* lays out a frame narrative in which Lemaire's *acteur* intervenes in a quarrel between two friends with differing opinions over the relative prestige of the French and Tuscan languages and their respective literary traditions. His intervention comes in the form of the Temple of Venus, written "à la fasson ytalienne" in *terza rima*, the interlocking three-line rhyme scheme [ABA, BCB, CDC, etc.] first used by Dante that Lemaire himself had previously used in the *Temple d'Honneur et de Vertus*, and the Temple of Minerva, a prosimetrum whose verses, like Gaston de Foix's epigraph, are in "ryme françoise que on dit alexandrine" (6) [the French verse called alexandrine]. The very structure of the *Concorde* associates Venus with Italian poetic convention and Pallas with French poetic convention in the service of historical exemplarity. The title assigned to it in manuscript and in print, "le traicté intitulé *La Concorde des deux langaiges*" [treatise titled *La Concorde des deux langages*], casts it in a political framework of peace and recalls Lemaire's more explicitly political tracts, like the *Traicté des schismes et des conciles*.[23] Indeed, the *acteur* states his desire to remedy the lack of concord between France and much of Italy, implying that Julius II's anti-French policy is to blame and associating Roman politics with Tuscan poetry in the Temple of Venus so as to hint at the deleterious effects of both: "Laquelle amistié ne féaulté ne se pourratrouver ou temple de Venus qui signifie lascheté et oisiveté, attendu qu'elle est trop amoureuse et accoincte de Mars, le grand dieu des batailles, lequel ne quiert si non semer division et zizanie entre loyaulx amans" (6) [This affection and fidelity cannot be found in the Temple of Venus, who signifies weakness and idleness, seeing as she is too enamored and intimate with Mars, the great god of battles who seeks only to sow discord and ill will among loyal lovers].

This Venus closely resembles her counterpart in Books One and Two of the *Illustrations*, who separates Paris from the faithful Oenone and drives him to a life of luxury, idleness, and "lascheté," which, according to Randle Cotgrave, can mean "unmanliness" as well as "weakness."[24] The Temple of Venus itself recalls the "logis de plaisance, magnifique et hautain à merveilles" [house of mirth, marvelously magnificent and haughty] that Paris erects in Troy after giving up the "vertus palladiennes" of his youth (2:2.128). It is the delightfulness of the Temple of Venus, and by extension, of the Italian poetry it represents, that makes it so dangerous:

> Trop bel y estoit son arroy merveilleux,
> Trop y avoit de grandz beaultéz insignes,
> Trop y fut tout plaisant et perilleux.
> (9.46–48)

> [Too lovely was its marvelous equipage,
> Too many great and renowned beauties were there,
> Too delightful and too perilous was everything in it.]

As in the case of Paris, sensual pleasure leads to "lascheté," and Lemaire drives home the parallel between the Trojan prince and his contemporary readers through the geographical situation of the Temple.

It is, of course, located in Lyon with its Fourvière, or *Forum Veneris* according to the false etymology commonly accepted at the time.[25] Lemaire insists on Lugdunum's antiquity and refers to it as the capital of Celtic Gaul, tying it to his account of the city's founding by Lugdus, the thirteenth king of Gaul, in Book One of the *Illustrations* (1:1.85–86). Even more to the point, he claims that it is "Reflourissant comme ung aultre Ilïon" [flourishing once again, like a second Ilium], a pun that simultaneously calls to mind the *translatio* at the heart of the *Illustrations* and suggests that, like the first Troy, this "second Ilium" could potentially be laid low by its adherence to Venus (13.137). After all, Lemaire interprets the fact that Venus sides with the Trojans in Homer's *Iliad* to mean that they were "plus adonnez à delices et à mignotises luxurieuses que n'estoient les Grecz" (2:2.168–69) [more given to luxurious delights and charms than the Greeks].

In the "Paradis corporel" [bodily paradise] at the center of the Temple stands a figure that has much in common with Lemaire's authorial persona, and that possesses similar skills, but uses them for purposes diametrically opposed to Lemaire's. This figure is none other than Genius, who brings the ambiguity of rhetoric to the fore once again. While this Genius is at least partly inspired by Jean de Meun's, he preaches procreation on behalf of Venus rather than of Nature, and is drawn more from Fulgentius and Boccaccio than from the *Roman de la Rose*. This is apparent even in the prologue of Book One of the *Illustrations*, where Mercury refers to himself as Charles's "Bonus genius," the equivalent of the Greek *daimôn*, a personal guardian deity that presides over an individual's destiny (1:1.6).[26] Genius claims that his father is Mercury and his mother is the nymph Lara, which matches Boccaccio's account of the Lares as the twin sons of Mercury and Lara (29–30.538–43).[27] Boccaccio notes that the terms "Genius" and "Lar" are interchangeable, and that everyone has a good and an evil Lar or Genius. While both Lemaire's persona and Genius are associated with Mercury as the god of eloquence, there are a number of subtle differences that indicate they are the two opposite sides of the same coin that Boccaccio describes.

When Genius identifies the wing-footed god as his father, he describes him as "eloquent, prompt et sade, / Le dieu d'engin et de toute trafficque" (29.539–40) [eloquent, nimble, and agreeable, / The god of craftiness and of all commerce]. As in the prologue of the *Illustrations*, Mercury is the god of eloquence, but unlike in the prologue, he is also revealed to be the god of commerce as seen in Fulgentius. Whereas this role of Mercury is suppressed in the *Illustrations*, it is underscored when Genius introduces himself in the *Concorde*, making it clear that Lemaire offers, but Genius sells. Anyone who tries to get at Venus's relics without forking over a generous offering "ja n'aura ne grace ne pardon, / Tant est le prebstre estrange de nature, / Qui tout debvroit presenter en pur don" (16.214–16) [will never obtain grace or pardon, / Of so cruel a nature is the priest / Who should offer everything purely as a gift].[28]

Genius's sermon, designed to win the good will of his audience by promising that he has their best interests at heart in accordance with the prescriptions of *captatio benevolentiae*, portrays him as a *bonus genius*:

> Genïus suis, vous suyvant en tous lieux
> Pour vous semondre et vous persuader
> Ce que je sçay qui vous affiert le mieulx.
> (29.529–31)

> [I am Genius, who follows you everywhere
> To bid and persuade you to do
> What I know suits you best.]

The verbs "semondre" and "persuader" connect Genius's nature as a guiding spirit to his rhetorical skill, but in such a way as to make the reader, who has been made aware of his venality, suspicious of this skill. Genius may claim to be good, and his audience may be willing to believe him, but he is really a *malus genius*, a wicked double of Lemaire who uses the *Rhétoriqueur*'s knowledge and abilities to line his own pockets at the expense of the French nation. He claims to be concerned with what is in his audience's best interests, but in making this claim, he defines these interests so as to profit all the more from his audience's credulity, assigning value to the relics he sells without the slightest regard for the moral implications for his buyers.[29] Appropriately, Lemaire introduces Genius's sermon as epideictic rhetoric (the praise of Venus) with a mind to garnering more offerings:

> Il s'appresta pour ung peu sermonner
> Et declairer de Venus les merites,
> Affin que ceulx qui d'offrir prestz se monstrent
> Ne fissent pas leurs ententes irrites.
> (22.360–63)

> [He prepared himself to speak a bit
> And declare Venus's merits,
> So that those who seemed ready to make an offering
> Would make good on their intentions.]

Genius does not praise to edify, but to flatter and profit, and as a result, his sermon conforms to Henry Guy's stereotypical assessment of *Rhétoriqueur* praise poems as "monuments to parasitism."[30]

What is perhaps even more striking than Genius's mercenary rhetoric is the way in which he manipulates his audience with strategies identical to Lemaire's shaping ideal readership through exemplarity. After describing those who owe him tribute, he informs his French audience that he is talking about them (31.568–580). His "praise" suggests that paying tribute is a necessary condition for those who wish to conform to the ideal image of Frenchness that he holds up. In elaborating this image, he borrows from the *Illustrations*, the "Epistre du Roy," and even from the prologue of the *Concorde*. He first praises the French as "Peuple de Gaule aussi blanc comme let" [people of Gaul, white as milk], drawing on the same Greek etymology of *Gallus* to which Lemaire points in the second chapter of Book One of the *Illustrations* (31.581).[31] He then alludes to the very title of the *Illustrations* in addressing his listeners as "Illustre sang, troyenne nation" (31.587) [illustrious bloodline, Trojan nation]. Finally, he breaks into *vers senés* [tautograms] that echo Lemaire's recurring alliterative variations on "France" and "franc" in the *Illustrations* and "Epistre du Roy":

> François faictiz, francz, fortz, fermes au fait,
> Fins, frecz, de fer, feroces, sans frayeur,
> Telz sont voz noms concordans à l'effect.
> (31.583–85)

> [Feat French, frank, fortitudinous, firm in deeds,
> Fine, fresh, ferrous, ferocious, fearless,
> These are your names, and they match the facts.]³²

Reinier Leushuis points to this device as evidence of how Genius mimes the author figure as a linguistic fertilizer of the French vernacular, and while the similarity is undeniable, it must be noted that the ensuing appeal to war against the Turks is not sincere, as it is in Lemaire's polemical works.³³

Genius's sermon flatters his listeners into complacency and certainty of future victory rather than urging them to immediate action, as indicated by the future tense:

> Grece a fiance en l'ardant auriflame
> Qui d'iceulx Turcz les yeulx esblouÿra;
> C'est tout l'espoir qu'elle attent et reclame.
> (32.601–3)

> [Greece has faith in the burning oriflamme
> That will dazzle these Turks' eyes;
> This is the only hope she expects and demands.]

He even appropriates exemplarity for his own purposes, presenting Venus and the Graces' flirtations as "ung grand signe et exemple" [a great sign and example] and urging his audience to "vacquer à l'exemple de Mars" [follow the example of Mars], who lays down shield and sword to embrace Venus (21.348; 33.614–16). The most characteristic components of Lemaire's writing are also in Genius's bag of tricks: knowledge of the origins of the Gauls, masterful use of rhetorical and poetic devices, and the ideal of exemplarity. Whereas Lemaire uses these tools to encourage the French to fight bravely against their enemies, Genius uses them to urge his audience to a life of idleness and ease, thereby performing his duty as the high priest of Venus by encouraging the people to imitate the misguided Paris of the *Illustrations*.

For its part, the members of Genius's audience, composed as it is of the "jeunesse gallicane et françoise" [Gallic and French youth] assembled at the Temple of Venus, bear a striking resemblance to the Trojan prince. This audience shares Paris's age as well as his temperament—Genius calls them "bien complexïonnez" [well-complexioned] and "Sanguins" [sanguine], and reminds them that they were born "Soubz l'horoscope et regart venericque" (31.569–72) [under the sign and watchful eye of Venus]. They are naturally predisposed to follow the goddess of love, which Genius tries to make into a necessity, like Venus does to Paris in the *Illustrations*. He does this through the theme of his *carpe diem* sermon, "Aetatis breve ver" [the springtime of life is brief], referring to the very same season connected to youth and sanguinity in humoral theory. However, Genius also offers an alternative explanation: either those who pay him tribute were born to do it, "ou d'eulx mesme ilz se y sont façonnéz" (31.573) [or they fashioned themselves to do it on their own]. His remark attributes this self-fashioning to free will in the same way that Lemaire has the golden apple represent Paris's freedom to choose. Even if the French youth are inclined toward the idle pursuit of Venus, they retain the ability to fashion themselves in a different manner.

Their reaction in the prose section directly following the conclusion of Genius's sermon shows how they choose to fashion themselves:

> Aux parolles de l'archiprebstre Genius, plusieurs personnaiges de jeunesse gallicane et françoise, esmeuz et entalentéz d'aller à l'offrande, sans attendre la fin du sermon, comme plains de fureur amoureuse, contraignirent ledict predicateur de syncoper sa collation, car, par ardeur tumultueuse et farousche, tant ainsi que se ilz se deussent entrebatre, chascun s'avança qui mieulx mieulx, tendant de baiser les relicques du temple veneriien. (34)

> [At the words of the high priest Genius, several of the Gallic and French youths, moved with great appetite to go make an offering without waiting until the end of the sermon, as they were full of amorous furor, compelled said preacher to cut his sermon short, for in their tumultuous and wild ardor, as great as if they were fighting one another, they climbed over one another to try and kiss the relics of Venus's temple.]

This stampede places the responsibility more on the French youth than on Genius, who, after all, only urges them to do what they came to the Temple of Venus to do in the first place. They are so eager that in their rush to plunk down their sumptuous gifts and get to kissing relics, they compel him to cut short his sermon, as conveyed by the abrupt suspension of the *terza rima* scheme at line 616. Even before Genius begins his sermon, he is astonished that so many people would come to him (13.207). They have chosen Venus by coming to the temple, and Genius is simply there to make a tidy profit by encouraging them. In so doing, they have fashioned themselves into animals rather than men, as suggested by Lemaire's description of the "wild" ["farousche"] ardor with which they fight one another to get to the relics.

The French youths' behavior suggests that, like Paris, they have chosen bestial love, that of the vulgar Venus of Marsilio Ficino's *Commentary on Plato's Symposium* to which Judy Kem convincingly points as a source for the *Illustrations*.[34] To wit, the *acteur*'s use of the term "farousche" recalls Juno's vituperation of Paris after the Judgment, where she calls him "homme brutal, beste transformee" (1:1.258) [brutal man, transformed beast]. Still, the Temple of Minerva and the historical exemplarity it represents have the power to transform them back into men:

> Dedens ce palais est de Mynerve le temple,
> Ouquel maint noble esprit en hault sçavoir contemple
> Les beaux faitz vertueux en cronicque et histoire,
> En scïence moralle et en art oratoire.
> (41.69–72)

> [In this palace is the Temple of Minerva,
> Where many noble minds contemplate in lofty knowledge
> Fair, virtuous deeds in chronicles and histories,
> In moral learning and in oratory art.]

The occurrence here of virtue calls to mind the question of masculinity that underscores the Judgment of Paris in the *Illustrations*, as well as the argument of another piece of Lemaire's, "Le dyalogue de Vertu militaire et de Jeunesse françoise" [Dialogue between Military Virtue and French Youth], found in the same manuscript as "A la louenge des princes et princesses qui ayment la science historialle," and "Histoire, que faiz-tu?" The "Dyalogue" is a debate between "Vertu militaire" and "Jeunesse" over what to do with the body they both inhabit. The former wishes to win glory without delay, while the latter would rather live a life of pleasure for the time being. It is through the coexistence of these two impulses in the French youth (the same French youth seen in the Temple of Venus) that the "Dyalogue" makes a case for historical exemplarity and the influence it may exert on young men: "Pour donner exhortation à ung chascun jeune et vertueux seigneur de la langue françoise de tendre à choses plushaultaines et plus memorables, à l'exemple des preux et vaillans princes tant du temps passé que moderne, mesmement du roy, nostre sire treschrestien et tresvictorieux" (1) [To exhort each and every young, virtuous French-speaking lord to strive for higher and more memorable things after the example of the worthy and valiant princes of both the past and present, especially that of our most Christian and most victorious King].

Whereas Genius's sermon typifies the sort of flattery that bolsters the "excuses de Jeunesse," historical examples of virtue and bravery spur young men on to fight.[35] By revealing Genius's audience to be malleable despite its inclinations, Lemaire shows that young readers not only can be influenced by historical exemplarity, but also *must* be influenced by it for their own good and that of their nation. As such, the aesthetic sumptuousness of Venus's description in the *Illustrations* and of the Temple of Venus in the *Concorde* serves not simply to titillate readers, but also to make them aware of their own vulnerability to the allure of voluptuousness, and consequently of their need for a *Rhétoriqueur* who will correct their tendencies rather than prey upon them. This correction comes in the form of the prudence and historical work represented by Minerva, "Qui lascheté destruict et les vices enerve / Et rend homme tout dur, qui paravant fut tendre" (42.102–3) [who destroys weakness and enervates vices, / And toughens up a man who previously was soft].

Yet, what makes this connection between the *Illustrations* and the *Concorde* even more revealing is the way in which Juno blames Paris's decision on his poor interpretation: "N'as tu eu vergongne de postposer la pardurable à la transitoire? de laisser le grain pour la paille, la seve pour l'escorce, le fruit pour les fueilles, et le gain pour la perte? De mespriser la vraye vivacité des images celestes, pour le fard colouré et teint sophistique, d'une statue plate et vuide?" (1:1.258) [Were you not ashamed to neglect the everlasting in favor of the transitory? To give up the seed for the straw, the sap for the bark, the fruit for the leaves, and gain for loss? To disdain the true vigor of celestial images for the colored makeup and sophisticated dye of a flat, empty statue?] In employing common metaphors for allegorical reading, Juno reproaches Paris for allowing himself to be won over by Venus's empty rhetoric, whose formal perfection matches the statue to which Juno compares it. This technical mastery, however, only masks its vacuity, and instead of contemplating the hidden beauty of Pallas, Paris is enthralled by the superficial beauty of Venus, and it is this failure to interpret correctly that reveals his bestial nature.

The same may be said of the French youth in the Temple of Venus, who heed Genius's rhetorical sophistry and rush to embrace Venus's relics, which Genius refers to as "statue[s] ou simulachre[s]" when warning his subdeacon Belacueil to keep anyone from approaching them before offering gold or a ring (21.339). Just prior to this moment, Lemaire's *acteur* speaks of the poetry that resonates throughout the Temple with "maincte couleur notable" (19.282) [many a noteworthy color]. In describing these "Liricques vers dont amours on blasonne" [lyric verses in praise of love] (19.294), the *acteur* emphasizes the beauty of their construction according to the rules of second rhetoric:

> Facteurs, rymeurs, maint beau dictier recordent
> A la louenge et bruit de la deësse,
> Et de beaux motz leurs ditz ourlent et bordent.
> (19.286–88)

> [Verse-makers and rhymers recite many a beautiful poem
> To the praise and glory of the goddess,
> And hem and embroider their poems with beautiful words.]

The rhetorical ornamentation with which the poems are decorated resonates with the "colored makeup and sophisticated dye" covering the empty statue to which Juno refers. It is beautiful enough to entrance the French youth in the Temple, just as Italian love poetry had the power to captivate the literary scene in Lyon, but to pursue it is to reveal oneself as caught up in appearances, and by the same token, as bestial. The reader of the *Concorde* who wishes to fashion himself into a man rather than a beast should refrain from imitating Paris and the French youth, and instead read something whose rhetorical construction is paired with an edifying internal message—something very much like the *Illustrations*, whose material, according to the prologue of Book One, is "toute riche de grans mysteres et intelligences poëtiques et philosophales, contenant fructueuse substance souz l'escorce des fables artificielles" (1:1.4) [utterly rich in grand mysteries and poetic and philosophical conceits, containing a fruitful substance beneath the rind of artful fables].

The depiction of readership in the *Concorde* elevates the *Illustrations* above Italian lyric poetry by showing how the former facilitates masculine self-fashioning through reading that seeks out the "sub cortice virtus" [virtue beneath the shell] that Lavinius praises in his liminary poem (4:1.437). Lemaire thus advertises for a mode of reading that treats the *Illustrations* as a source of allegorical truth and as a repository of historical exempla—that is, a mode of reading that confers upon the *Illustrations* the status of an authoritative text. By revealing through the French youth that readers are fashioned not just by what they read, but also by how they read it, Lemaire uses ideal readership to advertise the reception he envisions for his work.

Like the Judgment of Paris in the *Illustrations*, the *Concorde* is a mirror for readers of Lemaire's works that reveals the dire consequences of choosing unwisely and failing to display gratitude for services. As such, it complements Lemaire's insistence on grateful reception in the paratext of the concomitant Book Three. Grateful and ungrateful reception are personified in Genius's deacons, Belacueil and Dangier, respectively. While these allegorical personages, like Genius, are borrowed from Jean de Meun, the description of Dangier resonates with contemporary criticisms of the Church and of Julius II:

> Le diacre nommé Dangier, qui d'autre part tenoit pié ferme, ayant une grande et longue verge en la main, de dur mesplier poly et plain de neux, d'un visaige rebarbatif et d'une voix tonant et redoubtable menassoit ceulx qui s'efforçoient d'approucher à main vuide aux riches coussinetz sur lesquelz reposoient les belles ymaiges et symulachres feminins et venericques, et, de fait, les reboutoit rudement. (35)

> [The deacon named Dangier, who stood firm on the other side with a long, thick rod in his hand made of hard, polished medlar riddled with knots, was threatening with a grim countenance and a booming, fearful voice those who tried to approach empty-handed the rich cushions upon which the lovely statues and feminine, Venereal images rested, and was, in fact, brutishly driving them back.]

Dangier's rod is made of medlar, whose fruit, only edible when rotten, signifies corruption, and his "grim countenance" recalls Lemaire's description in the *Traicté des schismes et des conciles* of Julius at the siege of Mirandola as "tout martial et tout rebarbatif en son harnois" [utterly warlike and grim in his armor].[36] By rejecting the *acteur*'s gift, Dangier, "le rude diacre plain d'avarice sacerdotalle" [the churlish deacon full of priestly avarice], displays a trait commonly attributed to Julius in the French polemics of the time: ingratitude (35).

The *acteur*, seeing that the rest of the French youth are giving gifts of gold, silver, perfume, rings, and paintings of their amorous misadventures, offers up "ung petit tableau de mon industrie, assez bien escript et enluminé de vignettes et flourettes, lequel j'estimoye ung chief d'euvre" (35) [a small tablet of my own work, rather well-written and illuminated with vignettes and flourishes, that I regarded as a masterpiece]. The fact that this object is "rather well-written," as well as its illumination, suggests that it is a presentation copy, but in such a way as to invite comparison with the printed edition of the recueil-*Epistre*, whose capitals are characterized by vegetal or floral motifs, especially in the *Concorde* itself, which contains five such capitals.[37] Additionally, the existence of a copy printed on vellum of the *princeps* edition of Book Three followed by part of the recueil-*Epistre* suggests that Marnef's printing job was considered elegant enough to merit an expensive material usually reserved for luxury manuscripts.[38] In either case, readers are encouraged to associate the book they hold in their hands with Lemaire's "petit tableau de mon industrie"; the phrase may be understood as "tablet that I made myself" or as "register of my industry," and both the *Illustrations* and the recueil-*Epistre* constitute such a register in that they represent the work Lemaire performs as a historiographer.

True to their natures, Belacueil welcomes the gift with "quelque peu de faveur" [some degree of favor], but Dangier sees it as nothing but parchment bound in wood with no precious metals in it aside from the gold lettering (35). On strictly material grounds, despite the obvious care that has gone into its preparation, and despite the fact that its writer deems it his masterpiece, it cannot compare to the "richesse mondaine" [worldly wealth] proffered by the other members of the congregation, and Dangier tosses it aside without realizing that it could serve to honor and exalt Venus and her temple. Not unlike the French youth, he cannot see past the shell (*sub cortice*), and his rejection of the *acteur*'s gift makes him a double not only of the pope, but also of the ungrateful reader. By repudiating the *acteur*'s "petit tableau," he goes against the proviso on the title page of Book Three, in which Lemaire expresses his desire to ascertain that the French are not ungrateful for his "petiz labeurs" (2:3.247–48n1). However, Dangier is only one half of a pair; and Belacueil welcomes the *acteur*'s gift. Dangier and Belacueil are thus less tied to the Temple of Venus than they are to reception, as both are also found on the path to the Palace of Honor and Temple of Minerva: if a work in honor of Venus (love poetry) may be received favorably or unfavorably, so too may a work in honor of Minerva (history). Indeed, the presence on the path of rod-bearing monsters that bear a strong resemblance to Dangier serves as a deterrent to travelers. Those who persevere past these horrors are assured of "Belacueil," and this obstacle suggests that Lemaire's work itself cannot survive without the "fair welcome" of its readers (39–40.17–18, 25).

The *Acteur*'s Evolution from Amant Vert to Labeur Historien

The reader's fair welcome is solicited by the *acteur*'s journey from the Temple of Venus to the Temple of Minerva, and hence between the two poles represented by Genius and Lemaire. As he enters and proceeds through the Temple of Venus, the *acteur* more closely resembles Genius, but as he is rebuffed by Dangier and approaches the Temple of Minerva, he comes to resemble Lemaire's authorial persona. According to the incipit of the Temple of Venus, the *acteur* starts out young and entirely concerned with his own advantage:

> En la verdeur du mien flourissant aaige,
> D'Amours servir me vouluz entremettre,
> Mais je n'y euz ne prouffit n'avantaige.
> (7.1–3)

> [In the green of my flowering age,
> I desired to pour myself into serving Love,
> But I obtained neither profit nor benefit by it.]

He seems an ideal candidate to enter the Temple of Venus and learn at the feet of Genius along with the French youth, as he crafts verses, couplets, and meters in an effort to imitate "Le bon Petrarcque, en amours le vray maistre" (7.6) [Brave Petrarch, the true master in matters of love]. He follows the lesson of Genius's sermon even before reaching the Temple, as he was born in Hainaut, "pays enclin aux armes" [a country inclined toward arms], but left for Lyon to compose love poetry instead of epic: "Si changeay Mars au noble dieu d'amours, / Et chant bellicque aux amoureuses larmes" (7.14; 8.17–18) [And so, I exchanged Mars for the noble god of love, / And warlike song for love's tears]. These lines are a reminiscence of the incipit of Ovid's *Amores*, with the difference that Ovid humorously blames Cupid for stealing a foot from the dactylic hexameter he was about to write, while Lemaire's *acteur* willingly adopts *terza rima*.[39] He even makes ill use of exemplarity in the same way that Genius does, invoking Clio, the Muse of history, to relate the lofty deeds of Venus (12.131). One could thus describe Genius as the model to which the *acteur* initially aspires, as Genius has found a way to derive both "prouffit" and "avantaige" from serving Venus at the expense of the French youth who flock to him.

Certain aspects of the *acteur*'s self-presentation also harken back to the

Amant Vert. Like the parrot, the *acteur* leaves his native land to serve the lady of whom he is enamored, either his anonymous "amour lïonnoise" [love from Lyon] or Venus herself (7.15).[40] "Love's tears" and the "green" of the *acteur*'s youth also invite a comparison with the parrot, whose tomb, it will be remembered, is consecrated to Venus. Yet, just as the Amant Vert changes from the first to the second epistle, so too the *acteur* of the *Concorde* is in a stage of development and learning, as suggested by his invocation of Clio. In both the works of Fulgentius and Boccaccio, the nine Muses represent nine stages of learning and knowledge, with Clio representing the earliest stage.[41] Her name, Fulgentius explains, derives from the Greek *kléos* (fame/rumor), as one should not seek knowledge that does not redound honorably to one's reputation. In invoking the Muse of history, the *acteur* reveals that he possesses an inkling of the proper use of historical exemplarity, knowledge acquired and marshaled so as to exhort oneself and others to virtuous behavior through imitation. However, he is still in an early stage of learning how to become a proper historiographer, as he applies this rudimentary knowledge to Venus rather than to the more suitable Minerva.

Like the Amant Vert, the *acteur* learns by imitation, and in the Temple of Venus, he follows the instructions of Genius and the example of the French youth, making his offering to Venus "à l'exemple des autres" (35) [after the example of the others]. Dangier's disdain for his offering initially renders him despondent, but proves to be a blessing in disguise. It compels him to venture out into the wilderness, where the first trace he finds of the Temple of Minerva are "aucuns pas humains impriméz en la sablonniere seiche" (36) [a few human footprints pressed into the dry sand]. Only a select few have been capable of reaching the Temple of Minerva, and the *acteur* will follow in their footsteps. They are the "meilleurs indiciaires et historiographes" [best *indiciaires* and historiographers] of whom Lemaire claims to be the "treshumble disciple et loingtain imitateur" [most humble disciple and far-removed imitator] in the letter to Perréal before the *Épîtres de l'Amant Vert*.[42] This choice of the straight and narrow path distinguishes the *acteur* from Paris, who follows Venus's advice to "ensuis le grand chemin usité de la plus part des humains" [follow the wide path used by the majority of human beings] by giving himself over to a life of pleasure (1:1.247).[43] Moreover, the location of the Temple of Minerva within the Palace of Honor may be understood in relation to the *acteur*'s invocation of Clio, whose name inextricably links the pursuit of historical knowledge to the pursuit of an honorable reputation (*kléos*). Unfittingly evoked in the Temple of Venus, Clio is restored to her proper place in the Temple of Minerva inside the Palace of Honor. Finally, the fact that the footprints are "impriméz" into the sand is a subtle nod to Lemaire's status as a pioneer among the *Rhétoriqueurs* who made a foray into print.

Lemaire's authorial self-representation through the *acteur* thus lends perspective to the question of whether the *Concorde* is a farewell to poetry, and suggests that Lemaire, as Hervé Campangne and Daniel Ménager have argued, does not so much juxtapose prose to poetry as demonstrate how prose can comment on and translate poetry.[44] This relationship is seen in the work the *acteur* performs as a reader and writer. The concluding prose section opens as he transcribes the description of the Temple of Minerva and records the lines beginning with "Dedens ce palais est de Mynerve le temple" [In this palace is of Minerva the Temple], but he alters the syntax to make it more suitable for prose: "Dedens ce palais est le temple de Mynerve" [In this palace is the Temple of Minerva] (43). In so doing, he displays his ability to use prose to render authorities more clear and accessible, which means that, at the end of the *Concorde*, he is prepared to undertake a project like the *Illustrations*, a prose history based heavily on the adaptation of authoritative sources in both prose and verse.

As the *acteur* begins his transcription, the aptly named Labeur Historien shows up to guide him in this undertaking. This "esperit familier" is a *Bonus Genius* who contrasts neatly with the *Malus Genius* of the Temple of Venus. Like Jean de Meun's Genius, Labeur Historien is a servant not of Venus, but of Nature, "et ne s'appert jamais pour quelque conjuration qu'on luy face, sy non que dame Nature luy commande" (44) [and he never appears, no matter what kind of oath is made to him, unless Lady Nature commands him to]. If he has appeared to the *acteur*, it can only be because Nature has mandated it: his "grant affection et inclination naturelle" [strong affection and natural inclination] for loving Labeur Historien explains why Nature allows the spirit to appear to him and take him into his service (45). At this moment, the *acteur* finally resembles the Lemaire that readers know and love, the young Lemaire whom Mercury chooses to undertake the *Illustrations*. Though he initially seems meant to serve Venus, he is revealed to be naturally inclined toward historiography.

The *Concorde* does not conclude here, though. Labeur Historien then promises the *acteur* that if he finds him worthy of the Palace of Honor and Temple of Minerva, which can only occur after the *acteur*'s death, "que lors il feroit tant que j'auroie deux guides qui sont deux paranymphes arcangelicques, l'un nommé Repos et l'autre Guerdon, lesquelz me feront veoir à plain la tresvertueuse et tresnecessaire concorde des deux langaiges" (46) [then he would arrange for me to have two archangelic assistants as guides, one named

Repose and the other Recompense, who would allow me plainly to see the most virtuous and most necessary concord of the two languages]. Armstrong, describing the *Concorde* as "Lemaire's Consolation of Philology," reads the conclusion as an assertion that didactic and historical writing merits the consolation of immortal fame after death and an eternal scholarly existence.[45] While this is certainly a possibility, it is worth considering what the terms "repos" and "guerdon" connote in the context of Lemaire's *œuvre*.

The *acteur* does not actually meet Repos and Guerdon. Instead, Labeur Historien allows him to glimpse the two spirits, "dont en ung miroir artificiel, fait par art magicque, il me monstra les vifves ymaiges embrassans l'une l'autre en la presence de la deesse" (46) [whose living images he showed me embracing one another in the presence of the goddess in an artful mirror, magically constructed]. The mirror, emblematic of the didactic character of European literature in the late fifteenth and early sixteenth centuries, recalls the presentation of the *Illustrations* as a mirror for princes.[46] The final image of the *Concorde* is a mirror for princes, as well, one that holds up an image of an ideal ruler governed by the prudence and respect for history characterized by Minerva, and in this sense, Repos and Guerdon resonate above all with Lemaire's concerns over how his work is to be received and rewarded. For instance, in a 1509 letter to Margaret of Austria, he complains of her failure to allow him to take up residence in "some solitary place" to pursue his writing without distraction, whereas his former patron, Louis of Luxembourg, recognized that "le repos m'estoit necessaire pour mieulx labourer" [I needed rest in order to work better].[47] Even more to the point, Honor is described in the *Concorde* as a "roy puissant, juste, grandipotent, / Qui maintz riches guerdons à tous cueurs nobles tend" (41.67–68) [most powerful and just king / Who offers many rich rewards to all noble hearts]. In this sense, the *acteur*'s dream vision corresponds to the author's reality: Lemaire serves a just king who rewards those who serve him well and, as a result, Lemaire has been able to envision the "most virtuous and most necessary concord of the two languages" and put it into writing as the *Concorde des deux langages*. In this way, the *Concorde* advertises for Lemaire's continued service to Louis; by holding up Honor as a mirror for princes, the *Concorde* encourages Louis to conform to this ideal by continuing to reward Lemaire for the essential services he provides.

Beyond Louis, though, Repos and Guerdon advertise to anonymous readers by reminding them that to read Lemaire is to act out one's own Judgment of Paris. After all, "guerdon" is the term used *passim* in the *Illustrations* to refer to the rewards the three goddesses promise Paris and to the golden apple itself. Mercury even ironically sets Paris up for failure by vouching for him as a "droiturier retributeur de guerdons" (1:1.224) [equitable dispenser of rewards]. To prefer Lemaire's *Illustrations* to love poetry is to reward the deserving and to be rewarded for it in turn, but the real reward for the reader is perhaps less the continuation of Lemaire's literary production than the opportunity to fashion oneself after Honor and come to resemble the ideal reader that is the King of France. If sovereigns must prove their worth by recognizing the importance of historiography and rewarding it accordingly, then the anonymous reader is also given the chance to become magnanimous and kingly by doing the same.

What unifies Lemaire's body of printed work is his authorial persona and the Judgment of Paris that ties it to ideal readership. This persona imposes fixity upon an author whose political allegiances and attitude toward his courtly obligations, when considered strictly on the basis of his career and the text of his works, remain ambiguous. Lemaire may very well have been a political opportunist who regarded his duties toward his patrons as necessary evils impeding his more ambitious projects, and his correspondence with Margaret of Austria regarding his supervision of the monastery at Brou provides one instance where this was almost certainly the case. Yet, in his editions, he takes on the persona of a loyal servant who labors tirelessly for the good of his patron and his patron's subjects, expecting no greater reward than the "repos" and "guerdon" necessary to sustain his efforts.

If modern scholars tend to agree that Lemaire protests too much, it may be assumed that his patrons and his readers at court entertained their own doubts about his priorities. In this light, we may regard his loyal persona as a form of rhetorical anticipation (*praesumptio*): if the specter of Genius is raised in the *Concorde* only to act as a foil for Lemaire's persona and forestall suspicion, the fact that Genius so closely resembles this persona should give us pause. Time and time again, Lemaire disavows profit as a possible motivation for his work; the *Illustrations* are given as a gift to patrons and readers alike, Lemaire is identified with Boccaccio's Mercury rather than Fulgentius's, and, as a whole, the *Illustrations* and the recueil-*Epistre* set up an economy based not on commercial exchange like the kind that Genius orchestrates in the Temple of Venus, but on service freely given and duly rewarded out of gratitude. But this disavowal of profit calls attention to the paradoxical nature of *captatio benevolentiae*: to claim not to be concerned with profit is, of course, a good way to obtain even greater profit, just as the Antony of Shakespeare's *Julius Caesar* shows how effective an orator he is by proclaiming to the crowd that he is not an orator, and just as the air of effortlessness and nonchalance that Baldassare Castiglione calls *sprezzatura* is in fact the product of great effort and concern as to how one is perceived.

Lemaire's seemingly benevolent authorial persona exists in order to oblige the reader to approach the *Illustrations* as Lemaire says they should be approached, to conform to his conception of ideal readership. It is in this way that Lemaire imposes upon his reader through the Judgment of Paris the false freedom of self-fashioning, and indeed of advertising: the freedom to fashion oneself into something better by reading the *Illustrations* the way Lemaire wants them to be read, or to fashion oneself into something worse by reading Petrarchan poetry instead of the *Illustrations* or reading the *Illustrations* for amusement without recognizing them as a repository of sacred truths and an authoritative work on matters of great historical import. Readers may have the same freedom as Paris, but why would they want to make the same choice as he does?

Part II

Clément Marot, or Proteus in Print

CHAPTER 3

"Quel bien par rime on a"
Authorial and Printerly Personae in the *Adolescence clementine*

Although Jean Lemaire de Belges did his utmost to advertise his authorial persona in print, he was well aware of the possibility that printers could get in the way of his effort. In his liminary epistle to Guillaume Cretin in Book Three of the *Illustrations*, he takes printers to task for the inaccuracy of previous editions of his works: "Car à peine sauroit on garder les compositeurs de leurs incorrections (quelque diligence qu'on y fasse) mais les fautes soient imputees à eux. Et pensent les lecteurs et auditeurs que ce ne vient point du vice de l'acteur qui leur donne bons et vrays exemplaires" [For it is scarcely possible to keep the compositors from making mistakes, no matter how carefully they are supervised, but the errors should be imputed to them, and readers and listeners should not think that they are shortcomings on the part of the author, who provides the compositors with good and accurate copies].[1] Editions with an abundance of errors impress readers as careless, and if they blame this carelessness on the author rather than on the printer and his or her subordinates (in this case, compositors who make mistakes in assembling the characters), it ruins the image of the diligent, painstaking historian committed to truth and accuracy that is so crucial to the proper reception Lemaire envisions for his books. His complaint embodies the stakes of disputes between authors and those responsible for the execution of their editions: what is ultimately being contested is not just authority or control over the publication process, but also the image the printed book conveys of its producers.

This is one of the reasons why French poets after Lemaire did not unanimously follow his example in embracing print as a means of dissemination. Court poets in particular, like Mellin de Saint-Gelais or Jean Marot, showed little or no interest in having their works printed. In contrast, the investment in print of Jean Marot's son, Clément, has been well documented by critics, who have revealed not only the painstaking attention he devoted to the publication of his own works, but also the principles he adopted in preparing editions of his father and François Villon. In examining original editions of Marot, though, critics have been quick to obey Marot's own pronouncements as if they were the law and disavow unauthorized or dubious editions as bastard children. Gérard Defaux, whose standard edition of Marot's complete works established the 1538 Œuvres published by Étienne Dolet and Sébastien Gryphe as the definitive edition of Marot published during the poet's lifetime, particularly exhibits this tendency. Arguing that Marot valued the printing press above all as a way of spreading the evangelical faith, Defaux repeatedly decried the hindrances posed to his project by careless and unethical printers.[2] For Defaux, Marot strived in his editions to represent his unmediated self, to make of his poetry a mirror for the soul and the story of his life, and aspired to achieve the transparency sought after by evangelical writers.[3] This view does not mesh with the principles of poetic self-presentation exhibited in Marot's work as an editor of Villon.

The preface to Marot's 1533 edition of Villon's Œuvres may be seen as a model for the poet's approach to the publication of his own works.[4] Marot differs sharply from Villon in matters of *inventio*, and in particular, the Cadurcian poet disapproves of the Parisian poet's highly anecdotal subject matter and complains that one would have to have lived in Villon's Paris and have been familiar with the places, things, and people he describes in order to appreciate his craft.[5] Villon's *Lais* and *Testament* are wasted effort from the standpoint of posterity, as they will be forgotten along with the knowledge of Villon's Paris and its denizens—or so Marot thought, at least. Poets must endeavor to find a subject that ensures the survival of their work through the continued appreciation of a broad readership: "Pour ceste cause, qui vouldra faire une œuvre de longue durée, ne preigne son soubgect sur telles choses basses et particulieres" (OC 2:469; OPC 2:777) [For this reason, anyone who would craft a long-lasting work should not take such lowly and particular things as his subject].[6]

Marot approaches Villon as a poet familiar with the possibilities of print would approach a poet who was not and strives to adapt him to the kind of public that printing compels the author to envision. Rather than striving for immediacy and the unvarnished representation of the self and lived experience (though this is, of course, more a reflection of how Marot read Villon than of Villon himself), authors must pass their personae through the filter of their reading public, and Marot follows this principle in publishing his own works as well as in editing Villon. In fashioning a persona out of his lived experience, Marot plays a subtle game that makes the author into what Yves Delègue calls a "marionnette publique."[7] The figure of the poet presented to the reader in editions of Marot is just as much a puppet as the Villon of Marot's edition.

Marot's poetic "autobiography" is, in fact, the story of a persona rather than of a historical person.[8] More precisely, Marot appears in several different personae that remain distinct in spite of their commonalities: the *dépourvu* victimized by Fortune and unjustly imprisoned or separated from his wages by theft or neglect, the royal poet of France, the French Virgil, the militant evangelical, and the bawdy composer of profane songs.[9] This elusive, indefinite, ever-changing quality of Marot's authorial persona led François Rigolot, as previously stated, to compare the poet to Erasmus's Proteus and Pico's chameleon.[10] It is in this context of self-fashioning that Marot's persona must be understood, as the authorial persona is a self that can be and is fashioned differently from edition to edition. From this standpoint, unauthorized editions are every bit as valuable as authorized ones, because they reveal the role that editors, printers, and booksellers play in constructing personae not only for the author, but also for themselves in order to advertise for an edition and guide its reception.

Since it was in printers' and booksellers' best interests to clearly identify their product and its importance, it was often they who accented the importance of an author or even twisted an author's image to suit their own purposes. This sort of printerly intervention gave rise to a number of remarkable cases, as seen, for example, in Cynthia Brown's account of Jean Bouchet's dispute with the Parisian printer Antoine Vérard, who put the more famous Sebastian Brant's name on Bouchet's *Regnars traversans*—to say nothing of Mireille Huchon's controversial hypothesis that the author Louise Labé was actually a hoax meant to capitalize on the vogue for Sappho and Lyonnais print culture.[11] Even in less extreme cases, though, the authorial persona is still largely a function of printerly intervention.[12] In fact, if the prestige of a book was increasingly linked with authorial identity by the middle of the sixteenth century, this change in the author's status may be attributed as much to the pragmatism of printer/publishers as to the creative genius of authors.[13] The same may be said of Marot's persona in his editions, which enjoyed unparalleled popularity. Claude Mayer's bibliography lists eight editions of Marot, such as the 1531 *Opuscules* published in Lyon by Olivier Arnoullet, and anonymous *plaquettes* of the "Temple de Cupido" or "Epistre de Maguelonne" published prior to the August 12, 1532 *Adolescence clementine*, which means that, by the time he set out to produce an authorized edition, Marot's poems were already quite popular in print, to say nothing of manuscript circulation or oral transmission. The fact that Mayer lists 233 editions of Marot published before 1600, and that even more editions have been discovered since the publication of Mayer's bibliography, confirms the phenomenal success of Marot's works.

Popularity proved to be both a blessing and a curse for Marot, however. The preface of the *Adolescence* expresses the poet's displeasure "d'en ouir cryer et publier par les rues une grande partie, toute incorrecte, mal imprimée, et plus au proffit du Libraire, qu'à l'honneur de l'Autheur" (OC 1:35, OPC 1:17) [at hearing a large part of (his works) hawked and made public in the streets, completely erroneous, poorly printed, and more for the bookseller's profit than the author's honor]. His remark reveals not only his concern for his own reputation and his belief that he should have the final say in how his works are made public, but also his awareness that printing his works is a profitable venture, and that printers were more than willing to invest time and money in printing them and even advertising them with criers. In other words, there was no need to create demand for Marot's works, as they were already in high demand, but the profit motive still damaged his reputation by exploiting his success.

Because there was such considerable preexisting demand for the poet's works, Marot's editions favor prestige advertising and publicity. They do not advertise the product so much as the producers, dissociating the poet and printer/publisher's work from the profit motive and soliciting a given public or several distinct yet potentially overlapping publics, such as those who read Marot purely for entertainment or those more attuned to his humanist and evangelical inclinations. Marot's editions sell both themselves and forthcoming editions of the poet's works through the image they create of his career trajectory: the sense of what the poet was, is, and will be suggests to readers what they may expect of his future production. Indeed, to call a collection the *Adolescence* is to advertise for future works by offering a sample, a tactic similar to one commonly employed by French wine criers, and in referring to the *Adolescence* as "coups d'essay," Marot uses an artisanal metaphor that equates the collection with a work by which an apprentice's skill may be evaluated, a work whose main purpose is to demonstrate its maker's capabilities and promise.[14] Text, paratext, and the order of works in the *Adolescence* combine to create an image of this "youthful" work as a taste of better things to come or a sapling that will grow into a magnificent tree. This image persists and is reinforced in the numerous editions of the *Adolescence* and *Suite* published between August 12, 1532 and the summer of 1538, as well as in the 1538 *Œuvres*. It is perhaps to this tendency that Dolet refers when he acknowledges that Marot "tousjours laisse ung desir de soy" [always leaves something of himself to be desired] in his preface to Antoine Héroët's *Parfaicte amye*.[15]

The present chapters will examine how Marot's poetic persona and career trajectory are constructed and maintained in the paratext and order of editions of the *Adolescence, Suite,* and *Œuvres* from 1530 to 1538. By "order," I mean the order of poems within these collections and, to a lesser extent, within individual genre groupings; for unauthorized editions, this also includes changes made to the order of the *princeps* editions, as well as the inclusion of apocryphal or allographic works. I have elected to begin with the 1530 *Opuscules* because as one of only two known pre-1532 Marot collections in print, it may fruitfully be compared with the *princeps* edition of the *Adolescence*.[16] The end date of 1538 corresponds to the Dolet/Gryphe *Œuvres*. Like Lemaire's *Illustrations*, the editions examined in this period predicate ideal readership upon the favorable reception of the edition itself. In so doing, they aim to secure the reader's good will toward the printer/publisher as well as the author.

"Arres de ce mieulx": *L'Adolescence clémentine* as Sample

Olivier Arnoullet (c. 1486–1567) devoted his attention almost exclusively to vernacular works, showing a particular predilection for adaptations of *chansons de geste* like *Girart de Roussillon* and *Huon de Bordeaux*, devotional treatises, translations, and works of *Rhétoriqueurs* like Octavien de Saint-Gelais, Jean Meschinot, or Pierre Gringore.[17] It is not surprising, then, that he was the first to print a collection of Marot's works, probably in late 1530 or 1531. The title page of that collection reads: *Les Opuscules et petitz Traictez de Clement Marot de Quahors, Varlet de chambre du Roy. Contenens Chantz royaulx Ballades Rondeaulx Epistres Elegies avec le Temple de Cupido et la plaincte de Robertet ensemble plusieurs autres choses joyeuses et recreatives redigees en ung et nouvellement imprimees a Lyon par Olivier Arnoullet*.[18] The title is worth citing in its entirety because of how much it contrasts with that of the *Adolescence*: there is no indication whatsoever of chronology or development in Marot's œuvre, nor does the title lay out any lofty poetic ambitions for Marot, describing the contents as "choses joyeuses et recreatives" [merry, delightful things]. Given that the *Opuscules* were published in Lyon, far from the watchful eyes of the Sorbonne and Parlement of Paris, several years prior to the Affair of the Placards (October 17, 1534), there is little reason to believe that the title is meant to protect the book from the authorities. Rather, the emphasis is placed solely on the reader's enjoyment of an already well-known poet.

The novelty of this edition leads Guillaume Berthon to claim that, in spite of its many errors, inelegant *mise en page*, and inclusion of allographic works, it was made more for the author's honor than for the bookseller's profit, despite the poet's protests to the contrary in the *Adolescence*.[19] However, the title calls just as much attention to the work Arnoullet performs in bringing Marot to the reader by distinguishing the collection from the existing *plaquettes* of the "Temple de Cupido," "Epistre de Maguelonne," "Epistre du Camp d'Attigny," "Complainte de Semblançay," and "Déploration de Florimond Robertet." Here, Marot's works have been *redigees en ung*, collected into one handy octavo volume where they were previously scattered across quarto-sized *plaquettes*; Arnoullet has assembled the works of a famous poet for the convenience and enjoyment of a reader who enjoys Marot's humor and wit.

A very different picture of the poet is painted in the August 12, 1532 *princeps* edition of the *Adolescence clementine* printed by Geoffroy Tory and sold by Pierre Roffet, alias Le Faulcheur, a Parisian printer, binder, and bookseller. The little we know about Roffet does not make him an especially likely candidate to become the first exclusive vendor of authorized Marot editions. Setting up shop on the Île de la Cité in 1511 and working until his death in 1533, he focused principally on books of hours, missals, and breviaries, an expensive operation that he most often shared with other Parisian printers.[20] While Roffet's participation in Marot's first foray into print remains difficult to explain, Tory's does not. A humanist printer/publisher and translator, as well as the king's printer from July 1531 until his death in late 1533, he would have been familiar with Marot at court, had a similar taste in letters to Marot, and likely saw in the poet a strong pillar for the defense of the French language.[21] His involvement in the project went beyond printing, as he contributed a Latin epigraph and perhaps influenced the preface, as well.

The fruit of the collaboration between Marot, Tory, and Roffet is an octavo volume titled *L'Adolescence clementine, Autrement, Les Oeuvres de Clement Marot de Cahors en Quercy, Valet de Chambre du Roy, composes en l'eage de son Adolescence. Avec la Complaincte sur le Trespas de feu Messire Florimond Robertet. Et plusieurs autres Oeuvres faictes par ledict Marot depuis l'eage de sa dicte Adolescence. Le tout reveu corrige et mis en bon ordre*.[22] The title contains a wealth of information, beginning with its most prominent aspect, *L'Adolescence clementine*, appearing in capitals above the rest. The use of the term "adolescence" immediately associates the collection with Marot's development as a human being and as a poet. Defaux, drawing on Censorinus's *De die natali liber* and Charles du Fresne, sieur du Cange's *Glossarium*, identifies the *adolescens* as the second of five ages of man, corresponding to the period from fifteen to thirty years of age.[23] Sure enough, the period is referred to in the title as "l'eage de son Adolescence." For Marot, the year in which he left his adolescence behind (1526) corresponds closely to his assumption of his late father's post at court. The title, which equates the book's contents with the author's life in a way that the *Opuscules* do not, promises that the volume will exhibit both the work of a young, promising poet and the results of that poet's maturation, namely the "Déploration de Florimond Robertet" and the "autres Oeuvres faictes par ledict Marot depuis l'eage de sa dicte Adolescence" [other works composed by said Marot after the age of said adolescence]. It presents the volume as proof of maturation, which suggests that "adolescence" may be read as "growth" (*adolesco*) as well as "youth."

The title also stakes a claim to authoritativeness in the face of competing editions. The application of the term "œuvres" to the works of a vernacular writer is somewhat uncommon for this period, and serves to mark Marot as an author in the authoritative sense of the word, as the only person with the right to modify, correct, add to, or assemble his writings.[24] Most importantly, the title distinguishes the book from such preexisting editions of Marot as the *Opuscules* by stressing that it has been "reveu corrige et mis en bon ordre" [revised, corrected, and put in the proper order], intimating that it has been scrupulously compiled, where its predecessors were not. Finally, the title invites a comparison with the *Bucolica seu Adulescentia*, a collection of ten eclogues by the Carmelite monk Baptista Spagnuoli Mantuanus, commonly referred to as Mantuan. Sharing a birthplace with Virgil, Mantuan was regarded as a Christian successor of the Roman poet. Erasmus, for example, claimed in a letter to Henry of Bergen that Mantuan deserves every bit as much to be called "Christianus Maro" as Lactantius deserved to be called "Christianus Cicero," predicting that in time, his fame would surpass that of his illustrious predecessor.[25] Mantuan's most successful work, the *Adulescentia*, were even more of a bestseller north of the Alps and in England than in Italy: of 165 extant printings from 1498 to 1600, only ten are Italian.[26]

In France, the *Adulescentia* were first published in Paris by Jean Petit in 1503, edited and annotated by Josse Bade, and Michel d'Amboise's French translation appeared in 1530.[27] Nathalie Dauvois has pointed out the many similarities between the *Adulescentia* and Marot's *Adolescence*, including their titles, and their presentation of a general evolution from profane to sacred, as

Mantuan added to the original eight eclogues two more composed after he took up religious orders, and Marot's propensity for pastoral and the prominent position of the "Premiere eglogue de Virgile" (*OC* 1:38–43; *OPC* 1:21–26) at the beginning of the *Adolescence*. She also points out some key differences, notably the fact that Mantuan makes explicit his emendations of a youthful work and provides a much more linear progression than Marot.[28] Interestingly, Mantuan addresses the same problem in his preface that Marot addresses in his: the unwanted propagation of his works in print and his desire to exert control over their diffusion. Mantuan explains that in Bologna, he learned that a man of letters possessed a copy of a book he had written for fun while beginning his studies at Padua, a book named *Adulescentia* to reflect the age at which he wrote it:

> [Q]uod iam diu tamquam abortivum putabam abolitum. Ubi id rescivi, saturnina fame repente sum percitus, et cogitavi quonam pacto possem proli meae inferre perniciem. Iuvantibus ergo amicis libellum mihi vindicavi, ut perderem quem suspicabar erratis non posse non scatere. At ubi intellexi et alia quaedam exemplaria superesse, visum est praestare hoc quod vindicaram emendare emendatumque edere, ut eius editione caetera quae continent multa nimis iuvenilia deleantur.[29]

> [Born prematurely, as it were, it is a work that I thought had been destroyed long ago. So, when I learned of it, I was suddenly roused by Saturn's hunger and pondered the means by which I might be able to bring about my progeny's obliteration. Thus, through the help of friends I laid claim to my little book in order to suppress it, a work that I suspected could not help but abound in errors. But when I learned that certain other copies also existed, it seemed better to emend the one I had laid claim to and publish it so that through its publication the other copies, which contain much that is too youthful, might be destroyed.]

Mantuan, with the help of friends similar to Marot's "treschers Freres" [dearest brothers], seeks to gain control over his literary reputation by producing a definitive copy of a work he feels might reflect badly on him in its current state. Like Marot, he responds to preexisting demand (exhibited by the man of letters who owns a copy of the *Adulescentia* and the existence of other copies) by satisfying it with his own product, one that he believes will better guarantee his prestige. Mantuan's book, like Marot's, is equated with its author, as the poet urges his dedicatee, the Mantuan nobleman Paride Ceresara, to accept both book and author and use them as if they were his own according to his judgment. Both the *Adulescentia* and the *Adolescence* attempt to reconcile authorial prestige with readerly demand for works composed in an earlier period of the author's life, and as such, to put forth a specific image of the author. The main difference is that while both Marot and Mantuan address the demand for works already available, Marot also seeks to create demand for works to come.

This effort begins in earnest with Marot's oft-cited preface in the form of a dedication to "ung grant nombre de freres qu'il a, tous Enfans D'apollo" [a great many of his brothers, all children of Apollo]. In it, the poet employs an extended metaphor that acknowledges the tradition of *florilegia* while setting the *Adolescence* apart from it: "Ce n'est (en effect) aultre chose, qu'un petit jardin que je vous ay cultive de ce que j'ay peu recouvrer d'arbres, d'herbes et fleurs de mon primtemps" (OC 1:35; OPC 1:17) [Indeed, it is nothing other than a little garden I have cultivated for you from the trees, herbs, and flowers that I was able to recover from the springtime of my life]. Like a *florilegium*, the *Adolescence* consists of choice pieces culled from Marot's youthful production, and in this sense, it is not entirely different from the 1531 *Opuscules*. Much like Arnoullet's title page, Marot presents his work as having been performed for the benefit of readers: "a little garden I have cultivated for *you*." However, Marot insists that the collection, contrary to the *Opuscules*, is useful as well as enjoyable, in accordance with the Horatian *utile dulci*: "Lisez hardyment, vous y trouverez quelque delectation, et en certains endroictz quelque peu de fruict. Peu dis je, pource qu'arbres nouveaulx entez ne produisent pas fruictz de trop grande saveur" (OC 1:35; OPC 1:17) [Read boldly, for you will find some enjoyment in it, and in some places, a bit of fruitfulness. I say a bit because newly grafted trees do not yield very tasty fruit]. In other words, the *Adolescence* offers everything the *Opuscules* do, and more. The comparison of youthful works to unripe fruit further reinforces the message that the collection is but a taste of what Marot's mature works will be. The very least his readers should get out of the book is "passetemps" (OC 1:36; OPC 1:18). As Jean-Max Colard has shown, "passetemps," meaning either "pastime" or "the passing of time," encourages both an immediate reading based on pleasure and a reading that searches for signs of future maturity. The use of the term thus constitutes an editorial strategy that advertises not only for the *Adolescence*, but also for the works to be published in its wake.[30]

Marot directs the reader to look for signs of his literary evolution in the same way that Petrarch describes the early poems of the *Canzoniere* as a "primo giovenile errore" [first youthful error].³¹ In fact, the garden metaphor might explain the prevalence of the color green in the *Adolescence*, which is mentioned thirteen times, and that, for Marot as for Lemaire, denotes youth or inexperience.³² To provide a sample of Marot's evolution, the *Adolescence* includes some mature works at the end: "Esperant de brief vous faire offre de mieulx, et pour arres de ce mieulx, desja vous mectz en veue (a la fin de l'Adolescence) Ouvraiges de meilleure trempe et de plus polie estoffe" (*OC* 1:36; *OPC* 1:18) [In the hope of offering you something better shortly, and as a down payment for it, even now I am showing you works of a higher caliber and of more polished substance at the end of the *Adolescence*]. The term "arres," like the modern French *arrhes*, is of a particularly commercial nature; Randle Cotgrave defines it as "mony given for the conclusion, or striking up, of a bargaine."³³ Readers are asked to enter into an agreement to continue reading works that Marot will publish, and the more mature works appended to the *Adolescence* are the sample or down payment that both tantalizes readers and reassures them that there is indeed more to come.

"Mes freres (et vous autres nobles lecteurs)": Tory's Ideal Readership

The presentation of Marot's youthful works as a promise of mature ones is bolstered on the title page by Nicolas Bérault's Latin distich: "Hi sunt Clementis juveniles, aspice, lusus. / Sed tamen his ipsis est juvenile nihil" (*OC* 1:33, *OPC* 1:16) [Look, these are Clément's youthful diversions. / And yet, there is nothing youthful about them].³⁴ Bérault, a distinguished scholar and diplomat, was a correspondent and friend of Erasmus and Guillaume Budé, and one of France's premier humanists who was named a royal reader in Greek.³⁵ Bérault's name, the Latin of the distich, and the use of Roman type (the "lettres Attiques" of Tory's *Champ Fleury*) make clear the lofty humanist aspirations of this vernacular book and its producers. In fact, Florian Preisig has identified the title page as a site of tension between author and printer, claiming that the title page confers upon the collection loftier pretensions than those of its author, who first refers to the collected poems as "ces miennes petites jeunesses" (*OC* 1:35; *OPC* 1:17) [these little *juvenilia* of mine]. Preisig compares the title page to a humanist shop window that advertises the book to the readers Tory envisions, offering them an image of the author as humanist.³⁶

The verso of the title page contains two more Latin distiches. The first, by Pierre Brisset, reads: "Quae cecinit juvenis juvenili mente Marotus, / Testantur qualis Musa senilis erit" (*OC* 1:33) [What young Marot sang in his youthful state of mind / Is a testament to what his muse will be like in her old age].³⁷ It reinforces the notion that Marot is continuing to mature as a poet, drawing a distinction between what Marot's poetry used to be (the perfect "cecinit") and what it will eventually become (the future "erit"). Yet, Tory's distich that follows Brisset's would appear to nuance Preisig's assessment: "Vis lauros, cipryasque comas, charitesque, jocosque / Inde sales etiam nosse? Marotus habet" (*OC* 1:33) [Do you truly wish to know laurels, Cyprian foliage, the Graces, jests, / And wit to boot? Marot has them]. The distich, addressed to an unspecified reader ("Ad lectorem"), endorses the poetic *varietas* of the *Adolescence*: the laurels represent Marot's poetic glory and hint at his celebrations of French military victories, the myrtle ("cipryas comas") and the Graces denote the *Adolescence*'s many love poems and perhaps the "Temple de Cupido" specifically, the jests recall Bérault's "juveniles lusus" and Marot's penchant for light, humorous fare, and salt ("sales") represents Marot's particular knack for often biting satire. The collection is a sort of humanist royal banquet capable of pleasing readers with different predilections.³⁸ In fact, the use of the term "jocos" leaves the possibility open for readers to regard the *Adolescence* as a collection of youthful diversions akin to Mantuan's original *Adulescentia*, which is less clearly contradictory of Marot's representation of his work in the preface than Preisig implies. To be sure, the *Adolescence* is meant to be more appealing to a humanist audience than something like the Arnoullet *Opuscules* were, and the distich does represent Tory as a connoisseur and privileged interpreter of Marot who sees in the poet an eminent example of the illustration of the French vernacular.³⁹ At the same time, though, Tory seems to be well aware of the wide-ranging appeal that Marot would have even among the educated elite capable of reading his Latin epigraph, and his evocation of Marot's *varietas* preserves and encourages this appeal.

While Tory's distich acknowledges different modes of reception, Marot's preface aims to control reception through ideal readership. In addressing the community of his fellow humanists and poets whose existence is confirmed by the Latin epigraphs, or perhaps his evangelical *fratres charissimi in Christo* (dearest brothers in Christ), Marot acknowledges his entire readership while simultaneously singling out a model subset of it: "je vous supply (mes Freres) (et vous autres nobles lecteurs) ..." (*OC* 1:36; *OPC* 1:18) [I pray you, my brothers, and you other noble readers ...]. He breaks with the common practice of dedicating a book to a current or future patron, and instead appeals to a general public by encouraging it to live up to its most outstanding members, the ideal readership of the *Adolescence*—that is, if it is indeed Marot who is behind the preface.⁴⁰ Though it is often taken as Marot's manifesto on authorship, Tory may have exerted more influence on it than previously thought, as it reads quite similarly to the preface of the *Champ Fleury*, published three years earlier. This highly metadiscursive preface explains why the *Champ Fleury* is not dedicated to a prominent member of the nobility or clergy, but to all those capable of appreciating it. Tory acknowledges that poets, orators, and learned men customarily present their works to great lords or prelates so as to oblige them to give something in exchange, and he could easily have done the same with the *Champ Fleury*, but

> ... considerant que si je le presentoys plustost a quelcun que a ung autre, Il y porroit avoir quelque enuyeulx scrupule, j'ay avise que ce seroit honnestement faict a moy de vous en faire a tous ung present, O Devotz Amateurs de bonnes Lettres, sans preferer grant a petit, si non d'autant qu'il ayme plus les Lettres, et qu'il est plus intimé en vertus. Par ainsi les Prelats et grans Seigneurs, qui sont tous excellens en belles et bonnes vertus, y auront part en sorte que vous n'en perdres la vostre.[41]

> [... considering that if I presented it to one person rather than to another, there could arise some sort of troublesome difficulty, I thought it would be appropriate to give it as a gift to all of you devoted lovers of good letters, without preferring the great to the small unless they love letters more and are more thoroughly versed in virtues. This way, the prelates and great lords, who all excel in fair and good virtues, will have a share in it without you having to lose yours.]

Tory rejects outright the use of the preface to make a transaction with a patron and exchange praise for money, employment, or an ecclesiastical sinecure. What distinguishes this book's public is not rank, power, or wealth, but love of letters and virtue.[42] In fact, the language of the preface implies that Tory appeals especially to readers of the Third Estate, as it juxtaposes its addressee ("vous") against the "Prelats et grans Seigneurs" of the First and Second Estates.

The fact that the book is not offered exclusively to the rich and powerful does not make the preface any less of a representation of a transaction, however. Rather, the transaction has simply been extended to the unspecified reader, who must still prove himself or herself literate and virtuous by buying and reading the book. Tory holds up ideal readers as "Devotz Amateurs de bonnes Lettres" [devoted lovers of good letters], and reading the *Champ*

Fleury allows any reader to join this idealized community, regardless of station. Marot's preface employs the exact same strategy to secure the reader's good will: "Ne vous chaille (mes Freres) si la courtoysie des lecteurs ne nous excuse, le Tiltre du livre nous excusera" (*OC* 1:35; *OPC* 1:17) [Do not be concerned, brothers, if the courtesy of our readers does not excuse us, for the book's title will]. A courteous reader will appreciate the book as much as do the members of Marot's poetic community, which the anonymous reader may join by receiving the book favorably and in a manner that the author and all those involved in the book's publication approve.

Given their similarities, we should consider the possibility that Tory's preface served as a source for that of the *Adolescence*, and perhaps even that Tory played a role in the latter's composition. After all, the preface represents the publication of the *Adolescence* as a collective project in which many people have a stake.[43] Marot attributes the impetus for publishing the collection not only to his concern over unauthorized editions of his work, but also to the requests of his "brothers," whose demand was an even greater factor than his own indignation. Their influence even gives them an equal share in the results of the book's reception: "Puis donques que vous estes cause de l'évidence de l'oeuvre, je suis d'advis, s'il en vient blasme, que la moytié en tombe sur vous" (*OC* 1:35; *OPC* 1:17) [Since it was because of you that the work was made public, I am of the opinion that if fault is found with it, half the fault should be yours].

Order and Maturation in the *Adolescence*

If the preface's primary purpose is to present the *Adolescence* as a sample of greater things to come and garner favorable reception through ideal readership, its secondary and concomitant purpose is to assert that Marot's works should be published in a certain order. Here, the poet only specifies that the *Adolescence* should come first and begin with his translation of Virgil's first *Eclogue* (*OC* 1:36; *OPC* 1:18). Editions of Marot published during the poet's lifetime adhere to this principle, reconciling organization by chronology with organization by genre, but there remains the question of whether the text of the *Adolescence* supports the claims made in the paratext regarding Marot's capabilities or the promise of greater works to come. As it turns out, the images of the paratext resonate with the text in such a way as to suggest that the collection reflects the author's life and career, though this was not necessarily the case.

The poems that open the *Adolescence* serve as a guide for the rest of the collection. To be sure, the decision to begin with the translation of Virgil's first *Eclogue* invites the Marot-Maro comparison and implies that much of Marot's early career was devoted to mastering Latin through translation.[44] The *Eglogue*'s prominent position also heightens the sense of competition with Mantuan's *Adulescentia*: Perrine Galland-Hallyn suggests that beginning with the *Eglogue* may be a nod to Bérault, who worried that Mantuan was becoming more popular than Virgil.[45] The *Adolescence* supplants the "Christianus Maro" of the *Adulescentia*, offering readers both the original Maro (Virgil) and his legitimate successor and translator. According to Thomas Sébillet, who points to Marot as an example of how to translate in his *Art poëtique*, translations were then considered to be "le Poème plus fréquent et mieux reçu des estimés Poètes et des doctes lecteurs, à cause que chacun d'eux estime grand œuvre et de grand prix, rendre la pure et argentine invention des Poètes dorée et enrichie de notre langue" [the most frequent and well-received poems among esteemed poets and learned readers, because they all deem it a great work of much value to gild and enrich with our tongue the pure, silvery inventions of (ancient) poets].[46] The translation's prominent position matches the humanist framing of the paratext, and would seem to appeal above all to "doctes lecteurs" familiar with the image of Mantuan as Virgil's modern successor.

The eclogue also reflects the horticultural metaphors of the preface. Tityrus and Meliboeus's concern over soldiers using their fields instead of them, a subtle protest against civil war in Virgil, here echoes Marot's concern over the publication of his works:

> Las, pour qui est ce qu'avons semé noz champs?
> O Melibée, plante Arbres à la ligne,
> Ente Poyriers, mectz en ordre la Vigne:
> Las et pour qui?
>   (OC 1:43.150–53; OPC 1:25–26.151–54)

> [Alas, for whom did we sow our fields?
> Meliboeus, plant trees in a line,
> Graft pear trees, maintain an orderly vine:
> Alas, but for whom?]

The pear trees and vines recall Marot's proviso that newly grafted trees do not produce the tastiest fruit, but even more striking is the reappearance of the "ordre" insisted upon in the title page. Given that the preface insists that the *Adolescence* must begin with the "Eglogue," it is likely that it was written with this translation in mind, and the dichotomy between the wealthy Tityrus and the impoverished, but free Meliboeus evokes not only Marot's ambiguous feelings toward patronage, but also his claim to authority over his literary production.

The question of for whom the trees are planted has been answered in the prologue: "a little garden I have cultivated for *you*," and Tityrus's gesture of hospitality toward Meliboeus at the close of the poem mirrors the one Marot makes toward the reader:

> Tu pourras bien (et te pry que le vueilles)
> Prendre repos dessus des vertes fueilles
> Avecques moy, ceste nuyct seulement.
> J'ay à soupper assez passablement,
> Des pommes doulces, tout plain de bon frommage,
> Chastaignes molles, avec force laictage
>   (OC 1:43.163–68).[47]

> [You very well can—and I pray you will—
> Take your rest upon the green leaves
> With me, just for tonight.
> I have food passable enough for supper:
> Sweet apples, plenty of good cheese,
> Tender chestnuts, and plenty of white meat.]

Tityrus invites Meliboeus to enjoy the fruits of his garden with him, much as the reader is invited to enjoy the fruits of Marot's garden in the preface, and the parallel between this pastoral repast and the material book is implied by the "fueilles" under which the shepherds rest.

Other moments in the *Adolescence* reinforce the comparison of Marot's poetic career to ripening fruit, as well. The last two poems of the "Epistres," the "Epistre pour le capitaine Bourgeon à monseigneur l'escuyer la Rocque" [Epistle for Captain Bourgeon to My Lord Squire La Rocque] and the "Epistre faicte pour le Capitaine Raisin audict seigneur de la Rocque" [Epistle for Captain Raisin to said Lord La Rocque] constitute a humorous reference to Marot's poetic maturation through the ripening of the bud ("Bourgeon") into a grape ("Raisin") from one poem to the next (OC 1:100–103; OPC 1:88–91). Similarly, the first half of the *Adolescence*, the "Oeuvres Poetiques que Clement Marot ... composa en l'eage de son Adolescence" [poetic works that Clément

Marot... composed in the age of his adolescence] as opposed to the more mature works that follow, ends with a song celebrating Bacchus and wine, a product of ripened fruit (*OC* 1:187; *OPC* 1:195).

Among the mature works, the celebrated "Epistre au Roy par Marot estant malade à Paris" [Epistle to the King from Marot, sick in Paris] (better known by its 1544 title "Au Roy pour avoir esté dérobé" [To the King, on account of having been robbed]) similarly plays on expectations for Marot's career through its depiction of Marot's bout with the plague, which most likely occurred during an epidemic in mid- to late 1531. Plague imagery pervades the poem, even the description of the stock Gascon valet's larceny: the "venerable Hillot," seeing that Marot's purse "avoit grosse apostume" [had a great big bubo] after being filled with one hundred *écus* given by the king, runs away with the purse beneath his armpit, a site where buboes commonly appear (*OC* 1:227.17–20; *OPC* 1:320.17–20). Marot transmits his money to the Gascon as if it were the plague, then catches the actual plague himself, which he spends nearly thirty lines describing, and predicts that he is likely to die in winter: "Et en danger (si en yver je meurs) / De ne veoir pas les premiers raisins meurs" (*OC* 1:228.77–78; *OPC* 1:322.77–78) [And I am in danger, if I die in winter, / Of not seeing the first ripe grapes]. The reader, having seen Marot describe his youthful works as unripe fruit in the preface, may pick up on the echo and feel relieved that Marot has survived to maturity.

Maturation is also a prominent theme in the "Adolescence" proper: after the "Eglogue" comes a truly pivotal *dit*, the "Temple de Cupido, Et la Queste de Ferme Amour" (*OC* 1:44). The "Ferme amour" that the speaker eventually chooses over erotic and inconstant love, whether it is taken to mean simple constancy and fidelity or Pauline *agape*, is a central concept to Marot's *œuvre* and recurs throughout it.[48] As such, the "Temple" is a *dit* that not only imitates the *Roman de la Rose* and Lemaire's *Concorde des deux langages*, but also represents the poet's quest for his own poetics and personal style.[49] While the imagery in the "Temple" facilitates the allegory of love that is the Mass, it also anticipates the rest of the *Adolescence* and prepares the reader for it. The reference to the "faulx et desloyal Jason" [false and disloyal Jason] foreshadows the "Epistre de Maguelonne," just as the "brandon de Destresse, / Dont fut enflammée Dido" [torch of distress / With which Dido was enflamed] anticipates the acrostic rondeau following it (*OC* 1:49.202, 1:50.234–35; *OPC* 1:33.202, 1:34.234–35). The misgivings arising from the reference to the passions of Dido, Byblis, and Helen set up the speaker's embrace of Ferme Amour and Maguelonne's refusal to despair, which distinguishes her from the equally jilted Dido. The vaults made of Priapus's trellises from which hang "Bourgeons et raisins à plaisance" [all the buds and grapes you could want] echo the satirical last two poems of the Epistres, further encouraging the reader to draw a parallel between Marot's production and the speaker's journey in the "Temple" (OC 1:51.278; OPC 1:35.278).

The "Temple" may thus be seen as a microcosm of the *Adolescence,* and is strewn with references to the genres and *formes fixes* that make up the collection: the lessons sung in the Temple are rondeaus, ballads, and virelays (OC 1:52.328–29; OPC 1:36.328–29).⁵⁰ Perhaps even more striking is the Temple's cemetery, which connects the preface to the "Complainctes et epitaphes":

> Le Cymetiere est ung vert boys:
> Et les murs, Hayes, et Buissons.
> Arbres plantez, ce sont les Croix:
> *De profundis,* gayes Chansons.
>   (OC 1:52.313–16; OPC 1:36.313–16)

> [The cemetery is a green wood,
> And its walls, hedges and bushes.
> Planted trees are its crosses,
> And its *De profundis,* merry songs.]

In describing the cemetery as a wood with hedges and bushes for walls and trees for grave markers, Marot draws a parallel between the "little garden I have cultivated for you from the trees, herbs, and flowers that I was able to recover from the springtime of my life" and the "Complainctes et epitaphes."⁵¹ Yet, the description of the cemetery in terms highly reminiscent of the preface suggests that the *locus amoenus* characteristic of love poetry (the usual cemetery wall has been replaced with greenery) is, in fact, a space of death that fails to reflect the message of Christ's triumph over death and humanity's redemption through grace that figures so prominently in the "Déploration de Florimond Robertet." Trees cannot adequately mark graves or do justice to the deceased until they have been fashioned into crosses, wooden representations of Christ's sacrifice.

This comparison is not the only one of its kind in the *Adolescence.* A similar one occurs in the "Oroison contemplative devant le Crucifix" [Contemplative prayer before the Cross]:

> Et que mon corps soit tout fendu en bouches,
> Pour myeulx à plain, et en plus de manieres
> Te rendre grace, et chanter mes prieres.
>   (OC 1:75.72–74; OPC 1:62.72–74)

[And may my body be hewn into mouths
The more fully, and in more ways,
To thank you, and sing my prayers.]

The pun on "bouches" (mouths) and *bûches* (logs) drives home the notion that the poet, in his current state, is raw material that must be refined, much like a tree must be hewn into logs before it can be put to use. In the poet's case, he must come to voice prayers with many mouths by disseminating the word of God through print. Similarly, Psalm 130 (*De profundis*), used in the liturgy as a hymn to the faithful departed, has been replaced in the "Temple de Cupido" with "gayes Chansons" not unlike those with which the *Adolescence* concludes, such as Chanson 12:

Tant que vivray en aage florissant,
Je serviray amour, le dieu puissant,
En faictz et dictz, en chansons et accords.
 (*OC* 1:177.1–3; *OPC* 1:185.1–3)

[As long as I live in my flowering age,
I will serve love, the mighty god,
In deeds and words, in songs and chords.][52]

The "Temple," then, not only represents an early attempt by the young Marot to make his mark, but also hints at the mature Marot's dissatisfaction with his poetic production thus far and suggests that the poet is still seeking a poetry worthy of *Ferme Amour* that will eventually take the form of his Psalm translations.[53] Marot invites the reader through use of the first-person plural to search the collection for evidence of this quest: "Or taschons à trouver la chose, / Que je cherche au Temple d'Amours" (*OC* 1:54.422; *OPC* 1:39.422) [Now let us try to find / What I am searching for in the Temple of Love].

Imagery aside, does the order of poems in the *Adolescence* corroborate the maturation hinted at in the paratext and text? A great deal of critical attention has been devoted to this question, with the general consensus that there is some logic to the order of poems within genre divisions and within the *Adolescence* as a whole.[54] Studies have been primarily thematic in nature, as those that focus on specific genres have centered on how the themes in the "Ballades" mark a rupture with the "Epistres" and establish a continuity with the "Complainctes et epitaphes," on how they tell a story of salvation on a personal, national, and universal level, or on the theme of peace in the Epistres as an attempt to create a Christian (and likely evangelical) community across both the universal and particular planes of experience.[55] Although these accounts are attuned to definite tendencies of Marot's, they adhere strictly to the authorized edition and regard unauthorized editions as inadmissible precisely because they corrupt or threaten Marot's intended unity. In order to arrive at a clearer idea of how these unauthorized editions are compiled, we must first consider the aspect of the authorized edition's order that gives rise to them: the narrative of Marot's poetic career.

Edwin Duval has performed an extensive structural analysis of the *Adolescence* based on how the collection's two halves differ in terms of chronology: the *Adolescence* alludes to events that transpired prior to 1526 during Marot's career at the court of Marguerite de Navarre when she was still the Duchess of Alençon, whereas the *Autres Oeuvres* are works composed after 1526 at the royal court. The two sections are thus divided by the year in which Marot turned thirty and ceased to be an *adolescens*. However, while identifying this chronological principle, Duval challenges the notion that the order of poems in the *Adolescence* delivers on the promise of evolution or maturation. In his view, the poems of the *Autres Oeuvres*, notably the epistles concerning Marot's imprisonment, illness, and thieving valet, betray the evolution clearly laid out in the long poems at the beginning of the collection by indicating an autobiographical devolution and personal crisis.[56] The order of the collection implies that Marot's later difficulties prevented him from producing greater works; the *Adolescence* raises the reader's hopes only to dash them with excuses in the *Autres oeuvres*.

I do not agree that these greater works must necessarily meet Duval's criterion of "some kind of *Aeneid*," but the personal crisis represented in the last poems of the *Adolescence* does leave Marot's career in a state of suspense. The reader is left to wonder whether Marot, having survived imprisonment, theft, and plague, actually will produce works worthy of his mature skill or of his turn toward religion, depending on which reading one pursues. In examining subsequent editions of the *Adolescence*, we find that these same personal crises, especially his illness, provide printer/publishers with an answer to this question and a tool with which to satisfy readers' expectations.

Marot's "Jeunesse abusée": Unauthorized Editions of the *Adolescence*

In terms of paratext, the next three Tory-Roffet editions of the *Adolescence* are largely similar to the *princeps*, with the notable difference that they underscore the printer's role even further. The title page of the February 12, 1533 edition indicates that it is "Plus amples que les premiers imprimez de ceste ny autre impression" [Ampler than the first of this or any other printing], referring to the addition of some poems concerning Marot's illness.[57] The title page of the June 7, 1533 edition further notes that acute accents, apostrophes marking elisions, and cedillas have been added to the text, "Ce qui par cy devant par faulte d'advis n'a este faict au langaige françoys, combien qu'il y fust et soyt tresnecessaire" [Which heretofore, due to lack of judgment, has never been done for the French language, even though it was and still is most necessary].[58] This introduction of diacritical marks reflects some of the reforms proposed by Tory in the *Champ Fleury*, which leads Nina Catach to hypothesize that the printer convinced Marot to take his typographical reforms on board for this edition.[59] Berthon, however, points out that Marot never openly approved of the introduction of diacritical marks, and that his concern with correct printing had more to do with not corrupting the text than with any perceived inadequacies of typography.[60] The reforms are therefore almost certainly Tory's imposition, and are another example of how a printer can call attention to the services that he performs for the reader. Indeed, the title page places as much emphasis on Tory's enrichment of the French language through printing as on Marot; the marks have been added less for the benefit of Marot's poems than for the benefit of the French language, which is sorely in need of them.

The text of these editions corresponds to that of the *princeps* edition, with the exception of the aforementioned additional poems concerning Marot's illness appended to the end of the *Autres Oeuvres* under the heading "Autres Oeuvres faictes en sa dicte maladie" [Other works composed during said illness].[61] They prolong the suspense created by the introduction of Marot's sickness, but when examined piecemeal, they also reinforce the notion of maturity implied by the *Autres Oeuvres*, corroborating a reading of this maturity as growth in poetic skill and ambition or a reading of it as a religious conversion. The first of these, "Au Lieutenant de Bourges Gontier . . . ," heaps facetious praise on the verses of this "Gontier" [churl], verses "si haults, et arduz à tout prendre, / Que mon Esprit travaille à les comprendre" (*OC* 1:407.11–12; *OPC* 1:325.11–12) [so lofty and, in all, difficult to grasp / That my mind labors to understand them]. Marot's "apology" to Gontier for not replying more promptly positively drips with sarcasm, as he claims that his pen is too rustic for a bumpkin to appreciate. Any doubts about Marot's claim to divinely inspired poetic talent ("ung esprit Poëtique") are dissipated by his second "excuse":

> les Muses me contraignent
> Penser ailleurs et fault que mes Vers plaignent

> La dure mort de la Mere du Roy,
> Mon Mecenas.
>   (OC 1:408.23–26; OPC 1:326.23–26)
>
> [The Muses compel me to
> Direct my thought elsewhere, and my verses must lament
> The cruel death of the mother of the king,
> My Maecenas.]

It grieves the poet not to have been able to provide a lengthier reply, but he was inconvenienced with the bothersome task of composing the "Eglogue sur le trespas de treshaulte et tresillustre princesse ma Dame Loyse de Savoye" [Eclogue on the Passing of the Most Lofty and Illustrious Princess Madame Louise of Savoy] (OC 1:204–12; OPC 1:224–31). Unlike Gontier, Marot is not a *rimeur*, but a poet inspired by the Muses, and he invokes the Maro/Marot parallel by comparing Francis I to Maecenas, the protector of Horace and Virgil whose name is synonymous with patronage.

The ensuing poem to Vignals reinforces Marot's ironic praise of Gontier. Though he spares this *écolier toulousain* [Toulouse schoolboy] much of the spleen vented upon Gontier, the poet inserts yet another criticism of affected style:

> Ce neantmoins (Vignals) je pense bien
> Que tu congnois que le souverain bien
> De l'amytié ne gist en longues Lettres,
> En motz exquis, en grand nombre de Mettres,
> Ains en bon cueur et en vraye intention.
>   (OC 1:408.5–10; OPC 1:326.5–10)
>
> [Despite this, Vignals, I do think
> You know that the greatest good
> Of friendship lies not in long letters,
> Exquisite words, or a great number of meters,
> But in a good heart and in true intentions.]

The "bon cueur" continues the emphasis on simplicity and sincerity over excessive ornamentation from the response to Gontier and recalls the "Ferme Amour" of "Temple de Cupido," creating the impression that Marot's maturity has not led him to abandon one of the foundational principles of his poetry. By integrating Marot's illness with his poetic maturation, these two poems accentuate the danger posed by a malady that threatens to cut down the poet just as he begins to realize his full potential.

The poet's fear of imminent death is quite palpable in the set of poems labeled "Ce qu'il escrivit a ses Medecins en sadicte Maladie" [What he wrote to his doctors during said illness], and especially in the *huitain* to the physician Michel Amy, who had himself recently recovered from a serious illness.[62] The *huitain*'s internal rhymes underscore the contrast between the doctor's own convalescence and his inability to aid Marot's:

> Amy de nom, de pensée et de faict,
> Qu'ay je *meffaict* que vers moy ne prens voye?
> Graces à Dieu, tu es dru et *refaict*;
> Moy, plus *deffaict* que ceulx que morts on *faict*.
> Mort en *effect*, si Dieu toy ne m'*envoye*,
> Brief ne *pourvoye* au mal qui me *desvoye*.
>   (OC 1:439.1–6; OPC 2:221.1–6; emphasis mine).

> [Friend in name, thought, and deed,
> What have I done wrong to keep you from coming to me?
> Thank God you are hale and hearty,
> But I am more broken than those who are put to death.
> I am dead indeed if God does not send you my way,
> And you do not presently attend to the sickness that derails me.]

Marot's exhortation underscores his sickness as an interruption of his poetic maturation ("qui me desvoye"). At the same time, the poet calls attention to Amy's powerlessness to heal him and resigns himself to God's will, which is ultimately all that can determine whether he is to live or die. The additional poems thus begin to hint at the afflicted Marot's turn toward God in keeping with a conversion narrative. The last of the additional poems, the *dizain* to Pierre Vuyard, Claude of Lorraine's secretary, adds to this narrative by representing a speaker torn between the preservation of his body and the liberation of his spirit from its corporeal prison:

> Ce meschant Corps demande guerison,
> Mon frere cher: et l'Esprit, au contraire,
> Le veult laisser comme une orde Prison:
> L'ung tend au Monde et l'autre à s'en distraire.
>   (OC 1:440.1–4; OPC 2:222–23.1–4)

[This miserable body demands to be healed,
Dear brother, and on the other hand, the spirit
Wants to leave it like a filthy prison:
One reaches for the world, the other strives to depart from it.]

The connotation of *fratres charissimi in Christo* ("frere cher") imparts an evangelical flavor to the poem, which was included in Antoine Augereau's December 1533 edition of the *Miroir de treschrestienne princesse Marguerite de France* and assigned the title "Dizain d'ung Chrestien malade à son amy" [Dizain from a sick Christian to his friend].[63] Most importantly, the last line, "Du Seigneur Dieu la volunté soit faicte" [The Lord God's will be done], restates the speaker's submission to God's will in the letter to Amy by rendering the *Pater noster*'s "fiat voluntas tua" [thy will be done] (*OC* 1:610n143). This scrap of prayer translation anticipates the addition of parts or all of Marot's *Instruction et foy d'ung chrestien* to subsequent editions of the *Adolescence* and *Suite*.

The very first edition to add these translations appeared just over three months after the publication of the November 13th *Adolescence*. This was the first edition of the *Adolescence* to be printed in Lyon by one of the city's most celebrated printer/publishers, François Juste. Details on Juste's life are scarce, and any hypotheses as to the man's inclinations must be based upon his production, which, not unlike Arnoullet's, reflects a propensity for the vernacular. His early career also reflects his tendency to counterfeit successful works either unprotected by privilege or protected by Parisian privileges with no teeth in Lyon, which made the *Adolescence* a prime target.[64] Juste is also thought to have shared the evangelical leanings of the authors he is best known for printing, and Paul Lacroix goes so far as to suggest that Juste anonymously published a number of Protestant *plaquettes*, though the claim is unsubstantiated.[65] Nevertheless, given Juste's affinity for writers suspected of heresy like François Rabelais, Maurice Scève, and Marot, we may at least regard his evangelism as highly likely, and his editions of the *Adolescence* further substantiate this theory.

Juste's February 23, 1533 edition of the *Adolescence* closely follows the Roffet *princeps* edition in terms of the text, but appends four poems to the end of the *Autres Oeuvres*. The first two of these are "Le Pater noster, et le Credo en francoys faict et traduict pa[r] ledict C. M. et offert na guyeres a la Royne de Navarre" [The *Pater noster* and *Credo* in French, composed and translated by said Clément Marot and recently offered to the Queen of Navarre].[66] Like the aforementioned *dizain* to Vuyard, these French translations of the Lord's

Prayer and Apostles' Creed were printed in Antoine Augereau's edition of Marguerite's *Miroir de l'âme pécheresse* that same year, and had likely been offered to the queen earlier in manuscript form. Their inclusion here suggests that Juste took a particular interest in Marot's evangelical project of translating prayers into the vernacular, but their presence also has just as profound an effect on the representation of Marot's career in this volume of the *Adolescence* as the inclusion of the sickness poems does in the Roffet editions.

The evocation of Marguerite's name recalls Marot's role as poet of the royal family and underscores his participation in the queen's literary and religious circle. More significantly, the presence of these translations at the end of the *Autres Oeuvres* implies that Marot has finally found the greater calling evoked throughout the *Adolescence*, and that his poetic wood has finally been carved into crosses. Marot's rendering of the last lines of the Apostles' Creed dovetails with both the poet's sickness in the *Autres Oeuvres* and the poet's motto, "La mort n'y mord" [Death has no teeth], affixed to this translation: "Finablement croy la vie eternelle / Telle est ma foy, et veulx mourir en elle" (OC 1:434.7–8; OPC 1:391.7–8) [Lastly, I believe in life everlasting; / This is my faith, and I am willing to die in it]. The proximity of these lines to the account of the poet's near-death encounter with the plague fleshes out the conversion narrative hinted at in the Roffet editions, and in this context, "La mort n'y mord" seems to indicate the poet's willingness to face death strengthened by his faith in redemption in keeping with the "Déploration de Florimond Robertet."[67] Including these translations allows Juste to kill two birds with one stone: he can include additional works that hold a special appeal for an evangelically inclined audience, and he can make the book appear to deliver more fully on the *Adolescence*'s promise of greater things to come.

The edition does not conclude with Marot's translations, but with two allographic poems, a *chant royal* on fortune and worldly possessions and an epitaph of Marie, the eldest daughter of Geoffroy d'Estissac.[68] Both are signed "F. R.," which has led to the generally accepted hypothesis that they were penned by none other than François Rabelais, the former protégé of Estissac and tutor of his nephew Louis.[69] Their putative attribution to Rabelais is of less significance to the present study than their content and the manner in which they are presented to the reader. Thematically, they join seamlessly with Marot's prayer translations and the conversion narrative they introduce. The *chant royal* lends an especially evangelical flavor to the additional poems, as its vocabulary evokes the doctrines of predestination and justification by faith alone:

Sommes *esleuz* à la saincte assistence.
Puis se vestir de la ferme existence
De *foy*, qui l'homme orne tresnoblement.
   (OPC 2:758.30–36; emphasis mine)

[We are elected to be part of the holy audience.
Then, one must clothe oneself solidly
With faith, which most nobly adorns a man.]

The epitaph, in turn, contains clear parallels to both the *chant royal* and the volume's conversion narrative. Its speaker, the young Marie's soul, explains how she wished to die rather than remain in a mortal state permanently tainted by sin, a wish God granted her through premature birth and a swift departure from this vale of tears. Marie acts as a surrogate for Marot, suggesting that the poet truly has turned a corner, and, like the girl, would rather resign himself to death and redemption than persist in his youthful errors, just as he expresses his desire to abandon the "filthy prison" of his body in the *dizain* to Vuyard.

Marie's death crowns the conversion narrative of Juste's edition, and the "F. R." poems may be seen as the evangelical equivalent of the Latin distiches in the paratext of the *Adolescence*. The two groups of allographic poems frame Marot's poetic persona within an evangelical or a humanist context, respectively, presenting him as a French poet who is worthy of the ancients or who eventually turns to God and the Reformation. Furthermore, the coexistence of these two groups of liminary poems within this one edition implies that Juste's edition, like the image of Marot's career it conveys through the poet's persona, is simultaneously tailored to evangelical readers, humanist readers, and evangelical humanist readers. In every edition of the *Adolescence*, Marot's preface informs readers that the poet's garden was planted especially for them. The flexibility of Marot's persona allows printer/publishers like Juste to organize their editions so as to deliver on this promise for groups of readers with possibly conflicting orientations, all while giving each group sufficient reason to believe that Marot is *their* poet.

Juste did not stop there, either. In July 1533, he produced a second edition of the *Adolescence*, this one with many more additional pieces than the first. Defaux has pointed to this edition as evidence of collaboration between Marot, Juste, and Rabelais, claiming that Marot followed the court to Lyon in June and entrusted his poems on Francis I's banishment of the syndic Noël Béda the previous month to the good doctor for publication in Juste's edition.⁷⁰ As Berthon points out, not only is it unclear whether Marot was even in Lyon at this time, but in the absence of any tangible evidence, there is little reason to believe that Marot would have approved of an edition containing works that he later explicitly disavowed and others that did not reappear in the 1538 *Œuvres*.⁷¹ The edition is less a reflection of Marot's pre-Placards reformist ardor than of Juste's attempt to expand upon Marot's evangelical poetic persona with additional material.

A glance at the title page reveals that Juste, like a great many of his colleagues, was not above false advertising, as the reader is promised "plus de soixante nouvelles compositions lesquelles jamays ne furent Imprimees, comme pourrez veoire a la fin du livre" [over sixty new compositions, never before printed, as you will be able to see at the end of the book].⁷² In reality, there are forty additional works included, fourteen of which may be found in prior editions. At first glance, this mass of new material seems to corroborate Duval's characterization of post-1532 editions as adding archaic *formes fixes* in bulk without any concern for theme, genre, or chronology.⁷³ Upon closer inspection, however, much of it heightens the effects of the previous Juste edition. The Lyonnais printer/bookseller seems to have taken a cue from the Roffet re-editions, as the ten sickness poems now follow the *Autres Oeuvres*.

Directly following these are the "Epitaphe du Conte de Salles" [Epitaph of the Count de Salles] and "Complaincte de Dame Bazoche sur le trespas dudict Conte" [Lamentation of Lady Bazoche on the death of said Count], two poems that Marot condemned in 1538 as part of the "lourderies qu'on a meslées en mes Livres" (*OC* 1:384; *OPC* 1:10) [tomfooleries that have been mixed into my books]. Although the poet found them lacking, these poems contain as many remarkable parallels with the *Adolescence* and the sickness poems as do the "F. R." poems of the previous edition. The epitaph employs the same rhetoric of misfortune found in the *Autres Oeuvres* and sickness poems, and its affinity with both groups is made even clearer by an accounting metaphor:

> Parquoy laissay pour bon gaige ma vie,
> Dont j'ay quictance sans faulte ne mescompte
> Escripte au Roolle des mors d'epidimye.
>
> [So I put down my life as collateral,
> And was given a receipt, without mistake or error,
> Written in the register of those who died of the plague.]⁷⁴

The "gaige" recalls the *Adolescence*, which Marot has put down as "arres de ce mieulx," and the "Roolle" recalls the "Epistre à monseigneur le Chancellier du Prat, nouvellement Cardinal, envoyée par ledict Marot oublyé en l'estat du Roy" [Epistle to My Lord Chancellor du Prat, recently made a Cardinal, sent by said Marot, who was overlooked in the royal estate], in which Marot demands to be added to the salary register of the royal estate after having been omitted (*OC* 1:220–21; *OPC* 1:313–15). The death of this Count in an "epidimye," along with the ensuing *complainte* voiced by the personification of a theater company known for staging farces, implies that the joyous farces of Marot's youth are a thing of the past, swept away once and for all by his bout with the plague. In this context, we may see in the line "Car tel est bien hault juche qu'on desmonte" [For he who sits very high in the saddle is unhorsed] a reference to Luke 14:11 ("For all who exalt themselves will be humbled, and those who humble themselves will be exalted"): the "on" is none other than God, who lays Marot low to encourage him to humble himself in devotion.

The *complainte* is followed by two *rondeaux*. The first, "Au cueur ne peult ung chascun commander" [Not everyone can command the heart], reintroduces the heart topos central to the "Temple de Cupido" and the epistle to Vignals (*OC* 1:253; *OPC* 2:760–61). The second, "Juges, prevostz, bourgeoys, marchans, commun," addresses all three estates as if predicting an imminent apocalypse:

> Juges, prevostz, bourgeoys, marchans, commun,
> Nobles, vilains, et vous seigneurs d'Eglise,
> Amendez vous: sinon je vous advise
> Que ne verrez l'an cinq cens quarante un.
>   (*OC* 1:254.1–4; *OPC* 2:761.1–4)

> [Judges, provosts, burghers, merchants, commoners,
> Nobles, serfs, and you lords of the Church,
> Better yourselves: if you don't, I warn you
> That you will not see the year 541.]

In Rigolot's view, the moralizing warning is meant to have a comedic effect, as no one actually expects to live to the age of 541.[75] However, "l'an cinq cens quarante un" may refer to the year 1541 rather than to the age of 541, and in the context of a series of plague poems, the universal warning to people from all walks of life seems rather more like a *danse macabre* than a bit of comedy.

Moreover, the fact that the "seigneurs d'Eglise" are singled out by being mentioned last anticipates some of the more brazenly anticlerical poems to follow.

The same may be said of the next rondeau, "Nostre maistre Geoffroy Brulart," which abounds in theologically loaded vocabulary, notably "Nostre maistre" (a translation of the title *Magister Noster* given to theologians of the Sorbonne and other faculties) and "papelart" [hypocrite].[76] Addressing a theologian as if he were a physician, the poem connects the pieces on Marot's sickness with the three poems on Noël Béda; the narrative of Marot's physical illness and subsequent turn to a higher calling converges with a narrative of the Church's spiritual sickness and its subsequent cure through reform signaled by Béda's banishment, though the aftermath of the Affair of the Placards would disabuse French evangelicals of this hope. Marot's resignation to his illness is then recalled by the ensuing "Remede contre la peste" [Cure for the plague], a set of humorous instructions whose last two lines reveal its take on the inefficacy of medicine: "Continuez ung an ou deux; / De trois mois ne mourrez de peste" (OC 2:463.23–24; OPC 2:290.23–24) [Keep it up for a year or two, / And you won't die of the plague for three months].

The first of the next five poems, the rondeau "Qui ses besoignes veult bien faire" [If someone wants to do his job well], acknowledges that Marot must still attend to the business of being a court poet while indicating his increasing dissatisfaction with it:

> Le Herault ung peu contrefaire,
> Mais encore est il necessaire
> Estre beau parleur, et non lourd.
>   (OC 2:254.7–9; OPC 2:761.7–9)

> [Imitate the herald a bit,
> But you still have to
> Be a fair speaker, not a dull one.]

The comparison of court poet to herald suggests Marot's official duty to proclaim the king's accomplishments and the major events of his reign. While Marot retains his official capacity and his financial dependence on the king (as seen in the "Deux placets" included after the Béda poems), this rondeau conveys the sense that he regards his position as a burden that prevents him from pursuing his true calling, a sense that persists in the ensuing pieces.

After these five poems come the "Pater" and "Credo," as well as a "Benediction devant manger" that would not be included in the 1538 *Œuvres*, and that makes an implicit reference to the evangelical doctrine of *sola scriptura:* "Donne nous par ton escripture / Que noz esprits soient nourris" (*OC* 1:609n126; *OPC* 1:812) [Grant that by Your scripture / Our spirits be nourished]. Two devotional *rondeaux*, "O quel erreur, parfaictz esperitz" [O what an error, perfect spirits] and "O Bon Jesus de Dieu eternel filz" [O goodly Jesus, son of God everlasting], follow. This suite of religious poems is interrupted by what I would term the *Adieux* quarrel, consisting of the "A Dieulx nouveaux" [New farewells] and Marot's responses to its authors (though he may indeed have written it himself) and to the Parisian women who accuse him of impugning their honor. This second response is most pertinent, as it represents a Marot who distances himself from the *Adolescence* even further and bemoans his inability to undertake tasks worthy of his talent:

> N'ay je passé ma jeunesse abusée
> Autour de vous [?] laquelle j'eusse usée
> En meilleur lieu (peut estre en pire aussy)
> (*OC* 1:309–10.69–71; *OPC* 1:286.69–71)

> [Didn't I waste my youth
> Hanging around with you, which I could have spent
> Doing something better (or maybe worse)?]

"Jeunesse" refers not just to the image we have of Marot's youth in Paris from such poems of the *Adolescence* as the "Ballade de Marot du temps qu'il aprenoit à escrire au Palais à Paris" [Ballad by Marot from when he was learning to write at the Palais in Paris], but also to the *Adolescence* in its entirety, suggesting that Marot wasted his youthful compositions on women such as these (*OC* 1:117–18; *OPC* 1:113–14).

The poet goes on to explain that he is still prevented from writing what he wants, only this time by persecution rather than by impertinent Parisian women:

> Tant de broillys, qu'en Justice on tolere,
> Je l'escriroys mais je crains la collere.
> L'oysiveté des Prebstres et Cagotz,
> Je la diroys mais garde les fagotz.
> Et des abus, dont l'Eglise est fourrée,
> J'en parleroys, mais garde la bourrée.
> (*OC* 1:310.81–86; *OPC* 1:286.81–86)

[There is so much pettifoggery allowed by the judicial system
That I would write about, but I fear their anger.
Of the idleness of priests and dissemblers
I would write, but the stake keeps me from it.
And of the abuses the Church wears like furs
I would tell, were it not for those bundles of wood.]

The preterition of these lines and the fact that the poems on Béda's exile, which immediately follow this epistle, do indeed point to abuses of the clergy suggest that Marot, despite his claim to the contrary, composes and publishes poetry that might cost him his life at the stake. This edition defers what it ultimately provides, using Marot's role as court poet and involvement in a quarrel to delay the inevitable arrival of the expanded prayer translations and engagement in what was regarded as a major victory for the evangelical cause. By juxtaposing the "A Dieulx nouveaux" with prayer translations, devotional poems, and satires of oppressive Catholic orthodoxy, Juste makes it seem that Marot has indeed bid *adieu* to his frivolous youth and turned entirely toward God (*à Dieu*).

In fact, "Qui ses besoignes veult bien faire" may actually be seen as a testament to this putative victory: to portray the poet as "herald" makes him the king's mouthpiece, and in celebrating Béda's banishment, the king's poet publicly praises the king's seemingly reformist policy. Juste's edition thus merges the narrative of Marot's poetic persona with the narrative of the Reformation in France, capping their intersection with the same two "F. R." poems as in the previous edition. In so doing, it exemplifies how a printer/publisher can build upon and even manipulate an authorial persona to make it correspond all the more closely to the expectations of a certain group of readers. Marot himself, however, was not about to sit idly by while the persona he and his collaborators had worked so hard to build and publicize was tinkered with to appeal to readers who privileged a certain way of reading the poet's *œuvre*. After all, it was not in his best interest to allow himself to be represented as militantly evangelical, especially after his return from exile in Ferrara and Venice in the wake of the Affair of the Placards. While his stay at the court of the evangelically minded Renée of France and his improvement in Latin under the tutelage of Celio Calcagnini did lead to a sharper satirical edge and a more offensive stance in some works, notably his *coq-à-l'âne* and, later, the Sagon controversy, as Bernd Renner has shown, Marot nevertheless remained rather more circumspect in matters of crafting an authorial persona in collections of his works.⁷⁷ The manuscript he presented to the constable Anne de Montmorency, a noted conservative, proves that, as with his policies for editing Villon, he preferred to adapt his works and his persona to the circumstances.⁷⁸ And so, in terms of print, he decided to fight fire with fire, meeting demand for the additional works promised in the *Adolescence* with the succinctly named *Suite de l'Adolescence clémentine*.

CHAPTER 4

"Je n'en donne ung festu, pourveu qu'ayons son livre"
The Suite and the 1538 Œuvres

THE *SUITE* was first published in late 1533 or early 1534 by Louis Blaubloom, who went by the Latinized name Cyaneus, for the widow of Pierre Roffet.¹ As its title suggests, it is a continuation of the *Adolescence clementine* published to compete with counterfeit editions. It reproduces several of the poems that had already appeared in them, and encourages readers of the *Adolescence* to continue to expect greater works from Clément Marot. A much less impressively constructed volume than Geoffroy Tory's first printing of the *Adolescence*, it does not appear to be ordered anywhere near as carefully, but it surpasses its predecessor in terms of advertising Marot's editions and those of his printers to the anonymous reader.

Although the *Suite* contains less paratext than the *Adolescence*, the paratext that it does contain is more forceful in calling attention to the printer/publisher's role in making the author's work available to the public. This role is elaborated upon in three Latin epigraphs by France's two most eminent Neo-Latin poets at the time, the first and third by Salmon Macrin (with translations by Antoine Macault), and the second by Nicolas Bourbon. In his first epigraph, Macrin speaks to the reader as a reader, introducing an adversarial relationship between printer/publisher and poet in which the former serves as the reader's ally against the latter:

> Quos tu tantopere expetis, probasque,
> Demiransque stupes, amice lector,

> Clementi nisi surpuisset audax
> Maroto plagiarus libellos,
> Esset copia nulla nunc legendi.
> Proin si praemia danda sunt merenti,
> Fraudari suo honore fas nec ullum,
> Ipsi gratia non habenda vati est,
> Qui nobis sua durus invidebat:
> Sed furi magis illa publicanti,
> Hoc quem conspicis ordine ac paratu
> Non sane illepido: nec invenusto.
> Si authori editio haud placet, quid ad me?
> Ipsis dum liceat frui libellis?[2]

[There would be no copy to read of these books which you so desire, esteem, and marvel at in awe, dear reader, had a bold kidnapper not spirited them away from Clément Marot. Thus, if the deserving are to be rewarded, and if it is unjust to defraud someone of what he has earned, thanks should be given not to the cruel poet who begrudged us his works, but to the thief who makes them public in the not altogether unrefined or unappealing order and preparation that you see. If the author doesn't like the fact that it was published, what do I care, so long as these books may be enjoyed?]

Given that the poem reappears in the 1538 *Œuvres*, the epigraph does not reflect historical fact, but the commonplace of the stolen manuscript. The vocabulary ("copia," "publicanti," "editio") suggests that the kidnapper is actually the printer/publisher who distributes the work without the author's approval. This "kidnapper" is also given credit for the painstaking ordering and preparation ("ordine ac paratu") so important to Marot, whose satisfaction is less important than the reader's. This observation applies even more literally to unauthorized editions, whose motto very well could have been "so long as these books may be enjoyed." The *Suite* is a case of man bites dog in which an authorized edition imitates unauthorized editions offering never-before-seen works. Unable to beat these impostors, the *Suite* rhetorically joins them, but in so doing, legitimizes the sort of advertising that gives greater weight to the reader's desires than to the author's.

To wit, Antoine Macault's translation renders lines 10–12 as "... L'autre ce bien a faict, / Qu'en tresbon et bel ordre à ung chascun le livre" (*OC* 1:261; *OPC* 1:205). The phrase "à ung chascun" addresses an indeterminate public and represents the simultaneous humanist, evangelical, and popular appeal of the *Suite*: it is meant for anyone, even those unskilled at reading Latin, whose presence is acknowledged by Macault's French translation. The translation is followed by Nicolas Bourbon's brief epigraph "Ad lectorem," which also privileges the reader's enjoyment while reiterating the theme of the book as a sample from the *Adolescence*:

> Hic liber ignaro Domino volitare per orbem
> Inque tuas (lector) gaudet abire manus.
> Ex his conjicito, quae sint, et quanta futura
> Caetera, quae authoris lima severa premit.
>   (OC 1:262; OPC 1:206)

[Reader, this book rejoices in heading out, unbeknownst to its master, to fly around the world and into your hands. From it, you can infer how great the poems shaped by the author's strict revision are, and how great the rest will be.]

The image of the "lima," which figuratively means "revision" but literally means "file," recalls the artisanal metaphors (such as "coup d'essay") introduced in the preface of the *Adolescence*, and portrays the poet in a process of continual refinement. The volume has been produced by the "limae labor et mora" [toil and tedium of the file] whose neglect in Latin letters is lamented by Horace in the *Ars poetica*.[3] This neglect, Horace claims, is the only reason why Latium is more famous for feats of arms than for letters; the fact that Marot does not neglect this labor allows him to vie with his Roman predecessor, and Bourbon's epigraph accounts for Marot's delay (*mora*) in producing the better things promised to the reader in the *Adolescence* by turning it into a guarantor of literary quality.

In keeping with the Horatian intertext, the third Latin epigraph (Macrin's second) situates Marot's poetry firmly within the tradition of *translatio studii*, the transfer of knowledge from Ancient Greece and Rome to modern nations. Drawing on the customary Maro/Marot play on words, it states that just as Virgil excelled by preferring his native Latin to Homer's Greek, so too does Marot become the prince of French poets ("princeps") by writing in French instead of in Macrin's and Bourbon's Latin (OC 1:262; OPC 1:206).[4] Georges Soubeille has seen in the use of the word "princeps" another reference to Horace: "Libera per vacuum posui vestigia princeps, / non aliena meo pressi pede" [I was the first to plant free footsteps on a virgin soil; I walked not where others trod].⁵ Through this reference, Macrin concedes the superiority of French to Latin as a poetic language for the French, and acknowledges Marot's role as an innovator.⁶ The paratext of the *Suite* maintains the humanist image of Marot fostered in the paratext of the *Adolescence*, all while presenting the printer/publisher as more attentive to the reader's desires than to the author's and soliciting indeterminate readers who might otherwise be tempted to purchase and read a counterfeit edition.

The text of the *Suite*, in conjunction with the paratext, further blurs the distinction between private transaction and public consumption. In describing what he calls the "formlessness" of Marot's poetry, Robert Griffin stresses how the poet often represents himself as a poet, self-consciously engaged in the act of creating.⁷ When considered in light of the dissemination of Marot's poems in print, this poetic metadiscourse on the circumstances and techniques of creation serves a function similar to that of the Horatian "lima" in Bourbon's epigraph: it functions as prestige advertising that depicts the *Suite* as a meticulously prepared gift for the anonymous reader akin to a presentation manuscript. For example, the speaker of the eleventh elegy invites his recalcitrant mistress to "fai[re] recueil de" [favorably receive] his heart, or rather of the elegy that testifies to it, which he presents to her, and which is free

>De faulx penser, fainctise, ou trahison;
>Il n'a sur luy faulte, ne mesprison;
>En luy ne sont aucunes amour vaines.
>   (*OC* 1:282.15–19; *OPC* 1:251.15–19)

>[From traitorous thought, feigning, or betrayal;
>It is free from error and blame;
>There is no vain love in it.]

The parallel between the speaker's heart and the "recueil" [collection] that is the *Suite*, expurgated of errors by a poet who abandons "vaine amour" for "Ferme Amour" in the *Adolescence*, is clear.

An even more explicit conflation of presentation copy with printed edition occurs in the "Epistre à Monseigneur le Grant Maistre de Montmorency, par laquelle Marot luy envoye ung petit recueil de ses Oeuvres, et luy recommande le porteur" [Epistle to My Lord the Grand Maître de Montmorency, in which Marot sends him a small collection of his works and recommends the bearer to him].[8] The *recueil* offered to the future Constable bears a truly striking resemblance to the *Adolescence* as described in its preface:

> C'est ung amas de choses espendues,
> Qui (quant à moy) estoient si bien perdues,
> Que mon esprit n'eut onq à les ouvrer
> Si grant labeur comme à les recouvrer.
> Mais comme ardant à faire vostre vueil,
> J'ay tant cherché qu'en ay faict ung recueil
> Et un jardin garny de fleurs diverses,
> De couleur jaulne, et de rouges, et perses.
> Vray est qu'il est sans arbre, ne grant fruict.
> Ce neantmoins je ne vous l'ay construict
> Des pires fleurs qui de moy sont sorties.
> Il est bien vray qu'il y a des orties.
> Mais ce ne sont que celles qui picquerent
> Les Musequins qui de moy se mocquerent.
>   (OC 1:319.13–26; OPC 1:296.13–26)

> [It is a heap of scattered things
> That, as far as I'm concerned, were so completely lost
> That it was less of a mental labor
> To write them than it was to find them again.
> But, burning with a desire to fulfill your wish,
> I searched for so long that I've made a collection of them,
> A garden bedecked with various flowers,
> Some yellow, some red, some blue.
> True, it has neither trees nor much fruit,
> But I did not make it for you
> Out of the worst flowers to spring from me.
> There are indeed some nettles in it,
> But only the ones intended to sting
> The little fops who mocked me.]

First of all, it is important to note the conflict between the poet's perception of the works in this collection and his desire to please Montmorency. The poet, not unlike Mantuan in the *Bucolica*, is less than delighted at the prospect of recovering works that are better off lost as far as he is concerned, but his desire to please the Grand Maître wins out. As in Macrin and Bourbon's epigraphs, Marot's wish to restrict the distribution of his works is overshadowed by this reader's desire to acquire a copy of them. Additionally, the verb "recouvrer" ["find them again"] is the same one used to introduce the horticultural metaphor in the preface of the *Adolescence* ("ce que j'ay peu *recouvrer* d'arbres, d'herbes, et fleurs de mon primtemps" [the trees, herbs, and flowers that I was able to recover from the springtime of my life]), a metaphor which is itself applied to Montmorency's copy. There is even a similarity between the description of the presentation copy as bearing "neither trees nor much fruit" and the proviso in the preface of the *Adolescence* that newly grafted trees do not produce sweet-tasting fruit. Even the nettles that sting the "Musequins" who mock the poet recall the plethora of bitingly satirical poems directed at Marot's critics in both the *Adolescence* and *Suite*.[9] The epistle suggests that the *Suite* that readers hold in their hands is comparable in conception and execution to a manuscript collection submitted to a high-ranking noble with the power to grant offices in the king's household.[10] In so doing, it narrows the gap between a copy prepared for a specific, influential patron and a book meant for production in the thousands and a comparatively wide distribution; a copy of the *Suite* is every bit as much a presentation copy for its reader as Montmorency's collection is for him.

Even so, the effect of the *Suite* on the thematic and sequential coherence of Marot's poetic persona is less clear. While the *Adolescence* follows a definite chronological principle and represents the evolution of both the poet's career and the poet's vocation, the *Suite*, aside from its grouping by genre, does not present any distinct sense of ordering or maturation. If anything, the collection appears at first glance to disrupt the illness and conversion narrative hinted at in the Roffet and François Juste editions of the *Adolescence*. The "Elegies" are entirely devoted to love, both good and bad, as if to suggest that the poet, even after leaving his "adolescence" behind, remains a servant of the God of Love.[11] The *Suite* does not seem to move from lesser to greater works, either, as the title of the concluding "Menu" (from the Latin *minutus*, or "diminished") implies that the section is comprised of lesser pieces.[12]

The *Suite* does, however, contain subtle hints at the poet's continued maturation toward greater works, the most salient of which occurs in the twenty-first and final elegy. A reprise of the traditional theme of the *mal mariée*, the elegy closely resembles the "Epistre de Maguelonne" in both structure (especially the concluding rondeau) and theme, in that its speaker resigns herself to her situation and refuses to sin (here, taking a lover rather than following

Maguelonne's option to commit suicide). Instead, she appeals to the Virgin Mary, and following the advice of Matt. 5:39, resolves to turn the other cheek: "Je ne feray ne serviteur, n'amy, / Mais tiendray foy à mon grant ennemy" (*OC* 1:304.87–88; *OPC* 1:273.87–88) [I will not take a *serviteur* or a lover, / But I will remain faithful to my greatest foe]. The speaker then justifies turning to Mary with a reference to the opening lines of Psalm 41:

> Comme le Cerf, qui court à la fontaine,
> Cherchant remede à la soif qui le presse,
> Nature aussi ne veult que ailleurs m'adresse.
> (*OC* 1:305.96–98; *OPC* 1:273.96–98)

> [Just as the deer rushes to the fountain
> To quench its pressing thirst,
> Nature would not have me turn anywhere else.][13]

The "Elegies" do hint at a move toward religion, and specifically toward translation of the Psalms. This same sense of evolution toward the Psalms is adopted in subsequent editions as a way of reconciling the *Suite* with the *Adolescence*, and of establishing a more consistent trajectory for Marot's aspirations.

The March 7, 1534 Roffet edition of the *Adolescence*, a response to Juste's July 12, 1533 edition, makes just such use of the *Suite*. Like the Juste edition of the *Adolescence*, it includes the sickness poems, and after these, the remainder closely matches the content of Juste's edition, albeit with one significant exception: the prayer translations do not appear at the end of the *Adolescence*, but at the beginning of the accompanying *Suite*.[14] They are grouped under the heading "L'Instruction et foy d'ung chrestien," the same title affixed to them in the Augereau editions of Marguerite de Navarre where they first appeared in print, and here they include a translation of the *Ave Maria* and the "Graces pour ung enfant." They are also followed by Marot's translation of Psalm 6, whose "Argument" presents it as a song in which the speaker, "Affligé de longue Maladie" [long afflicted by illness] and terrified at the prospect of imminent death, prays for health and gives glory to God once more before dying (*OC* 1:435; *OPC* 1:392). It is as if the psalm were the inevitable outcome of the sickness poems and Marot's own "longue maladie"; the *Suite* picks up where the plague and conversion narrative of the *Adolescence* leaves off. The poet nearly succumbs to the plague, confronts death, and sees the error of his ways, resolving to sing God's praises and begging God not to punish him any further:

> N'en ta fureur terrible
> Me punir de l'orrible
> Tourment qu'ay merité.
>   (OC 1:435.4–6; OPC 1:392.4–6)
>
> [And in your terrible fury
> Do not punish me with the horrible
> Torment that I deserve.]¹⁵

This edition, like all the ensuing Roffet editions, compensates for the perplexing and potentially disappointing structure of the *Suite* by appending the *Instruction* and psalm to the beginning of the standard text to pique the interest of evangelical readers who would take the psalm as proof that Marot, in spite of what some aspects of the *Suite* might imply, has fully committed himself to their cause. Indeed, the title assigned to the psalm translation, which explains that it has been translated into French in accordance with the Hebrew, marks it as distinctly evangelical in orientation. It simultaneously stresses Marot's rendering of the psalm into a vernacular version accessible to all believers and the accuracy of this translation with respect to the original language of the Old Testament rather than to the Vulgate.¹⁶ The fact that the title recalls Marot's position as Groom of the King's Chamber may be seen as an assertion of evangelical ascendancy, as well. Francis I appointed François Vatable and Agazio Giudacerio as royal readers (*lecteurs royaux*) in Hebrew in March 1530, adding Paul Paradis (Paolo Canossa) in 1531, and the title of Marot's psalm translation alludes to these developments by implying that Francis's policies have made works like his possible. Simply put, Marot's psalm translation acts as a synecdoche for evangelical readers, a part that stands for the whole of the king's apparent espousal of the movement at that time.

If the Roffet editions of the *Suite* follow Juste's in making Marot into a representative of evangelism, they also take advantage of his chameleonic nature in the paratext, starting with the August 19, 1534 edition. An anonymous quatrain that outlines the place and purpose of each section within the *Suite* is inserted after the table of contents:

> Les Elegies suyvent L'adolescence.
> Non differant Epistres, Chantz divers,
> Le Cymetiere plaint apres tristes vers,
> Quant le Menu vient a convalescence.

[The *Elegies* follow the *Adolescence*,
Though they don't put off the *Epistres* and *Chantz divers* for too long.
After that, the *Cymetiere* laments with sad verses,
Until the *Menu* comes along to make everything better.][17]

The collection follows the *Adolescence* and is meant to be regarded as continuous with it, even if printed separately, much like Jean Lemaire de Belges's recueil-*Epistre* with respect to the *Illustrations*. The phrase "Though they don't put off the *Epistres* and *Chantz divers* for too long" implies that the *Suite*'s sections might have been of the greatest interest to many readers, whom the quatrain reassures that they will not have to wait long to reach them. It even implies that the troublesome *Menu* has a salutary role, that of providing joy and laughter to counteract the "sad verses" of the *Cymetiere*. While the edition is advertised to evangelical readers with the addition of the *Instruction* and psalm, it is also advertised in the paratext to readers primarily seeking entertainment.

Roffet's paratextual interventions thus continue to reveal the determining role that the printer/publisher can play in fashioning the persona of a protean author like Marot to appeal to multiple audiences. The printerly persona is itself defined by prestige advertising to such an extent that it often leads to outright false advertising. This is the case in Denis de Harsy's 1534 *Adolescence*, which takes a stand against editorial intervention and piracy.[18] After the preface, there is an anonymous *douzain* that laments outside interference in authoritative works since antiquity:

> Merveille n'est si es Auteurs antiques
> Tant en couleurs, qu'en fureur poetiques
> Maint Aristarque a sa dent impose.
> Merveilles n'est aux oeuvres authentiques
> De doulce prose ou biens plaisans Cantiques
> Des trespassez si tant ont transpose,
> Change, brouille, corrompu, suppose,
> Faulcifie, deprave, transpose,
> Car de Clement poete a stile fin,
> Qui en beau francoys maintz vers a compose
> En ses traictez a l'on interpose,
> Qu'il n'est pas mort, et si vivra sans fin.[19]

[It is no wonder that into the rhetorical colors
And poetic furors of ancient authors,

Many an Aristarchus has sunk his teeth.
It is no wonder that the excellent works
Of the dead, delightful prose or pleasant song,
Have been transposed, changed,
Scrambled, corrupted, forged,
Falsified, marred, and removed so much,
For the works of Clément, poet of refined style,
Who has composed many verses in his lovely French,
Have been intervened in
Even though he's not dead, and yet, he will live forever.]

The *douzain* sets up a parallel between the editors of Marot and Aristarchus of Samothrace, the grammarian and early editor of Homer whose name was synonymous with exacting criticism, and not necessarily in a good way. For Erasmus, Aristarchus typified harsh and even arbitrary criticism and editing, as he would reject passages in Homer that he deemed spurious or lacking in quality with an obelus (†) and approve of passages he thought authentic and worthy of Homer with an asterisk (*).[20] The *douzain*'s litany of alterations made to the works of ancient authors ("transposed, changed, / Scrambled, corrupted, forged, / Falsified, marred, and removed") positions the Harsy edition as a humanist effort to restore texts to their pristine state, uncorrupted by subsequent commentaries and accretions. The poem bears a striking resemblance to the accusations Marot levels against printers in his prefaces; we could even see in its final line a reference to Marot's motto, "La mort n'y mord" [Death has no teeth], and with it, an affirmation that Marot's poetic legacy is secure in spite of their interference. Philippe Desan tersely points to the *douzain* as proof that a text no longer belongs to its author once the editor transforms it into a book, and the irony is that even though the Harsy edition's prestige advertising depicts it as a bastion of fidelity to the authorial intention of a poet worthy of the ancients, it is itself an unauthorized edition whose textual content is pirated from the Roffet and Juste editions.[21] The Roffet editions themselves adopt the same strategy, as they spuriously claim to be free of "autres meschantes oeuvres mal composees, que on impose estre du dict acteur, les quelles il reprouve et desavoue" [those other paltry, badly written works that are imparted to the author, though he condemns and disavows them].[22]

Juste, for his part, did not remain inactive after Marot went into exile following the Affair of the Placards. In fact, the oppressive atmosphere that followed in the wake of the event, which included a temporary royal ban on printing, does not seem to have daunted him in the least if his December 12,

1534 *Adolescence* and its accompanying *Suite* are any indication, though, as previously stated, Lyon's distance from the capital afforded Juste greater freedom than could be enjoyed in Paris and its environs.²³ Not only does Juste keep the poems on Francis I's banishment of Noël Béda in the *Adolescence*, but he also adds a further two anti-Sorbonne poems at the end of the *Suite*. The first, the *huitain* "Le Roy, aymant la decoration," recommends that the Sorbonne be made into a stockyard ["place aux veaux"] as part of Francis I's renovations of Paris (OC 2:472.8; OPC 2:289.8). The ensuing *dizain* is even more risqué, as it goes beyond simple anticlerical satire to argue for the doctrine of salvation by faith alone. In it, a doctor of theology complains to his mistress that he cannot earn any favors from her ["Je ne peux rien meriter de vous, belle"], then preaches to his congregation that eternal life can be earned through words and deeds. The poet's ensuing argument against the efficaciousness of works is all the more effective for its parody of the language of scholastic disputation:

> *Arguo sic*: si *magister Lourdis*
> De sa Catin meriter ne peult rien,
> *Ergo* ne peult meriter Paradis
> Car pour le moins Paradis la vault bien.
>   (OC 2:471.7–10; OPC 2:288.7–10)

> [I argue thusly: if Master Thicky
> Can't earn any favors from his Katie,
> It follows that he cannot earn Heaven,
> Because Heaven is worth at least as much as she is.]²⁴

Given Marot's absence during the publication of this edition, it is unclear whether these poems are actually his, but their presence at the end of the *Suite* perpetuates the image of a Marot all the more committed to the evangelical cause despite the stunning reversal of its fortunes after the Affair of the Placards and his own exile.²⁵

After the poet's return from exile in late 1536, abjuration in Lyon, and (relatively fleeting) restoration to glory, he wasted little time in responding to this trend in his portrayal in the same way he responded to its previous iterations: by bringing out his *Œuvres* in 1538. The decisiveness of this gesture is respected in current scholarly consensus, which grants primacy to the *Œuvres* among editions of Marot's collected works, but what is often overlooked is the extent to which they appropriate the advertising strategies of the unauthorized editions they are meant to combat.

The Œuvres, a Product of Editorial Intervention

The publication of the *Œuvres* in Lyon by Étienne Dolet in July 1538 and by Sébastien Gryphe later that year represented both a departure from and an imitation of the practices of previous editions.[26] The full title of the *Œuvres* reads *Les Oeuvres de Clément Marot de Cahors, valet de chambre du Roy. Augmentées de deux Livres d'Epigrammes Et d'ung grand nombre d'aultres Oeuvres par cy devant non imprimées. Le tout songneusement par luy mesmes reveu, et mieulx ordonné* (OC 1:381) [The Works of Clément Marot of Cahors, Groom of the King's Chamber, augmented with two books of epigrams and a large number of other works never before printed, all carefully reviewed by the author and put in a better order]. It simultaneously indicates the additional and never-before-seen material contained in the volume, Marot's personal and painstaking revision of the edition, and the superior ordering of this edition compared to previous ones. These points are taken up again in Nicholas Bourbon's Latin epigraph to the *Œuvres*, which, much like his earlier epigraph to the *Suite*, represents the book going forth into the reader's hands, but this time in such a way as to advertise to the reader through ideal readership:

> Saepe quod inspersis nugis foedaverat ausus
> Quorundam, ut sunt haec candida Secla parum:
> En tibi, nunc Lector, patria fornace recoctum,
> Spectandumque; novo lumine prodit Opus.
> Hic nihil est, quod non sic elimaverit Autor,
> Ut metuat Momi judicis ora nihil.
> (OC 1:385; OPC 1:12).

[Behold, reader: this work, which the daring of certain people has often besmirched by interspersing trifles in it, as ours is hardly a Golden Age, now comes to you to be seen in a new light, reforged in its father's furnace. There is nothing here that the author has not polished, so it should fear nothing that judging Momus has to say.]

Momus, the god of mockery willing to find fault with anything and everything, deters readers from receiving the book unfavorably by serving as a foil akin to ingratitude in Lemaire's work. Readers who do manage to find fault with the book are, by implication, even pettier and more quarrelsome than a deity banished from Olympus when he mocked Poseidon for creating bulls with horns on top of their heads rather than under their eyes.[27] In this vein, perhaps poetic convention is not the only reason why Bourbon uses the plural "ora," as Momus is less a specific deity here than a metonymy for criticism in the same way that Vulcan and Ceres are often used as metonymies for fire and grain. Momus *qua* petty criticism is made up of thousands of wagging tongues, and readers' tongues wag with them if they find fault with the book.

As far as Marot's image is concerned, the reforged work once again portrays the poet as a wordsmith, with the verb "*eli*maverit" recalling the painstaking revision indicated on the title page of the *Œuvres* and the "lima severa" of Bourbon's epigraph for the *Suite*. Even more intriguing, though, is the use of the ablative absolute "inspersis nugis" as a reference to "nugae" [trifles] in an epigraph by a poet who had published his own *Nugae* in 1533, which hardly seems coincidental. In other words, the inclusion of the right kind of "nugae" is actually beneficial rather than detrimental to the work, and the poet's success still hinges on the contributions of those who prepare the volume. In the same vein, other aspects of the paratext point to the printer/publisher's responsibility for the text's perfection. This is especially the case in the Dolet edition, in which Dolet's mark, which directly follows the title, calls attention to the Orleanese humanist's role as editor: "Scabra, et impolita ad amussim dolo, atque perpolio" (*OC* 1:381) [That which is rough and unfinished, I hew with precision and polish]. The *doloire* [wagoner's axe/adze] resonates with Dolet's own name and the ruler or straightedge (*amussis*) to formulate an artisanal image of the editor who transforms the raw material of the text ("scabra, et impolita") into the finished book (fig. 4). Marot himself refers to carpenter's tools in the epistle "A Alexis Juré de Quiers en Piedmont" in a manner highly reminiscent of Dolet's mark:

> Mais il fault
> Ton deffault
> Raboter
> Pour oster
> Les gros noeudz
> Lours et neufz
> Du langage
> Tout ramage.
> Et que limes
> Quand tu rimes
> Tes Mesures
> Et Cesures.

(*OC* 1:415–16.29–40; *OPC* 1:334.29–40)

Figure 4. Dolet's mark, title page of 1538 Œuvres. (BNF Rés. Ye 1457; reprinted with permission of the Bibliothèque nationale de France)

[Your error
Has to be
Leveled smooth
To remove
The big knots
Fresh and thick
Of language
Most uncouth.
And polish,
When you rhyme,
Meters and
Caesuras.]

Dolet's work also mirrors the poet's own in an epigraph added to the paratext of the *Adolescence*, "Marot à son livre": "Racler je veulx (approche toy mon Livre) / Ung tas d'escriptz, qui par d'aultres sont faictz" (*OC* 1:386.1–2; *OPC* 1:14.1–2) [Come here, my book: I want to scrape away / A mass of writings made by others]. The verb "racler" likely refers to the erasure of manuscripts with a polishing or scraping tool.²⁸

In this respect, Marot's depiction of his own editorial work elevates the status of the printed book to that of the presentation manuscript, much like the poem on Montmorency's collection in the *Suite*. However, Dolet's Latin epigraph to Marot's book on the verso of the title page further stresses that an edition is the result of a collective effort:

> Autoris arte tui superbus in lucem
> Exi Liber: sed non minus superbe unguem
> Ostende cuilibet, nitore tam raro,
> Mendisque nullis exiens nunc in lucem.
> Exire sic te voluimus nonne Amici,
> Purum, nitidum, tersum, et carentem omni labe?
>   (OC 1:382; OPC 1:6)

[Go forth proudly in public, book, thanks to your author's art. But do not be any less proud to display your perfection to anyone, for its elegance is so rare, and you appear in public now free of faults. Is this not how we, your friends, wanted you to come out: pure, splendid, clean, and free from all defects?]

Like in Bourbon's epigraph for the *Suite*, Dolet puts Marot in competition with the ancients through a reference to the *Ars poetica*, indeed to the very same passage to which Bourbon refers: just after complaining of the absence of "toil and tedium of the file" in Latin letters, Horace instructs his Calpurnian correspondents to condemn any poem that has not been rigorously corrected ten times over "ad unguem" [to the test of the close-cut nail].²⁹ This level of polish is not the result of the author's work alone, but of the efforts of its "friends," both those involved in its publication and the larger community of "freres d'Apollon" evoked in the preface of the *Adolescence*.

The paratext of the *Œuvres* thus stresses the perfection of the volume and predicates ideal readership upon recognition of this perfection. Yet, Marot's preface to the *Œuvres* describes the volume as a sort of concession to the desire of his readers for more works, the very same desire that accounts for the propagation of so many unauthorized editions in the poet's absence. What might initially appear to be a magnanimous gesture on the part of the poet is actually prestige advertising that conditions readerly desire by claiming to be preoccupied with it. Put differently, the *Œuvres* employ the very same strategy that previous editions do in that they claim to have the reader's best interests at heart where other editions do not.

"[A]ffin que les Lecteurs ne se plaignent": The *Œuvres* as Concession to and Conditioning of Readerly Desire

In the preface, addressed to Dolet in Dolet's edition and to "ceux qui par cy devant ont imprime ses oeuvres" [those who have previously printed his works] in Gryphe's edition, Marot takes to task editors who have printed his works without permission.[30] They have stained Marot's honor and endangered his person: "car par avare couvoitise de vendre plus cher, et plustost, ce qui se vendoit assez, ont adjousté à icelles miennes Oeuvres plusieurs aultres qui ne me sont rien: dont les unes sont froidement et de maulvaise grace composées, mettant sur moy l'ignorance d'aultruy, et les aultres toutes pleines de scandale et sedition" (*OC* 1:383; *OPC* 1:9) [for in their avaricious longing to sell more quickly and at a higher price a book that was already selling well enough, they added to these works of mine several others that are anything but mine, some of which are coldly and inelegantly composed and make the ignorance of others out to be my own, and others of which are positively full of scandal and sedition]. Marot's adversaries, we are to believe, are motivated entirely by profit. Not content with counterfeiting a work that, as Marot claims and his publication history confirms, already sells a lot of copies, they have opted to add allographic works, some of which are not worthy of Marot's skill and damage the poet's reputation, and some of which are scandalous enough to imperil a poet with a penchant for getting into trouble.[31] Adding these works allows them to sell more copies and perhaps to charge more for them by virtue of novelty, and it is true that a great many editions of Marot advertise the presence of new material within them on their title pages.[32] Marot attributes these interventions to avarice in order to discredit the existing editions in the eyes of readers and allay their potential suspicions regarding his own motive for bringing out yet another collection of his works. In conjunction with the title page's insistence on the author's and the editor's care and attention to detail, Marot's accusation paints the additional material offered by competing editions as evidence not of their worth, but of their deficiency—by giving more, unauthorized editions are actually giving less.

The preface of the Dolet edition, in turn, uses unscrupulous printers as a foil for Dolet. The poet trusts him to reprint his book "non seulement ainsi correct que je le t'envoye mais encores mieulx" (*OC* 1:384; *OPC* 1:10) [not only as correctly as when I send it to you, but even better]. Whereas competitors are motivated only by gain and hence inclined to mutilate the text to sell more copies, Dolet claims to improve upon it, but when we consider that Dolet was himself notorious for putting out pirated editions (notably of Rabelais), and that Marot's own quarrel with Dolet led him to have the *Œuvres* printed by a competitor, it becomes clear that the preface reflects less the historical Dolet and his unethical business practices than an idealized image of the producer meant to sell the *Œuvres* to readers. In this regard, the *Œuvres* are not so different from the Harsy or Roffet editions and the crocodile tears they cry over unscrupulous printerly interventions.

The preface goes on to reintroduce the horticultural and agricultural metaphors familiar to readers of the *Adolescence:* "de tous ces miens Labeurs le proffit leur en retourne. J'ay planté les Arbres; ils en cueillent les fruictz. J'ay trayné la Charrue; ilz en serrent la moisson" (*OC* 1:383; *OPC* 1:9) [from all these labors of mine, the profit goes to them. I planted the trees; they pick the fruit. I pulled the plow; they gather up the harvest]. This iteration of the metaphor makes the connection between Marot's claim to authorial rights and Tityrus's and Meliboeus's lamentation over the misuse of their fields even clearer, suggesting that interlopers have been stealing the "fruit" that Marot promised his readers in the preface of the *Adolescence*. Unlike Lemaire, whose complaint of having to beat the bushes while others catch the birds focused on his own frustrated ambitions and lack of recognition, Marot laments the reader's loss as much as his own and thereby engages in prestige advertising for the *Œuvres*.

Though Marot does not single out any specific printers or booksellers, he does mention several specific works that have been appended to the *Adolescence*: the "Epitaphe du Conte de Sales," the "Complaincte de Dame Bazoche," and the "Alphabet du temps present," one or more of which appear in every edition of the *Adolescence* examined for the present study, beginning with the July 12, 1534 Juste edition. Additionally, the poet refuses to accept the inclusion even of allographic works he holds in high esteem, a practice he regards as tantamount to theft of the honor owed to their authors: "Encores ne leur a souffy de faire tort à moy seul mais à plusieurs excellens Poëtes de mon temps: desquelz les beaulx Ouvrages les Libraires ont joinctz avecques les miens, me faisant (maulgré moy) usurpateur de l'honneur d'aultruy" (*OC* 1:384; *OPC* 1:10) [And still, it wasn't enough for them to wrong me alone; they also had to wrong several excellent poets of my time, whose fine works the booksellers have joined with mine, making me a usurper of others' honor in spite of myself].[33] Even though the inclusion of allographic works can and perhaps has redounded to his honor, Marot's refusal to accept this honor distances his persona even further from dishonest printer/publishers: whereas they unscrupulously pursue profit, Marot treasures his own poetic craft more than any profit, symbolic or otherwise, to be gained by taking credit for the works of others.

However, the reader's insatiable desire for more works has also been accounted for in this new edition: "Toutesfois, au lieu des choses rejectées (affin que les Lecteurs ne se plaignent), je y ay mis douze fois aultant d'aultres Oeuvres miennes, par cy devant non imprimées: mesmement deux Livres de Epigrammes" (*OC* 1:384; *OPC* 1:10) [Yet, in place of the rejected items (so that readers do not complain), I have included twelve times as many of my other works that have not previously been printed, notably two books of epigrams]. Between the *Adolescence, Suite*, and *Epigrammes*, the *Œuvres* do, in fact, contain over 140 previously unprinted pieces, but in claiming that there are twelve times as many new works in the *Œuvres*, the preface employs the same hyperbolic advertising strategy seen in Juste's editions, addressing readers who have grown accustomed to purchasing and reading counterfeit editions with additional material. Dolet and Gryphe further contribute to this strategy by indicating "Les oeuvres de Marot augmentées" [Marot's works augmented] in the margins to further underscore the presence of this additional material.[34]

At the same time, the preface attempts to recondition the reader's priorities by emphasizing not only the edition's new material, but also its superior order. Marot sarcastically requests that printers ask him to make additions instead of publishing his works haphazardly the minute they get their hands on them: "Car si j'ay aulcunes Oeuvres à mettre en lumiere, elles tumberont assez à temps en leurs Mains, non ainsi par pieces comme ilz les recueillent çà et là, mais en belle forme de Livre" (*OC* 1:384; *OPC* 1:10) [For if I have some works to make public, they will fall into their hands in good time, not in the bits and pieces that they've been collecting here and there, but in the lovely form of a book].[35] Of course, this is not a warning that many printers or booksellers would have been inclined to heed, nor is it really directed at them. On the contrary, it is directed at the ideal reader of the *Œuvres*, who would prefer a well-crafted, well-ordered book to one with works added in a catch-as-catch-can fashion at the end. Real readers are thus encouraged to reorient their priorities accordingly.

In indicating changes made to the order of poems, the preface distinguishes between the *Adolescence* and the *Autres Oeuvres*, here repackaged as the *Suite*: "Lequel ordre (docte Dolet et vous aultres Lecteurs debonnaires) j'ay voulu changer à ceste derniere reveue, mettant l'Adolescence à part et ce qui est hors d'Adolescence tout en ung; de sorte que, plus facilement que paravant, rencontrerez ce que vouldrez y lire. Et, si ne le trouvez là où il souloit estre, le trouverez en reng plus convenable" (*OC* 1:384–5; *OPC* 1:10–11) [This order, learned Dolet and you other kindly readers, I wanted to change in this latest revision, separating out the *Adolescence* and combining everything outside of it into one, so that you will find what you want to read more easily than before. And if you do not find it where it used to be, you'll find it in a more appropriate place]. The division acknowledges that readers might be inclined to read selectively, preferring either the young or the mature Marot, and caters to this preference; the order of the *Œuvres* is just as tied to the desires of the collection's imagined public as it is to the author's desire to present himself in a certain manner. Indeed, these remarks address the printer/publisher as a reader who shares the concerns of the "aultres Lecteurs debonnaires." As usual, these readers are made to feel solicited, as if the collection was composed and then assembled with their proclivities and desires in mind.

Conversion or *Culetage?*

Perhaps so as to meet the expectations of readers who had grown accustomed to the conversion narrative so central to the Juste and Roffet editions, the order of the *Adolescence* and *Suite* displays a teleological orientation, giving the sense that Marot's poetic career takes a devotional turn. To wit, the *Suite* concludes with a section labeled "Oroisons" comprised both of the prayer translations originally published as the *Instruction et foy d'ung chrestien* and of Psalm 6. The section title has the added effect of establishing continuity between its contents and Marot's "Oroison contemplative devant le crucifix" [Contemplative prayer before the Cross], itself a translation from the Latin. The *Œuvres* do not merely adopt the position of these works, however. There are also several telling additions to the text of the *Suite* that reinforce this overarching narrative culminating in the "Oroisons."

The sickness narrative is abandoned in the *Suite*; of the ten poems that originally comprised the series, only three are added to the *Suite*, while six are added to the *Epigrammes*. However, two additional poems subtly recount Marot's career from the beginning through his exile and subsequent return so as to comment upon the goals of Marot's poetic career and the transformations that the *Œuvres* have undergone to reflect the accomplishment of these goals. The first poem is the epistle "Au Roy" in which Marot requests that the king erase his father's name on the salary register and replace it with his own (*OC* 1:409–12; *OPC* 1:327–30). Jean's deathbed speech to his son on why and how to pursue a poetic career reassures the reader of Marot's good intentions and presents the *Œuvres* as the fulfillment of his father's wish. Willing to his son the inheritance of his "peu de sçavoir" [scant knowledge], Jean reassures him that this knowledge is pure, innocent, and incapable of harming anyone, which distinguishes it from the sort of clerical and professional knowledge that might lead to a more lucrative career:

> Par Preschemens, le Peuple on peult seduire;
> Par Marchander, tromper on le peult bien;
> Par Plaiderie, on peult menger son bien;
> Par Medecine, on peult l'homme tuer;
> Mais ton bel Art ne peult telz coups ruer.
>   (*OC* 1:410.48–52; *OPC* 1:329.48–52)

> [With preaching, you can seduce the people;
> With trafficking, you can very well fool them;
> With litigation, you can eat them out of house and home;
> With medicine, you can kill a man;
> But your fair art cannot strike such blows.]

Priests seduce, merchants trick, lawyers defraud, and doctors charge for treatment that does more harm than good, but poets do no such thing.[36] Marot disavows the profit motive by representing his career as the realization of his father's advice against pursuing gain by taking up orders or a profession.

If "Au Roy" represents Marot's career as a turn away from parasitic professions, the "Chant de May," an addition to the *Suite*, represents it as the conversion of profane poetry to devotional poetry and translation. Gérard Defaux has compared this ballad to a *contrafactum* in that it adapts a genre usually associated with love poetry to the praise of God, and François Rigolot has noted its relevance to the Psalms as a hymn to the Creator and its exhibition of the poet's literary self-consciousness.[37] The imagery of the first stanza exhibits this self-consciousness in that it mirrors the structure of the *Œuvres*:

> En ce beau Moys delicieux
> Arbres, Fleurs et Agriculture,
> Qui durant l'Yver soucieux,
> Avez esté en Sepulture,
> Sortez, pour servir de pasture
> Aux Trouppeaulx du plus grand Pasteur:

Chascun de vous en sa nature
Louez le nom du Createur.
(*OC* 1:425.1–8; *OPC* 1:366.1–8)

[In this fair, delightful May,
You trees, flowers, and crops,
Who were entombed
During the worrisome winter,
Come out and provide pasture
For the greatest shepherd's flocks:
Each of you in your own way,
Praise the Creator's name.]

The "trees, flowers, and crops" recall the metaphor of the *Adolescence* as a garden, here reborn in the form of prayers that spiritually nourish the faithful and praise the Creator all the more effectively for their accessibility to the vernacular public. As in the "Oroison contemplative devant le crucifix," the raw material of the *Adolescence* eventually fuels the praise of God. The ballad's envoi also contains a choice of words that confirms the poem's metadiscursive nature and its parallel with the "Oroisons": "Et vous aussi, mon Escripture, / Louez le nom du Createur" (*OC* 1:426.27–28; *OPC* 1:366.27–28) [And you too, my scripture, / Praise the Creator's name]. The translations are indeed Marot's "Escripture" in that they are his translations of Scripture, which, in keeping with *sola scriptura*, ultimately constitutes the only proper way to praise God.

The order of the *Œuvres* and the metadiscourse of its texts are disposed in such a way as to confirm the evangelical arc of Marot's career. In fact, this disposition reinforces the conversion narrative so strongly that Guillaume Berthon compares it to the stories of saints' lives and Marot's various misfortunes to the turning points that characterize those narratives.[38] As such, the collection testifies to the poet's and the editor's awareness of the malleability of the authorial persona, which can, and indeed must, be shaped in such a way as to meet the reader's expectations as they have been conditioned by previous editions. In the *Œuvres* as in all things, Marot remains a chameleon, and the continual recurrence of the evangelical career arc does not change this fact; as Berthon points out, devotional poetry still made up a very small portion of Marot's production in 1538.[39] Marot got a lot of mileage out of this aspect of his persona, and his printers even more so, but at a particularly salient juncture of the collection, he calls the consequences of this malleability and of the accommodation of the reader into question, and challenges the validity of the very sort of literary advertising in which they all participate.

The "Cimetiere," which directly precedes the "Oroisons," concludes with the epitaph of Alix, one of Marot's bawdiest pieces. When originally published in the 1535 Juste edition of the *Suite*, it bore the title "Epitaphe d'Alys, fille de joye, extraict du second livre de la Priapee" [Epitaph of Alice, Lady of Pleasure, Excerpted from the Second Book of the *Priapeia*].[40] This lady of pleasure is most likely inspired not only by the *Priapeia*, a collection of songs celebrating Priapus, the god of the phallus and fertility, but also by the salacious Quartilla of Petronius's *Satyricon*, who cannot remember ever having been a virgin.[41] Simply put, the poem, which appears just before Marot's translation of the *Pater noster*, is an amplification of one of the raunchier passages of pagan literature and a celebration of a prostitute with an irrepressible propensity for bouncing her ass up and down during sex, "culetage" being a colorful synonym for fornication:

> Et inventa la bonne Dame
> Mille Tourdions advenans
> Pour culeter à tous venans.
> (OC 1:432–33.16–18; OPC 1:389.16–18)

[And the good lady discovered
A thousand comely contortions
To bounce her ass up and down on all comers.]

Even though Alice is no longer labeled a "fille de joye" in 1538, it is still clear that she is a skilled practitioner of the world's oldest profession.

To be sure, the close proximity of this poem to the "Oroisons" is jarring, and has not failed to astonish some *marotistes*. Rigolot, pointing out the fact that the Lord's Prayer comes right after this poem, compares the succession to the famous anecdote recounted in Novella 25 of the *Heptaméron* in which the future Francis I prays with exemplary devotion in church before heading to a tryst with the wife of a Parisian lawyer.[42] Nevertheless, if we are shocked by this juxtaposition, it is not only because we positivist moderns tend to see things more categorically than did our sixteenth-century predecessors, but also because we have bought into the prestige advertising that defines Marot's editions and encourages us to see the poet's career trajectory as a conversion narrative. In reality, Marot's trajectory was not a shift from the frivolous to the serious, but one in which the frivolous and the serious consistently worked in concert with one another. In this vein, David Claivaz points out that the gesture of putting the humble Alix's epitaph alongside those of the great and powerful is not incompatible with Marot's evangelical side, nor is his effort to describe humanity in all of its aspects incompatible with his humanist side.[43] Similarly, Berthon points to Alix as proof of Marot's commitment to aesthetic *varietas*, which is distinct from, but coexists alongside the constancy that defines the poet's ideology.[44]

Fittingly, Alix bears a strong resemblance to Marot's own highly inconstant and indeed adaptable poetic persona as seen in his editions. After all, she grows from *adolescence* to maturity and decides in her ripe old age to publish a *Livre de Culetage* and a *De Culetis* "... affin que le Monde vist / Son grand sçavoir" (OC 1:433.21–22; OPC 1:389.21–22) [... so that the world might see / Her vast expertise]. The association of court poets with courtesans is an intuitive and time-honored one, but I would draw a further parallel between Alice and Marot with respect not only to variety, but also to how accommodating they are. It is rather unusual that Alice uses the verb "inventer" (*inventio*) to describe her expansion of her sexual repertoire; it would seem that this is her own take on *captatio benevolentiae*. Just as Alice devises thousands of "comely contortions" to make her "culetage" more appealing to all interested parties, so too does Marot draw on a wide range of both sacred and profane subjects, appearing now as an evangelical humanist, now as "le pauvre Marot," in an effort to appeal to readers with varying tastes, interests, and ways of reading. The "comely contortions" call to mind certain stylistic traits of Marot, as well, not least the famous *rimes équivoquées* [holorhymes] of the "Petite epistre au Roy" or, closer at hand, the epitaph's improvisations on "culeter."

The poet pokes fun at his own body of work by comparing it to the body of a particularly enthusiastic woman of ill repute, capping the epitaph with a parody of the survival of the poet's voice after death as evoked by his motto, "La mort ny mord":

> Encor dit on, par grand merveille,
> Que si on veult mettre l'Oreille
> Contre la Tumbe et s'arrester,
> On oirra ses Os culeter.
>   (OC 1:433.29–32; OPC 1:389.29–32)

> [And they still say (oh, what a wonder!)
> That if you stop and put

> An ear to the tomb,
> You'll hear her bones twerking.]

The epitaph insists not only on variety, as Berthon argues, but also on the rhetorical adaptability that characterizes Marot's production and poetic persona. If the *Œuvres* respond to unauthorized editions by stressing the conversion narrative, then Alice's epitaph suggests that this apparent turn toward God is but another of the "comely contortions" executed to please as great a number of customers as possible. To invoke Yves Delègue's phrase, Marot's fashioning and refashioning of his poetic persona makes him not only a "marionette publique," but also a *femme publique*.

This puppet persona is the key to understanding how Marot calls advertising through the authorial persona into question even as he engages in it. Any edition of Marot's works could attract buyers by virtue of the poet's name alone, but to teach these readers to prefer their specific edition to the plethora of others available, Marot and his chosen producers, much like their unauthorized competitors, had to tailor their personae to the assumed desires of their readership. In this sense, Marot's protean nature may be seen not as an interpretive challenge to those who aim to make sense of his vast and varied body of work, but as a solution to the problem of the indefinite public, one that reveals its own rhetorical sleight of hand (or in Alix's case, sleight of ass) and lets astute readers in on the inner workings of advertising. To return to Elizabeth Eisenstein's phrase, books are unique "inventions" not just because they can advertise for themselves, but also because, at the same time, their authors can use them to deconstruct advertising through the creation of authorial personae and ideal readers.

Part III

The Cure Is the Disease

*Self-Fashioning and Charlatanism
in François Rabelais's Prologues*

> Est-il quelqu'un qui desire estre malade pour voir son medecin en besogne, et faudroit-il pas foyter le medecin qui nous desireroit la peste, pour mettre son art en practicque? [Is there anyone who wants to be sick in order to see his doctor at work, and shouldn't we whip any doctor who would wish us the plague in order to put his art into practice?]
> —Montaigne, *Essais*, "De mesnager sa volonté,"
> bk. 3, ch. 10, p. 1023; trans. Frame, 783

CHAPTER 5

The Prophylactic Prologues of *Pantagruel* and *Gargantua*

He gathered all the springs to birth
From the many-venomed earth;
First a little, thence to more,
He sampled all her killing store;
And easy, smiling, seasoned sound,
Sate the king when healths went round.
They put arsenic in his meat
And stared aghast to watch him eat;
They poured strychnine in his cup
And shook to see him drink it up:
They shook, they stared as white's their shirt:
Them it was their poison hurt.
I tell the tale that I heard told.
Mithridates, he died old.

—A. E. Housman, "Terence, this is stupid stuff"

CLÉMENT MAROT and François Rabelais have a lot in common, not just with respect to their views or the circles in which they moved, but in terms of their experience in publishing their works. Both enjoyed dazzling success, judging by the number of editions published during and after their lifetimes, both often found themselves the victims of counterfeiting and false attributions, and both devoted a significant amount of effort to their paratexts. However, Marot entered the world of print as the king's poet whose vernacular works were already in circulation, whereas Rabelais first entered it as a humanist editor whose vernacular works might at first glance have seemed incongruous with his reputation. The *Geste Pantagruéline* did not benefit from quite the same level of preexisting demand as the *Adolescence clementine*, and, consequently, Rabelais adopted a somewhat different advertising strategy than did Marot. As we have seen, Marot's aim—and that of those who produced his authorized and unauthorized editions—was to get readers to prefer a specific edition of his works. Consequently, his editions are characterized above all by prestige advertising and publicity: their primary stated goal is to please the reader, and they put forth an image of Marot tailored to what a given readership would want to see. Rabelais also took full advantage of prestige advertising, whether under the persona of Alcofrybas Nasier or of François Rabelais, Doctor of Medicine, but what sets him apart is his use and deliberate abuse of ideal readership.

In examining Rabelais's relationship with the reader, I do not claim to paint a comprehensive picture of Rabelais's production or of his publication history over the course of the four authorized books of the Geste as well as the Cinquiesme Livre.[1] Rather, my intention is to show how Rabelais uses rhetoric, self-fashioning, and medicine in his prologues to manipulate the reader by holding up an ideal toward which to strive. This manipulation coexists alongside Rabelais's appeal to the reader's curiosity and autonomy in the work of interpretation that grows clearer with each successive prologue, as noted by Bernd Renner in one of the more significant recent contributions to the interpretative controversy surrounding Rabelais's expectations for his readers.[2] These two dimensions of Rabelais's prologues are not mutually exclusive. On the contrary, Rabelais does indeed offer freedom to the reader, but it is a freedom defined by ideal readership in a manner akin to that of Jean Lemaire de Belges's and Marot's paratexts. As Cathleen Bauschatz has argued, even when Rabelais seems at first glance to promote an active role for the reader, he places limits on that power.[3] The freedom that Rabelais offers the reader is the illusory freedom of advertising.

At the same time, if Rabelais uses ideal readership to manipulate the reader, he does so in such a way as to make the reader aware of this manipulation through the medical aspects he ascribes to himself as an author and to the book. Roland Antonioli has shown how Rabelais grows increasingly skeptical toward the medical profession, especially in the Quart Livre and Cinquiesme Livre, and given that medicine and writing are intrinsically linked in the Geste, this skepticism is highly palpable in the prologues.[4] Beginning by presenting the book as a miracle drug with specific pharmacological and farcical resonances in Pantagruel and Gargantua, and shifting to a presentation of the author as a doctor concerned entirely with the reader/patient's well-being in the last three books, Rabelais reveals that curative medicine survives by perpetuating the problem it claims to solve. By exposing this dirty trick, Rabelais acts in accordance with Pantagruel's praise of preventative medicine in Chapter 29 of the *Tiers Livre*: good doctors, the giant explains, prefer to "donner tel ordre à la partie prophylactice et conservatrice de santé en leur endroict, qu'ilz n'ont besoing de la therapeutice et curative par medicamens" [set to rights the preventive and health-preserving part in their own regard so well that they have no need of the therapeutic and curative part by medications].[5] Rabelais offers the reader cures to eliminate the dependency on cures, and in this sense, his prologues act as a *pharmakon* with all the ambiguity that the Ancient Greek term carries in Plato's *Phaedrus* and *Phaedo*—both medicine and poison, they cure by doing harm.[6]

Treacle in Medicine and Farce

As detailed in Chapter 24 of *Gargantua*, one of the ways in which the young giant and his preceptor Ponocrates make good use of rainy days is to observe jugglers, conjurors, and "theriacleurs" (G, 24.72). Donald Frame renders this term as "sellers of quack medicines," but it more specifically connotes sellers of treacle, or *triacle* in French (61). In the sixteenth century, treacle was not the sticky sugar syrup akin to molasses that the term denotes today, but another term for theriac, a medicinal electuary partly composed of sugar syrup. In medicine and pharmacology from classical antiquity to the Renaissance and beyond, treacle was considered a potent drug, even a panacea. However, treacle and the "theriacleurs" who sold it were also closely associated with charlatanism, as reflected in Frame's choice of words and in Randle Cotgrave's definition of "Triaclerie" as "an imposture, deceit, sophistication."[7] This sinister side of treacle is what interests Gargantua and Ponocrates. In observing the "theriacleurs," they focus in particular on "leurs gestes, leurs ruses, leurs sobressaulx et beau parler" [their moves, their tricks, their somersaults and spiels]. Treacle is thus synonymous both with miracle cures and with false cures and the rhetoric ("beau parler") used to pass them off on the unwitting.

Rabelais himself undoubtedly encountered his fair share of "beau parler" in the form of street cries, whether the *cris de Paris*, the celebrated cries in verse of street vendors that rang out in Paris well into the nineteenth century, or similar cries that Rabelais would have heard at fairs in Fontenay-le-Comte, Saint-Maixent, Niort, and Lyon. In his landmark study of popular culture in the works of Rabelais, Mikhail Bakhtin even compares the prologue of *Pantagruel* to a *cri*.[8] This similarity, along with the evocation of "theriacleurs" in *Gargantua*, leads us to two questions: why would observing the sale of treacle be an important part of education, and what are the implications of treacle-selling for Rabelais's authorial persona when we consider that *Pantagruel* is advertised to the reader as a drug with miraculous effects? We may answer these questions by considering how Rabelais understood treacle in a medical and a literary context.

In classical medicine, treacle was understood to function as a kind of antidote, or more precisely as a means of inoculation. It was often synonymous with mithridate, or *metridal* in French, the eponymous compound that Mithridates VI of Pontus used to build up an immunity to poison, and whose recipe was provided by Pliny the Elder and Celsus.[9] It was commonly believed that Mithridates's recipe was later improved upon with the addition of viper flesh, which became the defining characteristic of treacle and lent its name to the concoction through the Greek term *therion*, or "wild beast." Galen lays out the preparation and use of this sort of theriac in *De antidotis* as well as in the *De theriaca ad Pisonem*, of dubious authenticity.[10] In his *Deux livres des venins*, a 1568 treatise on *materia medica* with a focus on poisons and antidotes, the physician and playwright Jacques Grévin gives a slightly different account of theriac. He broadly defines it as "touts medicaments propres, tant pour se contregarder, que pour guarir les morsures des bestes venimeuses: le vulgaire le nomme Triacles" [all medicines suitable for inoculation and treating the bites of venomous animals: the people call it "treacle"], and he uses the term "theriaque" both to refer to the specific compound described by Nicander, Pliny, Celsus, and Galen and as a synonym for "potion" or "medicinal compound."[11] He specifies that the term comes from the use of the original compound to treat snakebites, and that the notion that it contains viper flesh is erroneous (fig. 5). Finally, he distinguishes antivenins from antidotes that have a purgative effect; among the former, he includes "medicaments que nous nommons communement preservatifs, c'est à dire, propres pour nous contregarder" [medicines that we commonly call preventative, that is, suitable for inoculating us], of which mithridate and theriac are the most eminent and effective examples.[12]

As treacle became a prized and exotic object of commerce as early as the Middle Ages, charlatans hawking it and other miracle drugs inevitably found their way into the European literary tradition. Notable examples include Rutebeuf's *Dit de l'herberie* or Chaucer's *Canterbury Tales*, in which the Host is so moved to pity by the Physician's tale that he calls out for "triacle" to keep from having a "cardiacle," only to receive the Pardoner's Tale.[13] Perhaps the most telling literary avatar of the *theriacleur*, though, appears in the comic theater of the late fifteenth and early sixteenth centuries, where he becomes a stock character like Rutebeuf's hawker or Chaucer's Pardoner.

The *theriacleur* may be found in farces, *sotties*, and dramatic monologues

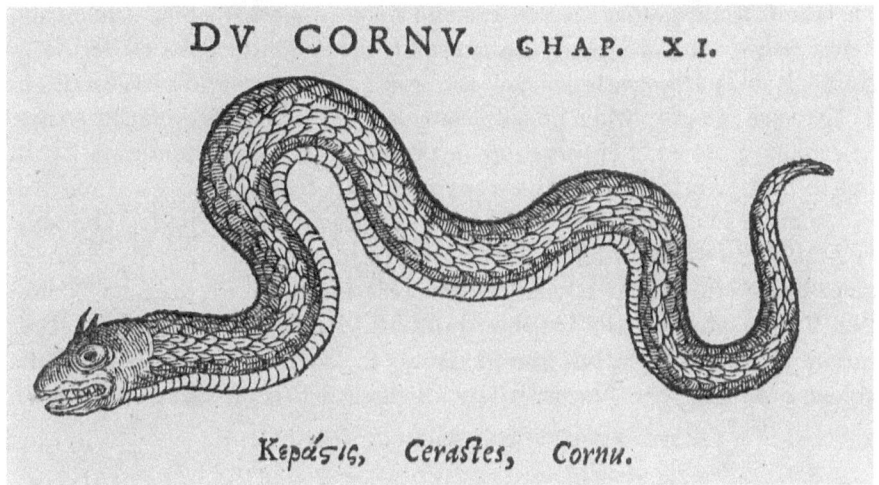

Figure 5. The "cornu," or horned viper (genus Cerastes), one of the snakes whose venom may be counteracted with theriac, according to Grévin. (University of Pennsylvania Special Collections FC55 G8694 568d [bk. 1, chap. 11, p. 79]; image courtesy of the Kislak Center for Special Collections, Rare Books, and Manuscripts, University of Pennsylvania)

in the tradition of the *dit*. A prime example of the latter, the *Ditz de Maistre Aliborum qui de tout se mesle* from the *Recueil du British Museum*, paints a more distinct picture of the kind of character that Gargantua and Ponocrates observe on rainy days. Aliborum belongs to a class of characters like the *Varlet à louër à tout faire*, the *Chambrière à louer à tout faire*, and *Watelet de tous mestiers*, all of whom resemble Beaumarchais's Figaro in the many different jobs they perform in a never-ending effort to scrape by. Among these, Aliborum works as a

> Fondeur, laveur, triacleur, basteleur,
> Saulteur, lucteur, danseur, apoticaire,
> Pescheur, pipeur, hasardeur, escrimeur,
> Bon advocat, procureur et notaire.
>
> [Caster, washer, treacle seller, juggler,
> Tumbler, wrestler, dancer, apothecary,
> Fisher, bird-catcher, adventurer, fencer,
> Good lawyer, prosecutor, and notary.][14]

He is at once a *theriacleur*, a *basteleur*, and a *pipeur*, literally a bird-catcher and figuratively a con man. He also conveys the theatricality of the *theriacleur* as seen in Rabelais's work, as he resolves to start carrying around a large snake in a bag to use as a prop when he sells "metridal" and "triacle," presumably so that he can make potential buyers think he derives his key ingredient from it.[15] In this respect, treacle is perfectly synonymous with snake oil.

Another stock *theriacleur* may be found in the *Recueil Trepperel*. The *Sottie de Maître Pierre Doribus* introduces us to a name commonly given to *theriacleurs* in Middle French, not unlike how cesspit cleaners were called "Maître Fifi." The spaghetti Latin "Doribus" not only lends an air of phony sophistication to the character, but also illustrates the comic disparity between the golden promises he makes and what he actually delivers. To wit, he opens the *Sottie* by declaring:

> Il me fault maintenant crier
> Mon mestier, pour dire le voir,
> Pour ung pou le faire valloir
> Soit avecque saiges ou sotz.
>
> [I must now hawk
> My trade, truth be told,
> To make it look good
> For both the wise and the foolish.][16]

His trade has no inherent value, but the manner in which he advertises it can confer value upon it in the eyes of those like the skeptical *sot* who subsequently confronts him.

By the time Rabelais began publishing his vernacular works, Doribus and Aliborum had become prominent enough to serve as points of reference for other *dits* like that of *Maistre Hambrelin, serviteur de Maistre Aliborum, cousin germain de Pacolet*. This piece can be dated to the 1530s or 1540s on the grounds that its author not only borrows from *Maistre Aliborum* and *Watelet de tous mestiers*, but also references Marot's Alix and Frippelippes, the "valet" who lambasts Marot's nemesis François Sagon in his master's stead. Like his predecessors, Hambrelin is a seller of "triacle" as well as a crier, and he knows how to prepare "pouldre d'oribus," a bogus concoction that shares its putative inventor's name.[17] The *theriacleur* had thus become a theatrical character with recognizable traits and a distinct vocabulary, and Rabelais frequently makes reference to both.

What is perhaps most interesting about the *thériacleur* of farces and *sotties* is less the frequency with which he appears than the prophylactic role he serves vis-à-vis the audience. This role is clearest in *Le pardonneur, le triacleur, et la tavernière*. The farce opens with the pardoner performing his pitch to the crowd and touting his relics, the ears of "Sainct Couillebault" [Saint Happysacks] and his sister, "Saincte Velue" [Saint Fuzzy], whose clearly sexual names are at odds with their supposedly saintly status. The *triacleur* then performs his pitch, and like Aliborum, he tries to attract the crowd's attention by passing off an eel named Margot as the poisonous adder from which he sources his medicine. He then touts his treacle as a potent antivenin:

> Car il n'y a poyson si forte,
> Soit reagal ou arceniq,
> Avant que vous eussiez dit: picq,
> Vous seriez guery trestout sain,
> Et feussiez-vous mors d'un aspicq.[18]

> [For there is no poison so strong,
> Not even aconite or arsenic,
> That, no sooner than you could say "pike,"
> You wouldn't be completely cured,
> Even if you had been bitten by an asp.]

The two charlatans then turn on one another, revealing their respective ruses to the audience: the *triacleur*'s ointment from the Holy Land is mere gruel, and the pardoner's seraphim wing is nothing more than the feathers of a goose he had for dinner. Having driven away their potential clients, the two miscreants decide to join forces, go to an inn, and con the innkeeper's wife.

At the inn, the pardoner pays for their meal with a box that he claims contains a bonnet that belonged to one of the Innocents, and before he and the *triacleur* take their leave, he warns the innkeeper's wife not to look at the holy relic inside. Once alone, the woman is overcome with Pandora's curiosity and opens the box, only to find that it contains not a bonnet, but a pair of shit-stained undergarments ("braies"). She realizes she has been duped and learns her lesson, exclaiming,

> Que de finesses cauteleuses
> Se font aujourd'huy par le monde!
> Je pry à Dieu qui les confonde.

[So many cunning tricks
Are played in the world today!
God confound them!][19]

She, and by extension the audience, has been inoculated against the false promises of charlatans through exposure to them. In this sense, the farce itself acts as a preventative *pharmakon* akin to treacle: the *triacleur*'s wares might be snake oil (or rather eel oil), but the farce that unmasks him is an effective antidote "suitable for inoculating us," as Grévin would say.

Alcofrybas, *Thériacleur* Extraordinaire

To return to Rabelais, we may assume his familiarity in his medical capacity with texts touching on treacle and mithridate such as Celsus's *De medica* and Galen's *De theriaca* and *De antidotis*, editions of which were published in Paris in the 1520s and 1530s.[20] Even more to the point, Rabelais refers to the practice of inoculation in Chapter 33 of *Pantagruel*, in which doctors travel through the sick giant's stomach and into his colon to clean out a mountain of excrement. Its odor is even more noxious than that of Mephitis, Roman goddess of swamp gas, the legendarily putrid marsh of Camarina in Sicily, or the lake of Serbonis, which Rabelais felicitously renders as "Sorbone." Fortunately, the doctors have prepared themselves for this contingency, "Et n'eust esté qu'ilz estoient tresbien antidotez le cueur, l'estomach, et le pot au vin (lequel on nomme la caboche) ilz feussent suffocquez et estainctz de ces vapeurs abhominables" (*P* 33.335) [and, had it not been that they had very well antidoted their heart, their stomach, and their wine-pot (which they call noggin), they would have been suffocated and snuffed out by these abominable vapors (Frame 243)]. Rabelais's use of "antidotez," the first attested occurrence of the term in French, indicates that while the doctors may be performing the sort of purgative function usually attributed to Rabelais's books *qua* medical treatment, they have themselves partaken of the preventative inoculation characteristic of treacle and of the *thériacleur*'s role in popular comic theatre.[21]

In this vein, Rabelais refers several times to the theatrical tradition of the *thériacleur* throughout the *Geste Pantagruéline*. The trickster Panurge's manifold abilities, and indeed his very name, which, as Dorothea Heitsch points out, could be read as a Greek version of "jack of all trades," are reminiscent of Aliborum or Hambrelin.[22] In Chapter 16 of *Pantagruel*, the reader learns that Panurge "avoit aultrefoys crié le theriacle" (*P* 16.276) [had hawked quack medicine (Frame 190)]. In Chapter 22, when Panurge plays a nasty trick on a

Parisian lady by dousing her with the pheromones of a bitch in heat, a pack of male dogs spray her front door with so much urine that it forms a brook "qui de present passe à sainct Victor, auquel Guobelin tainct l'escarlatte, pour la vertu specificque de ces pisse chiens, comme jadis prescha publicquement nostre maistre Doribus" (P 22.297) [that now passes by Saint-Victor, in which Gobelin dyes his scarlet, for the specific virtue of those pisshounds, as was once preached publicly by our master d'Oribus (Frame 209)].[23] Doribus reappears in Chapter 22 of *Gargantua*, where "la barbe d'oribus" [Gold-beard] is listed among the young giant's games (G 22.60, Frame 52). Finally, in Chapter 20 of the *Tiers Livre*, Panurge, exasperated with the increasingly invasive gestures of the deaf-mute Nazdecabre [Goatsnose], cries out, "Que Diable veult praetendre ce maistre Alliboron?" (*TL* 20.414) [What the devil does this Master Knowitall think he's doing? (Frame 316)].

Clearly, Rabelais was familiar with the *thériacleurs* of farces and *sotties*, and expected his reader to be familiar with them, as well, so when Rabelais's narratorial persona, Alcofrybas Nasier, speaks like a fairground hawker in the prologue of *Pantagruel*, he is more precisely speaking like a *thériacleur* of farce. Alcofrybas has recourse to the *thériacleur*'s vocabulary in describing the *Grandes et inestimables Chronicques de l'enorme geant Gargantua* as a wonder drug effective against colds, syphilis, and even toothache: "Aultres sont par le monde (ce ne sont fariboles) qui estans grandement affligez du mal des dentz, aprés avoir tous leurs biens despenduz en medicins sans en rien profiter, ne ont trouvé remede plus expedient que de mettre lesdictes chronicques entre deux beaulx linges bien chaulx, et les appliquer au lieu de la douleur, les sinapizand avecques un peu de pouldre d'oribus" (P 214) [There are others around the world (these are no silly tales) who, when in great pain from a toothache, after spending all their means on medicines with no profit, found no more expedient remedy than to wrap the said *Chronicles* between good hot cloths and apply them to the place where it hurt, sprinkling them with a little powdered dung (Frame 133)]. The seasoning of "pouldre d'oribus," which Frame renders as "powdered dung," firmly situates Alcofrybas's pitch within the context of *triaclerie*, as does the fact that he advertises for the *Chroniques* as a cure for toothaches. Both Aliborum and the Fool who aspires to be an "esprouveur de triacle" [treacle hawker] in the farce *Tout-Ménage* describe themselves as crying "à la malle dent" [tooth-pulling] along with their treacle and mithridate, and the innkeeper's wife in *Le pardonneur, le triacleur, et la tavernière* mentions that her deceased husband was himself a tooth-puller ["arracheur de dents"].[24]

Offering his audience another book "de mesme billon" [of the same caliber], Alcofrybas concludes the prologue by threatening potential readers of

Pantagruel with erysipelas, hellfire, and even sodomy if they do not believe every word of the chronicle (*P* 215, Frame 135). In so doing, he effectively addresses his readers as rustic dupes, claiming that he has taken his leave of his master Pantagruel to visit "pais de vache" [cow country]. This comical violence toward the reader has led François Rigolot to argue that just as we must distinguish between Alcofrybas the narrator and Rabelais the author, we must also distinguish between the narratees whom Alcofrybas addresses and the readers of *Pantagruel*.[25] Readers should distance themselves from the narratees and find amusement in how the latter might allow themselves to be abused by a charlatan such as Alcofrybas, whose fraudulence is made even clearer by the farcical subtext of the *thériacleur*.

In this sense, Rabelais accomplishes in the prologue of *Pantagruel* what one of his principal sources, Lucian, does in in the preface of the *True History*. Alcofrybas's hyperbolic insistence on truth, as well as the fact that he describes the *Chronicques* (and, by extension, *Pantagruel*) as reading for those who are otherwise unoccupied ["hors de propos"], distinctly calls to mind Lucian's prologue and its comparison of pleasure reading to rest as part of an exercise regimen.[26] Lucian justifies his tale, a parody of sea voyage epics like the *Odyssey* or *Argonautica*, as well as of histories like those of Herodotus or travel narratives like those of Ctesias and Iambulus, as a form of mental recreation. Just as relaxation is necessary to athletic training and leaves the athlete in better condition for future exertion, so too can a tale like the *True History* prove beneficial to students of more serious genres: "They will find it enticing not only for the novelty of its subject, for the humor of its plan and because I tell all kinds of lies in a plausible and specious way, but also because everything in my story is a more or less comical parody of one or another of the poets, historians and philosophers of old, who have written much that smacks of miracles and fables."[27] Lucian promises profitability despite, or rather because of, the humorous nature of his tale. By parodying the likes of Homer, Herodotus, and Ctesias, he "tell[s] all kinds of lies in a plausible and specious way" while insisting hyperbolically (and ironically) upon the truth of what he is about to recount. He thereby reveals to his readers the techniques used to lend credibility to incredible stories, such as when he specifies that his ship arrived at the moon after a wave lifted it approximately three hundred stadia into the air, parodying the use of precise details to impart an air of accuracy to something otherwise totally implausible. In so doing, he distances himself from his models by way of the liar's paradox: "But my lying is far more honest than theirs, for though I tell the truth in nothing else, I shall at least be truthful in saying that I am a liar. I think I can escape the censure of the world by my own admission that I am not telling a word of truth."²⁸ He is not so different from Pierre Doribus, then, who admits to his audience that he has to lie about his trade when he cries, "pour dire le voir" [truth be told].

Like Lucian, Rabelais has his narrator make false promises in such a way as to put the reader on guard against them, thereby providing inoculation against paratextual charlatanism; once exposed to specious rhetoric, the reader develops an immunity to it. Romain Menini, contending that Rabelais models the prologue of *Pantagruel* on Lucian's *True History* in response to the vogue for chronicles of suspect veracity in the first four decades of the sixteenth century, suggests that when confronted with the "maladie historienne" of his era, the good doctor offers not a cure, but a placebo that takes advantage of recent publishing trends.²⁹ While Menini's remarks may hold true when we consider the prologue from the standpoint of historical accuracy, considering it from the standpoint of farce and the *thériacleur* makes it clear that Rabelais is not offering a placebo, but rather a sort of literary treacle. It is not the miracle cure that Alcofrybas claims it is, but Alcofrybas's claims are precisely what allow it to protect the reader against the rhetorical poison of *captatio benevolentiae* and ideal readership.

Don't Read Like Thaumaste: Inoculation Against Ideal Readership

Terence Cave has discussed the connections Rabelais makes between linguistic or rhetorical inflation and the rampant economic inflation in sixteenth-century Europe brought on by the devaluation of old currencies and the influx of Spanish gold from the Conquista.³⁰ For Rabelais, rhetoric, like currency, loses its value if overused and overproduced with no regard for the actual value of what it represents, and while Cave focuses on Panurge's encounter with the merchant Dindenault and his overpriced sheep in Chapters 5–8 of the *Quart Livre*, his remarks on rhetorical inflation are equally applicable to all of the entries of the *Geste*, starting with the prologue of *Pantagruel*. The opening sentence of the prologue conforms to the *Rhetorica ad Herennium*'s instructions to dwell upon the audience's courage, wisdom, and good judgment:

> Tresillustres et Treschevalereux champions, gentilz hommes, et aultres, qui voluntiers vous adonnez à toutes gentillesses et honnestetez, vous avez n'a gueres veu, leu, et sceu, les *grandes et inestimables Chronicques de l'enorme geant Gargantua*: et comme vrays fideles les avez creues, gualantement, et y avez maintesfoys passé vostre temps avecques les honorables Dames et Damoyselles, leur en faisans beaulx et longs nar-

rez, alors que estiez hors de propos: dont estez bien dignes de grande louange, et mémoire sempiternelle. (P 213)

[Most illustrious and most valorous champions, who gladly devote yourselves to all things nice and honorable, not long ago you saw, read, and came to know the *Great and Inestimable Chronicles of the Enormous Giant Gargantua,* and, as true faithful, you had the courtesy to believe them, and you have spent your time many times with the honorable older and younger ladies, telling them beautiful long stories from these when you ran out of things to say, which makes you most worthy of great praise and eternal remembrance. (Frame 133)][31]

The *captatio* of this opening sentence is so patently obvious as to seem disingenuous, all the more so once the reader identifies Alcofrybas as a *thériacleur*: *captatio* and its praise of the audience are just another lure in the charlatan's bag of tricks.

The transformative experience of ideal readership offered by the book is similarly called into question. Indeed, it is farce, as we will see, that connects Alcofrybas the *thériacleur* with self-fashioning in *Pantagruel,* and particularly with the appetite for acquiring knowledge. Gérard Defaux has shown that Pantagruel's intellectual trajectory mirrors that of Pico della Mirandola, from the Florentine's overweening ambition in posting nine hundred theses in Rome in 1486 to his eventual repudiation of them. As such, *Pantagruel* warns Rabelais's fellow humanists against making a misguided attempt to attain divinity through human knowledge as exhibited in Panurge's declaration that "Autant vault l'homme comme il s'estime" [A man is as good as he thinks he is] (P 29.316, Frame 226), a phrase particularly reminiscent of Pico's *Oration on the Dignity of Man.*[32] *Pantagruel* equates an unrestrained adherence to self-fashioning with the sort of "science sans conscience" [science without conscience] so ruinous to the soul against which Gargantua warns his son in his famous letter (P 8.245, Frame 162).

In that very same letter, Gargantua urges Pantagruel to plunge headfirst into the "abysme de science" [abyss of knowledge] opened up by the new learning and its dissemination through print, recommending a course of study that includes the Talmud and Kabbalah and recalls Pico's syncretism, and even urging his son to defend his theses "en tout sçavoir publiquement envers tous et contre tous" (P 8.245) [in every branch of knowledge, publicly, before all comers and against all comers (Frame 161–62)]. Defaux and Gerard Brault, going against the usual scholarly assessment of Gargantua's letter as a humanist manifesto, have suggested that it reveals the giant's arrogance and ignorance, with Defaux calling it a "dance in front of the mirror" and Brault calling it the "overblown rhetoric of a pretentious fool."[33] While these assessments are attuned to the internal contradictions of Gargantua's letter, the letter also acknowledges the potentially dangerous appeal of humanist learning. After all, Gargantua's encouragement is accompanied by a warning to "Aye suspectz les abus du monde, ne metz ton cueur à vanité: car ceste vie est transitoire: mais la parolle de Dieu demeure eternellement" (*P* 8.245) [Hold suspect the abuses of the world; set not your heart on vanity, for this life is transitory, but the word of God abides eternally (Frame 162)]. In other words, vanity is less a problem for Gargantua than it is a potential one for Pantagruel.

Pantagruel does heed his father's advice insofar as he applies himself zealously to his studies, but immediately after meeting Panurge, he becomes an exaggerated parody of Pico as he tries to "essayer son sçavoir" [test out his learning]: "De faict par tous les carrefours de la ville mist conclusions en nombre de neuf mille sept cens soixante et quatre en tout sçavoir, touchant en ycelles les plus fors doubtes qui feussent en toutes sciences" (*P* 10.250) [Accordingly, at all the city's crossroads he posted conclusions in the number of nine thousand seven hundred and sixty-four, in all fields of learning, in these touching on all the gravest doubts there were in all these fields (Frame 167)]. The expansion of Pico's nine hundred theses to 9,764 already conveys Pantagruel's vainglory, which is only further confirmed when he begins to take pride in his growing reputation and *gloria mundi*: "Dont tout le monde commença à bruyre et parler de son sçavoir si merveilleux, jusques es bonnes femmes lavandieres, courratieres, roustissieres, ganyvetieres, et aultres, lesquelles quand il passoit par les rues disoient 'c'est luy,' à quoy il prenoit plaisir, comme Demosthenes prince des orateurs Grecz faisoit quand de luy dist une vieille acropie le monstrant au doigt, 'c'est cestuy là'" (*P* 10.251) [Whereat everyone began sounding off and talking about his marvelous learning, even to the gammers, washerwomen, women brokers, women roast meat sellers, penknife sellers, and others, who, when he passed in the street, used to say: "He's the one!" At which he took pleasure, as did Demosthenes, prince of Greek orators, when a huddled old woman, pointing her finger at him, said: "That's the one!" (Frame 167)]. Rabelais's allusion to the Erasmian adage "Monstrari digito" is not a compliment for Pantagruel: in it, Erasmus criticizes Demosthenes for being "gloriae avidum et moribus contaminatis" [glory-seeking and of polluted morals].[34]

Pantagruel falls even further into pride when he gets the opportunity to resolve the legal dispute between Baisecul [Kissass] and Humevesne [Sniffshit], whose nonsensical verbal diarrhea matches their names and produces a fitting reaction from all of the legal experts assembled to rule on the case: "Ainsi assemblez par l'espace de quarente et six sepmaines n'y avoyent sceu mordre, ny entendre le cas au net, pour le mettre en droict façon quelconques: dont ilz estoyent si despitz qu'ilz se conchioyent de honte vilainement" (*P* 10.251) [Thus assembled, for the space of forty-six weeks they had not been able to get their teeth into it or understand the case clearly to put it into law in any way whatever, at which they were so vexed that they were foully beshitting themselves for shame (Frame 168)]. When Pantagruel resolves the dispute by pronouncing an equally nonsensical judgment, the assembled councilors are so struck with admiration at "la prudence de Pantagruel plus que humaine" [the more than human wisdom of Pantagruel] that they need to be revived with vinegar and rosewater (*P* 13.262, Frame 177).[35]

Pantagruel and his easily impressed audience are convinced that he has fashioned himself into something "more than human" thanks to his assiduous humanist education, but in reality, he fails to follow the advice in his father's letter; instead of giving all glory to God and pursuing Christ through his study, he wins worldly glory by trafficking in shit. His problem, then, is not what he is learning, but what he decides to do with his knowledge, and as such, Pantagruel serves as a warning to Rabelais's humanist readers. As Nicolas Le Cadet has convincingly argued, Rabelais envisions an elite readership who shares Pantagruel's and his own interests, and who would therefore be especially susceptible to the sin of pride that tends to accompany these interests.[36] This danger is hammered home first through Pantagruel, and then through the English cleric Thaumaste.

Bruce Hayes, who has shown just how extensively Rabelais makes use of farce to advance his evangelical humanist agenda, places a particular emphasis on the ways in which the French Lucian appropriates the humiliating reversals that farces tend to visit upon characters with excessive appetites or ambitions, or who overstep their social bounds.[37] Thaumaste most certainly falls into this category, as he comes to Paris to test Pantagruel's knowledge publicly while debating "aulcuns passages de Philosophie, de Geomantie, et de Caballe" (*P* 18.282) [certain passages in philosophy, in geomancy, and in the Cabala (Frame 194)]. The Kabbalah, which Thaumaste also mentions at the beginning of Chapter 20, calls Pico's *Apologia* to mind, as does the Englishman's reference to the Florentine when proposing that the debate be conducted entirely in gestures. Thaumaste is both similar to and different from the Écolier limousin [Limousin schoolboy] in that he shares the young bachelor's misplaced sense of self-assurance, but whereas the Écolier is the product of a scholastic university education deficient in both useful learning and morals, Thaumaste epitomizes humanist interests and thirst for knowledge, much like Pantagruel.

Indeed, both parties bear a strong resemblance to one another on the night before the debate. Thaumaste mentions to his concierge that he has never before been so thirsty ("alteré") in his life: "'Il m'est (disoit il) advis que Pantagruel me tient à la gorge'" (P 18.283) ["I do believe," said he, "that Pantagruel has me by the throat" (Frame 196)]. Thaumaste's thirst plays on Pantagruel's origins as a saltwater demon in Simon Gréban's *Mystère des actes des apôtres*, but also recalls the fate of the Écolier limousin, who dies of thirst after constantly complaining that Pantagruel has him by the throat (P 7.235). Pantagruel, for his part, is equally transported, and spends the night cramming for the mute debate by reading a series of texts on nonverbal communication and interpretation:

> Le livre de Beda *de numeris et signis*.
> Le livre de Plotin *de inenarrabilibus*.
> Le livre de Procle *de magia*.
> Les livres de Artemidore *peri onirocriticon*.
> De Anaxagoras *peri semion*.
> D'Ynarius *peri aphaton*.
> Les livres de Philistion.
> Hipponax *peri anecphoneton*, et un tas d'aultres ...
> (P 18.283–84)

> [Bede's book *On numbers and signs*;
> Plotinus's book *On unnarratables*;
> Proclus's book *On magic*;
> The books of Artemidorus *On the meaning of dreams*;
> Of Anaxagoras *On signs*;
> Of Ynarius *On unutterables*;
> The books of Philistion;
> Hipponax *On things unpronounced*;
> and a pile of others ... (Frame 196)]

The list starts out promisingly enough, as the first four authors and works are authentic. However, the Venerable Bede's name does recall that of Noël Béda, the Sorbonne syndic and *bête noire* of evangelicals whose *De optimitate triparum* [*On the optimity of tripes*] may be found in the library of Saint-Victor (P 237, Frame 154). Pantagruel's reading list starts to look more and more like Saint-Victor's collection, both in form and in increasingly fanciful content: Anaxagoras, Philistion, and Hipponax are not known to have written the works attributed to them here, Ynarius is unknown and his name is likely a pun on *denarius* ["Mr. Money"], and the concluding "pile of others" implies that the reader has been spared a further list of even more ludicrous works.

However, there is a key difference between Pantagruel's reading list and the books of Saint-Victor. The latter is full of books like "*Ars honeste pettandi in societate* per M. Ortuinum" [*The art of farting decorously in society*, by Master Hardouin], "Tartaretus *de modo cacandi*" [Craparetus, *On the methodology of shitting*], and of course "*Des poys au lart cum commento*" [On peas with bacon, with commentary], whose titles are a mix of French and spaghetti Latin meant to disparage the scholasticism and non-Ciceronian Latin of the universities (*P* 7.236–37, Frame 153–54).[38] Pantagruel's list, on the other hand, is composed of authors and philosophers from antiquity (albeit with one probable interloper), and the titles are all in accurate Greek. The implication is that, in his effort to demonstrate his knowledge publicly for the sake of recognition and to probe for hidden secrets, the young prince has effectively made humanism into another version of scholasticism. This reading is different and more in line with the humanist call to return *ad fontes* [to the sources], but the result is the same.

It is at this moment that Panurge, seeing the giant's distress, volunteers to take his place and make Thaumaste "chier vinaigre devant tout le monde" (*P* 18.284) [I'll have him shitting vinegar in front of everybody (Frame 196)]. At the debate, Panurge regales the Englishman with a series of increasingly obscene gestures, which include making the sign of the horns, wiggling his codpiece, and sticking his finger up his anus. Thaumaste, driven by his lust for hidden knowledge, reads meaning into Panurge's gestures and works himself up into such a state of agitation that he "commença suer à grosses gouttes, et sembloit bien un homme qui feust ravy en haulte contemplation" (*P* 19.288) [started sweating great drops, and certainly looked like a man transported in lofty contemplation (Frame 199)]. Eventually, Thaumaste gets so worked up that he lets out a "gros pet de boulangier" [great baker's fart], so called because it is followed by "bran" (a pun on "bren," or shit), and he "se conchioit de angustie" [beshitting himself in his perplexity] (*P* 19.288, Frame 200). He thus meets with the same farcical humiliation as the Écolier limousin and the experts summoned to weigh in on Baisecul and Humevesne's case do. And yet, he takes his leave in gratitude, grateful to Pantagruel that his disciple has "ouvert le vray puys et abisme de Encyclopedie" [opened for me the true well and abyss of encyclopedic knowledge], which recalls the "abisme de science" of

Gargantua's letter to Pantagruel (*P* 20.290, Frame 201). In Thaumaste's case, however, the "abisme" has a more infernal connotation: the audience members have to plug their noses, because he "puoit comme tous les diables" (*P* 19.288) [stank like all the devils in hell (Frame 200)].

Thaumaste serves as a farcical scapegoat to allow Pantagruel and, by extension, the reader, to learn from his example about the dangers of pursuing self-fashioning through hidden knowledge. In fact, the language used to describe Thaumaste's ambition and punishment connects him not only to Pico, but also to the reader, or more precisely to the promises Alcofrybas makes to the reader in the prologue. Even in the first Claude Nourry and François Juste editions of *Pantagruel*, Alcofrybas asks the reader to become so absorbed with the *Chronicques* (and, by extension, the book at hand) that he abandons his own affairs "pour y vacquer entierement, sans que son esperit feust de ailleurs distraict ny empesché" (*P* 213) [to see to these entirely, without his mind being involved elsewhere (Frame 133)].[39] Alcofrybas would have readers approach *Pantagruel* in very much the same way that Thaumaste approaches the debate with Panurge just before he loses control of his bowels. Readers thus find themselves in a position similar to that of the innkeeper's wife in her dealings with the pardoner and the *triacleur*: though they are offered an object worthy of "lofty contemplation," they run the risk of ending up with nothing but a pair of soiled trousers.

Alcofrybas's connection to Thaumaste, as well as to Pico and self-fashioning, is made even stronger in the definitive 1542 Juste edition.[40] In a lengthy passage added to the debate between Panurge and Thaumaste in Chapter 19, the Englishman breaks the procedural rules of the debate by interjecting "Et si Mercure" [And if Mercury], alluding to Hermes Trismegistus, and by extension to the esoteric tradition of Hermeticism and *prisca theologia*, or true theological revelation granted directly to ancient man by God and partially reflected in all religions, associated with him and held in great reverence by Pico, Ficino, and other humanist luminaries. The allusion is reinforced by Panurge's "tresmegiste" [thrice great] codpiece (*P* 19.286–87).[41] The newly added hermetic vocabulary of this chapter underscores not only Thaumaste's mad quest for hidden knowledge, but also Alcofrybas's transformation on the title page (beginning with the 1534 Juste edition) from the vaguely Ovidian "maistre Alcofrybas Nasier" ("Nasier" echoing Ovid's cognomen, Naso) to "m. Alcofrybas abstracteur de quinte essence," which suggests an exotic alchemist—the preface "al-" calls to mind such highly regarded Arabic and Persian authorities as Avicenna and Albumasar—capable of extracting the most subtle parts from substances.[42] It also evokes the hermetic tradition, as quintessence was associated with Mercury, both the god and the element.⁴³ The reader is invited to approach Alcofrybas with the same sort of reverence with which Thaumaste approaches Panurge, with the difference that the reader is made aware through the Englishman's farcical plight of just what sort of fate awaits those who are easily fooled into grasping after self-fashioning through recondite knowledge. When Alcofrybas instructs readers in the 1542 edition to learn the *Chronicques* by heart and pass them down across generations "ainsy que une religieuse Caballe" [like some religious cabala], they know that he is effectively inviting them to repeat Thaumaste's mistake, and that Rabelais has his narrator address them this way so as to inoculate them against prologues that advertise for the book as a repository of self-fashioning.

When we recall Rabelais's evangelical orientation and the prologue's oft-cited claim that more copies of the *Chronicques* were sold in two months than copies of the Bible in nine years, it becomes clear that his lesson of caution is likely religious in nature.⁴⁴ It echoes the concerns expressed by Erasmus in the *Paraclesis*, which first appeared as one of the three prefaces to his 1516 Greek/Latin edition of the New Testament, the *Novum Instrumentum*.⁴⁵ Rabelais's admiration for and consistent use of Erasmus, to whom he refers as his spiritual father and mother in a November 30, 1532 letter, are well-established, and the *Paraclesis* is no exception. Raymond Lebègue lists Erasmus's prefaces for the *Novum Instrumentum* as one of three categories of sources for Rabelais, the other two being compendia like the *Adages* and *Apophtegmata* and Erasmus's original works.⁴⁶ Like *Pantagruel*, the *Paraclesis* raises the question of how print culture and humanism affect the tastes of the learned reading public, and attempts to recondition these priorities, which Erasmus, himself a master of self-promotion, sees as both theologically misguided and detrimental to his own publishing project.⁴⁷

The *Paraclesis* urges the study of what Erasmus calls the philosophy of Christ through reading the Scriptures. It begins by praising the advancement of human knowledge, but this praise is only meant to underscore the lack of attention to scriptural study that Erasmus feels has plagued Christendom to the point where Christians pride themselves on not reading the Bible, either because they feel such things are best left to the clergy or because they deem other pursuits more worthy of their attention: "At in ceteris disciplinis omnibus, quas humana prodidit industria, nihil est tam abditum ac retrusum, quod non pervestigarit ingenii sagacitas, nihil tam difficile, quod non expugnarit labor improbus. Qui fit autem, ut hanc unam philosophiam non his, quibus par est, animis amplectamur, quotquot ipso etiam cognimine Christi factionem profitemur?" [Moreover, in all other branches of learning which human industry has brought forth, nothing is so hidden and obscure which the keenness of genius has not explored, nothing is so difficult which tremendous exertion has not overcome. Yet how is it that even those of us who profess to be Christian fail to embrace with the proper spirit this philosophy alone?].[48] If this sorry state stems from people wanting to learn about anything but Christ and to read anything but the Bible, readers of *Pantagruel* might recall that the narratee whom Alcofrybas addressses has a taste for the *Chronicques*, which has sold many more copies than the Bible. Moreover, in versions of the prologue through 1537, the suckers whom Alcofrybas addresses believe what is written in the *Chronicques* as if it were the Gospel (1234). In lamenting this lack of interest in the Bible, Erasmus complains that, too often, readers are distracted from it by the lure of exoticism and the promise of hidden knowledge it implies: "Si quid a Chaldaeis aut Aegyptiis affertur, id ob hoc ipsum acrius avemus cognoscere, quod e peregrino sit orbe deportatum, et pretii pars est e longinquo venisse, et saepenumero in somniis homunculi, ne dicam impostoris, tam anxie distorquemur non solum nullo fructu, sed magno temporis dispendio" [If anything is brought to us from the Chaldeans or Egyptians, we desire more eagerly to examine it because of the fact that it comes from a strange world, and part of its value is to have come from far off; and oftentimes we are anxiously tormented by the fancies of an insignificant man, not to say an impostor, not only to no avail but with great loss of time].[49] As previously mentioned, the name "Alcofrybas" has a distinctly Arabic ring to it, promising the very kind of exotic novelty described by Erasmus. In spite of the fact that Alcofrybas is clearly a charlatan and a huckster, his narratees still pay attention to what he offers, allowing themselves to be "tormented by the fancies of an insignificant man, not to say an impostor," not unlike how Thaumaste sees in Panurge and his obscene gestures a hidden hermetic truth and the "true well and abyss of encyclopedic knowledge."

Rabelais does not reject outright the kind of self-fashioning exemplified in Erasmus's *De pueris instituendis*, nor, of course, does he reject the humanist enterprise and its hermetic tendencies. Rather, he grounds both of them within man's relationship with the word of God and places the onus on readers to fashion themselves for the better by searching for evangelical truths as they read. In keeping with the reformist tenet of *soli Deo gloria*, the point of self-fashioning through the pursuit of knowledge is to serve God, not one's own *philautia*, or blind, deluded self-love.[50] Pantagruel is given the chance to learn this lesson from Thaumaste's ordeal, and in turn, the reader is given the chance to learn it from Alcofrybas the *thériacleur* and to be put on guard against advertisements promising hidden knowledge as the key to becoming more than human.

Gargantua: Sileni and Self-Fashioning as Treacle

Self-fashioning is also at stake in the prologue of *Gargantua*, in which Alcofrybas continues to appear in the guise of a *thériacleur* at the same time as Rabelais's authorial persona begins to take on a more explicitly medical aspect. It does so in the paratextual *dizain* "Aux lecteurs," which first appears in Juste's 1535 second edition of *Gargantua*.[51] Here, Rabelais speaks as a doctor examining and diagnosing his patients, "Voyant le dueil, qui vous mine et consomme" [Seeing the grief that robs you of your rest], and prescribing a book that "ne contient mal ne infection" [holds no evil to corrupt the mind] (G 3, Frame 2). As a humanist doctor, he offers to treat both mind and body with a cure for grief in the form of laughter.[52] He presents himself as a practitioner concerned only with the well-being of the patient/reader, a foreshadowing of the persona he progressively adopts over the course of the remaining books.

If Rabelais appears increasingly solicitous of the reader's desires, the Alcofrybas of the prologue appears every bit as aggressive and manipulative as he does in the prologue of *Pantagruel*, concluding by calling his audience "vietz d'azes" [donkeypricks] and cursing them with "que le maulubec vous trousque" [may boils and blains rack you] (G 8, Frame 5).[53] Paradoxically, he also calls attention to his conformity to rhetorical prescriptions for *captatio benevolentiae*, only this time in such a way as to cast even more doubt on his case than he does in the prologue of *Pantagruel*. In describing the prologue as a "prelude, et coup d'essay" (G 6), he combines Marot's description of the *Adolescence clémentine* with a term taken straight from Aristotle's *Rhetoric*, which compares a speech's introduction to a musical prelude. The latter is particularly disconcerting, as Aristotle is quick to remind readers that introductions are especially useful for those whose case is weak, or looks weak.[54] When trying to convince his readers of the value of *Gargantua*, Alcofrybas promises that it contains "doctrine plus absconce, laquelle vous revelera de tres haultz sacremens et mysteres horrificques, tant en ce que concerne nostre religion, que aussi l'estat politicq et vie oeconomicque" [more abstruse doctrine, which will reveal to you some very lofty sacraments and horrific mysteries, concerning (our religion, as well as) our political state and domestic life], conforming verbatim to Cicero's instructions to make one's audience attentive by promising to discuss matters that pertain to the gods, the state, or the audience's personal affairs (G 7, Frame 4).[55] Through these references, the narrator calls attention to his rhetorical self-presentation and reminds readers that what they see is a carefully constructed persona intended to win their good will and make them overlook any possible deficiencies the book might have.

Furthermore, while much ink has been spilled over the prologue of *Gargantua*, surprisingly little has been written about the centrality of self-fashioning to a text so clearly Erasmian in inspiration. Self-fashioning is what ties the reader to the search for a "plus hault sens" [higher sense] and to the central metaphor of the *silenus* taken from Plato's *Symposium* and the Erasmian adage "Sileni Alcibiadis."[56] In the *Symposium*, Alcibiades compares Socrates to a statue of the aged, drunken satyr Silenus that looks amusingly ugly on the outside, but contains an image of a god on the inside.[57] Erasmus extends this comparison to Antisthenes, Diogenes, Epictetus, the Prophets, the Apostles, and especially to Christ, all of whom reveal their godliness through their very humility. These *sileni* contrast sharply with vulgar, trivial things (and, it is implied, with most representatives of the Church of Rome), which seem golden on the outside, but are leaden on the inside, which prompts Erasmus to call them inverted *sileni* ("praeposteri Sileni"). It is in this context that Alcofrybas addresses his readers, no longer calling them "Tresillustres et Treschevaleureux champions," but "Beuveurs tresillustres, et vous Verolez tresprecieux" (G 5) [Most illustrious topers, and you, most precious poxies (Frame 3)]. While this might appear to be an insult at first glance, it is actually flattery in the context of the Erasmian adage: in emphasizing the lowly, even risible appearance of his readers, Alcofrybas invites them to see themselves as *sileni*. In fact, not only is the original Silenus famous for his drunkenness, but Alcofrybas depicts Socrates as "tousjours beuvant d'autant à un chascun" [ever matching drink for drink]; if he addresses readers as drinkers, then he acknowledges that they are similar to Erasmus's Athenian saint (G 5).[58]

Inside every reader is an image of a god just waiting to be released—a point Alcofrybas drives home by alluding to the use of *sileni* as containers in which apothecaries would store "les fines drogues comme Baulme, Ambre gris, Amomon, Musc, zivette, pierreries: et aultres choses precieuses" (G 5) [fine drugs such as balm, ambergris, amomum, musk, civet, precious stones, and other valuables (Frame 3)]. While this allusion to the pharmacological use of *sileni* reinforces the inner/outer distinction central to the Erasmian adage and makes the book, to borrow a phrase from Montaigne, consubstantial with its reader, it also calls to mind the "pouldre d'oribus" of the previous prologue and Alcofrybas's comparison of the *Chronicques* and *Pantagruel* to wondrous drugs. In fact, storing supposedly luxurious or highly efficacious wares in boxes where no one can actually see them is a calling card of charlatans in farce: aside from the trope of keeping a snake (or an eel, as the case may be) in a bag, the pardoner tricks the innkeeper's wife by keeping his "bonnet of the Innocents" in a box, and the *triacleur* claims to keep a piece of Cerberus's head in a barrel.[59]

Alcofrybas goes on to describe Socrates as just such an apothecary's box containing "une celeste et impreciable drogue" [a heavenly drug beyond price], all while hinting at the ambition of self-fashioning by way of Socrates's "entendement plus que humain" [superhuman understanding] (G 5–6, Frame 3). Self-fashioning is exactly what Alcofrybas promises for readers willing to open the box and search the book for a "doctrine plus absconce." He emphasizes not only how to read the book (the question behind the interpretive controversy), but also the transformative effect that reading the book will have on the reader,[60] an effect conveyed by the celebrated metaphor of a dog breaking open a bone to suck out the marrow:

> À l'exemple d'icelluy vous convient estre saiges pour fleurer, sentir et estimer ces beaulx livres de haulte gresse, legiers au prochaz: et hardiz à la rencontre. Puis par curieuse leçon, et meditation frequente rompre l'os, et sugcer la sustantificque mouelle. C'est à dire: ce que j'entends par ces symboles Pythagoricques avecques espoir certain d'estre faictz escors et preux à ladicte lecture. (G 7)

> [After this example it behooves you to be wise enough to sniff out and assess these exquisite books, to be light footed in pursuit and bold in the encounter; then by careful reading and frequent meditation, break bone and suck out the substantific marrow—that is to say what I mean by these Pythagorean symbols, in the certain hope of being made more astute and brave by the said reading. (Frame 4)]

The passive "estre faictz" connects Alcofrybas's promise with the famous "homines non nascuntur, sed finguntur" [people are not born, but made] of Erasmus's *De pueris instituendis*.[61] From this standpoint, the text is not the end in and of itself, nor is the "higher sense" that the reader might discover in it, as the reader, while encouraged to search for it, is never told exactly what it is, and is forbidden to equate it with authorial intention. Rather, the text is the adjuvant described by Torben Vestergaard and Kim Schrøder, and the "certain hope" offered is the fashioning of readers into idealized versions of themselves made more intelligent and worthy by the act of reading: it is the promise of advertising.

In promising readers the ability to fashion themselves, however, Alcofrybas actually degrades them. Cathleen Bauschatz contends that the *abstracteur* attempts to gain control over readers by making them passive: "They will be made 'escors et preux' by a process which they must submit to in a fairly childlike manner."[62] Indeed, making listeners or readers willing to learn, or docile, is one of the principal aims of *captatio*, and Alcofrybas apparently aspires to make his readers as docile as trained dogs, even preceding his reference to Plato's dog by crying out "Caisgne!," an exclamation of wonderment that also means "bitch," as does its modern equivalent, *chienne*.[63] In other words, just after encouraging readers to aspire to "superhuman understanding," the narrator addresses them as less than human in a reversal reminiscent of the one visited upon Thaumaste, who, at the height of his rapture, reminds the world of his humanity in the basest, most animalistic way possible. After shitting his pants, he puffs up his cheeks "comme se il enfloit une vessie de porc" [as if he were blowing up a pig's bladder], continuing to do so until he "souffloit toujours comme une oye" [was still puffing like a goose], and when Panurge makes a popping noise by sticking his finger in his mouth and pulling it out nine times, Thaumaste cries out, "Ha messieurs, le grand secret: il y a mis la main jusqu'au coulde" [Aha! Gentlemen, the great secret. He put his hand in up to the elbow] (*P* 19.288–89, Frame 200).

In *Gargantua*, the reader's canine fate is confirmed by Alcofrybas's discovery in Chapter 1 of the manuscript containing the ensuing text, a "gros, gras, grand, gris, joly, petit, moisy livret" (*G* 1.10) [huge, stout, big, gray, pretty little moldy book (Frame 8)]. Rabelais uses this alliteration, which Pierre Fabri derides as a *cacephaton*, or a "barbare de rude langaige a ouyr" [barbarous, harsh language to hear], on more than one occasion.[64] Its effect is inevitably lost both in translation and in modern French, as the Middle French "r" was rolled. The Roman satirist Persius refers to the rolled "r" (also present in Latin) as the "littera canina" because it sounds like a dog's growl and even resonates in the nasal cavity like one.[65] This association was not lost on Geoffroy Tory, who cites Persius in a section of the *Champ Fleury* devoted to the "lettre canine": "Quant les chiens se despitent l'ung contre l'aultre, avant qu'ilz s'entremordent, en renfroignant leur geulle et retraignant leurs dents, ilz semblent qu'ilz pronuncent le R" [When dogs fight, and scowl and bare their teeth before they bite each other, they look like they're pronouncing the letter "r"].[66]

The manuscript containing the text Alcofrybas has been advertising is described in such a way as to force the reader to speak like a dog, thereby conforming ridiculously to Alcofrybas's instructions in the prologue. Then, before even getting to the actual tale of Gargantua, the *abstracteur* inserts the

"Fanfreluches antidotées" [antidoted Frigglefraggles], an enigmatic poem that he has included "par reverence de l'antiquaille" [out of reverence for antiquity] (G 1–2.10–11, Frame 8–9). M. A. Screech insists that the "Fanfreluches" must have been more comprehensible to Rabelais's contemporaries than to modern readers, as the author would not have frustrated the former's expectations so flagrantly by putting an incomprehensible text at the beginning of the book.[67] However, when we consider the "Fanfreluches" in light of how treacle functions in the prologue of *Pantagruel*, it becomes clear that frustrating the reader is not only admissible, but salutary. In reusing the neologism "antidotées" coined in the previous book, Rabelais once again calls to mind the pharmacological connotations of the term and effectively fulfills the promise Alcofrybas makes in the prologue to readers of *Gargantua*. The *silenus* that is the book does indeed contain a wondrous drug in the form of an antidote that inoculates readers against the sort of techniques used to lend an air of importance to a nonsensical text.

Posing as a scrupulous humanist editor who recounts the fortuitous discovery of a manuscript worthy of Poggio Bracciolini, Alcofrybas apologizes that the "Fanfreluches," found in an ancient tomb, have been partially eaten by rats and moths. The beginnings of the first five lines of the text are indeed totally or partially illegible, and Juste, who seems to have been willing to go along with the joke, contributes to the illusion with characters he most likely damaged prior to printing (fig. 6). The age and degradation of the text make it seem like Alcofrybas has done his readers and the humanist enterprise in general a great service by saving the "Fanfreluches" from oblivion, but the name "Fanfreluches" hints instead at its triviality or even its baseness. Cotgrave defines the term as "Loose threds, or hanging shreds in rags, and torne clothes; any such trash, excrement, riffraffe," and the alternate spelling "Finfreluches" as "Shales, or scales, or scalie excrements; as dandriffe," while Edmond Huguet defines "Finfreluche" as a synonym of "bagatelle."[68] Additionally, Rabelais humorously uses the verb "fanfrelucher" to denote the sex act, which might account for such bawdy elements of the poem as a calf's horns (connoting cuckoldry), the thousand other holes discussed along with those of Saint Patrick and Gibraltar, or the "braquemart" (a term of which Rabelais was particularly fond, which denotes either a sword or the male member) in the final stanza.[69]

Given the proximity of the "Fanfreluches" to the prologue, the term "Fanfreluches" may be seen as a lure akin to the *silenus*, a surface that appears trifling, but hides profound wisdom. The highly amphigoric series of *coq-à-l'âne*

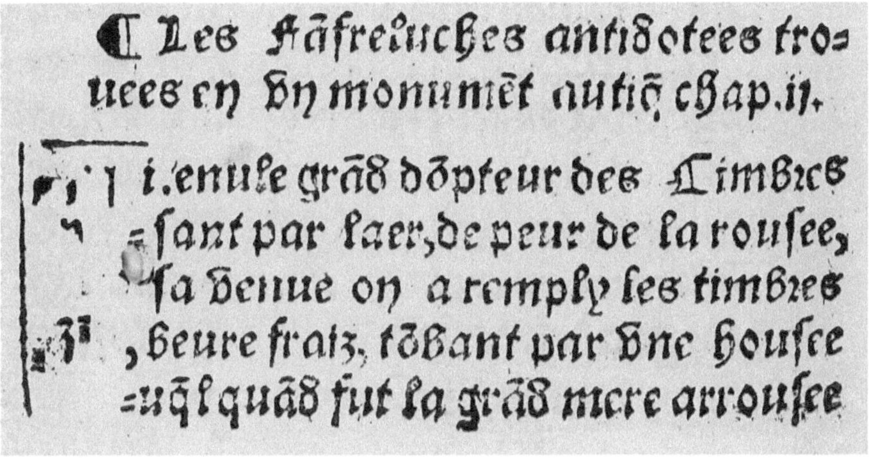

> ¶ Les fanfreluches antidotées trou-
> vees en vn monument antiq chap.ij.
>
> [i]enuse grãd dõpteur des Cimbres
> ſant par laer, de peur de la rousee,
> a venue on a remply les timbres
> , beure fraiz, tõbant par vne houſee
> =uq l quãd fut la grãd mere arrousee

Figure 6. Incipit of the "Fanfreluches antidotées." (BNF Rés. Y² 2130, f. A5v; reprinted with permission of the Bibliothèque nationale de France)

has indeed seen its share of critics who have sought to tease out its allusions with an impressive degree of erudition.[70] In spite of their efforts, the only clear allusions in the text are to the Pope and Charles V, which are hardly surprising given Rabelais's Gallican and evangelical religious and political orientation. The "Fanfreluches" are designed to invite this sort of exegesis not only by virtue of their apparent age, but also by virtue of their prophetic overtones, which confer upon them an air of urgency and suggest that they contain the "mysteres horrificques" promised in the prologue. In the eleventh stanza, the tense shifts abruptly from the past to the future as the enigma ceases to recount past events and begins to predict events to come, year by year. The first year, marked by such marvels as "d'un arc turquoys / De v. fuseaulx, et troys culz de marmite" [a Turkish bow, / Five spindles, and three bottoms-of-the-pot], will see the humiliation of a "roy trop peu courtoys" [king too crude to show], most likely Charles V. The remainder of the stanza takes on an even more apocalyptic tone, as suggested by the verb "engouffrer" [go down] and the last line, "Retirez vous au frere des serpens" [Go join the brother of the serpents brown], most likely Satan, while the next stanza predicts that the following year will see the peaceful reign of God ["cil qui est"] (G 2.13, Frame 11). The penultimate stanza promises a sort of return to the Ovidian golden age:

> Et durera ce temps de passe passe
> Jusques à tant que Mars ayt les empas.
> Puis en viendra un qui tous aultres passe
> Delitieux, plaisant, beau sans compas.
> (G 2.14)

> [And so this time of sleight-of-hand shall last,
> Until such time as Mars is chained for fair.
> Then comes one who all others has surpassed,
> Delightful, handsome, nice beyond compare.
> (Frame 11)]

This promise, along with the ensuing line, "Levez vos cueurs" [Lift up your hearts], a reference to the *sursum corda* of the mass, could be read as a coded message to evangelicals encouraging them to endure persecution and promising them that their cause will eventually win out, a possible interpretation that also applies to the paratextual *dizain* "Aux lecteurs" as well as to the "Enigme en prophetie" [Prophetic riddle] with which the book closes. Regardless, the importance of the "Fanfreluches" does not lie in their intended referents (if indeed there are any), but in the way in which they present themselves as an authoritative text worthy of the reader's attention and effort, all while serving as a shining example of what Rigolot calls Rabelais's "semantic plasticity," capable of justifying divergent interpretations.[71]

It is this combination of allure and "semantic plasticity" that allows us to classify the "Fanfreluches" as an enigma akin to the "Enigme en prophetie," which serves as the other bookend of Gargantua's narrative. The enigma, a poetic form quite popular in Rabelais's time, is described by Thomas Sébillet as an "allégorie obscure" [obscure allegory] whose appeal lies in posing an obstacle that the reader will want to overcome: "Lés plus cours sont lés plus élégans, et la vertu de l'énigme est l'obscurité tant dilucide que le bon esprit la puisse ésclercir après s'y estre quelque peu appliqué: et le vice est de faire téle déscription qu'elle se puisse adapter a plus d'une chose" [The shortest ones are the most elegant; an enigma is good if its obscurity is easy enough to see through for a good mind to be able to resolve it with a bit of effort, and bad if it produces a description that can apply to more than one thing].[72] According to Sébillet's definition, the "Fanfreluches" are a poor enigma by virtue of their length and obscurity. However, they are made to tempt the reader into believing that they contain a single solution, a hidden mystery that may be easily discerned by a "good mind." In other words, they pique the reader's curiosity and pride the way a good enigma would in Sébillet's assessment, but without offering the satisfaction of a clear answer.

Jacob Le Duchat, editor of the 1711 edition of Rabelais's works, sees the "Fanfreluches" in a similar light. In his view, they are nothing but "... un panneau tendu par Rabelais à ses lecteurs qui se piqueroient mal à propos de subtilité.... [Il] prévoioit fort bien que ce seroit cette obscurité même qui animeroit davantage les curieux à vouloir en pénétrer le mystère. Tel est le tour d'esprit de certains hommes, que plus les difficultez sont grandes, plus ils s'empressent à remporter l'honneur de les avoir surmontées" [... a trap Rabelais has set for readers who might become quite badly taken with subtleties.... (He) foresaw very well that it would be their very obscurity that would further compel the curious to want to fathom the mystery. Such is the frame of mind of some men that the greater the difficulties, the more fuss they make about trying to win the honor of overcoming them].[73] In this sense, the "Fanfreluches," not unlike the prologue of *Pantagruel*, place the reader in the position of a "curieux" who seeks to puff himself up through an interpretive *tour de force*. It is the very same situation in which Thaumaste finds himself when faced with Panurge's obscene gestures, and once again, the reader runs the risk of resembling the Englishman and sharing his fate by searching for "the great secret." It is in this way that the "Fanfreluches antidotées," in keeping with their name, serve as an antidote: by simultaneously appealing to and frustrating readers' desire to distinguish themselves through reading and interpretation, they inoculate readers against works that employ similar advertising strategies in an effort to draw in and control their audience through ideal readership.

Thus, while the prologue of *Gargantua* and the "Fanfreluches antidotées" promise readers the opportunity to fashion themselves through reading, they also make readers aware of their own vulnerability to allowing advertising to define their identities for its own purposes. In short, they advertise to the reader, but in such a way as to warn the reader against trusting advertising. In a similar vein, André Tournon points out that *pantagruélisme*, which comes to mean ideal readership *qua* charitable disposition toward the text over the course of the *Geste Pantagruéline*, does not entail being duped, much like Pantagruel, despite the *agape* he exhibits toward Panurge, is not fooled by his trickery. To refuse to reciprocate the text's generosity is to misunderstand it, but to fail to see the narrator's ruses and sophistry is equally misguided.[74] In this sense, *Gargantua* actually does deliver on Alcofrybas's promise: readers truly are made "escors" by reading it, as Cotgrave reminds us that the term can mean "warie" or "heedie" in addition to "wise."⁷⁵ Alcofrybas may peddle snake oil, but his snake oil inoculates the reader against the promises of advertising.

This simultaneous advertisement and warning against advertisement characterizes the rest of the *Geste*, as well. The *Tiers Livre*, in whose paratext Rabelais fully abandons the persona of Alcofrybas in favor of the persona of François Rabelais, medical doctor, incorporates prestige advertising through the comparison of author to doctor, as well as through an apparent insouciance as to whether the book is read. Yet, while the doctor may have replaced the *thériacleur*, he is every bit as much a charlatan.

CHAPTER 6

Rabelais, Doctor of Iatrosophism

B Y THE TIME the *Tiers Livre* was printed in 1546, the situation had changed drastically for François Rabelais and for France. The kingdom was wracked by political turmoil, as England and the Empire had pushed its territory back to its modern boundaries, and the costly Italian Wars had led to civil unrest like the revolt against the *gabelle* [salt tax] in the southwest. The religious landscape looked even more dire for evangelicals like Rabelais. Erasmus and Jacques Lefèvre d'Étaples, the two leading intellectual lights of the evangelical movement, both died in 1536, the same year in which Jean Calvin first published his *Institutes of the Christian Religion* in Latin; conciliation was giving way to schism and inevitable conflict. Royal support for reform was also a distant memory by 1546. Francis I had turned more and more against the movement after the Affair of the Placards, and near the end of his reign, he initiated or at least facilitated the horrors that would characterize the Wars of Religion: royal troops massacred the Waldensians at Cabrières and Mérindol in 1545, and in 1546, Étienne Dolet was burnt at the stake at Place Maubert in Paris. Meanwhile, Rabelais had lost his most staunch protector, Guillaume du Bellay, in 1543, and Guillaume's brother Jean saw his influence diminish significantly under Henri II.

This is not to say that Rabelais's writing started to become any less controversial with the *Tiers Livre*. However, he was cognizant of how precarious his situation had become, and consequently, he adopted a much more humble and dutiful authorial persona for the *Tiers Livre* and the remaining entries of the *Geste Pantagruéline*.¹ In the intervening years, Rabelais also had difficulties with the unauthorized and, as he saw it, deficient publication of his own works. This prompted him to adopt the same strategies that he would have witnessed in the works of Clément Marot, either when working as an editor for François Juste or simply as an enthusiastic reader who often quoted Marot in his own writing. Perhaps not surprisingly, the unscrupulous printer/publisher who occasioned this turn was none other than Étienne Dolet.

From the *Grands annales* to the *Tiers Livre*

In 1542, Dolet published his own editions of *Pantagruel*, the *Pantagrueline Prognostication*, and *Gargantua*.² Dolet's *Gargantua* preserves the original title in its *faux-titre*, but its title page reads *La Plaisante, et joyeuse histoyre du grand Geant Gargantua, Prochainement reveue, et de beaucoup augmentée par l'Autheur mesme* [*The pleasant, joyful history of the great giant Gargantua, recently revised and much expanded by the author himself*]. Not only is this claim not true, but the title affords the reader the choice to laugh off the "[p]laisante, et joyeuse" book. Dolet's biggest *faux pas*, however, is to include in his combined edition of *Pantagruel* and the *Pantagrueline Prognostication* the apocryphal *Navigations de Panurge*, also known as the *Disciple de Pantagruel*, a Lucianic sea voyage tale first published in 1538.³ An attempt to capitalize on Rabelais's success, it is most assuredly not his work, though he did borrow certain aspects of it, such as the giant Bringuenarilles, for the *Quart Livre*.

Rabelais's response to its inclusion dominates the next two editions of the *Geste*, the first published in Lyon by Juste's successor, Pierre de Tours, in 1542 and 1543, and the second in 1542 by an unidentified printer.⁴ They combine *Pantagruel* and *Gargantua* into the *Grands annales*, starting a precedent by organizing them according to the story's chronology and putting *Gargantua* before *Pantagruel*, and include a significant addition to their paratext in the form of a lengthy letter from the printer to the reader that appears in the same insert bearing the collective title.⁵ The letter, imputed to Rabelais by modern critics, is a vitriolic attack on a "plagiaire, homme encliné à tout mal" [plagiarist, a man inclined toward all manner of evil], namely Dolet.⁶ The complaint is directed at Dolet's hastily printed and unauthorized editions, which fail to omit controversial passages that Rabelais had altered or eliminated, and falsely attribute other works (e.g., the *Navigations*) to him: "Affin que tu ne prennes la faulse monnoye pour la bonne (amy lecteur) et la forme fardee, pour la nayve: et la bastarde, et adulterine edition du present oeuvre, pour la legitime et naturelle: Soies adverty que par avarice a esté soubstraict l'exemplaire de ce livre encores estant souz la presse" (¢2r) [So that you do not mistake fake money for real money, good friend reader, the embellished form for the natural one, and the bastard, adulterated edition of the present work for the legitimate, natural one, be warned that out of avarice, the copy of this book was stolen while it was still in press]. The caveat's vocabulary is strikingly similar to that of Marot's epistles to the "children of Apollo" in the *Adolescence* and, ironically, to Dolet's in the 1538 *Œuvres*. It recalls Marot's protests in the former regarding the sales of a large part of his works, "completely erroneous, poorly printed, and more for the bookseller's profit than the author's honor," and his disavowal of works excluded from the *Oeuvres* as "bastards" or "spoiled children."[7] The letter even goes on to level the very Marot-like accusation that Dolet's printings are "confusement amoncellées, ou elles estoient bien ordonnées" (¢2v) [piled together haphazardly, whereas they used to be properly ordered]. Worse still, it claims that Dolet sacrifices quality and honor for profit to such an extent that he gladly lets others use his ten-year comprehensive privilege for a fee and then tries to take credit for their work, or simply pirates their editions "pour donner a entendre que les Livres des bons autheurs, comme de Marot, de Rabelais, et plusieurs aultres, sont de sa facon" (¢3r) [to make people think that the books of good authors, like Marot, Rabelais, and several others, were made by him]. The letter's parting shot at Dolet's abuse of the French language casts further aspersions on his character and motivations, claiming that his linguistic "viedazeries" [donkey cock-ups] are "dignes d'estre baillees a mostardiers pour les publier par la ville" (¢4r) [worthy of being given to mustard-criers to distribute throughout the town]. Dolet's barbarisms bring him closer not only to the Écolier limousin of *Pantagruel*, but to mustard criers, a class of people who debase language in an effort to make money.[8]

Much like unauthorized editions of Marot's works set the stage for the *Œuvres*, Dolet's unauthorized editions and Rabelais's response in the *Grands annales* set the stage for the *Tiers Livre*, in which the good doctor adopts a beneficent, generous persona defined against the foil of the grasping, thieving Dolet. First printed in Paris by Chrestien Wechel in 1546, editions of the *Tiers Livre* are rather consistent in their titles.[9] From 1546 to 1552, all of them read (orthographical variants aside): *Le Tiers livre des faictz et dictz Heroïques du noble Pantagruel, composez par M. François Rabelais docteur en Medicine, et Calloïer des Isles Hieres*.[10] As has been noted, this title marks the first time that Rabelais signs his given name to an entry of the *Geste*, but more significant is the fact that Rabelais presents himself in his capacity as a doctor of medicine, introducing the connection between literature and healing that will be even further expounded upon in the two ensuing books. Yet, in leaving behind the *thériacleur* of his previous prologues, he puts himself in a potentially compromising position by tying his name to yet another bawdy and potentially controversial romance in the midst of the ninth Italian War. Now more than ever, he must justify his motivations for writing a book and convince readers to be interested in it, and to do so, he leans all the more heavily on classical rhetoric and its distinctions between different kinds of introductions. At the same time, he continues to encourage his reader to take a critical distance from his authorial persona: as Jerome Schwartz puts it succinctly, Rabelais's rhetoric is not the rhetoric of persuasion, but the rhetoric of irony.[11]

Rabelais's Medical Persona as *Insinuatio* in the *Tiers Livre*

If the mention of "M. François Rabelais docteur en Medicine" on the title page already gestures toward the author's benevolence, the prologue of the *Tiers Livre* drives the point home. Of all Rabelais's prologues, it is the one in which the role of rhetoric is most prominent, as the author excuses himself for writing another book of Pantagruel's adventures in wartime. His comparison of himself to Diogenes banging on his wine tub during the siege of Corinth, borrowed from Lucian's *How to Write History*, corresponds to the defensive measures taken in Paris after the fall of Saint-Dizier in 1544 during the Anglo-Imperial invasion of France.[12] Like Diogenes, Rabelais does not wish to be accused of being a "spectateur ocieux" [idle spectator] among those who play out the "insigne fable et Tragicque comedie" [notable fable and tragic comedy] of war.[13]

Rabelais fears that his readers might dismiss the *Tiers Livre* as superfluous, which means that according to the rules of classical rhetoric, his case belongs to the category that the *Rhetorica ad Herennium* calls "turpe" [discreditable] and that Cicero calls "admirabile" [incredible] in *De inventione*, in the sense that it is incredible that an orator would agree to argue it.[14] Cases like this call for *insinuatio*, the sidelong or subtle approach whose indirect nature distinguishes it from the more straightforward *exordium*. *Insinuatio* dictates that the orator open with an unexpected subject before arriving at the expected one, which is more delicate. The most effective means to achieve this rhetorical sleight of hand is to discuss one's own character instead of the case in question: Aristotle advises the orator to give more weight to a person's motive than to his or her actual deed, and the *Rhetorica ad Herennium* reminds the orator that one must encourage listeners to consider the person rather than the case.[15] The prologue of the *Tiers Livre* uses exactly this kind of *insinuatio*: it differs from the prologues of *Pantagruel* and *Gargantua* in that where they are concerned with the relationship between reader and book, it is concerned with the relationship between reader and author.[16] Through this substitution, Rabelais bases the reception of his book on the reception of his authorial persona.

Rabelais elaborates this persona and its fears by drawing on the anecdote of Ptolemy trying and failing to impress the Egyptians as related by Lucian in "To One Who Said, 'You're a Prometheus in Words.'"[17] In particular, he stresses the disparity between his intentions and the way in which his book might be received by readers: "en lieu de les servir, je les fasche: en lieu de les esbaudir, je les offense: en lieu de leurs complaire, je desplaise" (*TL* 351) [instead of serving them I offend them, instead of pleasing them I displease (Frame 258)]. His prologue manifests the anxiety of reception, his fear of being misunderstood and misread.[18] Why does he make this anxiety apparent, though? In light of rhetorical prescriptions for "turpe" or "admirabile" cases, the prologue seems less like a heartfelt outpouring of Rabelais's uncertainty than an aspect of his authorial persona that conforms perfectly to the goals of *insinuatio*. It stresses the author's desire to please the reader, and the anaphora of the phrase quoted above ("en lieu de ... je ...") marks the contrast between the potentially disappointing book on one hand and the author, who intends only to serve and please, on the other. In fact, this expression of anxiety recalls Cicero's *De oratore*, in which Crassus explains that an orator's uneasiness is actually a sure sign of skill: "Ut enim quisque optime dicit, ita maxime dicendi difficultatem, variosque eventus orationis, exspectationemque hominum pertimescit" [For the better the orator, the more profoundly is he frightened of the difficulty of speaking, and of the doubtful fate of a speech, and of the anticipations of the audience].[19] Crassus's seemingly modest admission of his own nervousness only wins him even more admiration from his interlocutors, who take it as proof of his "probitas" [integrity].[20] The same may be said for Rabelais: by making his anxiety apparent to the reader, he attests to his own integrity and generosity as an author, and in this way, *insinuatio* acts as prestige advertising.

This *insinuatio*, in turn, compels the reader to receive the *Tiers Livre* with the particular brand of benevolence that Rabelais calls "pantagruélisme," a term first associated with the reception of the *Geste* in the paratext of Juste's 1534 edition of *Pantagruel*, which adds after Hugues Salel's liminary *dizain* the phrase "Vivent tous bons pantagruelistes" [Long live all the good Pantagruelists], which would remain in editions through 1537. Its meaning is made clear by a simultaneous addition to Chapter 34, in which Alcofrybas warns his audience not to read the same way as "un grand tas de Sarrabovites, Cagotz, Escargotz, Hypocrites, Caffars, Frapars, Botineurs et aultres telles sectes de gens, qui se sont desguisez comme masques pour tromper le monde" (*P* 34.336–37) [a big bunch of Sarabaites, bigots, snails, hypocrites, fakers, bellybumpers, monks in buskins, and other such sects of people, who have disguised themselves like maskers to deceive people (Frame 244)]. These are, of course, the hypocritical members of the monastic orders and more specifically the censors of the Sorbonne, who read books like *Pantagruel* "non tant pour passer temps joyeusement, que pour nuyre à quelcun meschantement, sçavoir est, articulant, monorticulant, torticulant, culletant, couilletant, et diabliculant, c'est à dire callumniant" (*P* 34.337) [not so much to pass the time joyously as to harm someone wickedly, to wit by articulating, monorticulating, torticulating, buttock-wagging, ballock-shaking, and diaboliculating, that is to say calumniating (Frame 245)]. One wonders why these holy men spend all their time reading "livres Pantagruelicques" instead of Scripture, and even worse, why they read these books not for amusement, but with the more sinister aim of bringing accusations, twisting words to their purposes ("torticulant"), and figuratively defecating on them, as the recurrence of the syllable "cul" makes abundantly clear.[21]

The ensuing simile is also fecal in nature, as it compares these readers, in an amusing manifestation of the Latin proverb "Aurum ex stercore colligendum" [Gold may be collected from dung], to village scamps who pick through turds in search of cherry stones to sell to druggists who use them to make mahlab ["huille de Maguelet"] (*P* 34.337). These hypocrites convert their filthy criticisms into sweet-smelling mahlab, which was typically used in perfume, and use it to mask their own stench; by accusing innocent books of stinking of sulfur, they distract attention from their own infernal wickedness. Any reader can easily come to resemble them, and the chapter concludes with an imperative directing readers not to imitate them: "Iceulx fuyez, abhorrissez, et haissez aultant que je foys et vous en trouverez bien sur ma foy. Et si desirez estre bons pantagruelistes (c'est-à-dire vivre en paix, joye, santé, faisans tousjours grand chere) ne vous fiez jamais en gens qui regardent par un partuys" (*P* 34.337) [These shun, abhor, and hate as much as I do, and you will be well off for it, upon my word, and, if you want to be good Pantagruelists (that is to say to live in peace, joy, and health, always having a good time), never trust people who look out through a hole (Frame 245)]. The good cheer of "bons pantagruelistes" contrasts sharply with that of the monks, who have more than their share of good times, but hide it while attaching far too much significance to practices like fasting during Lent that they themselves do not bother to observe. They are reduced to "gens qui regardent par un partuys," an image that implies both the narrowness of their theological views and the voyeuristic pleasure they derive from scouring books for obscenity or heresy in the same way that peeping toms peer through windows hoping to see something naughty.[22]

Pantagruélisme, then, is Rabelais's definition of ideal readership in an evangelical context: whereas fault-finding is a sign of reprobation, *pantagruélisme*, as numerous scholars have discussed, is tantamount to the practice of Pauline *agape* in the act of interpretation.[23] Guy Demerson associates this charity with *captatio benevolentiae*—to display the benevolence required to enter the kingdom of the book is to adhere to *pantagruélisme*.[24] However, Rabelais alters the definition of *pantagruélisme* in the prologue of the *Tiers Livre* to better suit the new and increased dangers he faces as an author. Here, the definition consists not only of refusing to seek scandal in or take offense at the book, but more precisely of recognizing the author's good intentions:

> Je recongnois en eulx tous une forme specificque, et proprieté individuale, laquelle nos majeurs nommoient Pantagruelisme, moienant laquelle jamais en maulvaise partie ne prendront choses quelconques, ilz congnoistront sourdre de bon, franc, et loyal couraige. Je les ay ordinairement veuz bon vouloir en payement prendre, et en icelluy acquiescer, quand debilité de puissance y a esté associée. (*TL* 351)

> [I recognize in them all a specific form and individual property that our ancestors called Pantagruelism, on condition of which they never take in bad part things they know issue from a good, free, and honest heart. I have seen them ordinarily take good will in payment and be content with that, even when weakness in power has been associated with it. (Frame 258)]

The use of scholastic terminology ("forme specificque, et proprieté individuale") might be parodic, but the assimilation of *pantagruélisme* to the reader's acceptance is no less effective for it. Readers are encouraged to fashion themselves after the ideal *pantagruéliste* reader who gladly accepts the author's good intentions ("bon, franc, et loyal couraige," "bon vouloir") in lieu of a satisfying book, and who displays Pantagruel's charity and generosity toward Panurge when he absolves the author of his debts. *Pantagruélisme* is exactly what the *insinuatio* of the prologue aims to instill in the reader, and in this respect, prestige advertising and ideal readership depend upon one another.

By presenting himself as a lowly, fearful debtor, Rabelais closely follows the guidelines for *captatio benevolentiae;* the *Rhetorica ad Herennium,* for example, recommends that orators stress their disabilities, need, loneliness, and misfortune.[25] To do so is to compel one's readers to display their magnanimity, and accordingly, Rabelais compares himself to Euclio's rooster in Plautus's *Aulularia.* Euclio, the inspiration for Molière's Harpagon, is so afraid that his buried pot of gold will be found that he kills the rooster for scratching at the ground above it (*TL* 351).[26] His avarice and paranoia are so extreme that he imputes ill will to the animal and brutally butchers it, and the prologue of the *Tiers Livre* suggests that the reader who disdains Rabelais's book is no better than Euclio. Rabelais also changes a detail of Plautus's comedy: in *Aulularia,* Euclio bludgeons the rooster to death with a cudgel, whereas in *Tiers Livre,* the rooster dies of a "couppe guorgée" [cut throat]. This is, of course, one of Rabelais's famous *contrepèteries* [spoonerisms] that differs humorously from the expected "gorge coupée," but this spoonerism also transforms the rooster's cut throat into the overflowing cup of Psalms 23:5 ["calix meus inebrians"]. Much like in Lemaire's paratexts, to spurn the generosity of Rabelais's authorial persona is to spurn divine generosity and providence, and readers who disdain the *Tiers Livre* only display their own sinful ingratitude.

The prologue pursues the metaphor of the book as an inexhaustible source of wine, a parody of the Gospel according to John and yet another symbol of Rabelaisian liberality: "Tout beuveur de bien, tout Goutteux de bien, alterez, venens à ce mien tonneau, s'ilz ne voulent ne beuvent: s'ilz voulent, et le vin plaist au guoust de la seigneurie de leurs seigneuries, beuvent franchement, librement, hardiment, sans rien payer, et ne l'espargnent. Tel est mon decret" (*TL* 351) [Every worthy toper, every worthy goutie, when thirsty, coming to this barrel of mine, is not to drink if he doesn't want to; if they want to, and the wine pleases the taste of the Excellency of their Excellencies, let them drink freely, frankly, boldly, without paying a thing, and not spare it. Such is my decree (Frame 259)].[27] Rabelais's "decree" compares the book to a royal banquet, a simile also seen in Pierre de Ronsard's "Discours à Loys des Masures," which seems to grant the reader the freedom not to read the book:

> Ainsi ny par edict ny par arrest publique
> Je ne contrains personne à mon vers poëtique:
> Le lise qui voudra l'achete qui voudra.
>
> [Neither by edict nor by public injunction
> Do I compel anyone to my poetic verse:
> Read it if you want, buy it if you want.][28]

Nevertheless, Ronsard's apparent magnanimity betrays a preference for benevolent readers to the exclusion of others. The Vendômois poet uses the banquet simile in the context of his polemical *Discours des misères de ce temps* to assert his right to compose poems on profane or pagan subjects in the face of Huguenot accusations of impiety.

Invitations can exclude as well as invite, as is clear in Joachim Du Bellay's liminary epigram for the *Regrets*:

> Si gratum quid erit tuo palato,
> Huc conviva veni: tibi haec parata est
> Coena. Sin minus, hinc facesse, quaeso:
> Ad hanc te volui haud vocare coenam.
>
> [If you find something pleasing to your palate,
> Come, dear guest: this dinner was made
> For you. If you don't like it, then kindly begone:
> You're not the one I wanted to invite to this dinner.]²⁹

The same may be said for Rabelais, who performs what Bernd Renner calls "triage." After indicating "quelle maniere de gens j'invite" [what manner of people I invite], he chases away the "geants Doriphages" ["doriphagous giants" or "gift eaters," a reference to corrupt judges], "cerveaulx à bourlet grabeleurs de corrections" [hood-brained pettifoggers, the nitpicking sticklers for details, most likely the Sorbonne censors once again], and "Caphars" [pious hypocrites], whom he did not invite, not unlike how Diogenes, having called out for men, threatened with his stick all those who approached him, saying that he wanted men, not scoundrels (*TL* 352; Frame 259).³⁰

However, the prologue's profound irony must also be taken into account. Just as Diogenes mocks the Corinthians and their frenetic preparations for a siege (which turned out to be pointless, since Philip of Macedon did not attack the city in the end) with a Sisyphean gesture, Rabelais mocks the warlike folly of the French with his verbal gymnastics.³¹ Rabelais's irony extends to the prologue's *captatio*, as it subtly mocks readers who would allow themselves to be manipulated by the authorial persona and its constant flattery. Like any good orator, Rabelais praises his readers' noble extraction with an allusion to the myth of the Trojan origins of the French so near and dear to Lemaire: "vous estez tous du sang de Phrygie extraictz, (ou je me abuse) et si n'avez tant d'escuz comme avoit Midas, si avez-vous de luy je ne sçay quoy" (*TL* 345) [you're all sprung from Phrygian blood (or I'm mistaken), and, if you haven't as many gold crowns as Midas had, yet you do have a certain something of his about you (Frame 253)]. This "je ne sçay quoy" is, of course, the ass's ears, which Apollo inflicts upon the hapless Midas for siding with the satyr Marsyas in a music contest.[32] To intimate that one's readers have ass's ears (or to compare them to Midas at all) is already to impugn their judgment and intelligence, but the image of the ass recurs later in the prologue, when Rabelais complains of idle spectators who "chauvent des aureilles comme asnes de Arcadie au chant des musiciens, et par mines en silence signifient qu'ilz consentent à la prosopopée" (*TL* 349) [flapping their ears like Arcadian donkeys at the musicians' song and by their faces signifying in silence that they consent to the prosopopoeia (Frame 257)]. The Erasmian intertext of this simile, the adage "Asinus ad lyram" [An ass to the lyre], criticizes those who pretend to appreciate something they do not comprehend in the same way that an ass twitches its ears to the sound of music, even though it is incapable of understanding it.[33] Just as the reader of *Gargantua* is reduced to a dog, the French reader who descends from Midas and shares his "je ne sçay quoy" is reduced to an ass incapable of truly appreciating the *Tiers Livre*, which Rabelais associates with song by comparing the bottle/book to Helicon and the Hippocrene, the mountain and the spring sacred to the Muses (*TL* 349, Frame 257).

What is perhaps even more striking, though, is the use of the term "prosopopée," which should not be understood in the modern sense of a rhetorical figure whereby one speaks through someone or something else, but simply as a costume, a theatrical role, or indeed a persona. To wit, the "Briefve declaration," the glossary for the *Quart Livre*, defines "Prosopopée" as "Desguisement ou Fiction de persone" (*QL* 703) [disguise, impersonation (Frame 593)].[34] In the context of the *Tiers Livre*'s prologue, "prosopopée" denotes in part the "vaillans, disers, et chevalereux personnaiges" [valiant, eloquent, and knightly personages] who act out the "Tragicque comedie" of war, but also Rabelais's own "fiction de persone," the authorial persona (*TL* 349, Frame 256). This persona constantly advertises its own benevolence and good intentions toward the reader, but readers who "consent to the prosopopoeia" only reveal their own ignorance. Just as the ass wiggles its ears in time with music, the gullible reader accepts Rabelais's *insinuatio* without noticing its rhetorical blandishments or realizing that François Rabelais, medical doctor is not so different from Alcofrybas Nasier, after all.

Even so, to inform readers of how they risk being duped by *captatio* is to put them on guard against it and its prevalence in Renaissance paratexts; the prologue of the *Tiers Livre* is every bit as preventive as those of *Pantagruel* and *Gargantua*. It is through the narratee's transformation into an ass that the reader may realize that professions of goodwill, humility, and generosity can serve the same ends of manipulation and domination as the insults and threats of sodomy that Alcofrybas spews in the prologue of *Pantagruel*. Put another way, if "M. François Rabelais docteur en Medicine" uses *insinuatio* to make an ass of the narratee, then François Rabelais, in his capacity as an actual practitioner of medicine through writing, uses his prologues to inoculate readers against letting advertising make asses of them. The medical dimension becomes even more prevalent and central in the last two installments of the *Geste Pantagruéline*, but instead of adopting the persona of a *thériacleur*, Rabelais adopts the persona of an iatrosophist, a quack doctor who uses rhetoric to sell his art the same way the sophists of Ancient Greece sold their knowledge.[35] His persona is still that of a physician, but one who uses his knowledge for ill by imputing sickness to the reader/patient so that he may provide a cure.

The Triumph of Medicine?
Iatrosophism in the *Quart Livre* and *Cinquiesme Livre*

The paratexts of the 1548 and 1552 *Quart Livre* (*NRB* 41, 45) both use medicine as a way of justifying Rabelais in the face of detractors on both sides of the confessional divide, whether they were defenders of Catholic orthodoxy or Jean Calvin, who accused Rabelais and other writers of his ilk, such as Bonaventure des Périers, of irreligion in the 1550 treatise *De scandalis*. As in the prologue of the *Tiers Livre*, Rabelais opts for *insinuatio* and discusses his and his adversaries' character rather than the book itself. He first compares his detractors to devils, playing on the etymological connection between *diábolos* and calumny, then to gluttons who spit in other people's food in order to claim it for themselves, and finally to the "medecin d'eau doulce" [freshwater doctor] who only prescribes water and allows his patients to eat nothing but chicken necks "à fin que les malades n'en mangeassent, tout fust reservé pour sa bouche" (*QL* 718) [so that patients should not have any and the whole thing be preserved for his mouth (Frame 418)]. Those who hinder the dissemination of Rabelais's books pose an obstacle not only to the reader's pleasure, but also to the reader's healing through the act of reading: "Ilz les ont tolluz es malades, es goutteux, es infortunez, pour lesquelz en leur mal esjouyr, les avois faictz et composez. Si je prenois en cure tous ceux qui tomboient en meshaing et maladie, jà besoing ne seroit mettre telz livres en impression" (*QL* 719) [They have taken them away from the sick, the gouties, the unfortunate, for whom I had written them to cheer them up in their trouble. If I took on as patients all those who fell into disability or illness, there would be no longer any need to bring such books into light and print (Frame 419)]. Rabelais's only concern is for the health of his patients, and since he is unable to care for them all in person, he sends the *Quart Livre* in his stead. The book is thus less a form of medication than it is a replacement for the practitioner himself, combining treatment with a salutary bedside manner.

This is why Rabelais justifies the comical appearance of the *Quart Livre* with a reference to Hippocrates, who "commande rien n'estre au medecin (voyre jusques à particulariser les ongles) qui puisse offenser le patient: tout ce qu'est au medecin, gestes, visaige, vestemens, parolles, regardz, touchement, complaire et delecter le malade" (*QL* 719) [commands that nothing about the doctor—indeed, even to the fingernails—must offend the patient, and that rather, everything about the doctor (the gestures, the face, the clothes, the words, the looks, the touch) must please and delight the patient (Frame 419)]. In this way, the authorial persona resembles the medical persona insofar as both are intended to reassure the reader/patient of the author/doctor's good intentions and character: Rabelais and Hippocrates both strive after *captatio benevolentiae*.

In the 1552 edition, Rabelais relocates the medical metaphor from the prologue to the dedicatory epistle to Odet de Châtillon, his protector after the Du Bellay brothers, where he once again stresses his good intentions by insisting that he does not write his romances for glory or praise, but because he "seulement avois esguard et intention par escript donner ce peu de soulaigement que povois es affligez et malades absens, lequel voluntiers, quand besoing est, je fais es presens qui soy aident de mon art et service" (*QL* 517) [had intended and had regard only to give in writing what little relief I could to the absent sufferers and sick, which gladly, when there is need, I give to those who take help from my craft and service (Frame 421)]. The book still replaces the distant practitioner whose only intention is to heal the reader, a notion that Rabelais reinforces with a citation of Johannes Alexandrinus's commentary on Hippocrates's *Epidemics*: "Ainsi me suis je acoustré, non pour me guorgiaser et pomper: mais pour le gré du malade, lequel je visite: auquel seul je veulx entierement complaire: en rien ne l'offenser ne fascher" (*QL* 518) [Thus have I clad myself, not to show off and strut, but for the taste of the patient I am visiting, whom alone I want to please entirely, not offend or vex him in any way (Frame 422)].

Readers cannot heal unless they are delighted and reassured by the doctor's appearance, so this is exactly the appearance Rabelais adopts, comparing his effort to how Augustus's daughter Julia dresses provocatively for her husband and modestly for her father in Macrobius's anecdote.[36]

Rabelais's medical persona is not a one-way street, though. It obligates the reader to be as cooperative (i.e., *pantagruéliste*) as those who "take help from" his care; patients must allow themselves to be healed and adopt a persona to match the doctor's, as suggested by the comparison, dubiously attributed to Hippocrates, of medicine to a "farce jouée à trois personnages: le malade, le medecin, la maladie" (*QL* 518) [farce played by three personae: the patient, the doctor, and the illness (Frame 421)]. Rabelais assumes the reader's cooperation from the beginning of the new prologue, which is no longer addressed to the customary "Beuveurs tresillustres, et vous goutteurs tres precieux" [Most illustrious drinkers, and you, most precious poxies], but to "lecteurs benevoles" [readers of good will] and "Gens de bien" [good people] (*QL* 715, 523, Frame 415, 425).[37] The reader's benevolence is now a necessary condition for reading, and when he addresses the reader/patient once again at the conclusion of the prologue, Rabelais further restricts the latter's expectations: "C'est, Goutteux, sus quoy je fonde mon esperance, et croy fermement, que (s'il plaist au bon Dieu) vous obtiendrez santé: veu que rien plus que santé pour le present ne demandez" (*QL* 535) [That, gouties, is what I base my hope on, and I firmly believe that, if the good God please you, you will obtain health, seeing as you demand nothing more than health for now (Frame 435)]. Physical and spiritual health is all the book has to offer, but all that readers should expect from it, contenting themselves with mediocrity (in the sense of the golden mean, or *aurea mediocritas*) in the same way that Couillatris turns down the axes of gold and silver that Mercury offers him in favor of his own (*QL*, 531–32). To read, then, is to recognize one's own sickness and submit to the healing offered by the author.

In the context of the *Quart Livre*, though, to play patient to the author's "Docteur en medicine" is to "consent to the prosopopoeia"; Rabelais even calls attention to the theatricality of the medical persona by calling it a "prosopopée" (*QL* 518) [costume (Frame 422)]. Additionally, medicine is not compared to just any genre of play, but to a farce, which calls to mind the medical charlatans of plays like *Le pardonneur, le triacleur, et la tavernière*. The context of farce should make the reader wonder as to Rabelais's motivations in presenting himself as a doctor, and even more so as to why he seems to perform a medical examination at the conclusion of the prologue: "Or en bonne santé toussez un bon coup, beuvez en trois, secouez dehait vos aureilles, et vous oyrez dire merveilles du noble et bon Pantagruel" (*QL* 535) [Now, in good health cough one good cough, drink three drinks, give your ears a cheery shake, and you shall hear wonders about the good and noble Pantagruel (Frame 435)]. If Rabelais acknowledges his readers' "good health" at the opening of the prologue, why does he ask them to cough as he would a sick patient? Is he diagnosing an existing condition or inventing one in order to heal it with the ensuing romance? Here, as in the prologue of the *Tiers Livre*, Rabelais makes an ass of the reader by requesting that he twitch his ears like the ignorant donkey of Erasmus's adage.

Rabelais adopts an equally ambiguous persona in the *Cinquiesme Livre*, whose prologue is so similar to those of the two preceding books that it is most likely a draft of them.[38] Unlike those two prologues, though, this one focuses on the book rather than the author, on the medication rather than the doctor. Based on the proverbial expression "le monde n'est plus fat," [the world's not so fatuous anymore], Rabelais expresses his confidence that there will be no fear of "la fleur des febves en la prime vere, c'est-à-dire, comme pouvez le voirre au poing, et les larmes à l'œil pitoiablement croire, en caresme" (CL 725) [the flower of beans in the springtime; that is to say (as you may pitiably believe, glass in hand and tears in your eyes), in Lent (Frame 610)]. The bean, a vegetable foodstuff typical of the Lenten diet, becomes a metaphor for the book's curative laughter and for allegorical reading whose contrast between interior germ and exterior shell recalls the *sileni* of the prologue of *Gargantua*. As with the discussion of that prologue in the previous chapter, my interest here is less in the legitimacy of the interpretative controversy than in the fact that the incitation to allegorical reading is presented to the reader as an opportunity for self-fashioning.

Rabelais compares "febves en gousse" [beans in the pod] to the "joyeux et fructueux livres de pantagruelisme, lesquels sont pour ce jourd'huy en bruit de bonne vente, attendant le periode du Jubilé subsequent, à l'estude desquels tout le monde s'est adonné, aussi est-il sage nommé. Voilà vostre problesme solu et resolu, faictes vous gens de bien là-dessus" (CL 725) [joyous fruitful books of Pantagruelism, which for this present day are in renown for their good sale, awaiting the next Jubilee, to the study of which everyone has devoted himself: and so they are called wise. There is your problem solved and resolved: make yourselves good people on the strength of it (Frame 611)]. The prologue of *Gargantua* offers readers "l'espoir certain d'estre faictz escors et preux à ladicte lecture" [the certain hope of being made more astute and brave by the said reading] (G 7, Frame 4), and in turn, the prologue of the *Cinquiesme Livre* guarantees them the possibility to "make [them]selves good people on the strength of it." To offer readers the "bonne et belle pannerée" [nice handsome basketful] of beans that is the *Cinquiesme Livre* is not so much a sign of generosity as an attempt to reduce the readers to nothing so as to force them to fashion themselves through reading. In other words, readers are indeterminate beings who must fashion themselves through reading, just as the prologue of the *Quart Livre* addresses readers as patients who need to be healed through reading. Rabelais's munificence in the *Cinquiesme Livre* is the munificence of an iatrosophist.[39]

The prologue's iatrosophism is confirmed by the episode of the Fredon friar in Chapters 26–28. The friar, who answers Panurge's questions exclusively in monosyllables, nevertheless manages to paint far too detailed a picture of his amorous pursuits. We learn that he is at his randiest in March, that is, during Lent, a period ostensibly meant to inspire remorse and penitence. This seeming paradox does not surprise Pantagruel and Epistemon, who explain that although Lent is supposed to help mortify sensual pleasures, it occurs in the springtime, a season in which heat circulates more freely throughout the body and stimulates libidinal tendencies. Lent only exacerbates the symptoms of these natural tendencies by imposing a diet that consists mainly of aphrodisiacs (*CL* 28.797, Frame 676).[40] Lent, which was upheld by the Council of Trent in 1547, fails because it does not account for human nature, much like other orthodox Catholic traditions such as celibacy to which evangelicals were largely, though not categorically, opposed.

According to Epistemon, though, the real problem with Lent is medical rather than theological in nature, and physicians should oppose it on the grounds that it contributes to infirmity, but they do not. On the contrary, they approve of it: "Car sans le quaresme seroit leur art en mespris, rien ne gaigneroient, personne ne seroit malade" (*CL* 28.798) [For without Lent their craft would be held in disdain, and they wouldn't earn anything, and no one would be sick (Frame 677)]. An oath to do no harm is ultimately less important to medical practitioners than a steady source of income is; no more Lent means no more sickness and no more need for cures. Doctors are therefore quite happy to perpetuate a misguided practice that makes it possible for them to sell their services, and it is no surprise that in the *Quart Livre*, Rabelais calls the monstrous Quaresmeprenant [Fastilent] the "pere et nourrisson des medecins" (*QL* 29.606) [father and nursling of the physicians (Frame 499)].

Seen in this light, Rabelais's medical persona in the prologue of the *Cinquiesme Livre* is not so different from the unscrupulous doctors discussed by Epistemon, who goes on to list the foods responsible for Lenten lubricity. The first four are "febves, poix, phaseols, chiches" [beans, peas, kidney beans, chickpeas] (*CL* 28.797, Frame 676), yet another reminiscence of Quaresmeprenant, himself a "grand avalleur de poys gris" [great swallower of gray peas] (29.606, Frame 499). The prologue instructs readers to make themselves into good people by peeling and eating the basketful of "beans in the pod" that is the *Cinquiesme Livre*, but as Epistemon explains, beans engender sickness and the need for cures. He echoes Panurge's complaint in the *Tiers Livre* when

Pantagruel suggests that he consult with a theologian, a physician, and a jurist that most theologians are heretics, lawyers never bring suits against one another, and doctors abhor medicines and never take them (*TL* 29.444). Perhaps, then, readers are "infatigables" in the sense of being "insatiable" rather than in the sense of being "invulnerable to dupery": like sick believers trapped in the vicious cycle of Lent, they keep coming back to books whose authorial personae continually try to convince them that they are sick and need the book the author so generously offers them.

Rabelais's iatrosophism could be compared to how Lemaire uses masculinity and ideal readership in the *Illustrations*, as Lemaire threatens the reader's masculinity to convince him that he needs to fashion himself into a man by reading the *Illustrations* allegorically, as if they were "beans in the pod" to be shelled and eaten. Of course, as with Rabelais's medical persona, one might wonder whether Lemaire is simply creating a problem in order to advertise a solution for it. Yet, Rabelais tips his hand much more so than does Lemaire, so much so that we should consider the possibility that Rabelais's use of the interpretative controversy is a parody of the *Illustrations*, or at the very least of works like the *Illustrations*. Peter Gilman and Abraham Keller have devoted a series of three articles to the hypothesis that *Pantagruel*'s prologue and opening chapters are parodies of Lemaire, and while the connections they draw are rather tenuous, the question deserves further attention.[41] After all, Rabelais was well aware of Lemaire and his reputation, and the *Rhétoriqueur* finds his way into the *Geste* on more than one occasion. In the same descent into Hell where he sees Xerxes hawking mustard, Epistemon also sees "maistre Jean le maire qui contrefaisoit du pape, et à tous ces pauvres roys et papes de ce monde faisoit baiser ses piedz, et en faisant du grobis leur donnoit sa benediction, disant 'Gaignez les pardons coquins, guaignez, ilz sont à bon marché. Je vous absoulz de pain et de souppe, et vous dispense de ne valoir jamais rien'" (*P* 30.236) [Master Jean Lemaire impersonating the pope, and he had all those poor kings and popes of this world kiss his feet; and putting on the dog, he gave them this blessing, saying: "Get your pardons, scoundrels, get them, they're cheap. I absolve you of bread and dips, and dispense you from ever being good for anything" (Frame 235)]. Rabelais clearly saw Lemaire as a predecessor of the evangelical movement on account of his endorsement of ecumenical councils and criticism of Julius II and ecclesiastical corruption, but this does not preclude the possibility that he also saw Lemaire with a more critical eye. The fact that Lemaire "fai[t] du grobis" [puffs himself up] in front of the humbled kings and popes makes him a likely candidate for the inspiration behind the poet Raminagrobis in the *Tiers Livre*, who hails from near Villaumere (*TL* 21.416).[42]

If Rabelais does indeed poke fun at Lemaire in his prologues, then his target is less Lemaire's mythology than it is his advertising through ideal readership. Lemaire advertises in earnest, whereas Rabelais advertises ironically, and this difference may be attributed to the respective situations with which each author was faced. Lemaire, as we have seen, had compelling reasons to use masculinity to advertise for the *Illustrations*: he felt that he had an essential role to play as a historiographer in the political landscape of the Italian Wars and wanted his patrons and reading public to realize that, and he rightly feared competition from Italian histories and poetry. To put it another way, Lemaire knew that Louis XII's foreign policy, as well as his own political loyalties and work as a *Rhétoriqueur*, was a morally gray area, and he advertised his authorial persona and masculine self-fashioning to make things seem more appealingly black and white. Rabelais, on the other hand, found himself in a period when politics and especially religion were moving more and more toward black and white, and his Erasmian non-schismatic evangelism and pacifism motivated him, like Marot, to cultivate gray areas in the form of interpretative complexity and perplexity.

Renner has shown how Rabelais increasingly cultivates Menippean paradox, which presents multiple possibilities or solutions to a problem without giving preference to any after the example of Lucian's *Icaromenippus*, across the *Geste* and especially in the *Tiers Livre*. The fact that Panurge is never given the straight answer he so desperately desires to his question of whether he should marry drives home the point that interpretation is necessarily subjective, and that readers must take responsibility for, and question, their own interpretations.[43] As Stéphan Geonget puts it in his account of the legal and theological background of perplexity, this is the way in which Rabelais sets the *Geste* apart from medieval and Renaissance didactic dialogues in which a master expounds upon the subject at hand so as to clear up his student's perplexity. Pantagruel has no clear answers to give Panurge and, in truth, the fact that he doesn't claim to give him any is the surest sign of his honesty and his love for Panurge.[44] This is also the way in which Rabelais distances himself from the advertising strategies he parodies. He adopts the persona of a *thériacleur* hawking a miracle drug or of a kindly physician offering his care to a sick patient, and in so doing, he encourages the reader to be docile and to search for hidden meaning in the text. However, he makes it clear at the same time that his promises of self-fashioning through reading might be empty.

His readers must take responsibility for their own interpretive tendencies and acknowledge their own susceptibility to advertising that holds up a book or a specific mode of reading as a clear-cut answer, a product that will make them "more than human" or simply "good people."

Afterword
The Triumph of Advertising

WHEN I BEGAN working on the dissertation that eventually led to this book, I was haunted by the fear that my approach was fundamentally anachronistic. As I continued to work on it, I came to realize that the problem was not the inapplicability of advertising to earlier periods, but the narrow definition of advertising as a phenomenon unique to the Industrial Revolution and the age of consumerism. When we see advertising as a set of persuasive techniques that fashion the selves of the producer and the consumer to promote a product, a service, or an image, it becomes clear that advertising can be and has been widely used in many different domains, especially literature. Literary self-promotion and self-fashioning were extremely prominent in the Renaissance, but they are far from unique to the period, and French literary history from the Middle Ages to the present is strewn with examples of both. The present study is, of course, not a history of advertising the self from the early modern period to the present, but it makes the case that such a history would certainly be a worthy project, as would projects smaller in scope that examine the implications of the malleable self for rhetoric and reception. By way of conclusion, I would like to offer a single, brief example from the twentieth century, one with implications beyond the literary realm.

Jules Romains's comedy *Knock, ou le triomphe de la médecine* was first performed on December 14, 1923 at the Comédie des Champs-Élysées in a masterful staging by Louis Jouvet, who also played the title character. Knock is a physician who arrives in the small provincial canton of Saint-Maurice to take over the business of the lackadaisical Docteur Parpalaid, who hesitates to provide any treatment beyond prescribing chamomile tea and reassuring his patients that they will be back on their feet in no time. Knock, on the other hand, adopts as his motto, "Les gens bien portant sont des malades qui s'ignorent" [Healthy people are sick; they just don't know it yet]; in this respect, he bears a strong resemblance to the iatrosophist of Rabelais's prologues.[1] Knock makes a point of advertising his services and insisting on his own generosity and concern as a medical practitioner. Immediately after replacing Parpalaid, he hires the town's drummer to spread the word about his free consultations:

> Le docteur Knock, successeur du docteur Parpalaid, présente ses compliments à la population de la ville et du canton de Saint-Maurice, et a l'honneur de lui faire connaître que, dans un esprit philanthropique, et pour enrayer le progrès inquiétant des maladies de toutes sortes qui envahissent depuis quelques années nos régions si salubres autrefois... il donnera tous les lundis matin, de neuf heures trente à onze heures trente, une consultation entièrement gratuite, réservée aux habitants du canton. Pour les personnes étrangères au canton, la consultation restera au prix ordinaire de huit francs. (2.1.64)

> [Doctor Knock, Doctor Parpalaid's successor, sends his compliments to the people of the town and canton of Saint-Maurice, and is honored to let them know that in the spirit of philanthropy, and in order to halt the disturbing progress of all sorts of illnesses that for several years now have been invading our regions, which used to be so healthy... on Monday mornings from 9:30 to 11:30, he will give consultations *gratis*, but only to residents of the canton. For persons from outside the canton, the consultation will remain at the usual price of eight francs.]

Knock's announcement is prestige advertising at its finest. He claims to be concerned with nothing but the well-being of the canton's inhabitants, as he is motivated by "the spirit of philanthropy." He also draws a distinction between the canton and everything outside of it, both the diseases that invade their formerly healthy lands and the outsiders who aren't entitled to Knock's free consultations. In so doing, he makes his free consultations seem like a privilege and a distinction for the canton's residents, but at the same time, he calls their health into question and creates a need for his services. One wonders whether these "foreign diseases" are quite the problem that Knock makes them out to be, as in the previous act, Parpalaid mentions that given the region's harsh climate, inhabitants who survive past infancy are "des gaillards durs à cuire" (1.1.41) [tough cookies].

Sure enough, throughout the course of the play, Knock uses his free consultations to convince everyone that they are gravely ill and in need of treatment, starting with the drummer himself and ending with Parpalaid at the play's conclusion, by which point Knock has succeeded in hospitalizing nearly the entire canton. In the process, he comes to see himself as a sort of god who confers existence upon people by diagnosing them with some condition or another: "Vous me donnez un canton peuplé de quelques milliers d'individus neutres, indéterminés. Mon rôle, c'est de les déterminer, de les amener à l'existence médicale. Je les mets au lit, et je regarde ce qui va pouvoir en sortir : un tuberculeux, un névropathe, un artérioscléreux, ce qu'on voudra, mais quelqu'un, bon Dieu! quelqu'un" (3.6.114) [You gave me a canton populated by several thousand neutral, indeterminate individuals. My role is to determine them, to bring them into medical existence. I prescribe them bed rest, and I see what can make of them: a tuberculitic, a neuropath, an arteriosclericic, whatever you like, but someone, good God! Someone]. As Knock sees it, people don't exist until he defines them, or rather fashions them, with his diagnoses. He assumes a "neutral, indeterminate" self that must be shaped by diagnosis and treatment—regardless, of course, of whether the patient is actually ill—in the same way that advertising posits an indeterminate self that must be defined by the products the consumer chooses to purchase.

Knock is not just a vehicle for Romains's unanimism, but also a thought experiment that applies the intensive advertising campaigns of the early twentieth century to the domain of medicine, a fact that has not been lost on the play's critics. For example, Gérard Gatinot, in an article on a 1960 revival of the comedy, states that "ce 'triomphe de la médecine' semble plutôt être celui de la publicité" [this "triumph of medicine" seems, rather, to be the triumph of advertising].[2] Its satirical take on modern iatrosophism and medical advertising is one of the things that guarantees its legacy and continued relevance, especially given that excessive or unnecessary treatment is still very much an issue in contemporary society.[3] However, *Knock* is also a play of its time that anticipates the rise of fascism in Europe. In his military takeover of the canton, which culminates in him pointing to the remaining pockets of healthy people on a map the way a general would draw up battle lines, Knock uses advertising to make the residents complicit in his rise to power. By frightening them with threats of foreign invaders in their midst and convincing them that they have no real existence without the medical care he offers, he effectively fashions them into the perfect subjects for his new health regimen, or rather regime. Needless to say, this kind of political rhetoric certainly did not disappear from the West after World War II, and will be instantly recognizable to anyone familiar with the rise of right-wing nationalism in Europe and America.

Knock thus serves as an example of how understanding advertising in the context of rhetoric and self-fashioning can provide what Kenneth Burke calls "equipment for living," the capability of literature to evaluate social situations and suggest strategies for dealing with them.[4] Renaissance texts are especially well suited to this purpose, as their authors were intensely aware of the dangers of rhetoric and self-fashioning both in general and in their own enterprises, so much so that they exhibit what François Rigolot calls a "sentiment de culpabilité" [sense of guilt] characteristic of sixteenth-century French writers.[5] Marot and Rabelais exhibit this guilt in the attention they call to the manipulation and manipulativeness of their authorial personae, and in the perplexity they inspire in readers through the ambiguous self-fashioning they offer them. Even Lemaire knows and acknowledges that his enterprise could be used for ill, though he is convinced that he himself is using it for good. In short, there are many good reasons why Lemaire, Marot, and Rabelais are still worth reading today, but not least among them is the fact that they can put us on guard against advertising in whatever form it takes.

Appendix
Marot Editions and Their Contents

This appendix lists the contents of Marot editions examined up to 1538 to catalogue how they differ from the authorized 1532 *Adolescence clementine* (Mayer 9) and 1533–34 *Suite* (Mayer 15). Numbers are those found in C. A. Mayer, *Bibliographie des éditions de Clément Marot publiées au XVIe siècle* (Paris: Nizet, 1975). The Rutgers editions, not listed in Mayer, are designated R1 and R2. For ambiguous cases, I provide references to Guillaume Berthon, *L'Intention du poète: Clément Marot "autheur"* (Paris: Garnier, 2014).

6. *Les Opuscules et petits Traictez*. Lyon: Olivier Arnoullet, n.d. (1530–31). BNF Rés. p Ye 736.
a1v–a2v: Chant Royal de Marot (*OC* 1:213–14; *OPC* 1:357–58).
a2v–a3v: Champ [sic] royal faict par Clement Marot sur le refrain donné par le Roy sur Desbender l'arc ne guarist point la playe (*OC* 1:214–16; *OPC* 1:359–60).
a3v–a5r: Epistre de Marot envoyee au Roy (*OC* 1:222–24; *OPC* 1:316–17).
a5r–a6r: A monsieur le Cardinal de Sens Chancelier de France Clement Marot donne treshumble salut (*OC* 1:220–21; *OPC* 1:313–15).
a6r: [Audict Seigneur pour se plaindre de Monsieur le Tresorier Preudhomme, faisant difficulté d'obeir à l'Acquit despesché] (*OC* 1:222; *OPC* 1:315).
a6r–a6v: Au conte d'Estampes (*OC* 1:118–19; *OPC* 1:114–15).
a6v–a7r: Balade sur la venue des enfans de France (Apocryphal; see Berthon, *Intention du poète*, 282).
a7r–a8r: Balade à la louenge de ma dame Alienor Royne de France (Guillaume Bochetel? See Berthon, *Intention du poète*, 282).
a8r–b1v: A monsieur le cardinal de Lorraine (*OC* 1:224–26; *OPC* 1:318–20).
b1v–c5r: Le temple de Cupido, faict et composé par maistre Clement Marot, facteur de la Royne de France (*OC* 1:44–57; *OPC* 1:27–42).
c5v–d8r: Deploration sur le trespas de feu messire Florimond Robertet seigneur d'Alluye, jadis chevalier, Conseiller du Roy, Tresorier de France, Secretaire des finances (*OC* 1:188–203; *OPC* 1:207–23).
d8r–e2v: Epistre du Coq à l'Asne faicte par Clement Marot (*OC* 1:216–19; *OPC* 1:310–13).

e2v–e3v: Chant Royal sur le grant decret que le pape ordonna (Jean Fillastre; see Berthon, *Intention du poète*, 282–83).

e3v–e8v: Epistre de Maguelonne à son amy Pierre de Provence elle estant à l'hospital (*OC* 1:78–85; *OPC* 1:65–71).

9. *Ladolescence clementine*. Paris: Geoffroy Tory for Pierre Roffet, Aug. 12, 1532. BNF Rés. Ye 1532.

11. *Ladolescence clementine*. Paris: Geoffroy Tory for Pierre Roffet, Nov. 13, 1532. BNF Rés. Ye 1533.

1r–115v: Content identical to Mayer 9.

116r–116v: Aultres Oeuvres faictes en sadicte maladie: "Au Lieutenant de Bourges Gontier qui luy escrivit en Ryme" (1:407–8; *OPC* 1:325–26), "A Vignals Thoulousan Escholier à Bourges, qui luy escrivit en prose avec ung Rondeau" (*OC* 1:408; *OPC* 1:326–27).

116v–118r: Ce qu'il escrivit a ses Medecins en sadicte Maladie: "Huictain à Monsieur Braillon" (*OC* 1:438; *OPC* 2:220), "Mart. Acakiae ad Clementem Maronem Tetrastichon" (*OPC* 2:1009–10n1), "Huictain responsive aux vers precedens" (*OC* 1:438–39; *OPC* 2:221), "Sizain à Monsieur le Coq qui par une lettre responsive promectoit guerison audict Marot" (*OC* 1:439; *OPC* 2:221), "Autre sizain audict Coq" (*OC* 1:439; *OPC* 2:222), "Huictain à Monsieur L'Amy aussi Medecin, nouvellement sorty de maladie" (*OC* 1:4339; *OPC* 2:222), "Marot malade à mon Seigneur de Guise passant par Paris" (*OC* 1:409; *OPC* 2:327), "Dizain à Pierre Vuyard secretaire dudict Seigneur" (*OC* 1:440; *OPC* 2:222–23).

12. *Ladolescence clementine*. Paris: Geoffroy Tory for Pierre Roffet, Feb. 12, 1533. BNF Rés Ye 1535. Content identical to Mayer 11.

13. *Ladolescence clementine*. Lyon: François Juste, Feb. 23, 1533. BNF Rothschild 59 (IV.5.41).

1r–114r: Content identical to Mayer 9.

114v–117r: Le Pater noster, et le Credo en françoys (*OC* 1:433–34; *OPC* 1:390–91), Chant Royal de la fortune et biens mondains, composé par ung des amys de C. Marot (*OPC* 2:757–59), Epitaphe de Marie fille aisnee de monsieur d'Estissac, compose par le susdict (*OPC* 2:759–60).

14. *Ladolescence clementine*. Paris: Geoffroy Tory for Pierre Roffet, June 7 1533. [BNF Rés. Ye 1537]. Content identical to Mayer 11, 12.

14bis. *Ladolescence clementine*. Lyon: François Juste, Jul. 12, 1533. Munich, Bayerische Staatsbibliothek Rar. 1780.

1r–113v: Content identical to Mayer 9.

113v–116r: Aultres Oeuvres faictes en sadicte maladie (cf. Mayer 11).

116r–117v: Epitaphe du Conte de Salles (apocryphal), Complaincte de Dame Bazoche sur le trespas dudict Conte (apocryphal).

117v–118v: Rondeaux: "Au cueur ne peult ung chascun commander" (*OC* 1:253; *OPC* 2:760–61), "Juges, prevostz, bourgeoys, marchans, commun" (*OC* 1:254; *OPC* 2:761), "Nostre maistre Geoffroy Brulart" (*OC* 2:464; *OPC* 2:290).

118v–119r: Remede contre la Peste, faict par Clement Marot (*OC* 2:463; *OPC* 2:289–90).

119r–119v: Rondeau ("Qui ses besoignes veult bien faire") (*OC* 1:254; *OPC* 2:761), Advice of "Raison" "Conseil" and "Vertu" (apocryphal).

119v: De la statue de Venus endormie sur le portal d'ung logis (*OC* 1:371; *OPC* 2:219).

119v–120r: Ung dizain du trop saoul, et de l'affamé (apocryphal).

120r: Sur Juppiter ex alto (*OC* 2:466; *OPC* 2:293).

120r–121r: La foy d'ung chrestien: Pater noster (*OC* 1:433; *OPC* 1:390), Credo in deum/ Credo in spiritum (*OC* 1:434; *OPC* 1:391), Benediction devant manger (apocryphal; *OC* 1:609n126; *OPC* 1:812).

121r: Rondeau ("O quel erreur, par finiz esperitz") (*OC* 1:255; *OPC* 2:762).

121r–121v: Rondeau ("O Bon Jesus de Dieu eternel filz") (*OC* 1:255–56; *OPC* 2:762).

121v: Les a Dieu nouveaulx (*OC* 1:372–73).

121v–126v: Clement Marot, aux gentilz veaulx / Qui ont faict les adieu nouveaulx (*OC* 1:306–7; *OPC* 1:282–84), Epistre de Clement Marot à troys sortes de Dames parisiennes (*OC* 1:308–14; *OPC* 1:284–90).

127r–127v: Ce que aulcuns Theologiens plaquerent à Paris, quand Beda fut forbanny, voulans esmouvoir le peuple à sedition contre le Roy (*OC* 2:464–65; *OPC* 2:291), Responce de Clement marot à l'escripteau cy dessus (*OC* 2:465; *OPC* 2:292), Dizain à ce propos (*OC* 2:466–66; *OPC* 2:292–93).

128r: Huictain sus la contenance du Lieutenent Criminel de Paris, quant il menoyt pendre Samblançay (*OC* 1:440–41; *OPC* 2:223–24).

128r–128v: Les deux placetz qu'il fist au Roy: "Plaise au Roy, ne reffuser point" (*OC* 1:440; *OPC* 2:223), "Plaise au Roy, nostre sire" (*OC* 1:365–66; *OPC* 2:212–13).

128v–129r: Rondeau de l'honneur des dames (*OC* 1:256; *OPC* 2:763).

129r: Epitaphe de feu maistre Alexandre president de Barroys (*OC* 1:352; *OPC* 1:375–76).

129r–129v: Rondeau sus les couleurs de ma dame duchesse de Lorraine, violet, et blanc, significans amour et foy (*OC* 1:365; *OPC* 1:173).

129v–130r: Quadrins respondans à ce que monsieur de sainct Ambroys le reprint sus le mot de viser, disant que regarder estoit plus propre (*OC* 1:326; *OPC* 2:224–25).

130v–132r: Chant Royal de la fortune et biens mondains (*OPC* 2:757–59), Epitaphe de Marie (*OPC* 2:759–60).

15. *La Suite de l'adolescence Clementine*. Paris: (Louis Cyaneus for) the widow of Pierre Roffet, n.d. (late 1533—early 1534). BNF Rés. Ye 1534; BNF Rés. Ye 1536.

16. *L'Adolescence clementine*. Paris: Louis Cyaneus for the widow of Pierre Roffet, Mar. 7, 1534. BNF Arsénal Rés. 8° BL 8712; BNF Rothschild 601 (II.5.37).

1–245: Content identical to Mayer 9.

245–50: Aultres Oeuvres faictes en sadicte maladie (cf. Mayer 11); Marot envoye le livre de son Adolescence à une Dame, et luy mande (*OC* 1:386; *OPC* 1:13).

251–54: Chant Royal de la fortune et biens mondains (*OPC* 2:757–59), Epitaphe de Marie (*OPC* 2:759–60).

254–61: Epitaphe du Conte de Salles through Advice of "Raison" "Conseil" and "Vertu" (cf. Mayer 14bis, 116r–119v).

261–62: Ung dizain du trop saoul, et de l'affamé (apocryphal), Sur Juppiter ex alto (*OC* 2:466; *OPC* 2:293).

17. *La Suite de l'Adolescence Clementine.* Paris: Louis Cyaneus for the widow of Pierre Roffet, n.d. (1534). BNF Rothschild 601 (II.5.37).
1–6: L'Instruction et Foy d'ung Chrestien: Pater noster (*OC* 1:433; *OPC* 1:390), Ave Maria (*OC* 1:434; *OPC* 1:390–91), Credo in deum/Credo in spiritum (*OC* 1:434; *OPC* 1:391), Benediction devant manger (apocryphal; *OC* 1:609n126; *OPC* 1:812), Graces pour ung enfant (*OC* 1:434–35; *OPC* 1:392), Le VI. Pseaulme de David, translaté en Françoys selon l'Hebrieu, par Clement Marot, Valet de chambre du Roy (*OC* 1:435–36; *OPC* 1:392–94).
7–146: Content identical to Mayer 15.
19. *L'Adolescence clementine.* Paris: Louis Cyaneus for the widow of Pierre Roffet, Aug. 19, 1534. BNF Rés. Ye 1561.
1–262: Content identical to Mayer 16.
262: Rondeau ("O Bon Jesus de Dieu eternel filz") (*OC* 1:255–56; *OPC* 2:762).
263: Placet au Roy pour Marot ("Plaise au Roy, ne reffuser point"; *OC* 1:440; *OPC* 2:223).
263–68: L'epistre de l'Asne au Coq, responsive à celle du Coq en l'Asne (*OC* 1:249–53; *OPC* 2:744–47).
268–69: Rondeau à nostre Dame (*OC* 1:256; *OPC* 2:763–64).
269: Epitaphe de Martin (apocryphal).
269: Rondeau du Guay (*OC* 1:257; *OPC* 2:764).
269–70: Dizain de l'Ymage de Venus armee R.F. (*OC* 2:471; *OPC* 2:760).
270–71: Le different de beaulté, force, et amour (apocryphal).
271–73: L'alphabet du temps present (apocryphal).
20. *La Suite de l'Adolescence Clementine.* Paris: (Louis Cyaneus for) the widow of Pierre Roffet, 1534. BNF Rés. Ye 1562.
1–144: Content identical to Mayer 17.
145: Dixain adjousté, extraict de l'Unziesme livre de la Priapeie (*OC* 2:27; *OPC* 2:220).
145–52: Accession d'une Epistre de complaincte à une qu'a laissé son amy (Jacques Colin? See Berthon, *Intention du poète,* 352).
R1. *Ladolescence Clementine.* N.p. (Lyon: Denis de Harsy), 1534. Rutgers University Library SPCOL X PQ1635.A6 1534.
4r–158v: Content identical to Mayer 11.
158v–159r: Epitaphe du Conte de Salles.
159v–160r: Rondeaux: "Au cueur ne peult ung chascun commander" (*OC* 1:253; *OPC* 2:760–61), "Juges, prevostz, bourgeoys, marchans, commun" (*OC* 1:254; *OPC* 2:761), "Nostre maistre Geoffroy Brulart" (*OC* 2:464; *OPC* 2:290).
160v–161r: Remede contre la Peste (*OC* 2:463; *OPC* 2:289–90).
161r–162r: Rondeau: "Qui ses besoignes veult bien faire" (*OC* 1:254; *OPC* 2:761), Debate between "Raison" and "Conseil" (apocryphal).
162r–162v: Ung dizain du trop saoul, et de l'affamé (apocryphal), Sur Juppiter ex alto (*OC* 2:466; *OPC* 2:293).
162v–163v: La foy d'ung Chrestien: Pater noster (*OC* 1:433; *OPC* 1:390), Credo in deum/Credo in spiritum (*OC* 1:434; *OPC* 1:391), Benediction devant manger (apocryphal; *OC* 1:609n126; *OPC* 1:812).

APPENDIX 193

163v–164v: Rondeaux: "O quel erreur, par finiz esperitz" (*OC* 1:255; *OPC* 2:762), "O Bon Jesus de Dieu eternel filz" (*OC* 1:255–56; *OPC* 2:762).

165r–166r: Ce que aulcuns Theologiens plaquerent à Paris (*OC* 2:464–65; *OPC* 2:291), Responce de Clement marot à l'escripteau cy dessus (*OC* 2:465; *OPC* 2:292), Dizain à ce propos (*OC* 2:466–66; *OPC* 2:292–93).

166v: Placet au Roy pour Marot ("Plaise au Roy, ne reffuser point") (*OC* 1:440; *OPC* 2:223).

167r–168v: Chant Royal de la fortune et biens mondains (*OPC* 2:757–59), Epitaphe de Marie (*OPC* 1:759–60).

169r–175r: L'epistre de l'Asne au Coq through L'alphabet du temps present (cf. Mayer 19, 263–73).

24. *Ladolescence clementine*. Lyon: François Juste, Dec. 12, 1534. BNF Rothschild 600 (II.7.28). Content identical to Mayer 14bis.

25. *La suyte de ladolescence Clementine*. Lyon: François Juste, 1534. BNF Rothschild 600 (II.7.28).

2r–61r: Content identical to Mayer 15, minus Clement Marot, aux gentilz veaulx / Qui ont faict les adieu nouveaulx (*OC* 1:306–7; *OPC* 1:282–84) and Epistre de Clement Marot à troys sortes de Dames parisiennes (*OC* 1:308–14; *OPC* 1:284–90), plus Epistre de complaincte à une qu'a laissé son amy (Jacques Colin? See Berthon, *Intention du poète*, 352) and Macrin and Bourbon epigraphs and translations.

61v: Dizain sus le propoz d'une nouvellement mariee (*OC* 1:441, *OPC* 2:224).

62r: Huitain: "Le Roy, aymant la decoration" (*OC* 2:472; *OPC* 2:289), Dizain sus le dict d'un Theologien (*OC* 2:471; *OPC* 2:288).

31. *Ladolescence clementine*. Lyon: François Juste, Feb. 6, 1535. BNF Rothschild 602 (II.7.27). Content identical to Mayer 14bis/24.

32. *L'Adolescence clementine*. Paris: The widow of Pierre Roffet, Jun. 20, 1535. BNF Arsénal Rés. 8° BL 8713. Content identical to Mayer 19.

33. *La Suite de l'Adolescence Clementine*. Paris: The widow of Pierre Roffet, 1535. BNF Arsénal Rés. 8° BL 8713. Content identical to Mayer 20.

34. *La suyte de ladolescence Clementine*. Lyon: François Juste, 1535. BNF Rothschild 602 (II.7.27).

1r–62r: Content identical to Mayer 25.

62r–62v: Epitaphe d'Alys, fille de joye (*OC* 1:432–33, *OPC* 1:388–89).

R1. *La suyte de ladolescence Clementine*. N.p. (Lyon: Denis de Harsy), 1535. Rutgers University Library SPCOL X PQ1635.A6 1534.

a2r–k8v: Content identical to Mayer 20, except for the omission of the "Second Chant d'Amour fugitif" (*OC* 1:336–38; *OPC* 1:344–46).

R2. *Ladolescence Clementine*. N.p. (Lyon: Denis de Harsy), 1535. Rutgers University Library SPCOL X PQ1637.M3A6 1535. Content identical to R1.

R2. *La Suyte de Ladolescence Clementine*. N.p. (Lyon: Denis de Harsy), 1535. Rutgers University Library SPCOL X PQ1637.M3A6 1535.

A2r–L3r: Content identical to Mayer 15.

L3r: Dixain adjousté, extraict de l'Unziesme livre de la Priapeie (*OC* 2:27; *OPC* 2:220).

L3v: Dixain sur le propos d'une nouvellement mariee (*OC* 1:441, *OPC* 2:224).

L4r–L4v: French translations of Latin epigraphs.

L5r–M1v: Certaines oeuvres, que Marot fei en la prison, lesquelles n'avoient encores estees mise en lumiere jusques à present: Le rondeau qui fut cause de sa prinse (*OC* 1:395; *OPC* 1:176–77), La Ballade qu'il feit en prison (*OC* 1:392; *OPC* 1:126), Epistre qu'il envoya à Bouchard, docteur en Theologie (*OC* 1:388–89; *OPC* 1:91–92), Rondeau parfaict composé apres sa delivrance et envoyé à ses amis (*OC* 1:395; *OPC* 1:177–78), Epistre à son amy Lion (*OC* 1:389–91; *OPC* 1:92–94), Dixain à ses amys, quant en laissant la Royne de Navarre fut receu en la maison et estat de ma dame Renee, Duchesse de Ferrare (*OC* 2:213–14; *OPC* 2:297), Dixain au Duc de Ferrare par Clement Marot à son arrivee Mil. CCCCCXXXV. (*OC* 2:322; *OPC* 2:296), Huictain faict à Ferrare (*OC* 2:214; *OPC* 2:251).

36. *Ladolescence clementine*. Paris: The widow of Pierre Roffet, 1536. BNF Rés. p Ye 664.

1r–124v: Content identical to Mayer 19.

125r–127r: S'ensuivent les regrectz et complainctes de la ville de [Venise] quant le Roy la conquesta (apocryphal).

36. *La Suite de ladolescence Clementine*. Paris: The widow of Pierre Roffet, 1536. BNF Rés. p Ye 664. Content identical to Mayer 20.

38. *Ladolescence clementine*. Paris: Antoine Bonnemère, 1536. BNF Rés. Ye 1539. Content identical to Mayer 19.

39. *La suite de ladolescence clementine*. Paris: Antoine Bonnemère, 1536. BNF Rés. Ye 1540. Content identical to Mayer 20.

55. *Ladolescence Clementine*. N.p. (Paris: Denis Janot), 1537. BNF Rés. Ye 1542.

4r–143v: Content identical to Mayer 11.

143v–144r: Epitaphe du Conte de Salles.

144r–145r: Rondeaux: "Au cueur ne peult ung chascun commander" (*OC* 1:253; *OPC* 2:760 61), "Juges, prevostz, bourgeoys, marchans, commun" (*OC* 1:254; *OPC* 2:761), "Nostre maistre Geoffroy Brulart" (*OC* 2:464; *OPC* 2:290).

145r–145v: Remede contre la Peste (*OC* 2:463; *OPC* 2:289–90).

145v: Sur Juppiter ex alto (*OC* 2:466; *OPC* 2:293).

146r: Les a Dieu nouveaulx (*OC* 1:372–73).

146v: Placet au Roy pour Marot ("Plaise au Roy, ne reffuser point") (*OC* 1:440; *OPC* 2:223).

147r–148v: La foy d'ung Chrestien: Pater noster (*OC* 1:433; *OPC* 1:390), Ave Maria (*OC* 1:434; *OPC* 1:390–91), Credo in deum/Credo in spiritum (*OC* 1:434; *OPC* 1:391), Benediction devant manger (apocryphal); *OC* 1:609n126; *OPC* 1:812), Graces pour ung enfant (*OC* 1:434–35; *OPC* 1:392).

148v: Rondeau: "O Bon Jesus de Dieu eternel filz" (*OC* 1:255–56; *OPC* 2:762).

149r–149v: Rondeau à nostre Dame (*OC* 1:256; *OPC* 2:763–64).

149v–150v: Epistre de Clement Marot à tresillustre Princesse ma Dame la Duchesse de Ferrare (*OC* 2:313; *OPC* 2:77–78).

151r–151v: Apocryphal dizains: "Vous vous plaignez de mon audace," "Du baiser qu'avez soubdain prins," "De ce que ne chet soubz ung pris."

15v: Dizain de l'Abbé et du varlet (*OC* 1:441, *OPC* 2:225).
56. *La suyte de Ladolescence Clementine*. N.p. (Paris: Denis Janot), 1537. BNF Rés. Ye 1543.
A2r–K2r: Content identical to Mayer 15.
K2r–K2v: Dixain adjousté, extraict de l'Unziesme livre de la Priapeie (*OC* 2:27; *OPC* 2:220).
K2v: Dixain sur le propos d'une nouvellement mariee (*OC* 1:441, *OPC* 2:224).
K3r–K3v: French translations of Latin epigraphs.
K3v–M1v: Certaines oeuvres, que Marot feit en la prison, lesquelles n'avoient encores estees mise en lumiere jusques à present: Le rondeau qui fut cause de sa prinse (*OC* 1:395; *OPC* 1:176–77), La Ballade qu'il feit en prison (*OC* 1:392; *OPC* 1:126), Epistre qu'il envoya à Bouchard, docteur en Theologie (*OC* 1:388–89; *OPC* 1:91–92), Rondeau parfaict composé apres sa delivrance et envoyé à ses amis (*OC* 1:395; *OPC* 1:177–78), Epistre à son amy Lion (*OC* 1:389–91; *OPC* 1:92–94), Dizain faict a monsieur le Daulphin avant son partement de France (*OC* 1:457–58; *OPC* 2:247), Dixain à ses amys, quant en laissant la Royne de Navarre fut receu en la maison et estat de ma dame Renee, Duchesse de Ferrare (*OC* 2:213–14; *OPC* 2:297), Dixain au Duc de Ferrare par Clement Marot à son arrivee Mil. CCCCCXXXV. (*OC* 2:322; *OPC* 2:296), Huictain faict à Ferrare (*OC* 2:214; *OPC* 2:251).
63. *Ladolescence Clementine*. Paris: Denis Janot, 1538. BNF Rés. Ye 1551. Content identical to Mayer 55.
64. *La suyte de l'adolescence Clementine*. Paris: Denis Janot, 1538. BNF Rés. Ye 1552.
a1v–l3r: Content identical to Mayer 56.
l3v–l4r: Le Dieu gard de Marot à la court (*OC* 2:238–40; *OPC* 2:133–35).
66. *Ladolescence clementine*. Paris: Antoine Bonnemère, 1538. BNF Rothschild 604 (II.5.44). Content identical to Mayer 19.
67. *La suite de ladolescence clementine*. Paris: Pierre Sergent, 1538. BNF Rothschild 604 (II.5.44). Content identical to Mayer 20.

Notes

Introduction

1. For more on Rabelais as the "French Lucian," see Lucien Febvre, *Le problème de l'incroyance au XVIe siècle: La religion de Rabelais* (Paris: Albin Michel, 1968), 64–78.

2. Lucian, "To One Who Said, 'You're a Prometheus in Words,'" in *Lucian, Vol. 6*, trans. K. Kilburn (London: William Heinemann, 1959), 423. Accustomed as they were to the one-humped dromedary, Ptolemy's Egyptian subjects were likely shocked not only at the Bactrian camel's unusual color, but also at its dual humps.

3. François Rabelais, *Œuvres complètes*, ed. Mireille Huchon (Paris: Gallimard, 1994), *TL*, 351; François Rabelais, *The Complete Works of François Rabelais*, trans. Donald M. Frame (Berkeley: University of California Press, 1991), 258.

4. Carlo Vecce, "La 'mort de l'auteur' à la Renaissance," in *L'Auteur à la Renaissance: L'altro que è in noi*, eds. Rosanna Gorris Camos and Alexandre Vanautgaerden (Turnhout, Belgium: Brepols, 2009), 87.

5. Desiderius Erasmus, *Adages Ii1 to Iv100*, ed. R. A. B. Mynors, trans. Margaret Mann Phillips, vol. 31 of *Collected Works of Erasmus* (Toronto: University of Toronto Press, 1982), chap. 1, cent. 9, adage 30.

6. Richard Copley Christie, Dolet's biographer and apologist, suggests that Dolet might have authored the letter rather than Juste. See Richard Copley Christie, *Étienne Dolet: The Martyr of the Renaissance* (London: MacMillan, 1880), 282.

7. Baldassare Castiglione, *Le Courtisan de messire Baltazar de Castillon nouvellement reveu et corrigé*, trans. Jacques Colin, ed. Étienne Dolet (Lyon: François Juste, 1538), P6v.

8. *Le Courtisan, nouvellement traduict de langue ytalicque en françoys* (Paris: Jean Longis, 1537), and *Les quatre livres du courtisan du conte Baltazar de Castillon, reduyct de langue ytalicque en françoys* (Lyon: Denis de Harsy, 1537).

9. Castiglione, *Le Courtisan*, P7r.

10. Malcolm Walsby, "La voix de l'auteur? Autorité et identité dans les imprimés français au XVIe siècle," in *L'Auteur à la Renaissance*, 73–76, 81.

11. Rudolf Hirsch, *Printing, Selling and Reading, 1450–1550* (Wiesbaden, Germany: Harrassowitz, 1967), 36.

12. Natalie Zemon Davis, *Society and Culture in Early Modern France* (Stanford, CA: Stanford University Press, 1975), 211–12.

13. Elizabeth Armstrong, *Before Copyright: The French Book-Privilege System, 1498–1526* (Cambridge: Cambridge University Press, 1980), 182.

14. The element of risk inherent to printing any work is apparent in what we know of print runs at the time. Runs of a given edition tended to be rather small, even for smashing successes; only 1,800 copies of a 1515 Froben edition of Erasmus's *Praise of Folly* were printed, and the initial printing of Luther's Bible was only four thousand copies. Consequently, the only reliable gauges of a work's success and diffusion are the number of different editions of it and the geographical and chronological distribution of these editions. See Lucien Febvre and Henri-Jean Martin, *L'apparition du livre* (Paris: Albin Michel, 1971), 310.

15. Roger Chartier, *L'ordre des livres: Lecteurs, auteurs, bibliothèques en Europe entre XIVe et XVIIIe siècle* (Aix-en-Provence: Alinéa, 1992), 8. See also Michel Jeanneret, "La Lecture en question: Sur quelques prologues comiques du seizième siècle," *French Forum* 14, no. 3 (Sept. 1989): 281.

16. For example, see: Jennifer Wicke, *Advertising Fictions: Literature, Advertisement, and Social Reading* (New York: Columbia University Press, 1988); Sara Thornton, *Advertising, Subjectivity and the Nineteenth-Century Novel* (Basingstoke: Palgrave Macmillan, 2009); and Urs Meyer, *Poetik der Werbung* (Berlin: Erich Schmidt, 2010).

17. Andrew Cowell, "Advertising, Rhetoric, and Literature: A Medieval Response to Contemporary Theory," *Poetics Today* 22, no. 4 (Winter 2001): 795–827.

18. Elizabeth Eisenstein, *Divine Art, Infernal Machine: The Reception of Printing in the West from First Impressions to the Sense of an Ending* (Philadelphia: University of Pennsylvania Press, 2011), 10.

19. Charlton T. Lewis and Charles Short, *A Latin Dictionary Founded on Andrews' Edition of Freund's Latin Dictionary* (Oxford: Clarendon, 1975), s.v. "adverto."

20. Frank Presbrey, *The History and Development of Advertising* (New York: Doubleday, 1929), 9–18.

21. Elizabeth Eisenstein, *The Printing Press as an Agent of Change: Communications and Cultural Transformations in Early-Modern Europe* (Cambridge: Cambridge University Press, 1979), 1:59.

22. Andrew Pettegree, *The Book in the Renaissance* (New Haven, CT: Yale University Press, 2010), 75.

23. Raymond Williams, "Advertising: The Magic System," in *The Cultural Studies Reader*, ed. Simon During (New York: Routledge, 1993), 328–29; Bernard Cathélat, *Publicité et société* (Paris: Payot, 1987), 49–50.

24. Williams, "The Magic System," 329.

25. Torben Vestergaard and Kim Schrøder, *The Language of Advertising* (Oxford: Blackwell, 1985), 132–33.

26. Poggio did not rediscover Quintilian entirely, but rather a complete manuscript of the *Institutio oratoria*. For a list of Renaissance editions of Aristotle, Cicero, and Quintilian, see Lawrence D. Green and James J. Murphy, *Renaissance Rhetoric Short-Title*

Catalogue, 1460–1700 (Aldershot, UK: Ashgate, 2003). For more on the rise of Aristotle's, Cicero's, and Quintilian's rhetorical treatises in the Renaissance, see François Rigolot, "Prolégomènes à une étude du statut de l'appareil liminaire des textes littéraires," *L'Esprit Créateur* 27, no. 3 (Fall 1987): 8–9.

27. Pierre Fabri, *Le grand et vrai art de pleine rhétorique*, ed. A. Héron (Geneva: Slatkine Reprints, 1969), 55.

28. Aristotle, *Rhetoric* (*Rh.*), 1.2.1356a. In citations of Aristotle, the third numbers refer to the page and column in Immanuel Bekker's standard 1831 Greek edition.

29. *Rhetorica ad Herennium* (*Rhet. Her.*). 1.7. Cf. Cicero, *De Inventione* (*Inv. rhet.*), 1.16.23, and Quintilian, *Institutio Oratoria*, 4.1.5. The distinction between attentiveness and willingness to learn seems to be a Roman one, as Aristotle only mentions good will and attentiveness; see Aristotle, *Rh.*, 3.14.1415a.

30. *Rhet. Her.* 1.7–8, Cicero, *Inv. rhet.*, 1.16.22. Cf. Aristotle, *Rh.*, 1.6.1362a, and Fabri, *Rhétorique*, 58.

31. Cicero, *Orator*, 8.24; "Orator," in *Cicero, vol. 5*, trans. H. M. Hubbell (Cambridge, MA: Harvard University Press, 1962), 323.

32. *Rhet. Her.* 1.8; Fabri, *Rhétorique*, 59. Cf. Lewis and Short, *A Latin Dictionary*, s.v. "persona," and Edmond Huguet, *Dictionnaire de la langue française du seizième siècle* (Paris: Champion, 1925–67), s.v. "personnage."

33. Aristotle, *Rh.*, 1.9.1366a–b.

34. Deborah Losse, *Sampling the Book: Renaissance Prologues and the French Conteurs* (Lewisburg, PA: Bucknell University Press, 1994), 62.

35. Castiglione, *Le Courtisan*, P7r.

36. Leah L. Chang, *Into Print: The Production of Female Authorship in Early Modern France* (Newark: University of Delaware Press, 2009), 36; Desiderius Erasmus, *Adages IIi1 to IIvi100*, ed. R. A. B. Mynors, trans. Margaret Mann Phillips, vol. 33 of *Collected Works of Erasmus* (Toronto: University of Toronto Press, 1991), chap. 2, cent. 1, adage 1. Eisenstein notes in *Divine Art* that Erasmus's optimism in the 1508 edition of the *Adages* gives way to disillusionment in successive versions, to the point where the praise of Aldus is more or less eclipsed by complaints about how the glut of new books leads to the neglect of old authors (25).

37. Pettegree, *The Book in the Renaissance*, 53. Precedents of this dilemma may also be found in the Middle Ages. For studies of how late medieval authors deal with broadening and potentially hostile readership, see Deborah McGrady, *Controlling Readers: Guillaume de Machaut and His Late Medieval Audience* (Toronto: University of Toronto Press, 2006), and Daniel Hobbins, *Authorship and Publicity Before Print: Jean Gerson and the Transformation of Late Medieval Learning* (Philadelphia: University of Pennsylvania Press, 2009).

38. Floyd Gray, "Rabelais's First Readers," in *Rabelais's Incomparable Book*, ed. Raymond C. La Charité (Lexington, KY: French Forum, 1986), 26; Eisenstein, *Agent of Change*, 63.

39. Philippe Desan, *L'imaginaire économique de la Renaissance* (Mont-de-Marsan, France: Editions Interuniversitaires, 1993), 202. See also Jean-Max Colard, "L'apparition

du paratexte," in *L'inscription du regard: Moyen Âge, Renaissance*, eds. Michèle Gally and Michel Jourde (Fontenay-aux-Roses, France: ENS éditions, 1995), 315–36.

40. Desan, *Imaginaire économique*, 204; Eisenstein, *Agent of Change*, 59. Gérard Genette first introduces the concept of paratext in *Introduction à l'architexte* (Paris: Seuil, 1979), and takes it up again in *Palimpsestes: La littérature au second degré* (Paris: Seuil, 1982), but develops it most fully in *Seuils* (Paris: Seuil, 1987), where he defines the paratext as everything that makes a text into a book and presents it as such to its public (7–8). He also subdivides the paratext into *péritexte*, which is attached to the physical volume, and *épitexte*, which is not, and includes things like book reviews or authors' correspondences in that category. This study focuses on *péritexte*, but in keeping with common usage, I simply refer to it as paratext.

41. Rigolot, "Prolégomènes," 10. Similarly, George Hoffmann ties the redefinition of the book's audience as the generic reader to the rise of the commercial notion of a buying public, and ultimately to "the dawn of modern business practices per se" and "the moment at which commercialism became intertwined with culture"; Hoffmann, "About Being about the Renaissance: Bestsellers and Booksellers," *Journal of Medieval and Renaissance Studies* 22, no. 1 (Winter 1992): 88. See also Cynthia J. Brown, *Poets, Patrons and Printers: Crisis of Authority in Late Medieval France* (Ithaca, NY: Cornell University Press, 1995), 11.

42. *The Reader in the Text: Essays on Audience and Interpretation*, eds. Susan R. Suleiman and Inge Crosman (Princeton, NJ: Princeton University Press, 1980), 9.

43. William J. Kennedy, "Petrarchan Audiences and Print Technology," *Journal of Medieval and Renaissance Studies* 14, no. 1 (Spring 1984): 5.

44. For more on the ideal reader in Joyce, Valéry, and Hofmannstahl, see Jan Kammerbeek, Jr., "Le concept du 'lecteur idéal,'" *Neophilologus* 61, no. 1 (Jan. 1977): 2–7, and Erwin Wolff, "Der intendierte Leser," *Poetica* 4, no. 2 (1971): 141–66.

45. Wolfgang Iser, *The Act of Reading: A Theory of Aesthetic Response* (Baltimore: Johns Hopkins University Press, 1978), 38. See also Iser, *The Implied Reader: Patterns of Communication in Prose Fiction from Bunyan to Beckett* (Baltimore: Johns Hopkins University Press, 1974).

46. For a survey of theoretical accounts of reading and the reader, including Iser's "implied reader" concept and its critics, see Gerald Prince, "Reader," in *Handbook of Narratology*, 2nd ed., eds. Peter Hühn, Jan Christoph Meister, John Pier, and Wolf Schmid (Berlin: De Gruyter, 2014), 744–47.

47. Aristotle, *Rh.*, 3.14.1415b.

48. Guy Demerson, *Humanisme et facétie: Quinze études sur Rabelais* (Caen: Paradigme, 1994), 238.

49. Lowry Nelson, Jr., "The Fictive Reader and Literary Self-Reflexiveness," in *The Disciplines of Criticism: Essays in Literary Theory, Interpretation, and History*, eds. Peter Demetz, Thomas Greene, and Lowry Nelson, Jr. (New Haven, CT: Yale University Press, 1968), 175–77.

50. Wayne Booth, *The Rhetoric of Fiction*, 2nd ed. (Chicago: University of Chicago Press, 1983), 138.

51. Michel Jeanneret, *Perpetuum mobile: Métamorphoses des corps et des œuvres de Vinci à Montaigne* (Paris: Macula, 1997), 165. See also Thomas Greene, "The Flexibility of the Self in Renaissance Literature," in *The Disciplines of Criticism*, 241–64.

52. Stephen Greenblatt, *Renaissance Self-Fashioning: From More to Shakespeare*, 2nd ed. (Chicago: University of Chicago Press, 2005), 162.

53. John Berger, *Ways of Seeing* (London: BBC and Penguin, 1977), 132.

54. Vestergaard and Schrøder, *The Language of Advertising*, 29.

55. Jean Baudrillard, *Le système des objets* (Paris: Gallimard, 1968), 215.

56. Judith Williamson, *Decoding Advertisements: Ideology and Meaning in Advertising* (London: Marion Boyars, 1978), 70. Of course, Sartrean existentialism itself owes much to Renaissance humanism, or at least to the common modern conception of it, hence *L'existentialisme est un humanisme*.

57. The *Rhétoriqueurs* date from approximately 1460 to 1520, and are generally divided into twelve "Grands Rhétoriqueurs" (Georges Chastellain, Octovien de Saint-Gelais, Jean Robertet, Jean Meschinot, Jean Molinet, Jean Lemaire de Belges, André de La Vigne, Guillaume Cretin, Jean Marot, Jean d'Auton, Pierre Gringore, and Jean Bouchet) and several secondary authors. Though they have been grouped together in literary history, they differ from one another not only in that they belong to different generations, but also in their divergent political loyalties: Burgundian *Rhétoriqueurs* like Molinet were effectively the enemies of French *Rhétoriqueurs* like Cretin or Marot. Lemaire, for his part, played both sides over the span of his career. See François Rigolot, "Rhétoriqueurs," in *Dictionnaire des lettres françaises: Le XVIe siècle*, ed. Michel Simonin (Paris: LGF, 2001), 1015. Moreover, these poets never actually referred to themselves as *Rhétoriqueurs*, a term that stems from Charles d'Héricault's reading of a line from Guillaume Coquillart's *Droits nouveaux* (1481) out of context; see Pierre Jodogne, "Les 'rhétoriqueurs' et l'humanisme: problème d'histoire littéraire," in *Humanism in France at the End of the Middle Ages and in the Early Renaissance*, ed. A. H. T. Levi (Manchester: Manchester University Press, 1970), 153–54. In spite of these inconsistencies, the term has continued to stick in academic discourse.

58. Gérard Defaux, *Le Poète en son jardin: Étude sur Clément Marot et L'Adolescence clémentine* (Paris: Champion, 1996), 128.

59. Clément Marot, *Œuvres complètes*, ed. François Rigolot (Paris: Garnier, 2007–9), vol. 1, p. 7.

60. See, for example, Brown, *Poets, Patrons, and Printers*, 247–53.

61. In this sense, my approach is similar to what Adrian Armstrong, borrowing a term from Pierre Bourdieu's *Esquisse d'une théorie de la pratique*, calls a "praxeological" approach, which dictates that literature cannot adequately be studied through texts alone, as it is through books that texts are transmitted and perceived. See Adrian Armstrong, *Technique and Technology: Script, Print, and Poetics in France, 1470–1550* (Oxford: Clarendon, 2000), 21. See also Chartier, *L'ordre des livres*, 21.

62. Romain Menini, *Rabelais altérateur: "Græciser en François"* (Paris: Classiques Garnier, 2014), 76, 80. "Tantaltération" is a portmanteau of "Tantale" (Tantalus) and "altération" (thirst).

1. The Judgment of the Reader in the *Illustrations de Gaule et singularitez de Troye*

This chapter is based in part on *"Virilior Sensus*: Allegorical Reading as Masculine Reading in the *Illustrations de Gaule et singularitez de Troye*" (paper presented at the Kentucky Foreign Language Conference, Lexington, KY, April 23–25, 2015), and on "Publicité et masculinité chez Jean Lemaire de Belges" (paper presented at "Médiation, promotions, et effets publicitaires dans la littérature de la première modernité," University of Toronto, Toronto, ON, February 19, 2016).

1. Henry Guy, *Histoire de la poésie française au XVIe siècle. Tome I: L'école des Rhétoriqueurs* (Paris: Champion, 1968), 44.

2. Cynthia J. Brown, *The Shaping of History and Poetry in Late Medieval France: Propaganda and Artistic Expression in the Works of the Rhétoriqueurs* (Birmingham, AL: Summa, 1985), 150, and *Poets, Patrons, and Printers: Crisis of Authority in Late Medieval France* (Ithaca, NY: Cornell University Press, 1995), 11.

3. Michael Sherman, "Political Propaganda and Renaissance Culture: French Reactions to the League of Cambrai, 1509–10," *The Sixteenth Century Journal* 8, no. 2 (1977): 105. For more on writers' involvement in propaganda campaigns during the Italian Wars, see Sherman, "The Selling of Louis XII: Propaganda and Popular Culture in Renaissance France, 1499–1514" (PhD diss., University of Chicago, 1974).

4. Jean Lemaire de Belges, *Lettres missives et épîtres dédicatoires*, ed. Anne Schoysman (Brussels: Académie Royale de Belgique, 2012), 183. See also Adrian Armstrong and Sarah Kay, *Knowing Poetry: Verse in Medieval France from the* Rose *to the* Rhétoriqueurs (Ithaca, NY: Cornell University Press, 2011), 52.

5. Olivia Rosenthal, "L'auteur devant son œuvre: l'exemple de Jean Lemaire de Belges," *Nouvelle Revue du Seizième Siècle* 17, no. 2 (1999): 190.

6. Adrian Armstrong, *Technique and Technology: Script, Print, and Poetics in France, 1470–1550* (Oxford: Clarendon, 2000), 9, and "Paratexte et autorité(s) chez les Grands Rhétoriqueurs," in *L'Écrivain éditeur*, ed. François Bessire (Geneva: Droz, 2001), 1:82.

7. Brown, *Poets, Patrons, and Printers*, 57.

8. Richard M. Berrong, "Les *Illustrations de Gaule et singularitez de Troye*: Jean Lemaire de Belges' Ambivalent View of 'Eloquence,'" *Studi Francesi* 78 (Sept.–Dec. 1982): 400.

9. Tom Conley, "Un tombeau de mélanges: Les 'Epistres de l'amant vert' dans le livre imprimé des *Illustrations de Gaule et singularitez de Troie* (1512–1513)," in *Ouvrages miscellanées et théories de la connaissance à la Renaissance*, ed. Dominique de Courcelles (Paris: Ecole Nationale des Chartes, 2003), 82.

10. See Jacques Abélard, *Les* Illustrations de Gaule et singularitez de Troye *de Jean Lemaire de Belges: Etude des éditions—Genèse de l'œuvre* (Geneva: Droz, 1976), 15, and Jean Lemaire de Belges, *Epistre du roy à Hector et autres pièces de circonstances (1511–1513)*, eds. Adrian Armstrong and Jennifer Britnell (Paris: STFM, 2000), XLVII and 71n2.

11. Frederic J. Baumgartner, *Louis XII* (New York: St. Martin's, 1994), 227; Bernard Quilliet, *Louis XII, Père du Peuple* (Paris: Fayard, 1986), 419.

12. See Marian Rothstein, "Jean Lemaire de Belges' *Illustrations de Gaule et Singular-*

itez de Troye: Politics and Unity," *BHR* 52, no. 3 (1990): 593–609, and Jacques Abélard, "Les *Illustrations de Gaule* de Jean Lemaire de Belges: Quelle Gaule? Quelle France? Quelle nation?," *Nouvelle Revue du Seizième Siècle* 13, no. 1 (1995): 7–27.

13. Jean Lemaire de Belges, *Traicté de la différence des schismes et des conciles de l'Église*, ed. Jennifer Britnell (Geneva: Droz, 1997), 150.

14. Pierre Jodogne, *Jean Lemaire de Belges: Ecrivain franco-bourgignon* (Brussels: Académie Royale de Belgique, 1972), 419–23; Georges Doutrepont, *Jean Lemaire de Belges et la Renaissance* (Brussels: Lamertin, 1934), 287.

15. Jean Lemaire de Belges, *Œuvres*, ed. J. Stecher, 4 vols. (Geneva: Slatkine Reprints, 1969), vol. 2, bk. 2, p. 244. References to the *Illustrations*, hereafter cited in text, are to the volume of the Stecher edition, the book of the *Illustrations*, and the page number in Stecher.

16. Mireille Huchon, *Louise Labé: Une créature de papier* (Geneva: Droz, 2006), 19–21; Jean Lemaire de Belges, *La Concorde des deux langages*, ed. Jean Frappier (Geneva: Droz, 1947), p. 20, line 310.

17. François Cornilliat, *Sujet caduc, noble sujet: La poésie de la Renaissance et le choix de ses arguments* (Geneva: Droz, 2009), 191–99. See also Elise Rajchenbach-Teller, "*Mais devant tous est le Lyon marchant*": *Construction littéraire d'un milieu éditorial et livres de poésie française à Lyon (1536–1551)* (Geneva: Droz, 2016), 230–31.

18. Judy Kem, *Jean Lemaire de Belges's* Les Illustrations de Gaule et singularitez de Troye: *The Trojan Legend in the Late Middle Ages and Early Renaissance* (New York: Peter Lang, 1994), 47–66.

19. See Kathleen Wilson-Chevalier, "Feminising the Warrior at Francis I's Fontainebleau," in *Masculinities in Sixteenth-Century France: Proceedings of the Eighth Cambridge French Renaissance Colloquium, 5–7 July 2003*, eds. Philip Ford and Paul White (Cambridge: Cambridge French Colloquia, 2006), 23–59, and Todd Reeser, *Moderating Masculinity in Early Modern Culture* (Chapel Hill: North Carolina Studies in the Romance Languages and Literatures), 2006.

20. Gilbert Gadoffre, *La Révolution culturelle dans la France des humanistes: Guillaume Budé et François Ier* (Geneva: Droz, 1997), 23.

21. David P. LaGuardia, *Intertextual Masculinity in French Renaissance Literature* (Aldershot, UK: Ashgate, 2008), 4.

22. Randle Cotgrave, *A Dictionarie of the French and English Tongues* (Columbia: University of South Carolina Press, 1950), s.v. "moriginé."

23. Fulgentius, *Mythologies* 2.1.

24. Giovanni Boccaccio, *De genealogia*, 6.22; Aristotle, *Ethica Nicomachea*, 1.5.1095b.

25. Margaret J. Ehrhart, *The Judgment of the Trojan Prince Paris in Medieval Literature* (Philadelphia: University of Pennsylvania Press, 1987), 200.

26. François Cornilliat, *Or ne mens: Couleurs de l'Éloge et du Blâme chez les "Grands Rhétoriqueurs"* (Paris: Champion, 1994), 844–45. Similarly, Donald Stone interprets Minerva in the *Concorde des deux langages* as "the intelligence that allows man to respond to unforeseen events." See Stone, "Some Observations on the Text and Possible Meanings of Lemaire de Belges' *La Concorde des deux langages*," *BHR* 55, no. 1 (1993): 71.

27. Boccaccio, *De genealogia*, 12.62.

28. For more on *adiaphora* in the Reformation, see: Anne-Pascale Pouey-Mounou, *Panurge comme lard en pois: Paradoxe, scandale et propriété dans le Tiers Livre*, ER 53 (Geneva: Droz, 2013); Bernard Verkamp, *The Indifferent Mean: Adiaphorism in the English Reformation to 1554* (Athens: Ohio University Press, 1977); Gary Remer, *Humanism and the Rhetoric of Toleration* (University Park: The Pennsylvania State University Press, 1996); Ross Dealy, *The Stoic Origins of Erasmus' Philosophy of Christ* (Toronto: University of Toronto Press, 2017); and Scott Francis, "Marguerite Nicodémite? *Adiaphora* and Intention in *Heptaméron* 30, 65, and 72," *Renaissance and Reformation/Renaissance et Réforme* 39, no. 3 (Summer 2016): 5–31.

29. Cornilliat, *Or ne mens*, 827. See also Ann Moss, *Poetry and Fable: Studies in Mythological Narrative in Sixteenth-Century France* (Cambridge: Cambridge University Press, 1984), 34–36.

30. Jodogne, *Écrivain franco-bourgignon*, 420. The *putto*, the small, chubby, occasionally winged boy commonly found in the art of classical antiquity and later conflated with cherubs in the Baroque period, is commonly thought to have been reintroduced to European art in the *Quattrocento* by Donatello, hence its likely Italian resonance for Lemaire.

31. Little is known of Baland, except that he seems to have been an expert printer to whom other printer/booksellers entrusted contracts on a number of occasions. He did have a predilection for editions of and commentaries on classical authors, which might account for his interest in the *Illustrations*. See H.-L. Baudrier, *Bibliographie lyonnaise*, 12 vols. (Lyon: Librairie ancienne d'Auguste Brun, 1895–1921), 11:2.

32. "Exegi monumentum aere perennius" [I have erected a monument more everlasting than bronze]; Horace, *Carmen Saeculare* 3.30.1.

33. Deborah McGrady, "Printing the Patron's Pleasure for Profit: The Case of the *Epîtres de l'Amant Vert*," *Journal of the Early Book Society* 2 (1999): 108.

34. Jean Lemaire de Belges, *La Concorde du genre humain*, ed. Pierre Jodogne (Brussels: Académie Royale de Belgique, 1964), 80.

35. Phaedrus, *Fables*, 3.17; emphasis mine. Note that Phaedrus plays on the polysemy of "fructus," which literally means "fruit," but figuratively denotes enjoyment or profit.

36. Armstrong, *Technique and Technology*, 148.

37. Bern Bürgerbibliothek cod. 241, 1r. See Abélard, *Étude des éditions*, 110.

38. See Baumgartner, *Louis XII*, 187; Nicole Hochner, *Louis XII: Les dérèglements de l'image royale (1498–1515)* (Seyssel, France: Champ Vallon, 2006), 186–89; and Robert W. Scheller, "Gallia Cisalpina: Louis XII and Italy, 1499–1508," *Simiolus* 15, no. 1 (1985): 40.

39. Richard Cooper, *Litterae in tempore belli: études sur les relations littéraires italo-françaises pendant les guerres d'Italie* (Geneva: Droz, 1997), 276, and Jodogne, *Écrivain franco-bourgignon*, 66–67.

40. For more on gift economies in Renaissance France, see Natalie Zemon Davis, *The Gift in Sixteenth-Century France* (Madison: University of Wisconsin Press, 2000).

41. "Felix" most properly means "fruit-bearing," "fruitful" or "fertile," though it is commonly used to mean "fortunate" or "happy" as in the modern sense of "felicity"; cf.

Charlton T. Lewis and Charles Short, *A Latin Dictionary Founded on Andrews' Edition of Freund's Latin Dictionary* (Oxford: Clarendon, 1975), s.v. "felix."

42. Fulgentius, *Mythologies* 1.18; Boccaccio, *De genealogia*, 12.62.

43. Virgil, *Aeneid*, 1.565.

44. Ibid., 4.238–78.

45. 1500 was also the year in which Archduke Charles was born, and the reference to the year may be less an accurate account of when Lemaire began to write the *Illustrations* than an homage to Charles and his aunt, Margaret of Austria; see Rothstein, "Politics and Unity," 600.

46. Lucretius, 3.11–12; *On the Nature of Things*, trans. W. H. D. Rouse, rev. Martin F. Smith (Cambridge, MA: Harvard University Press, 1992).

47. Lemaire, *Lettres missives et épîtres dédicatoires*, 103, 133.

48. Lemaire, *Concorde du genre humain*, 49.

49. Lemaire, *Lettres missives et épîtres dédicatoires*, 220.

50. Jennifer Britnell looks to Lemaire's publication history for insight into the uncertain circumstances surrounding his death, reasoning that he must have died around 1517 due to the sharp decline in the quality of his editions beginning in this year. See Britnell, "La mort de Jean Lemaire de Belges, l'édition de 1514 du *Traité des schismes et des conciles*, et les impertinences d'un éditeur," *BHR* 56, no. 1 (1994): 127–33. Evidence has surfaced, however, placing Lemaire's death closer to 1524; see Pascale Chiron and Grantley McDonald, "The Testament of Jean Lemaire, 1524," *BHR* 71, no. 3 (2009): 527–33.

51. Jean Lemaire de Belges, *Les troys Livres des Illustrations de Gaule et singularitez de Troye* (Paris: Pierre Vidoue for Galliot du Pré, 1531), a2r.

52. Ibid., b7v.

53. Philipp August Becker, *Jean Lemaire: Der erste humanistische Dichter Frankreichs* (Strasbourg: Karl J. Trübner, 1893), 382.

54. *Les Illustrations de Gaule et Singularitez de Troye* (Paris: Jean Réal for Jean Bonfons [Shared edition], 1548), ddd8r. Cf. Lemaire, *Œuvres*, 4:437.

55. Ibid., ggg5v–ggg6r. Cf. ibid., 4:438.

56. *Le Triumphe de l'Amant vert, comprins en deux épistres fort joyeuses, envoyées à Mme Marguerite Auguste, composées par Jehan Le Maire de Belges* (Paris: Denis Janot, 1535); *Les Illustrations de Gaule et Singularitez de Troye, par maistre Jean le Maire de Belges. Avec la Couronne Margaritique, et plusieurs autres oeuvres de luy, non jamais encore imprimees* (Lyon: Jean de Tournes, 1549). See Rajchenbach-Teller, "*Lyon marchant*," 228–49.

57. Mary B. McKinley, "Parrots and Poets: Writing Alterities in Scève and Lemaire de Belges," in *Self and Other in Sixteenth-Century France: Proceedings of the Seventh Cambridge French Renaissance Colloquium, 7–9 July 2001*, eds. Kathryn Banks and Philip Ford (Cambridge: Cambridge French Colloquia, 2004), 7.

58. See François Rigolot, *Poésie et Renaissance* (Paris: Seuil, 2002), 89–91.

59. Jean Lemaire de Belges, *Les Épîtres de l'Amant Vert*, ed. Jean Frappier (Geneva: Droz, 1948), 3–4. References to the *Épîtres de l'Amant Vert*, hereafter cited in text, are to

the page and line numbers of Frappier's edition. For more on Lemaire's relationship with Perréal, see Jodogne, *Écrivain franco-bourguignon*, 123–25.

60. McGrady, "Printing the Patron's Pleasure," 108.

61. François Rigolot, *Le Texte de la Renaissance: Des Rhétoriqueurs à Montaigne* (Geneva: Droz, 1982), 82. See also Lawrence Kritzman, "The Rhetoric of Dissimulation in *La première epistre de l'Amant Vert*," *Journal of Medieval and Renaissance Studies* 10, no. 1 (Spring 1980): 39.

62. Pliny, *Historia Naturalis*, 3.10.60.121–23.

63. This same quatrain appears in a 1509 letter from Lemaire to Margaret; Lemaire, *Lettres missives et épîtres dédicatoires*, 67.

64. Lemaire, *Œuvres*, 3:16n3.

65. Yvonne LeBlanc, "Death and Remembrance: The Immortality of the Word and the *Epîtres de l'Amant Vert*," *Medieval Perspectives* 8 (1993): 117.

66. Statius, *Silvae*, trans. D. R. Shackleton Bailey (Cambridge, MA: Harvard University Press, 2003), 101.

67. Adrian Armstrong, "Is This an Ex-Parrot? The Printed Afterlife of Jean Lemaire de Belges' *Epîtres de l'Amant Vert*," *Journal de la Renaissance* 5 (2007): 326–27.

68. Lemaire, *Œuvres*, 3:16n3; Statius, *Silvae*, 2.4.1–3, 25, 29–30; trans. Bailey, 143–45.

69. Hesiod, *Opera et Dies*, 286–92.

70. Homer, *Odyssey*, 19.560–70; Virgil, *Aeneid*, 6.893–96.

2. Lemaire's Genius in the *Concorde des deux langages*

This chapter is based in part on "'Ung petit tableau de mon industrie': *La Concorde des deux langages* and Gratitude for Historiography" (paper given at the Fifty-Eighth Annual Meeting of the Renaissance Society of America, Washington, D.C., March 22–24, 2012).

1. Lemaire procured a new privilege in May 1512, which he transferred from Étienne Baland to Marnef prior to the publication of Book Two of the *Illustrations* in August 1512. Marnef, like his brothers Enguilbert I and Jean I, was a *libraire-juré* of the University of Paris, and seems to have shown an interest in *Rhétoriqueur* works prior to Lemaire, such as his 1506 edition of Pierre Gringore's *Folles entreprises*; see Brigitte Moreau, *Inventaire chronologique des éditions parisiennes du XVIe siècle, d'après les manuscrits de Philippe Renouard*, 5 vols. to date (Paris: Imprimerie municipale, Service des travaux historiques de la ville de Paris, 1972–), 1:194, no. 72, and Philippe Renouard, *Répertoire des imprimeurs parisiens, libraires, fondeurs de caractères et correcteurs d'imprimerie depuis l'introduction de l'Imprimerie à Paris (1470) jusqu'à la fin du seizième siècle* (Paris: Minard, 1965), 296–97.

2. Cynthia J. Brown, *The Shaping of History and Poetry in Late Medieval France: Propaganda and Artistic Expression in the Works of the Rhétoriqueurs* (Birmingham, AL: Summa, 1985), 105–6.

3. Jean Lemaire de Belges, *Epistre du roy à Hector et autres pièces de circonstances (1511–1513)*, eds. Adrian Armstrong and Jennifer Britnell (Paris: STFM, 2000), 71. All

references to the recueil-*Epistre*, with the exception of the *Concorde des deux langages* and Cretin's "Plaincte sur le trespas de messire Guillaume de Byssipat," are to page numbers and, where relevant, to line numbers in Armstrong and Britnell's edition, hereafter cited in text.

4. Adrian Armstrong, *Technique and Technology: Script, Print, and Poetics in France, 1470–1550* (Oxford: Clarendon, 2000), 147.

5. D'Auton's epistle is reproduced in Armstrong and Britnell's edition (77–103). Yvonne LeBlanc groups D'Auton's and Lemaire's epistles within a category she calls "dead hero letters," in which a mythical hero or deceased prince writes to a living successor or his former subjects with advice. See Yvonne LeBlanc, *"Va Lettre Va": The French Verse Epistle (1400–1550)* (Birmingham, AL: Summa, 1995), 113. See also Jennifer J. Beard, "Letters from the Elysian Fields: A Group of Poems for Louis XII," *BHR* 31 (1969): 27–38.

6. Brown, *The Shaping of History and Poetry*, 103, 106.

7. The accusation of ingratitude also figures in D'Auton's epistle (96.499–501).

8. Jean Lemaire de Belges, *Œuvres*, ed. J. Stecher, 4 vols. (Geneva: Slatkine Reprints, 1969), vol. 2, bk. 3, lines 308–9, 317–22. References to the *Illustrations*, hereafter cited in text, are to the volume of the Stecher edition, the book of the *Illustrations*, and the page number in Stecher.

9. For the connection between epideictic rhetoric, glory, and exemplarity, see O. B. Hardison, *The Enduring Monument: A Study of the Idea of Praise in Renaissance Literary Theory and Practice* (Chapel Hill: University of North Carolina Press, 1962), 27.

10. BNF ms. fr. 25295, designated "Pa" by Armstrong and Britnell in *Epistre du Roy*.

11. Lemaire, *Epistre du Roy*, 64n5.

12. Ibid., XXXI.

13. Jean Lemaire de Belges, *La Concorde des deux langages*, ed. Jean Frappier (Geneva: Droz, 1947), 43. References to the *Concorde*, hereafter cited in text, are to the page numbers and, where relevant, to line numbers from Frappier's edition.

14. Nicole Hochner, "Un héros liminaire: Gaston de Foix," in *Voir Gaston de Foix (1512–2012): Métamorphoses européennes d'un héros paradoxal*, eds. Joana Barreto, Gabriele Quaranta and Colette Nativel (Paris: Publications de la Sorbonne, 2015), 68.

15. Rosenbach Museum and Library, ms. 232/II.

16. Ibid., [7r]. Alexander's reign was actually much closer to thirteen years (336–323 BCE).

17. Similarly, the prologue of the *Concorde* in the *princeps* edition indicates that Cretin is the prince of French poets, a phrase that does not figure in the Carpentras manuscript (4).

18. Guillaume Cretin, *Œuvres poétiques*, ed. Kathleen Chesney (Paris: Firmin-Didot et Cie, 1932), p. 74, line 28. References to the "Plaincte," hereafter cited in text, are to the page and line numbers from Chesney's edition.

19. Cynthia J. Brown, "Jean Lemaire's *La concorde des deux langages*: The Merging of Politics, Language and Poetry," *Fifteenth Century Studies* 3 (1980): 35.

20. François Cornilliat, *Or ne mens: Couleurs de l'Éloge et du Blâme chez les "Grands Rhétoriqueurs"* (Paris: Champion, 1994), 742. For other examples of moralizing readings,

see: Ann Moss, "Fabulous Narrations in the *Concorde des deux langages* of Jean Lemaire de Belges," in *Philosophical Fictions and the French Renaissance*, ed. Neil Kenny (London: The Warburg Institute, 1991), 17–28; Donald Stone, "Some Observations on the Text and Possible Meanings of Lemaire de Belges' *La Concorde des deux langages*," *BHR* 55, no. 1 (1993): 65–76; Michael Randall, "The Flamboyant Design of Jean Lemaire de Belges' *La Concorde des deux langages*," *L'Esprit Créateur* 28, no. 2 (Summer 1988): 13–24; and Cynthia Skenazi, *Le poète architecte en France: Constructions d'un imaginaire monarchique* (Paris: Champion, 2003). For an example of a synthetic reading, see Robert Griffin, "*La concorde des deux languages*: Discordia concors," in *Literature and the Arts in the Reign of Francis I: Essays Presented to C. A. Mayer*, eds. Pauline M. Smith and I. D. McFarlane (Lexington, KY: French Forum, 1985), 54–81. For an example of an estheticizing reading, see Floyd Gray, *La Renaissance des mots* (Paris: Champion, 2008), pt. 5, chap. 1.

21. Paul Imbs, "Jean Lemaire de Belges: *La Concorde des deux langages*," *Bulletin de la Faculté des Lettres de l'Université de Strasbourg* 26, no. 6 (Apr. 1948): 183–85. Frappier and Robert Griffin also cast aspersions on autobiographical readings; see Lemaire, *Concorde*, 2, and Griffin, "Cosmic Metaphor in *La concorde des deux langages*," in *Pre-Pléïade Poetry*, ed. Jerry C. Nash (Lexington, KY: French Forum, 1985), 20.

22. Moss, "Fabulous Narrations," 27. See also David Cowling, *Building the Text: Architecture as Metaphor in Late Medieval and Early Modern France* (Oxford: Clarendon, 1998), 201, and Adrian Armstrong, "Songe, vision, savoir: l'onirique et l'épistémique chez Molinet et Lemaire de Belges," *Zeitschrift für romanische Philologie* 123, no. 1 (2007): 64.

23. Brown, "Politics, Language and Poetry," 30.

24. Randle Cotgrave, *A Dictionarie of the French and English Tongues* (Columbia: University of South Carolina Press, 1950), s.v. "laschété." Similarly, Robert Estienne gives "Effœminate" [effeminately] for "laschement"; Estienne, *Dictionnaire françois-latin* (Paris: R. Estienne, 1549), s.v. "laschement."

25. "Fourvière" actually derives from *Forum vetus* [old forum].

26. For more on this conception of Genius, see: Ulrike Bergweiler, *Die Allegorie im Werk von Jean Lemaire de Belges* (Geneva: Droz, 1976), 96; Robert D. Cottrell, "Allegories of Desire in Lemaire's *Concorde des deux langages*," *French Forum* 23, no. 3 (Sept. 1998): 295; and Jean Lecointe, *L'Idéal et la différence: La perception de la personnalité littéraire à la Renaissance* (Geneva: Droz, 1993), 714. For more on the differences between Jean de Meun's and Lemaire's respective Geniuses, see Guy Raynaud de Lage, "Natura et Genius, chez Jean de Meung et chez Jean Lemaire de Belges," *Le Moyen Âge* 58 (1952): 125–43.

27. Boccaccio, *De genealogia*, 12.65. Cf. Lemaire, *Œuvres*, 1:1.211.

28. In "Discordia concors," Griffin connects Genius with the sale of indulgences, and even suggests that the character anticipates the infamous couplet "Wenn die Münze im Kästlein klingt, / die Seele in den Himmel springt" [When the coin in the coffer rings, / the soul from purgatory springs] dubiously attributed to the German commissioner of indulgences, Johann Tetzel (63).

29. François Cornilliat, "'Comme ung aultre Ilïon': Échec poétique et Renaissance ly-

onnaise dans *La concorde des deux langages*," in *Lyon et l'illustration de la langue française à la Renaissance*, ed. Gérard Defaux (Lyon: ENS Éditions, 2003), 384, and Cornilliat, *Sujet caduc, noble sujet: La poésie de la Renaissance et le choix de ses arguments* (Geneva: Droz, 2009), 242. See also Skenazi, *Le poète architecte*, 61, and Hervé Campangne, *Mythologie et rhétorique aux XVe et XVIe siècles en France* (Paris: Champion, 1996), 109.

30. Henry Guy, *Histoire de la poésie française au XVIe siècle. Tome I: L'école des Rhétoriqueurs* (Paris: Champion, 1968), 62.

31. Cf. Lemaire, *Œuvres*, 1:1.16.

32. Cf. ibid.: "Francus luy fut donné pour la franchise, noblesse et ferocité de son courage" (2:3.276) [He was named Francus after the frankness, nobility, and ferocity of his heart]. Cf. also Lemaire, *Epistre du Roy*, 47.477–80.

33. Reinier Leushuis, "Fertilizing the French Vernacular: Procreation, Warfare and Authorship in Jean de Meun, Jean Lemaire de Belges, and Rabelais," in *Sexuality in the Middle Ages and Early Modern Times*, ed. Albrecht Classen (Berlin: Walter de Gruyter, 2008), 799. See also Moss, "Fabulous Narrations," 25, and Cornilliat, *Sujet caduc*, 372.

34. Judy Kem, *Jean Lemaire de Belges's Les Illustrations de Gaule et singularitez de Troye: The Trojan Legend in the Late Middle Ages and Early Renaissance* (New York: Peter Lang, 1994), 76–82. For more on Lemaire's Platonism, see Lemaire, *Concorde*, XLVII, and François Rigolot, "Jean Lemaire de Belges: Concorde ou discorde des deux langages?," *Journal of Medieval and Renaissance Studies* 3 (1973): 169.

35. Cornilliat, *Sujet caduc*, 229; Skenazi, *Le poète architecte*, 58.

36. Jean Lemaire de Belges, *Traicté de la différence des schismes et des conciles de l'Église*, ed. Jennifer Britnell (Geneva: Droz, 1997), 84.

37. Jean Lemaire de Belges, *Lepistre du Roy a Hector de Troye. Et aucunes aultres oeuvres Assez dignes de veoir* (Paris: For Geoffroy de Marnef, Aug. 1513), Folger Shakespeare Library, Washington, DC, 234–555q, B6r, C1r, D1v, D2v, D4r.

38. BNF Vélins 1175; the copy contains the entirety of Book Three and the recueil-*Epistre* up through Gaston's epitaph. The copy has ruling in red ink and rubrication in gold paint, making it look even more like a manuscript, though it is difficult to determine whether these effects were added shortly after printing or by a later collector, as the copy's pages were also cut and dyed gold in the nineteenth century.

39. Ovid, *Amores*, 1.1–4.

40. Doranne Fenoaltea connects this wandering with the historical Lemaire leaving Margaret's service for Anne's. See Fenoaltea, "Doing It with Mirrors: Architecture and Textual Construction in Jean Lemaire's *La concorde des deux langages*," in *Lapidary Inscriptions: Renaissance Essays for Donald A. Stone*, eds. Barbara C. Bowen and Jerry C. Nash (Lexington, KY: French Forum, 1991), 29.

41. Fulgentius, *Mythologies*, 1.15; Boccaccio, *De genealogia*, 11.2.

42. Jean Lemaire de Belges, *Les Épîtres de l'Amant Vert*, ed. Jean Frappier (Geneva: Droz, 1948), 3.

43. "Ensuis" is erroneously rendered as "enfuis" by Stecher; it is "enſuis" in both the *princeps* edition and in the 1549 Antoine Du Moulin edition that serves as Stecher's base.

44. Campangne, *Mythologie et rhétorique*, 106; Daniel Ménager, "La *Concorde des deux langages*: Vers et prose chez Jean Lemaire de Belges," in *Prose et prosateurs de la Renaissance: Mélanges offerts à M. le Professeur Robert Aulotte* (Paris: SEDES, 1988), 22.

45. Adrian Armstrong, "Yearning and Learning: Spaces of Desire in Jean Lemaire de Belges' *Concorde des deux langages* (1511)," in *The Erotics of Consolation: Desire and Distance in the Late Middle Ages*, eds. Catherine E. Léglu and Stephen J. Milner (New York: Palgrave, 2008), 91–92.

46. François Rigolot, *Le Texte de la Renaissance: Des Rhétoriqueurs à Montaigne* (Geneva: Droz, 1982), 25. In "Flamboyant Design," Randall suggests that the pronoun "dont" can refer either to Repos and Guerdon or to the two languages (22). While this is grammatically admissible, I find that the context of the phrase makes it clear that Labeur Historien is showing the *acteur* images of the Repos and Guerdon he will eventually receive.

47. Jean Lemaire de Belges, *Lettres missives et épîtres dédicatoires*, ed. Anne Schoysman (Brussels: Académie Royale de Belgique, 2012), 62–63.

3. "Quel bien par rime on a"

1. Jean Lemaire de Belges, *Œuvres,* ed. J. Stecher, 4 vols. (Geneva: Slatkine Reprints, 1969), vol. 2, bk. 3, p. 257.

2. Gérard Defaux, "Trois cas d'écrivains éditeurs dans la première moitié du XVIe siècle: Marot, Rabelais, Dolet," in *L'Écrivain éditeur,* ed. François Bessire (Geneva: Droz, 2001), 1:96.

3. Gérard Defaux, *Le Poète en son jardin: Étude sur Clément Marot et L'Adolescence clémentine* (Paris: Champion, 1996), 163. In the same study, however, Defaux points to certain changes that Marot makes to his poems for the *Adolescence*, notably the replacement of the Compte d'Étampes with Marguerite de Navarre in the "Ballade a Ma dame la Duchesse d'Alençon," as evidence of how Marot forges a persona and substitutes fiction for biographical truth (116). For more on the pitfalls of Defaux's approach, see Guillaume Berthon, "Clément Marot et la tentation biographique," *Cahiers parisiens* 4 (2008): 550.

4. Jacqueline Cerquiglini-Toulet, for example, notes the similarities with regard to chronological organization, as Marot chooses to put the *Lais* before the *Testament* based on the fact that it was composed five years earlier; see Cerquiglini-Toulet, "Clément Marot et la critique littéraire et textuelle: Du bien renommé au mal imprimé Villon," in *Clément Marot, "Prince des poëtes françois," 1496–1996: Actes du Colloque international de Cahors en Quercy, 21–25 mai 1996,* eds. Gérard Defaux and Michel Simonin (Paris: Champion, 1997), 159–60. For more on how Marot makes Villon palatable for sixteenth-century readers, see Pascale Chiron, "L'édition des *Œuvres* de Villon annotée par Clément Marot, ou comment l'autorité vient au texte," *Littératures classiques* 64 (Spring 2008): 33–51.

5. Clément Marot, *Œuvres complètes,* ed. François Rigolot, 2 vols (Paris: Garnier, 2007–9), 2:469; *Œuvres poétiques complètes,* ed. Gérard Defaux, 2 vols (Paris: Bordas,

1990–93), 2:777. References to Marot, hereafter cited in the text, will be to the volume, page, and line numbers of Rigolot's and Defaux's editions, abbreviated as *OC* and *OPC*, respectively.

6. See François Rigolot, "Authorial Authority in the Early Age of Printing: Clément Marot (1496–1544)," *Princeton University Library Chronicle* 70, no. 1 (Autumn 2008): 42, and *Poésie et Renaissance* (Paris: Seuil, 2002), 102.

7. Yves Delègue, *Le Royaume d'exil: Le sujet de la littérature en quête d'auteur* (Paris: Obsidiane, 1991), 34.

8. Robert Melançon, "La personne de Marot," in *"Prince des poëtes françois,"* 524.

9. Florian Preisig, *Clément Marot et les métamorphoses de l'auteur à l'aube de la Renaissance* (Geneva: Droz, 2004), 106.

10. Rigolot, "Présentation," *OC* 1:5–7.

11. Cynthia J. Brown, *Poets, Patrons, and Printers: Crisis of Authority in Late Medieval France* (Ithaca, NY: Cornell University Press, 1995), *passim*; Mireille Huchon, *Louise Labé: Une créature de papier* (Geneva: Droz, 2006). Recently, Anne Réach-Ngô has raised a similar hypothesis regarding Hélisenne de Crenne by situating her works in the print culture of the early sentimental novel; see Réach-Ngô, *L'Écriture éditoriale à la Renaissance: Genèse et promotion du récit sentimental français (1530–1560)* (Geneva: Droz, 2013).

12. For an especially good example, see Leah L. Chang, *Into Print: The Production of Female Authorship in Early Modern France* (Newark: University of Delaware Press, 2009).

13. Rudolf Hirsch, *Printing, Selling and Reading, 1450–1550* (Wiesbaden, Germany: Harrassowitz, 1967), 8; Andrew Pettegree, *The Book in the Renaissance* (New Haven, CT: Yale University Press, 2010), 166; Anne Réach-Ngô, "De l'espace du livre à l'espace de l'œuvre: la consécration du fait littéraire à la Renaissance," in *Le livre et ses espaces*, eds. Alain Milon and Marc Perelman (Paris: Presses Universitaires de Paris 10, 2007), 73.

14. Frank Presbrey, *The History and Development of Advertising* (New York: Doubleday, 1929), 11; André Tournon, "Ce sont coups d'essai: L'ironie poétique," in *Clément Marot, L'Adolescence clémentine: Actes de la journée d'étude du 8 novembre 1996*, ed. Simone Perrier (Paris: Université Paris-Diderot, 1997), 118. Audrey Duru notes that the term *"coup d'essay"* is commonly used in prefaces and other paratexts, but the examples she cites are all from the second half of the sixteenth century, such as Guillaume Du Bartas and Jean de Sponde; see Duru, "Les *Essais poétiques*: Emplois et sens du mot *essai(s)* dans les titres de recueils poétiques à la fin du XVIe siècle et au début du XVIIe siècle," in *Le lexique métalittéraire français (XVIe–XVIIe siècles)*, eds. Michel Jourde and Jean-Charles Monferran (Geneva: Droz, 2006), 134. It seems, then, that Marot's use of the term in this context is an innovation, and one to which Rabelais makes reference in *Gargantua* when he has Alcofribas call the prologue a "prelude, et coup d'essay"; François Rabelais, *Œuvres complètes*, ed. Mireille Huchon (Paris: Gallimard, 1994), 6. Randle Cotgrave substantiates the connection between a work produced for evaluation and a sample meant to pique interest, as he defines "coup d'essay" as the "Maister-peece of a young workeman, or of one thats but newly come out of his years," and as "a flourish, or pre-

amble, whereby a tast of a thing is given, or taken"; Cotgrave, *A Dictionarie of the French and English Tongues* (Columbia: University of South Carolina Press, 1950), s.v. "essay."

15. Antoine Héroët, *La Parfaicte Amye*, ed. Christine M. Hill (Exeter: University of Exeter, 1981), 2.

16. The other collection of Marot's works from before the *Adolescence* is the *Petit traicte contenant plusieurs chantz royaulx, Balades, et Epistres, faictes et composees par Clement Marot de Quahors en quercy, varlet de chambre du Roy, Ensemble le Temple de Cupido, Avec la Deploration sur le trespas de feu messire Florimond Robertet, jadis chevalier, Conseillier du Roy, Tresorier de France, Secretaire des finances dudict seigneur, seigneur Dalluye, faicte par ledict Marot* (Paris: The Widow of Jean Saint-Denis, [1532]). Aside from advertising the deceased Robertet as much as it advertises Marot, it copies the content of the *Opuscules*, adding the "Epistre au Roy par Marot estant malade à Paris" (*OC* 1:226–30; *OPC* 1:320–23) and the "Huictain à ce propos" (*OC* 1:230; *OPC* 1:324); see Claude Mayer, *Clément Marot* (Paris: Nizet, 1972), 229.

17. See H.-L. Baudrier, *Bibliographie lyonnaise*, 12 vols. (Lyon: Librairie ancienne d'Auguste Brun, 1895–1921), 10:29.

18. Clément Marot, *Les Opuscules et petits Traictez* (Lyon: Olivier Arnoullet, n.d. [1530–31]), a1r.

19. Guillaume Berthon, "'L'intention du Poète': Du pupitre à la presse, Clément Marot *autheur*" (PhD diss., Université Paris-Sorbonne, 2010), 283.

20. Brigitte Moreau, *Inventaire chronologique des éditions parisiennes du XVIe siècle, d'après les manuscrits de Philippe Renouard*, 5 vols. to date (Paris: Imprimerie municipale, Service des travaux historiques de la ville de Paris, 1972–), vol. 3, nos. 520, 717, 681, 835, 836, 1276, 1277, 1285, 1390, 1864, 2216, 2217 and vol. 4, no. 239.

21. I. D. McFarlane, "Clément Marot and the World of Neo-Latin Poetry," in *Literature and the Arts in the Reign of Francis I: Essays Presented to C. A. Mayer*, eds. Pauline M. Smith and I. D. McFarlane (Lexington, KY: French Forum, 1985), 108; François Rigolot, "D'un libraire, l'autre: Marot, de Tory à Dolet via Montmorency," in *Les poètes français de la Renaissance et leurs "libraires": Actes du Colloque international de l'Université d'Orléans (5–7 juin 2013)*, eds. Denis Bjaï and François Rouget (Geneva: Droz, 2015), 313–18.

22. Clément Marot, *Ladolescence clementine* (Paris: Geoffroy Tory for Pierre Roffet, Aug. 12, 1532), +1.

23. *OPC* 1:410.

24. Olivia Rosenthal, "L'œuvre et ses éditeurs au début du XVIe siècle," in *L'Autre de l'œuvre*, ed. Yoshikazu Nakaji (Paris: Presses Universitaires de Vincennes, 2007), 24.

25. Desiderius Erasmus, *Opus epistolarum Des. Erasmi Roterodami*, vol. 1, ed. P. S. Allen (Oxford: Clarendon, 1906), ep. 49, p. 163.

26. Mantuan, *Adulescentia: The Eclogues of Mantuan*, ed. and trans. Lee Piepho (New York: Garland, 1989), XXV.

27. *Bucolica seu adolescentia in decem aeglogas divisa* (Paris: Jean Petit, 1503); *Les bucoliques de Frere Baptiste Mantuan* (Paris: Denis Janot, 1530).

28. Nathalie Dauvois, "Portrait du jeune poète en berger: Adolescence et bucolique,"

in *En relisant L'Adolescence Clémentine: Actes de la journée d'étude du 24 novembre 2006 organisée par Marie-Madeleine Fragonard, Pascal Debailly et Jean Vignes*, ed. Jean Vignes (Paris: Université Paris-Diderot, 2007), 21. See also McFarlane, "World of Neo-Latin Poetry," 127n15.

29. Mantuan, *Adulescentia*, 2; trans. Piepho, 3.

30. Jean-Max Colard, "L'écriture comme passetemps," in *Clément Marot*, 86. See also Rigolot, "Authorial Authority," 41.

31. Francesco Petrarch, *Petrarch's Lyric Poems: The* Rime Sparse *and Other Lyrics*, trans. Robert M. Durling (Cambridge, MA: Harvard University Press, 1976), poem 1, line 3; trans. Durling, 37.

32. Annie Bertin, "Les couleurs dans *L'Adolescence clémentine*," in *Clément Marot: À propos de* L'Adolescence clémentine. *Actes des quatrièmes Journées du Centre Jacques de Laprade tenues au Musée national du château de Pau les 29 et 30 novembre 1996*, eds. James Dauphiné and Paul Mironneau (Biarritz, France: J & D Editions, 1996), 41.

33. Cotgrave, *Dictionarie*, s.v. "arres."

34. Note the similarity of the vocabulary to Mantuan's; "juveniles" recalls the "multa nimis iuvenilia" of the original *Adulescentia*, which Mantuan claims to have composed for fun ("ludens excuderam").

35. For more on Bérault's relationship with Marot, see: McFarlane, "World of Neo-Latin Poetry," 106; Preisig, *Métamorphoses de l'auteur*, 56–57; and Mayer, *Clément Marot*, 167.

36. Preisig, *Métamorphoses de l'auteur*, 57. Corinne Noirot also argues that Marot's successive editors make consistent use of section titles, especially those with classical resonances, in order to promote the poet as *Maro Gallicus*; Noirot, *"Entre deux airs": Style simple et* ethos *poétique chez Clément Marot et Joachim Du Bellay (1515–1560)* (Quebec, QC: Les Presses de l'Université Laval, 2011), 107.

37. Little is known of Brisset, except that he was most likely a friend of Marot.

38. Joachim Du Bellay includes a similar "Ad lectorem" at the beginning of his *Regrets* and *Poemata*:

> Quem, Lector, tibi nunc damus libellum,
> Hic fellisque simul simulque mellis
> Permixtumque salis refert saporem

[This little book that we now give you, reader, tastes of gall, honey and salt all at once]

Joachim du Bellay, *Les Antiquités de Rome, Les Regrets*, vol. 2 of *Œuvres poétiques*, ed. Henri Chamard (Paris: STFM, 1993), 45.

39. Rigolot, "D'un libraire, l'autre," 317.

40. Though he agrees that Marot addresses a more or less universal reader, Preisig claims in *Métamorphoses de l'auteur* that the "noble" in "noble Lecteurs" necessarily means "of the nobility" (52), pointing out a similarity with Marot's *dizain* from the preface to Claude de Seyssel's translation of Thucydides (*OC* 2:457, *OPC* 2:322–33). I see no reason why this must be the case; the term's polysemy seems rather to invite identification

from readers noble by birth as well as from readers who believe themselves to be noble in letters or virtue.

41. Geoffroy Tory, *Champ Fleury* (Paris: Geoffroy Tory and Giles Gourmont, 1529), a2v.

42. Tory's preface exemplifies the shifting literary conception of glory described by Françoise Joukovsky: as humanism grows in influence, glory becomes less a reflection of worldly power and possessions—which Joukovsky refers to as "gloriole" and attributes largely to the *Rhétoriqueurs*—than of moral and intellectual superiority; Joukovsky, *La gloire dans la poésie française et néolatine du 16e siècle* (Geneva: Droz, 1969), 195.

43. Frank Lestringant, *Clément Marot: De L'Adolescence à L'Enfer* (Padua: Unipress, 1998), 25.

44. McFarlane, "World of Neo-Latin Poetry," 105.

45. Perrine Galland-Hallyn, "Marot, Macrin, Bourbon: 'Muse naïve' et 'tendre style,'" in *La génération Marot: Poètes français et néo-latins (1515–1550). Actes du Colloque international de Baltimore, 5–7 décembre 1996*, ed. Gérard Defaux (Paris: Champion, 1997), 234.

46. Thomas Sébillet, *Art poétique françoys*, ed. Félix Gaiffe (Paris: Droz, 1932), bk. 2, ch. 14, p. 140.

47. In the 1538 *Œuvres*, lines 167–68 become "Pommes, Pruneaux, tout plein de bon fructage, / Chastaignes, Aulx, avec force laictage" [Apples and plums full of ripe fruit, / Chestnuts, garlic, and plenty of white meat] making the connection with the fruit trees of the preface even clearer (*OPC* 1:26.168–69).

48. For an account of the *Temple* and of "Ferme amour" as Marot's choice of *agape* over erotic love, see Gérard Defaux, "Les deux amours de Clément Marot," *Rivista di Letterature moderne e comparate* 46, no. 1 (Jan.–Mar. 1993): 1–30, and Defaux, "Marot et 'Ferme Amour': Essai de mise au point," in *Anteros: Actes du colloque de Madison (Wisconsin) mars 1994*, eds. Ullrich Langer and Jan Miernowski (Orléans, France: Paradigme, 1994), 137–67.

49. Richard Crescenzo, "L'antique, l'ancien et le nouveau dans le *Temple de Cupido*," in *À propos de* L'Adolescence clémentine, 78; Danièle Duport, "'De pensée joyeuse' ou *Le Temple de Cupido* de Clément Marot," in *Nature et Paysages: L'émergence d'une nouvelle subjectivité à la Renaissance*, ed. Dominique de Courcelles (Paris: École Nationale des Chartes, 2006), 147.

50. Cf. lines 383–85:

> De *Requiem* les messes sont aubades,
> Cierges, rameaulx et sieges, la verdure
> Où les Amans font rondeaulx et ballades.
>
> [The *Requiem* masses are aubades,
> The candles, boughs, and the seats, the green grass
> Where lovers compose rondeaus and ballads.]

51. The corresponding section of the *Suite* is entitled "Le Cimetiere, autrement les epitaphes" (*OC* 1:348).

52. Ehsan Ahmed, *Clément Marot: The Mirror of the Prince* (Charlottesville, VA: Rookwood Press, 2005), 9.

53. Gérard Defaux, "Rhétorique, silence et liberté dans l'œuvre de Marot: Essai d'explication d'un style," *BHR* 46, no. 2 (1984): 320, and Defaux, *Marot, Rabelais, Montaigne: L'écriture comme présence* (Paris: Champion, 1987), 95. Similarly, Edwin Duval argues that until he finally reaches *Ferme Amour*, the speaker of the "Temple" essentially wastes his time pursuing the lure of erotic love; see Duval, "Marot, Marguerite, et le chant du cœur: Formes lyriques et formes de l'intériorité," in *"Prince des poëtes françois,"* 561. François Cornilliat also interprets the "Temple" as an interior quest for *Ferme Amour*, adding that Marot refuses to abandon love poetry in undertaking this quest, which marks a conscious departure from Lemaire's separation of poetry and history in the *Concorde des deux langages*; see Cornilliat, *Sujet caduc, noble sujet: La poésie de la Renaissance et le choix de ses arguments* (Geneva: Droz, 2009), 280–83.

54. Among scholars who have written on the 1532 *Adolescence*, Cécile Alduy is somewhat of an exception, as she claims that Marot is only concerned with order in the paratext of the *Adolescence*, and not in the text, whereas the 1538 *Œuvres* constitute a serious effort to impose order; see Alduy, "*L'Adolescence* de Marot mise en recueil: ordre du livre, fiction d'auteur," *L'Information littéraire* 58, no. 3 (2006): 11.

55. Claude Blum, "'L'ordre de mes livres': Les *Ballades* dans *L'Adolescence clémentine* de Marot," in *Désirs et plaisirs du livre: Hommage à Robert Kopp*, eds. Regina Bollhalder Mayer, Olivier Millet, and André Vanoncini (Paris: Champion, 2004), 75; Franck Bauer, "Ballades clémentines: L'ordre du sens," in *En relisant L'Adolescence Clémentine*, 150; Francis Goyet, "Sur l'ordre de *L'Adolescence clémentine*," in *"Prince des poëtes françois,"* 602.

56. Edwin Duval, "*L'Adolescence clémentine* et l'œuvre de Clément Marot," *Etudes françaises* 38, no. 3 (2002): 17–18, 21.

57. Clément Marot, *Ladolescence clementine* (Paris: Geoffroy Tory for Pierre Roffet, Feb. 12, 1533), a1r.

58. Ibid.

59. Nina Catach, *L'Orthographe française à l'époque de la Renaissance* (Geneva: Droz, 1968), 57. Rigolot also notes in "D'un libraire, l'autre" that these editions are contemporaneous with the *Briefve Doctrine pour deuement escripre selon la proprieté du langaige francoys* published by Antoine Augereau in Paris, which may possibly have been authored by Tory or Marot (318).

60. Berthon, "Intention," 317. See also Pauline M. Smith, "Clément Marot and the French Language," in *Literature and the Arts*, 169.

61. Marot, *Ladolescence clementine* (Paris: Geoffroy Tory for Pierre Roffet, Nov. 13, 1532), 112v. In the 1538 *Œuvres*, these poems all appear in the *Suite* or the *Premier livre des epigrammes*, with the exception of Martin Akakia's Latin quatrain. The June 7, 1533 edition (see above, n54) also includes the brief "Marot envoye le livre de son Adolescence a une dame, et luy mande" [Marot sends the book of his *Adolescence* to a lady, and entrusts it to her], which would be placed in the paratext just before the *Adolescence* in 1538 (*OC* 1:386; *OPC* 1:15).

62. The other three physicians to whom these poems are addressed, Louis Braillon, Guillaume Lecoq, and Akakia, are also mentioned in the "Epistre au Roy par Marot estant malade à Paris" (*OC* 1:228.71; *OPC* 1:322.71). Only Braillon could actually have been a "médecin du roi" in 1531; no documents list Lecoq as a royal doctor, and Akakia only became one in 1545; see Jean Dupèbe, "Un ami de Clément Marot, le médecin Michel Amy," in *Cité des hommes, Cité de Dieu: Travaux sur la littérature de la Renaissance en l'honneur de Daniel Ménager*, eds. Jean Céard, et al. (Geneva: Droz, 2003), 191n12. These poems, like the rest of Marot's "life story," are likely heavy on fabrication.

63. For more on Augereau's edition of the *Miroir*, see William Kemp, "Marguerite of Navarre, Clément Marot, and the Augereau editions of the *Miroir de l'âme pécheresse* (Paris, 1533)," *Journal of the Early Book Society* 2 (1999): 113–56.

64. See Sybille von Gültlingen, *Répertoire bibliographique des livres imprimés en France au seizième siècle*, 12 vols. to date (Baden-Baden, Germany: Valentin Koerner, 1992–), 4:201–22, and Berthon, "Intention," 370.

65. Paul Lacroix (Le Bibliophile Jacob), "François Juste: Libraire et Imprimeur à Lyon," *Bulletin du Bibliophile* (1869): 634.

66. Clément Marot, *Ladolescence clementine* (Lyon: François Juste, Feb. 23, 1533), 114v–115r.

67. For the polyvalence of "La mort n'y mord," which can be read as an affirmation of poetic glory or of Pauline faith in redemption, see Rigolot, "Authorial Authority," 41, and Rigolot, "Clément Marot et l'émergence de la conscience littéraire à la Renaissance," in *La génération Marot*, 33–34.

68. Marot, *Ladolescence clementine* (Lyon: François Juste, Feb. 23, 1533), 115v, 116v.

69. See Claude Mayer and C. M. Douglas, "Rabelais poète," *BHR* 24 (1962): 42–46. Mireille Huchon reproduces these poems and the dubious "Dizain de l'ymage de Venus armée" in her edition of Rabelais, *Œuvres complètes*, 1027–30. In her biography of Rabelais, she argues that the good doctor is responsible for the organization of Juste's editions of Marot; see Huchon, *Rabelais* (Paris: Gallimard, 2011), 178–81.

70. Defaux, *Poète en son jardin*, 122–23. See also Adalbert Hämel, "Clément Marot und François Juste," *Zeitschrift für französische Sprache und Literatur* 50 (1927): 132, and Pierre Villey, "A propos d'une édition de Marot," *Revue du seizième siècle* 15 (1928): 159–60. For more on the unrest in Paris following Gérard Roussel's sermons and the banishment of Béda, see R. J. Knecht, *Renaissance Warrior and Patron: The Reign of Francis I* (Cambridge: Cambridge University Press, 1994), 308–11.

71. Berthon, "Intention," 380. We should not, however, rule out the possibility of at least an initial collaboration between Marot and Juste, as Marot expresses regret in the 1538 preface of the *Œuvres* at having given his copies to printers who went on to show their ingratitude (*OC* 1:383; *OPC* 1:9).

72. Clément Marot, *Ladolescence clementine* (Lyon: François Juste, July 12, 1533), a1r.

73. Duval, "L'Adolescence clementine," 22.

74. Marot, *Ladolescence clementine* (Lyon: François Juste, July 12, 1533), 116v. For more on the rhetoric of misfortune that Marot deploys under the guise of the *dépourvu* [destitute], see Christine Scollen-Jimack, "Marot and Deschamps: The Rhetoric of

Misfortune," *French Studies* 42 (Jan. 1988): 21–32, and Scollen-Jimack, "Clément Marot: Protestant Humanist, or Court Jester?," *Renaissance Studies* 1, no. 2 (June 1989): 134–46.

75. Rigolot, *OC* 1:575n785.

76. Of course, "*papelart*" also often carries the connotation of "papist."

77. Bernd Renner, "'Clément devise dedans Venise': Marot's Satirical Poetry in Exile," in *Multicultural Europe and Cultural Exchange in the Middle Ages and Renaissance*, ed. James P. Helfers (Turnhout, Belgium: Brepols, 2005), 154. For a fine recent take on the Sagon controversy, see Robert Hudson, "Marot vs. Sagon: Heresy and the Gallic School, 1537," in *Representations of Heresy in French Art and Literature*, eds. Gabriella Scarlatta and Lidia Radi (Toronto: University of Toronto Press, 2017), 159–87.

78. Rigolot, "D'un libraire, l'autre," 327–29. The manuscript in question, the only surviving manuscript written or at least closely supervised by the poet himself, is Bibliothèque et Archives du Musée Condé de Chantilly ms. 524 (748); for a scholarly edition, see Clément Marot, *Recueil inédit offert au Connétable de Montmorency en mars 1538*, ed. François Rigolot (Geneva: Droz, 2010).

4. "Je n'en donne ung festu, pourveu qu'ayons son livre"

1. Clément Marot, *La Suite de l'adolescence Clementine* (Paris: [Louis Cyaneus for] the widow of Pierre Roffet, n.d. [late 1533—early 1534]).

2. Clément Marot, *Œuvres complètes*, ed. François Rigolot, 2 vols. (Paris: Garnier, 2007–9), 1:261; *Œuvres poétiques complètes*, ed. Gérard Defaux, 2 vols. (Paris: Bordas, 1990–93), 1:205. References to Marot, hereafter cited in the text, will be to the volume, page, and line numbers of Rigolot's and Defaux's editions, abbreviated as *OC* and *OPC*, respectively.

3. Horace, *Satires, Epistles, Ars Poetica*, trans. H. R. Fairclough (Cambridge: Harvard University Press, 1929), *Ars P.*, 291, trans. Fairclough, 475.

4. The Maro/Marot pun is the entire theme of two further unattributed epigraphs, the "A. C. Distichon" and "M. A. Tetrastichon," found in the paratext of late 1534 editions of the *Adolescence* and *Suite* published by Guillaume Boullé and François Juste. Their authorship remains uncertain, though Defaux suggests that "M. A." could be Antoine Macault; see Gérard Defaux, "'Vivre je veulx pour l'honneur de la France': Marot, Tory, Rabelais et le cas Étienne Dolet," in *Lyon et l'illustration de la langue française à la Renaissance*, ed. Gérard Defaux (Lyon: ENS Éditions, 2003), 420n5. Guillaume Berthon proposes that "M. A." could be either Martin Akakia or Michel Amy; see Berthon, "'L'intention du Poète': Du pupitre à la presse, Clément Marot *autheur*" (PhD diss., Université Paris-Sorbonne, 2010), 165n1.

5. Horace, *Epist.* 1.19.21–22, trans. Fairclough, 383. These are the very same lines, incidentally, that Pierre de Ronsard cites in the preface to the 1550 *Odes*.

6. Georges Soubeille, "Amitiés de Salmon Macrin parmi les poètes de langue vernaculaire," in *Neo-Latin and the Vernacular in Renaissance France*, eds. Grahame Castor and Terence Cave (Oxford: Clarendon, 1984), 102. See also Pauline M. Smith, "Clément Marot and Humanism," in *Humanism and Letters in the Age of François Ier: Proceedings of*

the Fourth Cambridge French Renaissance Colloquium, 19–21 September 1994, eds. Philip Ford and Gillian Jondorf (Cambridge: Cambridge French Colloquia, 1996), 137.

7. Robert Griffin, *Clément Marot and the Inflections of Poetic Voice* (Berkeley: University of California Press, 1974), 246.

8. For more on Marot's relationship with Anne de Montmorency, see Clément Marot, *Recueil inédit offert au Connétable de Montmorency en mars 1538*, ed. François Rigolot (Geneva: Droz, 2010), 159–64.

9. Randle Cotgrave amusingly renders "Musequin" as "an effeminate, or perfumed Courtier, that makes love to every wench he accompanies"; Cotgrave, *A Dictionarie of the French and English Tongues* (Columbia: University of South Carolina Press, 1950), s.v. "musequin." The epistles "A celluy qui l'injuria par escript, et ne se osa nommer" [To one who insulted him in writing, but didn't dare name himself] and "A celluy qui devant le Roy dist que ce mot, viser, (dont Marot usa) n'estoit bon langage" [To one who said in front of the King that the word "viser" (which Marot used) was not proper language], which follow shortly after the epistle to Montmorency particularly come to mind (*OC* 1:325–26; *OPC* 1:302–3, 2:224–25).

10. Cf. the "Dizain de Marot à Monsieur le Grant Maistre pour estre mys en l'estat" [Dizain by Marot to My Lord the Grand Maître, asking to be added to the estate] in the "Menu" (*OC* 1:366; *OPC* 2:213).

11. Edwin Duval, "L'*Adolescence clémentine* et l'œuvre de Clément Marot," *Etudes françaises* 38, no. 3 (2002): 22.

12. It is perhaps for this reason that the term "Menu" is dropped in the 1538 *Œuvres*.

13. Cf. Ps. 41:2: "Quemadmodum desiderat cervus ad fontes aquarum ita desiderat anima mea ad te Deus" [As a deer longs for flowing streams, so my soul longs for you, O God].

14. Clément Marot, *L'Adolescence clementine* (Paris: Louis Cyaneus for the widow of Pierre Roffet, Mar. 7, 1534); *La Suite de l'Adolescence Clementine* (Paris: Louis Cyaneus for the widow of Pierre Roffet, n.d. [1534]).

15. Cf. Psalms 6:1: "Domine ne in furore tuo arguas me neque in ira tua corripias me" [O Lord, do not rebuke me in your anger, or discipline me in your wrath].

16. In a similar vein, scholars have noted that Marot's psalm translations are written in a low style so as to reflect the concept of divine accommodation; see George Joseph, *Clément Marot* (Boston: Twayne, 1985), 120, and Corinne Noirot, *"Entre deux airs": Style simple et ethos poétique chez Clément Marot et Joachim Du Bellay (1515–1560)* (Quebec, QC: Les Presses de l'Université Laval, 2011), pt. 1, chap. 4.

17. Marot, *La Suite de l'Adolescence Clementine* (Paris: [Louis Cyaneus for] the widow of Pierre Roffet, 1534), *2r.

18. Clément Marot, *Ladolescence Clementine* (n.p. [Lyon: Denis de Harsy], 1534). Like all of Harsy's editions of Marot, this one does not list the publisher or place of publication, but does contain Harsy's mark, a foot soldier holding a shield with a face on it, in the colophon. Harsy published an edition of Mantuan's *Bucolica* in 1523, and as his career progressed, he shifted focus from breviaries and missals to editions and translations of ancient and modern authors writing in Latin, including Seneca, Petrarch,

Erasmus, Bembo, Juvenal, Horace, Lucan, and Quintilian. Harsy's editions of Marot mark a departure from his usual fare, and may represent an attempt to expand his market beyond humanists and clerics. See Sybille von Gültlingen, *Répertoire bibliographique des livres imprimés en France au seizième siècle*, 12 vols. to date (Baden-Baden, Germany: Valentin Koerner, 1992–), 4:101–53.

19. Marot, *Ladolescence Clementine* (n.p. [Lyon: Denis de Harsy], 1534). Pierre Villey reproduces this *douzain* in its entirety, as does Philippe Desan. Both critics, unaware of the Rutgers copy, claim that it first appeared in the 1537 Denis Janot edition, which is in fact a counterfeit of the Harsy editions, as is the accompanying *Suite*. See Villey, *Tableau chronologique des publications de Marot* (Paris: Champion, 1921), 61, and Desan, *L'imaginaire économique de la Renaissance* (Mont-de-Marsan, France: Editions Interuniversitaires, 1993), 159.

20. Desiderius Erasmus, *Adages Ii1 to Iv100*, ed. R. A. B. Mynors, trans. Margaret Mann Phillips, vol. 31of *Collected Works of Erasmus* (Toronto: University of Toronto Press, 1982), "Stelli signare, obelo notare," chap. 1, cent. 5, adage 57.

21. Its most original contribution to Marot's publication history, aside from the *douzain*, comes in the form of generic woodcuts before each poem, which Janot also copied.

22. Clément Marot, *L'Adolescence clementine* (Paris: [Louis Cyaneus for] the widow of Pierre Roffet, Aug. 19, 1534), 1r. This edition contains many of the apocryphal works first printed in Juste's July 12, 1534 *Adolescence*, and adds several more, including the "Alphabet du temps present" that Marot would disavow in 1538. To be fair, they are preceded by a heading that reads, "S'ensuyent aucunes oeuvres qui ne sont de la facon dudict Marot" (250) [Here follow other works not made by said Marot]. However, not only is this header misleading, as several of these works would later be included in the *Suite* or *Œuvres*, but its attribution of the works to poets other than Marot does not change the fact that the section belies the title page.

23. Clément Marot, *Ladolescence clementine* (Lyon: François Juste, Dec. 12, 1534); *La suyte de ladolescence Clementine* (Lyon: François Juste, 1534).

24. Defaux suggests that the spaghetti Latin *"magister Lourdis"* could refer to Béda's potbelly, though "lourd" probably means "dull-witted" here rather than "heavy" (*OPC* 2:1088n3).

25. Juste's next editions of the *Adolescence* and *Suite* are nearly identical in terms of content: Clément Marot, *Ladolescence clementine* (Lyon: François Juste, Feb. 6, 1535); *La suyte de ladolescence Clementine* (Lyon: François Juste, 1535).

26. Clément Marot, *Les Oeuvres de Clement Marot* (Lyon: [François Juste for] Étienne Dolet, 1538); *Les Oeuvres de Clement Marot* (Lyon: [François Juste for] Sébastien Gryphe, 1538). For Marot's quarrel with Dolet and Juste's involvement as printer, see Gérard Defaux, "Trois cas d'écrivains éditeurs dans la première moitié du XVIe siècle: Marot, Rabelais, Dolet," in *L'Écrivain éditeur*, ed. François Bessire (Geneva: Droz, 2001), 91–118, and Defaux, "Marot et ses éditions lyonnaises: Étienne Dolet, Sébastien Gryphe et François Juste," *Revue d'Histoire Littéraire Française* 93, no. 6 (1993): 819–49. See also Jeanne Veyrin-Forrer, "Les Œuvres de Clément Marot: Questions bibliographiques," in *Humanism and Letters*, 151–70, and Veyrin-Forrer, "Les premières éditions collectives de

Clément Marot publiées à Lyon," in *Clément Marot, "Prince des poëtes françois," 1496–1996: Actes du Colloque international de Cahors en Quercy, 21–25 mai 1996*, eds. Gérard Defaux and Michel Simonin (Paris: Champion, 1997), 699–711. The Dolet edition is the base for both *OC* and *OPC*, whereas Frank Lestringant's edition of *L'Adolescence clémentine* (Paris: Gallimard, 1987) is based on Gryphe.

27. In François Rabelais's *Tiers Livre*, Panurge refers to this anecdote when relating his prophetic dream; Rabelais, *Œuvres complètes*, ed. Mireille Huchon (Paris: Gallimard, 1994), *TL*, chap. 14, p. 393. Cf. Erasmus, *Adages Ii1 to Iv100*, "Momo satisfacere," chap. 1, cent. 5, adage 74.

28. Jean-Charles Monferran, "Va, mon Livre: Quelques jalons pour une histoire de la destination," *Nouvelle Revue du XVIe Siècle* 21, no. 1 (Jan. 2003): 138. "Racler" is replaced with "Oster" [remove] in the Gryphe edition, likely in order to eliminate any trace of Dolet. For more on the *lima* as artisanal metaphor, see Guillaume Berthon, *L'Intention du poète: Clément Marot "autheur"* (Paris: Garnier, 2014), 320.

29. Horace, *Ars P.*, 294, trans. Fairclough, 475. Horace also employs the phrase in the *Satires*, describing Fonteius Capito as an "ad unguem factus homo" [man fashioned to the test of the close-cut nail] (1.5.32–33). Fairclough notes that the metaphor originates in sculpture, where the artist would pass his fingernail over marble to test its smoothness (66nb). Randle Cotgrave gives the equivalent French expression of "conduire à l'ongle," "to finish, or bring unto perfection; to leave no jot undone of"; Cotgrave, *Dictionarie*, s.v. "conduire à l'ongle." Erasmus, for his part, lists the adages "Ad amussim" and "Ad unguem" next to one another: Erasmus, *Adages Ii1 to Iv100*, chap. 1, cent. 5, adages 90–91.

30. See *OC* 1:598–99nn1–15 for a list of variants between the respective prefaces of the two editions. For the Gryphe preface in its entirety, see Marot, *L'Adolescence clémentine*, ed. Lestringant, 37–38.

31. It is unclear just which works Marot believes to be "positively full of scandal and sedition." The July 12, 1533 and December 12, 1534 Juste editions of the *Adolescence* and *Suite*, which contain the "Gracieux adieux faictz aux Dames de Paris" [Gracious farewells to the ladies of Paris] as well as the anti-Sorbonne poems, seem like probable candidates, though the latter actually satirize theologians who themselves encourage sedition over a perceived lack of respect for orthodoxy on the part of the king. Interestingly, the June 20, 1535 Roffet *Adolescence* (*L'Adolescence clementine* [Paris: The widow of Pierre Roffet, June 20, 1535]), whose authority is questionable due to the fact that it was published during Marot's exile, contains a proviso on its title page whose language is quite reminiscent of the 1538 preface. It claims that the works it contains have been reviewed and corrected by the author against counterfeit printings,

> ... ausquelles a son grant deshonneur ont este adjoustees aulcunes oeuvres scandaleuses mal composees et incorrectes, desquelles craignant yceluy non seulement le blasme de chose si mal faicte, aussy le grant dommaige qui luy pourroit venir a cause desdictes oeuvres scandaleuses, apres avoir desavoue lesdictes oeuvres a obtenu privilege oultre les troys ans premiers deulx autres ans qui sont cinq ans, commencans a la date de la premiere Impression (1r).

[... to which have been added, to the considerable disgrace of the author, several scandalous, poorly-written, and incorrect works; for fear not only of being blamed for such ill-made things, but of the considerable harm that he could come to on account of said scandalous works, the author, after disavowing these works, obtained a privilege for two years beyond the original three, making it valid for five years from the date of the first printing.]

32. This is the case for all of Juste's editions and the Guillaume Boullé, Harsy, Janot, and 1538 Antoine Bonnemère/Pierre Sergent editions of the *Adolescence*.

33. Once again, it is difficult to identify the works or poets to which Marot is referring. Defaux points to the "Epistre de Complaincte a une qu'a laissé son amy" [Epistle with lamentation to a woman who left her lover] by Jacques Colin (who, of course, is not named in the editions), which first appears in the August 19, 1534 Roffet edition of the *Suite* (OPC 1:405n6).

34. Marot, *Oeuvres* (Lyon: [François Juste for] Étienne Dolet, 1538), a2v; *Oeuvres* (Lyon: [François Juste for] Sébastien Gryphe, 1538), a2v.

35. For more on this expression, see Jean Vignes, "'En belle forme de livre': La composition de *L'Adolescence clémentine*," *Op. cit.* 7 (Nov. 1996): 79–86.

36. The proximity of priests to merchants here might be a reference to the 1534 *Livre des marchans* attributed to Antoine Marcourt, a polemical tract against the sale of indulgences that compares the clergy to merchants who are so crafty that they can sell invisible things to their customers. For a scholarly edition, see Antoine Marcourt, *Le Livre des Marchans d'Antoine Marcourt: Une satire anticléricale au service de la Réforme*, ed. Geneviève Gross (Paris: Champion, 2016).

37. Defaux, *OPC* 1:780; Rigolot, *OC* 1:606n104. *Contrafacta* are new songs meant to be sung to a preexisting tune that is already well-known, and they often contain a religious dimension not present in the previous songs.

38. Berthon, *L'Intention du poète*, 526.

39. Ibid., 540.

40. Marot, *Ladolescence clementine* (Lyon: François Juste, Feb. 6, 1535), f. 62r.

41. Clément Marot, *Œuvres complètes*, ed. Claude Mayer, 5 vols. (London: Athlone Press, 1958–70), 4:227.

42. Rigolot, *OC* 1:608n122. Similarly, the Chantilly manuscript, which also contains the "Epitaphe d'Alix," ends with a series of bawdy epigrams, notably the *cinquain* "Janeton a du teton" [Jane has big tits], which prompted Gustave Macon, the curator of the Musée Condé who first publicized the manuscript in 1898, to bemoan the fact that the volume concludes with such a "pauvreté"; see Marot, *Recueil inédit*, 304n12. It should also be noted that Alix's epitaph appears shortly after that of Françoise de Foix, Francis I's mistress prior to the Duchess of Étampes ...

43. David Claivaz, *Ce que j'ay oublié d'y mettre: Essai sur l'invention poétique dans les coq-à-l'âne de Clément Marot* (Fribourg: Éditions Universitaires, 2000), 156.

44. Berthon, *L'Intention du poète*, 550–51.

5. The Prophylactic Prologues of *Pantagruel* and *Gargantua*

This chapter is based in part on "Treacle and Rabelais's Prologues as *pharmakon*" (paper given at the Sixteenth Century Society and Conference, San Juan, PR, October 24–27, 2013).

1. The authenticity of the *Cinquiesme Livre* has been a point of contention among *rabelaisants* since the early seventeenth century. Mireille Huchon adopts and convincingly demonstrates the theory that the *Cinquiesme Livre* is the work of an editor or group of editors who assembled various unfinished drafts left behind by Rabelais after his death, though the chapter on the Apedeftes, present in some editions of the *Cinquiesme Livre* and absent in others, is probably not Rabelais's work. Though it is not my goal to argue about the *Cinquiesme Livre*'s authorship one way or the other, the fact that its prologue uses the same advertising strategies seen in previous books would seem to lend credence to Huchon's theory. For a history of the various arguments for and against the authenticity of the *Cinquiesme Livre*, see: Huchon, *Rabelais grammairien: De l'histoire du texte aux problèmes d'authenticité* (Geneva: Droz, 1981), 413–16; Alfred Glauser, *Le faux Rabelais, ou De l'inauthenticité du* Cinquième Livre (Paris: Nizet, 1975), 25–40; and Richard Cooper, "L'authenticité du *Cinquiesme Livre*: État présent de la question," in *Le* Cinquiesme Livre: *Actes du colloque internationale de Rome (16–19 octobre 1998)*, ed. Franco Giacone (Geneva: Droz, 2001), 9–22.

2. Bernd Renner, "Changes in Renaissance Epistemology: The Dialogism of Rabelais's Prologues," in *Charting Change in France around 1540*, ed. Marian Rothstein (Selinsgrove, PA: Susquehanna University Press, 2006), 187, and Renner, *Difficile est saturam non scribere: L'herméneutique de la satire rabelaisienne*, ER 45 (Geneva: Droz, 2007), 56–57. The interpretative controversy, which centers in particular on the prologue of *Gargantua*, first pitted Leo Spitzer against what he derisively referred to as *rabelaisants*, or critics like Abel Lefranc and Claude Mayer who insisted on seeing a deeper meaning in the prologue and in the *Geste* as a whole, whereas Spitzer thought Rabelais's evocations of a "higher sense" were meant to be a humorous red herring; see Spitzer, "Rabelais et les 'rabelaisants,'" *Studi Francesi* 4 (1960): 401–23, and "Ancora sul prologo al primo libro del *Gargantua* di Rabelais," *Studi Francesi* 9, no. 3 (1965): 423–34. In the 1980s, the debate came to reflect the controversial role of deconstruction in literary criticism; see Gérard Defaux, "D'un problème l'autre: herméneutique de l'*altior sensus* et *captatio lectoris* dans le prologue de *Gargantua*," *Revue d'Histoire Littéraire de la France* 85, no. 2 (Mar.–Apr. 1985): 195–216, the response by Terence Cave, Michel Jeanneret, and François Rigolot in "Sur la prétendue transparence de Rabelais," *Revue d'Histoire Littéraire de la France* 86, no. 4 (Jul.–Aug. 1986): 709–16, and Defaux's riposte in the same issue, "Sur la prétendue pluralité du Prologue de *Gargantua*: Réponse d'un positiviste naïf à trois 'illustres et treschevaleureux champions,'" 716–22. See also Gérard Defaux, *Marot, Rabelais, Montaigne: L'écriture comme présence* (Paris: Champion, 1987), 101–42, and Defaux, *Rabelais agonistes: du rieur au prophète* (Geneva: Droz, 1997), 362–82. As fierce as this debate was, both sides had more in common than perhaps they let on at

the time; see François Cornilliat, "On Words and Meaning in Rabelais Criticism," *ER* 35 (Geneva: Droz, 1998): 7–28.

3. Cathleen M. Bauschatz, "'Une description du jeu de paulme soubz obscures parolles': The Portrayal of Reading in *Pantagruel* and *Gargantua*," *ER* 22 (Geneva: Droz, 1988): 75.

4. Roland Antonioli, *Rabelais et la médecine*, *ER* 12 (Geneva: Droz, 1976), 209–10.

5. François Rabelais, *Œuvres complètes*, ed. Mireille Huchon (Paris: Gallimard, 1994), *TL* 29.444; *The Complete Works of François Rabelais*, trans. Donald M. Frame (Berkeley: University of California Press, 1991), 348. References to Rabelais, hereafter cited in the text, are to chapter (where relevant) and page number in Huchon's edition, and to page number in Frame's translation. For Huchon's edition, *Gargantua* will be referred to as G, and *Pantagruel* will be referred to as P. All translations are Frame's, except where otherwise noted.

6. Romain Menini, *Rabelais et l'intertexte platonicien*, *ER* 47 (Geneva: Droz, 2009), 143; Tristan Dagron, "Silènes et statues platoniciennes, à propos du prologue du *Gargantua*," *Rabelais pour le XXIe siècle: Actes du colloque du Centre d'études supérieures de la Renaissance (Chinon-Tours, 1994)*, ed. Michel Simonin (Geneva: Droz, 1998), 84.

7. Randle Cotgrave, *A Dictionary of the French and English Tongues* (Columbia: University of South Carolina Press, 1950), s.v. "Triaclerie."

8. Mikhail Bakhtin, *Rabelais and His World*, trans. Hélène Iswolsky (Bloomington: Indiana University Press, 1984), 167. Lazar Sainéan also points out the similarity between several recorded *cris* and certain passages in Rabelais; see Sainéan, *La langue de Rabelais* (Geneva: Slatkine Reprints, 1976), 274–75. For a collection of *cris*, see *La vie privée d'autrefois: L'annonce et la réclame*, ed. Alfred Franklin (Paris: Plon, 1887).

9. Pliny the Elder, *Naturalis Historia*, 7.25.3.5–7, 8.29.24–25; Celsus, *De Medicina*, 5.23.3.

10. For a summary of ancient accounts of mithridate and theriac, see Laurence Totelin, "Mithridates' Antidote: A Pharmacological Ghost," *Early Science and Medicine* 9 (2004): 1–19. For a similar summary with a focus on Galen, see Demetrios Karaberopoulos, Marianna Karamanou, and George Androutsos, "The Theriac in Antiquity," *The Lancet* 379, no. 9830 (May 26, 2012): 1942–43.

11. Jacques Grévin, *Deux livres des venins, ausquels il est amplement discouru des bestes venimeuses, theriaques, poisons, et contrepoisons* (Antwerp: Christophe Plantin, 1568), 41.

12. Ibid., 193–94.

13. Geoffrey Chaucer, *The Riverside Chaucer*, ed. Larry D. Benson (Oxford: Oxford University Press, 2008), 194, lines 313–14. Pierre de Ronsard, for his part, proclaims in the preface to the *Franciade* that "Il y a autant de différence entre un Poëte et un versificateur, qu'entre un bidet et un genereux coursier de Naples, et, pour mieux les accomparer, entre un venerable Prophete et un Charlatan vendeur de triacles" [there is as big a difference between a poet and a rhymer as there is between a pony and a noble Neapolitan charger, or to make an even more accurate comparison, between a venerable

prophet and a charlatan hawking treacle]; Ronsard, Œuvres complètes, eds. Jean Céard, Daniel Ménager, and Michel Simonin, 2 vols. (Paris: Gallimard, 1993–94), 1:1164.

14. "Les Ditz de Maistre Aliborum qui de tout se mesle," in Recueil de poésies françoises des XVe et XVIe siècles, vol. 1, ed. Anatole de Montaiglon (Paris: P. Jannet, 1855), 37.

15. Ibid., 41.

16. "Sottie de Me Pierre Doribus," in Le Recueil Trepperel: Les sotties, ed. Eugénie Droz (Paris: Droz, 1935), 245, lines 2–5.

17. "Maistre Hambrelin, serviteur de maistre Aliborum, cousin germain de Pacolet," in Recueil de poésies françoises des XVe et XVIe siècles, vol. 13, ed. Anatole de Montaiglon (Paris: P. Jannet, 1878), lines 214–18. The modern equivalent of "poudre d'oribus" is "poudre de perlimpinpin," an expression that recently rose to prominence when Emmanuel Macron used it in the 2017 French presidential second-round debate to mock Marine Le Pen's proposed closed border policy.

18. "Le pardonneur, le triacleur, et la tavernière," in Recueil de farces (1450–1550), ed. André Tissier, 13 vols. (Geneva: Droz, 1989), 5:253–54, lines 97–101.

19. Ibid., 5:273, lines 312–17.

20. Celsus, De re medica libri octo (Paris: Simon de La Haye, 1528), Aurelii Cornelii Celsi De re medica libri octo (Paris: Chrétien Wechel, 1528–29); Galen, De antidotis libri duo (Paris: Simon de Colines, 1533), and De theriaca ad Pisonem liber (Paris: Simon de Colines, 1531).

21. For a particularly useful account of purgation and its uses in Rabelais, see Jeffery C. Persels, "'Straitened in the bowels,' or Concerning the Rabelaisian Trope of Defecation," ER 31 (1996): 101–12.

22. Dorothea Heitsch, Writing as Medication in Early Modern France (Heidelberg: Universitätsverlag Winter, 2017), 84.

23. "[P]isse chiens" likely means the urine rather than the dogs, which M. A. Screech conveys by translating it as "dog-piddles"; François Rabelais, Gargantua and Pantagruel, trans. M. A. Screech (London: Penguin, 2006), 117.

24. "Ditz de Maistre Aliborum," 41; "Tout-Ménage," in Recueil de farces, 5:295–96, lines 83–86; "Le pardonneur, le triacleur, et la tavernière," 269, line 269.

25. François Rigolot, "Vraisemblance et Narrativité dans le Pantagruel," L'Esprit Créateur 21, no. 1 (Spring 1981): 56–59. See also Bernd Renner, Difficile est saturam non scribere, 65, Bettina Rommel, Rabelais zwischen Mündlichkeit und Schriftlichkeit: Gargantua, Literatur als Lebensführung (Tübingen: Niemeyer, 1997), 62, and Raymond C. La Charité, "Lecteurs et lectures dans le prologue du Gargantua," French Forum 10, no. 3 (Sept. 1985): 262. For more on the concept of the narratee, see Gérard Genette, Figures III (Paris: Seuil, 1972), 265–67, and Gerald Prince, "Introduction à l'étude du narrataire," Poétique 14 (1973): 178–96.

26. Huchon glosses "hors de propos" as "inoccupés" (P 213nB).

27. Lucian, "A True Story," in Lucian, vol. 1, trans. A. M. Harmon (London: William Heinemann, 1953), 249–51.

28. Ibid., 253. For more on Rabelais's use of Lucian's *True History* to combat the reader's credulity, see Nicolas Le Cadet, "Le *topos* lucianesque des 'histoires vraies' et la poétique du *Quart Livre*," *Réforme Humanisme Renaissance* 74 (Jun. 2012): 7–24, and "'Beuveurs tresillustres et vous verolez tresprecieux': Rabelais et les anagnostes," *Revue d'Histoire Littéraire de la France* 115, no. 2 (2015): 267–68.

29. Romain Menini, *Rabelais altérateur: "Græciser en François"* (Paris: Classiques Garnier, 2014), 232–36.

30. Terence Cave, *Pré-Histoires II: Langues étrangères et troubles économiques au XVIe siècle* (Geneva: Droz, 2001), 160–62.

31. Cf. *Rhetorica ad Herennium (Rhet. Her.)* 5.8. For more on the prologue of *Pantagruel* as a parody of the rhetorical exordium, see Deborah N. Losse, *Rhetoric at Play: Rabelais and Satirical Eulogy* (Bern: Peter Lang, 1980), 36, and Paul J. Smith, "Le prologue du *Pantagruel*: Une lecture," *Neophilologus* 68, no. 2 (Apr. 1984): 163.

32. Gérard Defaux, "Un 'extraict de haulte mythologie' humaniste: Pantagruel, Picus redivivus,'" *ER* 14 (1977): 260.

33. Gérard Defaux, *Pantagruel et les Sophistes: Contribution à l'histoire de l'humanisme chrétien au XVIe siècle* (The Hague: M. Nijhoff, 1973), 76; Gerard J. Brault, "Ung abysme de science," *BHR* 28 (1966): 631. See also Defaux, *Rabelais agonistes*, 312–21. For examples of the celebratory take on Gargantua's letter, see: Michael B. Kline, *Rabelais and the Age of Printing*, *ER* 4 (Geneva: Droz, 1963), 14; M. A. Screech, *Rabelais* (London: Duckworth, 1979), 64–68; and Edwin Duval, "The Medieval Curriculum, The Scholastic University, and Gargantua's Program of Studies (*Pantagruel*, 8)," in *Rabelais's Incomparable Book*, ed. Raymond C. La Charité (Lexington, KY: French Forum, 1986), 30–44.

34. Desiderius Erasmus, *Adages Ivi1 to Ix100*, ed. R. A. B. Mynors, trans. Margaret Mann Phillips, vol. 32 of *Collected Works of Erasmus* (Toronto: University of Toronto Press, 1989), chap. 1, cent. 10, adage 43.

35. The dispute and Pantagruel's judgment are likely inspired by the adage "Surdaster cum surdastro litigabat, judex autem erat utroque surdior" [Two deaf men had a legal dispute, but the judge was deafer than either of them]; Desiderius Erasmus, *Adages IIIiv1 to IVii100*, ed. John N. Grant, trans. Denis L. Drysdall, vol. 35 of *Collected Works of Erasmus* (Toronto: University of Toronto Press, 2005), chap. 3, cent. 4, adage 83.

36. Le Cadet, "Rabelais et les anagnostes," 269–76. See also Mireille Huchon, *Rabelais* (Paris: Gallimard, 2011), 150–54.

37. E. Bruce Hayes, *Rabelais's Radical Farce: Late Medieval Comic Theater and Its Function in Rabelais* (Aldershot, UK: Ashgate, 2010), 124–28.

38. "M. Ortuinum" is, of course, a reference to Hardwin von Grätz (Ortuinus Gratius), the scholar and theologian at the University of Cologne to whom the satirical *Epistolae Obscurorum Virorum (Letters of Obscure Men)* are addressed.

39. François Rabelais, *Pantagruel* (Lyon: Claude Nourry, n.d. [1531 or 1532]), *NRB* 1; *Pantagruel* (Lyon: François Juste, 1534), *NRB* 8.

40. François Rabelais, *Pantagruel* (Lyon: François Juste, 1542), *NRB* 12.

41. "Thrice great" is my own translation. Frame's "supercolossal" (198) accurately

conveys the exaggerated size of Panurge's codpiece, but occludes the allusion to the hermetic tradition. Conversely, Screech's "trismegistical" (104) makes the allusion to Hermes Trismegistus clear, but misses out on the physical humor.

42. François Rigolot, *Les langages de Rabelais*, 2nd ed. (Geneva: Droz, 1996), 21; Heitsch, *Writing as Medication*, 100. For more on "Nasier" as an allusion to Ovid, see Raymond C. La Charité, "Rabelais and the Silenic Text: The Prologue to *Gargantua*," in *Rabelais's Incomparable Book*, 80. For more on the alchemical context of "quinte essence," see Léo Mérigot, "Rabelais et l'alchimie," *Les Cahiers d'Hermès* 1 (1947): 50–64.

43. Cf. Dom Antoine-Joseph Pernety, *Dictionnaire mytho-hermétique* (Paris: Denoël, 1972), 306. Mercury was also used to treat syphilis, which invites a connection with the "Verolez tresprecieux" of the prologue of *Gargantua*.

44. Lars Schneider sees in the claim, and in the entire prologue, an ironic commentary on the state of the book market in Lyon and its concern with selling above all else; Schneider, *Medienvielfalt und Medienwechsel in Rabelais' Lyon* (Münster: LIT, 2008), 115.

45. Erasmus changed the name to the more conventional *Novum Testamentum* in 1519. The three prefaces are the *Paraclesis*, an exhortation to the more assiduous and widespread reading of the Bible, the *Methodus*, in which Erasmus lays out his views on theology and interpretation, and the *Apologia*, in which he justifies his approach to editing and translating the text of the New Testament.

46. "Patrem te dixi, matrem etiam dicerem, si per indulgentiam mihi id tuam liceret" (998) [I have said you are my father; I would also say you are my mother, if your indulgence permitted me]; see Raymond Lebègue, "Rabelais, the Last of French Erasmians," *Journal of the Warburg and Courtauld Institutes* 12 (1949): 92–93. See also Marcel Françon, *Autour de la lettre de Gargantua à Pantagruel* (Rochecorbon, France: Gay, 1957), 43, 47, and Charles A. Béné, "Erasme et le Chapitre VIII du premier *Pantagruel*," *Paedagogica historica* 1, no. 1 (1961): 53–54.

47. For more on Erasmus's self-promotion in print, see Lisa Jardine, *Erasmus, Man of Letters: The Construction of Charisma in Print* (Princeton, NJ: Princeton University Press, 1993).

48. Desiderius Erasmus, "Paraclesis," in *Ausgewählte Werke*, eds. Hajo Holborn and Annemarie Holborn (Munich: C. H. Beck'sche, 1933), 140; "Paraclesis," in *Christian Humanism and The Reformation: Selected Writings*, ed. and trans. John C. Olin (Gloucester, MA: Peter Smith, 1973), 94.

49. Erasmus, "Paraclesis," 141; "Paraclesis," trans. Olin, 99–100.

50. In the same vein, Stephen Greenblatt specifies that self-fashioning necessarily entails submission to an authority, either human or divine; Greenblatt, *Renaissance Self-Fashioning From More to Shakespeare*, 2nd ed. (Chicago: University of Chicago Press, 2005), 9.

51. François Rabelais, *Gargantua* (Lyon: François Juste, 1535), NRB 20. It is impossible to know whether Juste's first edition of *Gargantua* contains the *dizain*, since the only surviving copy (BNF Rés. Y²2126) is missing its first leaf.

52. Antonioli, *Rabelais et la médecine*, 332–33.

53. Raymond C. La Charité takes a similar view of Alcofrybas, calling him a boastful, hostile, distrustful little tyrant who only seeks to impose his will on the reader; La Charité, "Du *Pantagruel* au *Quart Livre*: Projet narratif et lecteurs," in *Rabelais pour le XXIe siècle*, 363.

54. Aristotle, *Rhetoric*, 3.14.1414b.

55. Cicero, *De Inventione* (*Inv. rhet.*), 1.16.23; *Rhet. Her.* 4.7–8. Frame's translation omits "nostre religion, que aussi."

56. Desiderius Erasmus, *Adages IIvii1 to IIIiii100*, ed. R. A. B. Mynors, trans. Margaret Mann Phillips, vol. 34 of *Collected Works of Erasmus* (Toronto: University of Toronto Press, 1992), chap. 3, cent. 3, adage 1.

57. Plato, *Symposium* 216d–217b. Number and letters in references to Plato are the Stephanus pagination, and correspond to the page numbers and column letters in Jean de Serres's 1578 edition of Plato's complete works published by Henri Estienne.

58. *Gargantua and Pantagruel*, trans. Screech, 206. Frame does not translate this phrase.

59. Rabelais, "Le pardonneur, le triacleur, et la tavernière," 258–59, lines 157–61.

60. Schneider, *Medienvielfalt und Medienwechsel*, 133.

61. *Declamatio de pueris statim ac liberaliter instituendis*, ed. and trans. Jean-Claude Margolin (Geneva: Droz, 1966), 388.

62. Cathleen M. Bauschatz, "From 'estudier et profiter' to 'instruire et plaire': Didacticism in Rabelais's *Pantagruel* and *Gargantua*," *Modern Language Studies* 19, no. 1 (Winter 1989): 46.

63. Fittingly, Frame renders "Caisgne" as "Son of a bitch!" (4); Screech opts for "Dawg!," which seems somewhat out of place (*Gargantua and Pantagruel*, 207).

64. Pierre Fabri, *Le grand et vrai art de pleine rhétorique*, ed. A. Héron (Geneva: Slatkine Reprints, 1969), 118. Cf. *Quart Livre*, 41.635 ["un grand, gras, gros, gris pourceau"]. See also Gérard Milhe Poutingon, "Rabelais, Érasme, et le pourceau," *ER* 39 (2000): 39–57.

65. Persius, *Satires*, 1.109–10.

66. Geoffroy Tory, *Champ Fleury* (Paris: Geoffroy Tory and Gilles Gourmont, 1529), 55r.

67. M. A. Screech, *Rabelais* (London: Duckworth, 1979), 131.

68. Edmond Huguet, *Dictionnaire de la langue française du seizième siècle*, 7 vols. (Paris: Champion, 1925–67), s.v. "finfreluche"; Cotgrave, *Dictionarie*, s.v. "fanfreluches" and "finfreluches." Under the former heading, Cotgrave also defines "Fanfreluches antidotées" as "Vanities, fopperies, fooleries, fond tricks."

69. Cf. *P* 23.298–99: "Ainsi les compaignons joyeusement partirent, et pource qu'ilz estoyent frays et de sejour ilz fanfreluchoient à chasque bout de champ, et voylà pourquoy les lieues de France sont tant petites" [They set out joyously, and because they were fresh and rested, they friggle-fraggled at every little field, and that is why the leagues in France are so short (Frame 210)].

70. See, for example, Claude Gaignebet, *A plus hault sens: L'Ésotérisme spirituel et charnel de Rabelais*, 2 vols. (Paris: Maisonneuve et Larose, 1986), 2:230–42, and Jacques

Pons, "Recherches sur les 'Fanfreluches antidotées' (suite)," *Bulletin de l'association des amis de Rabelais et de La Devinière* 6, no. 8 (1999): 471–84.

71. Rigolot, *Langages de Rabelais*, *3.

72. Thomas Sébillet, *Art poétique françoys*, ed. Félix Gaiffe (Paris: Droz, 1932), bk. 2, chap. 11, p. 176.

73. Quoted in Gaignebet, *A plus haut sens*, 2:233.

74. André Tournon, "Le pantagruélisme, mode de lecture du *Tiers Livre*," *Littératures* 33 (Autumn 1995): 9. For more on *pantagruélisme* as ideal readership, see Edwin Duval, *The Design of Rabelais's Pantagruel* (New Haven, CT: Yale University Press, 1991), 144, and *The Design of Rabelais's Tiers livre de Pantagruel*, ER 34 (Geneva: Droz, 1997), 190–91. See also: Le Cadet, "Rabelais et les anagnostes," 277–82; Guy Demerson, *Humanisme et facétie: Quinze études sur Rabelais* (Caen: Paradigme, 1994), 332; Jan Miernowski, "Literature and Metaphysics: Rabelais and the Poetics of Misunderstanding," *ER* 35 (1998): 131–51; James Helgeson, "'Ce que j'entends par ces symboles pythagoricques': Rabelais on Meaning and Intention," *ER* 42 (2003): 75–100; and Helgeson, *The Lying Mirror: The First-Person Stance and Sixteenth-Century Writing* (Geneva: Droz, 2012).

75. Cotgrave, *Dictionarie*, s.v. "escors."

6. Rabelais, Doctor of Iatrosophism

This chapter is based in part on "The *Grands Annales*: Marot, Dolet, and the Evolution of Rabelais's Authorial Persona" (paper given at the Sixteenth Century Society and Conference, Cincinnati, OH, October 25–28, 2012), and on "La publicité iatrosophiste de Rabelais: *Captatio benevolentiae* et *persona* de l'auteur," *L'Année Rabelaisienne* 1 (Paris: Classiques Garnier, 2017): 183–202.

1. Walter Kaiser, *Praisers of Folly* (Cambridge: Harvard University Press, 1963), 106–8. See also E. Bruce Hayes, "A Decade of Silence: Rabelais's Return to Writing in a More Dangerous World," *ER* 46 (2008): 101–13.

2. Stephen Rawles and M. A. Screech, *A New Rabelais Bibliography* (*NRB*), *ER* 20 (Geneva: Droz, 1987), 13, 24.

3. Its full title is *Le voyage et navigation que fist Panurge, Disciple de Pantagruel aux Isles incongneues et estranges* (Paris: Denis Janot, [1538]). For a modern edition, see *Le Disciple de Pantagruel*, eds. Guy Demerson and Christiane Lauvergnat-Gagnière (Paris: STFM, 1982).

4. *NRB* 25, 26.

5. This letter does not appear in Mirielle Huchon's edition, nor, to my knowledge, in any other recent editions of Rabelais. A facsimile of it is provided in Rawles and Screech, *A New Rabelais Bibliography*, 151–53; quotations, with references in text, are from *Gargantua, Pantagruel, Pantagrueline prognostication* (N.p., 1542), *NRB* 26. 1542 was a year of intense competition between Dolet and Tours, with Dolet publishing his editions of Rabelais in response to Juste's 1542 editions, and Tours publishing the *Grands annales* and his own edition of Antoine Héroët's *Parfaicte Amye*, first published by Dolet in that same year. For more on Tours, see Sybille von Gültlingen, *Répertoire bibliogra-*

phique des livres imprimés en France au seizième siècle, 12 vols. to date (Baden-Baden and Bouxwiller: Valentin Koerner, 1992–), 9:6–13.

6. For more on Rabelais's authorship of the letter, see Michael B. Kline, *Rabelais and the Age of Printing*, ER 4 (Geneva: Droz, 1963), 21–24, and Mireille Huchon, *Rabelais* (Paris: Gallimard, 2011), 284–89.

7. Clément Marot, *Œuvres complètes*, ed. François Rigolot, 2 vols. (Paris: Garnier, 2007–9), 1:35, 385, and Marot, *Œuvres poétiques complètes*, ed. Gérard Defaux, 2 vols. (Paris: Bordas, 1990–93), 1:17, 11.

8. The association of mustard with "senseless gibbering" was a common one at the time, and one to which Rabelais refers on multiple occasions; see Emily Butterworth, *The Unbridled Tongue: Babble and Gossip in Renaissance France* (Oxford: Oxford University Press, 2016), 44n19. Criers are also often associated with punishment in Rabelais, especially in *Pantagruel*. In Chapter 30, Epistemon, having recovered from his decapitation, recounts what he saw in Hell, which includes great princes and generals reduced to humble states, including Xerxes, who is forced to work as a mustard crier, and in the following chapter, Pantagruel punishes Anarche, the vanquished king of the Dipsodes, by making him into a crier of green sauce; François Rabelais, *Œuvres complètes*, ed. Mireille Huchon (Paris: Gallimard, 1994), *Pantagruel* 30.322, 31.329; *The Complete Works of François Rabelais*, trans. Donald M. Frame (Berkeley: University of California Press, 1991), 235, 237. References to Rabelais, hereafter cited in the text, are to chapter (where relevant) and page number in Huchon's edition, and to page number in Frame's translation. For references to Huchon's edition, *Pantagruel* will be referred to as *P*, and *Gargantua* as *G*. All translations are Frame's, except where otherwise noted.

9. NRB 28–37. For more on Wechel, see Kline, *Rabelais and the Age of Printing*, 35, and Brigitte Moreau, *Inventaire chronologique des éditions parisiennes du XVIe siècle, d'après les manuscrits de Philippe Renouard*, 5 vols. to date (Paris: Imprimerie municipale, Service des travaux historiques de la ville de Paris, 1972–), 3:675, 4:468–69, and 5:603.

10. The title of "Calloïer des Isles Hieres," which also appears in the title of the 1548 *princeps* edition of the *Quart Livre*, is rather perplexing. In her edition, Huchon notes that the Hyères islands, off the coast of Var in the Mediterranean, were frequented by outlaws and pirates, especially when they were made into an asylum under Francis I, and were also the site of several attempts at establishing monasteries (1360–61n2). The archipelago's peculiar (or perhaps not so peculiar) blend of monasteries and iniquity, as well as its remarkable avian population (two of its islands are currently national parks for this reason), may have been the inspiration for the Isle Sonante in the *Cinquiesme Livre* (chaps. 1–8). As for "Calloïer," Frank Lestringant points to the existence of a symbolic "île du Caloyer" that lent itself to allegory or moral discourse and was readily interchangeable with Hesiod's Rock of Virtue, the same one that inspired Lemaire's Temple of Minerva: see Frank Lestringant, "L'Insulaire de Rabelais ou la fiction en archipel: Pour une lecture topographique du *Quart Livre*," ER 21 (1988): 268–73. Whatever the case may be, the title disappears in the 1552 editions of both the *Tiers* and *Quart Livre*.

11. Jerome Schwartz, "Rhetorical Tensions in the Liminary Texts of Rabelais's *Quart Livre*," ER 17 (1983): 34.

12. For more on these events, see R. J. Knecht, *Renaissance Warrior and Patron: The Reign of Francis I* (Cambridge: Cambridge University Press, 1994), 334–41 and 490–94.

13. Rabelais, *Œuvres complètes*, TL 349; *The Complete Works of François Rabelais*, trans. Frame, 256. "Tragicque comedie" should not be understood as "tragicomedy" in the modern sense of the term, but as a play ("comedie") with a lofty subject and characters suited to tragedy.

14. *Rhetorica ad Herennium* (*Rhet. Her.*) 1.5; Cicero, *De inventione* (*Inv. rhet.*), 1.15.20.

15. Aristotle, *Rhetoric*, 3.15.1416a; *Rhet. Her.* 1.9; Cf. Cicero, *Inv. rhet.*, 1.17.23–25.

16. Terence Cave, "'Je pareillement . . .': Instances de la première personne chez Rabelais," in *Rabelais: Actes de la journée d'étude du 20 octobre 1995, Cahiers Textuel* 34/44, no. 15 (Paris: Equipe Tradition antique et modernités de l'UFR "Sciences des textes et documents," 1996), 9.

17. See above, Introduction, n2.

18. Richard Regosin, "Opening Discourse," in *François Rabelais: Critical Assessments*, ed. Jean-Claude Carron (Baltimore: Johns Hopkins University Press, 1995), 146.

19. Cicero, *De oratore*, 1.120; *On the Orator, Books 1–2*, trans. E. W. Sutton and H. Rackham (Cambridge, MA: Harvard University Press, 1948), 85.

20. Ibid., 1.122; trans. Sutton, 87.

21. The repetition of "culs" might also be a subtle echo of Matt. 23:24, in which Jesus takes the Pharisees to task: "Duces caeci, excolantes culicem, camelum autem glutientes" [You blind guides! You strain out a gnat but swallow a camel]. Cf. Desiderius Erasmus, *Adages IIviii to IIIiii100*, ed. R. A. B. Mynors, trans. Margaret Mann Phillips, vol. 34 of *Collected Works of Erasmus* (Toronto: University of Toronto Press, 1992), "Culicem colant," chap. 3, cent. 10, adage 91.

22. Randle Cotgrave defines "gens qui regardent par un pertuis" as "Monkes, or Fryers (by reason of their Cowles)"; Cotgrave, *A Dictionarie of the French and English Tongues* (Columbia: University of South Carolina Press, 1950), s.v. "pertuis."

23. See Edwin Duval, "Interpretation and the 'doctrine absconce' of Rabelais's prologue to *Gargantua*," ER 18 (1985): 15, *The Design of Rabelais's Pantagruel* (New Haven, CT: Yale University Press, 1991), 144, and *The Design of Rabelais's Tiers livre de Pantagruel*, ER 34 (Geneva: Droz, 1997), 190–91. See also: François Rigolot, "Hybridity, Exemplarity, and Dialogism in a Historical Perspective: Rabelais's Dialogue on Dialogue with Lucian," in *Der Dialog im Diskursfeld seiner Zeit: Von der Antike bis zur Aufklärung*, eds. Klaus W. Hempfer and Anita Traninger (Stuttgart: Franz Steiner, 2010), 212–14; Antónia Szabari, "Rabelais *Parrhesiastes*: The Rhetoric of Insult and Rabelais's Cynical Mask," *Modern Language Notes* 120 Supplement (2005): S117; Michel Jeanneret, "Signs Gone Wild: The Dismantling of Allegory," in *Critical Assessments*, 57–70; and Erica Weems, "Charity and Interpretation in the *Heptaméron* and the *Tiers Livre*" (PhD diss., Columbia University, 2013). It should be noted that Tristan Vigliano provides a dissenting voice to this kind of reading, as, in his view, nothing could be less charitable than putting the charity of others on trial: see Vigliano, "Pour en finir avec le prologue de *Gargantua*," @nalyses 3.3 (Fall 2008), https://uottawa.scholarsportal.info/ojs/index.php/revue-analyses/article/view/704/605.

24. Guy Demerson, *Humanisme et facétie: Quinze études sur Rabelais* (Caen, France: Paradigme, 1994), 332. See also Gérard Defaux, *Rabelais agonistes: du rieur au prophète* (Geneva: Droz, 1997), 380.

25. *Rhet. Her.* 1.8; *Rhetorica ad Herennium*, trans. Harry Caplan (Cambridge, MA: Harvard University Press, 1954), trans. Caplan, 15. Cf. Cicero, *Inv. rhet.*, 1.16.22.

26. Plautus, *Aulularia*, 3.4.465–71.

27. Cf. John 7:37.

28. Pierre de Ronsard, *Œuvres complètes*, eds. Jean Céard, Daniel Ménager and Michel Simonin, 2 vols. (Paris: Gallimard, 1993–94), 2:1017, lines 29–31. For the banquet *topos*, see Michel Jeanneret, "Banquets poétiques et métaphores alimentaires," in *Ronsard en son IVe centenaire*, vol. 2, eds. Yvonne Bellenger, et al. (Geneva: Droz, 1989), 79.

29. Joachim du Bellay, *Les Antiquités de Rome, Les Regrets*, vol. 2 of *Œuvres poétiques*, ed. Henri Chamard (Paris: STFM, 1993).

30. Bernd Renner, *Difficile est saturam non scribere: L'herméneutique de la satire rabelaisienne*, ER 45 (Geneva: Droz, 2007), 71; Diogenes Laërtius, 6.32. Romain Menini sees this as an allusion to the Diogenes of Lucian's "Philosophies for Sale"; Menini, *Rabelais altérateur: "Græciser en François"* (Paris: Classiques Garnier, 2014), 425–26.

31. Duval, *Design of Rabelais's* Tiers Livre, 17. See also Kaiser, *Praisers of Folly*, 120–21.

32. Ovid, *Metamorphoses*, 11.172–79.

33. Desiderius Erasmus, *Adages Ii1 to Iv100*, ed. R. A. B. Mynors, trans. Margaret Mann Phillips, vol. 31 of *Collected Works of Erasmus* (Toronto: University of Toronto Press, 1982), chap. 1, cent. 4, adage 35.

34. For the nuances of the term "prosopopée" in Rabelais, see Claude La Charité, "La prosopopée chez Rabelais," in *Savoirs et fins de la représentation sous l'Ancien Régime*, eds. Annie Cloutier, Catherine Dubeau, and Pierre-Marc Gendron (Quebec, QC: Les Presses de L'Université Laval, 2005), 9–19, and Blandine Perona, *Prosopopée et persona à la Renaissance* (Paris: Garnier, 2013), 99–127.

35. Menini, *Rabelais altérateur*, 102.

36. Macrobius, *Saturnalia*, 2.5.

37. "Bonnes gens" is also added to the beginning of the prologue of the 1552 *Tiers Livre* (345).

38. Mireille Huchon, *Rabelais grammairien: De l'histoire du texte aux problèmes d'authenticité* (Geneva: Droz, 1981), 450–56.

39. Similarly, Menini argues in *Rabelais altérateur* that the references to beans are inspired by Lucian's denunciation of Pythagoras's beans (which followers of his school were forbidden from eating) as instruments for duping the naive in "Philosophies for Sale" and "The Rooster" (888).

40. These remarks are similar to those of Jean Riolan in the *Methodus medendi* (1548) and Guillaume Rondelet in the *Methodus curandorum omnium morborum* (1556); see Roland Antonioli, *Rabelais et la médecine*, ER 12 (Geneva: Droz, 1976), 210–11. Anne-Pascale Pouey-Mounou sees in them an allusion to Erasmus's 1522 *Epistola apologetica de interdicto esu carnium*; Pouey-Mounou, *Panurge comme lard en pois: Paradoxe, scandale et propriété dans le Tiers Livre*, ER 53 (Geneva: Droz, 2013), 124.

41. Peter Gilman and Abraham C. Keller, "Who is Pantagruel?" *ER* 22 (1988): 77–100, Gilman and Keller, "Rabelais, the 'Grandes Chronicques,' and Jean Lemaire de Belges," *ER* 29 (1993): 93–103, and Gilman and Keller, "The 'Grosses Mesles,'" *ER* 29 (1993): 105–26. For a more solid and accepted account of Lemaire's and Rabelais's commonalities with respect to myth, see Walter Stephens, *Giants in Those Days: Folklore, Ancient History, and Nationalism* (Lincoln: University of Nebraska Press, 1989).

42. See Rabelais, *Œuvres complètes*, 1404n5.

43. Bernd Renner, "'Ni l'un ni l'autre et tous les deux à la fois': Le paradoxe ménippéen inversé dans le *Tiers Livre* de Rabelais," *Romanic Review* 97, no. 2 (2006): 166, and *Difficile est saturam non scribere*, 57. See also: Dorothy Coleman, *Rabelais: A Critical Study in Prose Fiction* (Cambridge: Cambridge University Press, 1971), 84–110; André Tournon, "Le Paradoxe ménippéen dans l'œuvre de Rabelais," *ER* 21 (1988): 309–17; and Marcel Tetel, "Rabelais et Lucien: De deux rhétoriques," in *Rabelais's Incomparable Book*, ed. Raymond C. La Charité (Lexington, KY: French Forum, 1986), 137.

44. Stéphan Geonget, *La notion de perplexité à la Renaissance* (Geneva: Droz, 2006), 381.

Afterword

1. Jules Romains, *Knock, ou le Triomphe de la Médecine*, ed. Annie Angremy (Paris: Gallimard, 1993), act 1, sc. 1, p. 46. Further references to *Knock*, hereafter quoted in text, are to the act, scene, and page number of Angremy's edition.

2. Gérard Gatinot, "*Knock* (ou le triomphe... de la publicité)," *L'Humanité* (Feb. 8, 1960), 2.

3. See, for example, Atul Gawande, "Overkill," *New Yorker* (May 11, 2015).

4. Kenneth Burke, "Literature as Equipment for Living," in *The Philosophy of Literary Form* (Baton Rouge: Louisiana State University Press, 1941), 304.

5. François Rigolot, "Clément Marot et l'émergence de la conscience littéraire à la Renaissance," in *La génération Marot: Poètes français et néo-latins (1515–1550). Actes du Colloque international de Baltimore, 5–7 décembre 1996*, ed. Gérard Defaux (Paris: Champion, 1997), 34. See also Thomas Greene, "The Flexibility of the Self in Renaissance Literature," in *The Disciplines of Criticism: Essays in Literary Theory, Interpretation, and History*, eds. Peter Demetz, Thomas Greene, and Lowry Nelson, Jr. (New Haven, CT: Yale University Press, 1968), 241–64.

Bibliography

Manuscripts

LEMAIRE
Carpentras, Bibliothèque Inguimbertine ms. 412
Burgerbibliothek Bern cod. 241
Rosenbach Museum and Library, ms. 232/II

MAROT
Chantilly ms. 524 (748)

Printed Editions

LEMAIRE

Illustrations
Alphanumeric designations are Abélard's; Munn's alphanumeric designations are also given in parentheses.

A1 (Munn 8): *Les Illustrations de Gaule et Singularitez de Troye.* Lyon: Étienne Baland for Jean Richier, n.d. (May 1511). Bibliothèque Municipale d'Orléans, Rés. E2707.1.

B1 (Munn 10): *Les Illustrations de Gaule et Singularitez de Troye.* Lyon: Étienne Baland for Jacques Maillet, n.d. (May 1511–Nov. 12, 1512). BNF Rés. 4° La² 4A(I); BNF Arsénal 4° H 3663.

C1 (Munn 14): *Les Illustrations de Gaule et Singularitez de Troye.* Paris: Geoffroy de Marnef, Jan. 1512. BNF Rés. 4° La² 3A.

D1 (Munn 12a): *Les Illustrations de Gaule et Singularitez de Troye.* Paris: Geoffroy de Marnef, Sept. 1512. BNF Rés. 4° La² 4 (I); BNF Rés. 4° La² 4α (I).

E1 (Munn 13a): *Les Illustrations de Gaule et Singularitez de Troye.* Paris: Geoffroy de Marnef, Sept. 1512. British Library G.10249 (1).

G1 (Munn 18): *Les Illustrations de Gaule et Singularitez de Troye.* Paris: Enguilbert et Jean de Marnef, 1519. British Library 634.k.6.

H1 (Munn 19a): *Les Illustrations de Gaule et Singularitez de Troye.* Paris: Enguilbert et Jean de Marnef, 1521. BNF Rés. La² 5 (I).

I1 (Munn 21a): *Les Illustrations de Gaule et Singularitez de Troye.* Paris: François Regnault (Shared edition), 1523. BNF Rés. La² 6.

J (Munn 23a): *Les illustrations de Gaule et Singularitez de Troye.* Paris: Philippe Le Noir, Jul. 1524. BNF Rés. La² 8.

L (Munn 27a): *Les Illustrations de Gaule et singularitez de Troye.* Lyon: Antoine du Ry, 1528. ENS LF p 256 8°.

M (Munn 28a): *Les Illustrations de Gaule et singularitez de Troye.* Paris: François Regnault, 1528. BNF La² 8 A; BNF Rés. Ye 998.

N1 (Munn 29a): *Le premier livre des Illustrations de Gaule et Singularitez de Troye.* Paris: (Julien Hubert for) Ambroise Girault, 1529. British Library C 39 g 4.

O (Munn 30): *Les troys Livres des Illustrations de Gaule et singularitez de Troye.* Paris: Pierre Vidoue for Galliot du Pré, 1531. BNF Rés. La² 10.

Z (Munn 49): *Les illustrations de Gaule et Singularitez de Troye.* Paris: François Regnault, n.d. (1533–34?). BNF Rés. La² 7.

P (Munn 33): *Le premier livre des Illustrations de Gaule et Singularitez de Troye.* Paris: Nicolas Higman for Ambroise Girault, 1533. BNF Rés. La² 11.

Q (Munn 37): *Les Illustrations de Gaule et Singularitez de Troye.* Paris: Jean Longis (Shared edition), 1540. Princeton University Library 3217.58.349.

R (Munn 45): *Les Illustrations de Gaule et Singularitez de Troye.* Paris: Jean Réal for Jean Bonfons (Shared edition), 1548. BNF Rés. 4° La² 12.

S (Munn 47): *Les Illustrations de Gaule et Singularitez de Troye, par maistre Jean le Maire de Belges. Avec la Couronne Margaritique, et plusieurs autres oeuvres de luy, non jamais encore imprimees.* Lyon: Jean de Tournes, 1549. ENS H F omc 1 F°.

Recueil-Epistre

Letter designations are those found in *Epistre du roy à Hector et autres pièces de circonstances (1511–1513)*, ed. Armstrong and Britnell; Munn's alphanumeric designations are also given in parentheses.

A (Munn 12e): *Lepistre du Roy a Hector de Troye. Et aucunes aultres oeuvres Assez dignes de veoir.* Paris: For Geoffroy de Marnef, Aug. 1513. BNF Rés 8° Z Don 594(566); BNF Vélins 1175; Folger Shakespeare Library 234–555q.

B (Munn 12e): *LEpistre du Roy a Hector de Troye. Et aucunes aultres oeuvres Assez dignes de veoir.* Paris: For Geoffroy de Marnef, Aug. 1513. BNF Arsénal 4° H 3663.

C (Munn 13/16): *Lepistre du Roy a Hector de Troye. Et aucunes oeuvres Assez dignes de veoir.* Paris: (Nicolas Higman for) Geoffroy de Marnef, Jul. 1516. British Library G.10249(6).

E (Munn 18): *Lepistre du Roy a Hector de Troye. Et aucunes aultres oeuvres Assez dignes de veoir.* Paris: For Enguilbert and Jean de Marnef, Aug. 1519. British Library 634.k.6.

F (Munn 19e/20e): *LEpistre du Roy a Hector de Troye. Et aucunes autres oeuvres assez dignes de veoir.* Paris: For Enguilbert and Jean de Marnef, Aug. 1521. BNF Rés. La² 5(5).

G (Munn 21e): *LEpistre du Roy a Hector de Troye. Et aucunes autres oeuvres assez dignes de veoir.* Paris: For François Regnault, 1523. BNF Rés. La² 6(4).

J (Munn 23d): *LEpistre du roy a hector de troye et aucunes autres oeuvres assez dignes de veoir*. Paris: Philippe Le Noir, Jul. 1524. BNF Rés. La² 8.

L (Munn 27d): *Lepistre du roy a Hector de troye. Et aulcunes aultres oeuvres assez dignes de veoir*. Lyon: Antoine du Ry, 1528. ENS LF p 256 8°.

M (Munn 28e): *Lepistre du Roy a Hector de Troye et aucunes autres oeuvres assez dignes de veoir*. Paris: François Regnault, 1528. BNF Rés. Ye 998.

N (Munn 29d): *LEpistre du roy a Hector de troye. Et aucunes aultres Oeuvres assez dignes de veoir*. Paris: (Julien Hubert for) Ambroise Girault, 1529. Princeton University Library 3217.58.349.1528.

Z (Munn 49d): *LEpistre du roy a Hector de troye*. Paris: François Regnault, n.d. (1533–34?). BNF Rés. La² 7.

P (Munn 33e): *Lepistre du roy a Hector de Troye et aucunes autres oeuvres assez dignes de veoir*. Paris: Nicolas Higman for Ambroise Girault, 1533. BNF Rés. La² 11.

Q (Munn 37e): *Sensuit Lepistre du roy a Hector de Troye, et aulcunes aultres oeuvres assez dignes de veoir*. Paris: Jean Longis (Shared edition), 1540. Princeton University Library 3217.58.349.

R (Munn 45): *Sensuit Lepistre du roy, envoyee a Hector de Troye, et aulcunes aultres œuvres assez dignes de veoir*. Paris: Jean Réal for Jean Bonfons (Shared edition), 1548. BNF Rés. 4° La² 12.

S (Munn 47): *Les Illustrations de Gaule et Singularitez de Troye, par maistre Jean le Maire de Belges. Avec la Couronne Margaritique, et plusieurs autres oeuvres de luy, non jamais encore imprimees*. Lyon: Jean de Tournes, 1549. ENS H F omc 1 F°.

MAROT

Numbers are those found in Mayer, *Bibliographie des éditions de Clément Marot publiées au XVIe siècle*. The Rutgers editions, not listed in Mayer, are designated R1 and R2. For a summary of contents of unauthorized editions, see above, Appendix.

6. *Les Opuscules et petits Traictez*. Lyon: Olivier Arnoullet, n.d. (1530–31). BNF Rés. p Ye 736.

9. *Ladolescence clementine*. Paris: Geoffroy Tory for Pierre Roffet, Aug. 12, 1532. BNF Rés. Ye 1532.

11. *Ladolescence clementine*. Paris: Geoffroy Tory for Pierre Roffet, Nov. 13, 1532. BNF Rés. Ye 1533.

12. *Ladolescence clementine*. Paris: Geoffroy Tory for Pierre Roffet, Feb. 12, 1533. BNF Rés Ye 1535.

13. *Ladolescence clementine*. Lyon: François Juste, Feb. 23, 1533. BNF Rothschild 597 (IV.5.41).

14. *Ladolescence clementine*. Paris: Geoffroy Tory for Pierre Roffet, Jun. 7, 1533. BNF Rés. Ye 1537.

14bis. *Ladolescence clementine*. Lyon: François Juste, Jul. 12, 1533. Munich, Bayerische Staatsbibliothek Rar. 1780.

15. *La Suite de l'adolescence Clementine*. Paris: (Louis Cyaneus for) the widow of Pierre Roffet, n.d. (late 1533—early 1534). BNF Rés. Ye 1534; BNF Rés. Ye 1536.

16. *L'Adolescence clementine*. Paris: Louis Cyaneus for the widow of Pierre Roffet, Mar. 7, 1534. BNF Arsénal Rés. 8° BL 8712; BNF Rothschild 601 (II.5.37).
17. *La Suite de l'Adolescence Clementine*. Paris: Louis Cyaneus for the widow of Pierre Roffet, n.d. (1534). BNF Rothschild 601 (II.5.37).
19. *L'Adolescence clementine*. Paris: Louis Cyaneus for the widow of Pierre Roffet, Aug. 19, 1534. BNF Rés. Ye 1561.
20. *La Suite de l'Adolescence Clementine*. Paris: (Louis Cyaneus for) the widow of Pierre Roffet, 1534. BNF Rés. Ye 1562.
R1. *Ladolescence Clementine*. N.p. (Lyon: Denis de Harsy), 1534. Rutgers University Library SPCOL X PQ1635.A6 1534.
24. *Ladolescence clementine*. Lyon: François Juste, Dec. 12, 1534. BNF Rothschild 600 (II.7.28).
25. *La suyte de ladolescence Clementine*. Lyon: François Juste, 1534. BNF Rothschild 600 (II.7.28).
31. *Ladolescence clementine*. Lyon: François Juste, Feb. 6, 1535. BNF Rothschild 602 (II.7.27).
32. *L'Adolescence clementine*. Paris: The widow of Pierre Roffet, Jun. 20, 1535. BNF Arsénal Rés. 8° BL 8713.
33. *La Suite de l'Adolescence Clementine*. Paris: The widow of Pierre Roffet, 1535. BNF Arsénal Rés. 8° BL 8713.
34. *La suyte de ladolescence Clementine*. Lyon: François Juste, 1535. BNF Rothschild 602 (II.7.27).
R1. *La suyte de ladolescence Clementine*. N.p. (Lyon: Denis de Harsy), 1535. Rutgers University Library SPCOL X PQ1635.A6 1534.
R2. *Ladolescence Clementine*. N.p. (Lyon: Denis de Harsy), 1535. Rutgers University Library SPCOL X PQ1637.M3A6 1535.
R2. *La Suyte de Ladolescence Clementine*. N.p. (Lyon: Denis de Harsy), 1535. Rutgers University Library SPCOL X PQ1637.M3A6 1535.
36. *Ladolescence clementine*. Paris: The widow of Pierre Roffet, 1536. BNF Rés. p Ye 664.
36. *La Suite de ladolescence Clementine*. Paris: The widow of Pierre Roffet, 1536. BNF Rés. p Ye 664.
38. *Ladolescence clementine*. Paris: Antoine Bonnemère, 1536. BNF Rés. Ye 1539.
39. *La suite de ladolescence clementine*. Paris: Antoine Bonnemère, 1536. BNF Rés. Ye 1540.
55. *Ladolescence Clementine*. N.p. (Paris: Denis Janot), 1537. BNF Rés. Ye 1542.
56. *La suyte de Ladolescence Clementine*. N.p. (Paris: Denis Janot), 1537. BNF Rés. Ye 1543.
58. *Ladolescence Clementine*. N.p. (Lyon: Denis de Harsy), 1537. BNF Rés. Ye 1547.
59. *La suyte de Ladolescence Clementine*. N.p. (Lyon: Denis de Harsy), 1537. BNF Rés. Ye 1548.
63. *Ladolescence Clementine*. Paris: Denis Janot, 1538. BNF Rés. Ye 1551.
64. *La suyte de l'adolescence Clementine*. Paris: Denis Janot, 1538. BNF Rés. Ye 1552.

66. *Ladolescence clementine*. Paris: Antoine Bonnemère, 1538. BNF Rothschild 604 (II.5.44).
67. *La suite de ladolescence clementine*. Paris: Pierre Sergent, 1538. BNF Rothschild 604 (II.5.44).
70. *Les Oeuvres de Clement Marot*. Lyon: (François Juste for) Étienne Dolet, 1538. BNF Rés. Ye 1457–1460.
71. *Les Oeuvres de Clement Marot*. Lyon: (François Juste for) Sébastien Gryphe, 1538. BNF Rés. Ye 1461–1464.

RABELAIS

Numbers and abbreviated titles are those assigned by Rawles and Screech in the *NRB*; Plan's numbers are also given in parentheses wherever applicable.

1 (Plan 18). *Pantagruel*. Lyon: Claude Nourry, n.d. (1531 or 1532). BNF Rés. $Y^2$2146.
3 (Plan 20). *Pantagruel*. N.p. (Paris or Poitiers, Jean and Enguilbert de Marnef), 1533. BNF Rés. $Y^2$2147.
4 (Plan 19). *Pantagruel*. Paris: Jean Longis, n.d. BNF Rothschild 1508 (II.5.38).
5 (Plan 21). *Pantagruel*. N.p., n.d. (Late 1533, early 1534?). BNF Rés. $Y^2$2143.
6. *Pantagruel*. N.p., n.d. British Library G10420.
8 (Plan 24). *Pantagruel*. Lyon: François Juste, 1534. BNF Rothschild 3063 (VI.2.35).
12 (Plan 39). *Pantagruel*. Lyon: François Juste, 1542. BNF Rés. $Y^2$2135.
13 (Plan 41 and 48). *Pantagruel, Pantagrueline prognostication, Navigation*. Lyon: Étienne Dolet, 1542. BNF Rés. $Y^2$2145.
19 (Plan 31). *Gargantua*. N.p., n.d. (Lyon: François Juste, 1534–35). BNF Rés. $Y^2$2126.
20 (Plan 32). *Gargantua*. Lyon: François Juste, 1535. BNF Rés. $Y^2$2130.
23 (Plan 38). *Gargantua*. Lyon: François Juste, 1542. BNF Rés. $Y^2$2134.
24 (Plan 40). *Gargantua*. Lyon: Étienne Dolet, 1542. BNF Rés. $Y^2$2144.
26 (Plan 42 and 43). *Gargantua, Pantagruel, Pantagrueline prognostication*. N.p., 1542. BNF Rés. $Y^2$2137–38.
27 (Plan 86). *Gargantua, Pantagruel, Pantagrueline progostication*. Lyon: Pierre de Tours, n.d. BNF Rés. $Y^2$2140.
28 (Plan 67). *Tiers Livre*. Paris: Chrestien Wechel, 1546. BNF Rés. $Y^2$2159.
29 (Plan 71). *Tiers Livre*. Lyon: n.n., 1546. BNF Rothschild 3199 (IV.9.58).
31 (Plan 68 and 69). *Tiers Livre*. Paris: n.n., 1546. BNF Rothschild 1512 (VI.2.52).
32 (Plan 72). *Tiers Livre*. Lyon: n.n. (Pierre de Tours?), 1547. BNF Rés. $Y^2$2161.
33 (Plan 86). *Tiers Livre*. Lyon: Pierre de Tours, n.d. BNF Rés. $Y^2$2141.
36 (Plan 74). *Tiers Livre*. Paris: Michel Fezandat, 1552. BNF Rés. $Y^2$2162.
37 (Plan 75). *Tiers Livre*. Lyon: Jean Chabin (i.e. Paris, n.n.), 1552. BNF Rés. $Y^2$2163.
41 (Plan 77). *Quart Livre*. Lyon: n.n. (Pierre de Tours), 1548. BNF Rés. $Y^2$2160bis.
42 (Plan 76). *Quart Livre*. Lyon: n.n. (Pierre de Tours), 1548. BNF Rothschild 1513 (V.7.78).
45 (Plan 78). *Quart Livre*. Paris: Michel Fezandat, 1552. BNF Rothschild 1514 (VI.4.50).
46 (Plan 78). *Quart Livre*. Paris: Michel Fezandat, 1552. BNF Rés. $Y^2$2164.

48 (Plan 81). *Quart Livre.* Lyon: Baltasar Aleman, 1552. BNF Arsénal 8° BL 19595 Rés.
52 (Plan 83). *Quart Livre.* N.p. (Paris), 1553. BNF Rés. Y²2167.
53 (Plan 87). *L'isle Sonante.* N.p., 1562. BNF Rés. pY²1349.
54 (Plan 88). *Cinquiesme Livre.* N.p., 1564. BNF Rés. Y²2168.
55 (Plan 89). *Cinquiesme Livre.* N.p. (Paris?), 1565. BNF Rés. Y²2171.
56 (Plan 90). *Cinquiesme Livre.* Lyon: Jean Martin, 1565. BNF Rés. Y²2170.

OTHER PRINTED WORKS

Castiglione, Baldassare. *Le Courtisan de messire Baltazar de Castillon nouvellement reveu et corrigé.* Trans. Jacques Colin. Ed. Étienne Dolet. Lyon: François Juste, 1538. BNF Rés. R. 2049.
Estienne, Robert. *Dictionnaire françois-latin.* Paris: Robert Estienne, 1549.
Grévin, Jacques. *Deux livres des venins, ausquels il est amplement discouru des bestes venimeuses, theriaques, poisons, et contrepoisons.* Antwerp: Christophe Plantin, 1568. University of Pennsylvania Libraries Special Collections FC55 G8694 568d.
Marguerite de Navarre. *Le miroir de tres chrestienne princesse Marguerite de France, royne de Navarre, duchesse d'Alençon et de Berry, auquel elle voit son neant et son tout.* Paris: Antoine Auguereau, 1533. BNF Rés. Ye 1631.
Tory, Geoffroy. *Champ Fleury.* Paris: Geoffroy Tory and Giles Gourmont, 1529. BNF Rés. V. 595.
Le Triumphe de l'Amant Vert. Paris: Denis Janot, 1535. BNF Rés. Ye 1389.

Critical Editions

Aristotle. *The Complete Works of Aristotle.* Vol. 2. Edited by Jonathan Barnes. Bollingen Series. Princeton: Princeton University Press, 1984.
Boccaccio, Giovanni. *Opere.* Vols. 7–8. Edited by Vittore Branca. Milan: Mondadori, 1998.
Celsus. *On Medicine.* Vol. 2. Translated by W. G. Spencer. LCL 304. Cambridge: Harvard University Press, 1938.
Chaucer, Geoffrey. *The Riverside Chaucer.* 3rd ed. Edited by Larry D. Benson. Oxford: Oxford University Press, 2008.
Cicero. *On Invention, Best Kind of Orator, Topics.* Translated by H. M. Hubbell. LCL 386. Cambridge: Harvard University Press, 1949.
———. *On the Orator, Books 1–2.* Translated by E. W. Sutton and H. Rackham. LCL 348. Cambridge: Harvard University Press, 1948.
———. "Orator." Translated by H. M. Hubbell. In *Cicero,* vol. 5. LCL 342, 295–509. Cambridge: Harvard University Press, 1962.
[Cicero]. *Rhetorica ad Herennium.* Translated by Harry Caplan. LCL 403. Cambridge: Harvard University Press, 1954.
Cretin, Guillaume. *Œuvres poétiques.* Edited by Kathleen Chesney. Paris: Firmin-Didot et Cie, 1932.

Diogenes Laërtius. *Lives of Eminent Philosophers.* Vol. 2. Translated by R. D. Hicks. *LCL* 185. Cambridge: Harvard University Press, 1925.

Le Disciple de Pantagruel. Edited by Guy Demerson and Christiane Lauvergnat-Gagnière. Paris: STFM, 1982.

Droz, Eugénie, ed. *Le Recueil Trepperel: Les sotties.* Paris: Droz, 1935.

Du Bellay, Joachim. *Les Antiquités de Rome, Les Regrets. Œuvres poétiques,* vol. 2. Edited by Henri Chamard. Paris: STFM, 1993.

Erasmus, Desiderius. *Adages Ii1 to Iv100.* Edited by R. A. B. Mynors. Translated by Margaret Mann Phillips. Vol. 31 of *The Collected Works of Erasmus.* Toronto: University of Toronto Press, 1982.

———. *Adages Ivi1 to Ix100,* Edited by R. A. B. Mynors. Translated by Margaret Mann Phillips. Vol. 32 of *The Collected Works of Erasmus.* Toronto: University of Toronto Press, 1989.

———. *Adages IIi1 to IIvi100,* Edited by R. A. B. Mynors. Translated by Margaret Mann Phillips. Vol. 33 of *The Collected Works of Erasmus.* Toronto: University of Toronto Press, 1991.

———. *Adages IIvii1 to IIIiii100,* Edited by R. A. B. Mynors. Translated by Margaret Mann Phillips. Vol. 34 of *The Collected Works of Erasmus.* Toronto: University of Toronto Press, 1992.

———. *Adages IIIiv1 to IVii100.* Edited by John N. Grant. Translated by Denis L. Drysdall. Vol. 35 of *The Collected Works of Erasmus.* Toronto: University of Toronto Press, 2005.

———. *Declamatio de pueris statim ac liberaliter instituendis.* Edited and translated by Jean-Claude Margolin. Geneva: Droz, 1966.

———. *Opus epistolarum Des. Erasmi Roterodami.* Vol. 1. Edited by P. S. Allen. Oxford: Clarendon, 1906.

———. "Paraclesis." In *Ausgewählte Werke,* edited by Hajo Holborn and Annemarie Holborn, 139–49. Munich: C. H. Beck'sche, 1933.

———. "Paraclesis." In *Christian Humanism and The Reformation: Selected Writings,* edited and translated by John C. Olin, 92–106. Gloucester: Peter Smith, 1973.

Fabri, Pierre. *Le grand et vrai art de pleine rhétorique.* Edited by A. Héron. Geneva: Slatkine Reprints, 1969.

Franklin, Alfred, ed. *La vie privée d'autrefois: L'annonce et la réclame.* Paris: Plon, 1887.

Fulgentius. *Opera.* Edited by Rudolf Helm. Leipzig: Teubner, 1898.

Héroët, Antoine. *La Parfaicte Amye.* Edited by Christine M. Hill. Exeter: University of Exeter, 1981.

Horace. *Satires, Epistles, Ars Poetica.* Translated by H. R. Fairclough. *LCL* 194. Cambridge: Harvard University Press, 1929.

Lemaire de Belges, Jean. *La Concorde des deux langages.* Edited by Jean Frappier. Geneva: Droz, 1947.

———. *La Concorde du genre humain.* Edited by Pierre Jodogne. Brussels: Académie Royale de Belgique, 1964.

———. "Epistre du roy à Hector" et autres pièces de circonstances (1511–1513). Edited by Adrian Armstrong and Jennifer Britnell. Paris: STFM, 2000.

———. Les Épîtres de l'Amant Vert. Edited by Jean Frappier. Geneva: Droz, 1948.

———. La Légende des Vénitiens. Edited by Anne Schoysman. Brussels: Académie Royale de Belgique, 1999.

———. Lettres missives et épîtres dédicatoires. Edited by Anne Schoysman. Brussels: Académie Royale de Belgique, 2012.

———. Œuvres. Edited by J. Stecher. 4 vols. Geneva: Slatkine Reprints, 1969.

———. Le Temple d'Honneur et de Vertus. Edited by Henri Hornik. Geneva: Droz, 1957.

———. Traicté de la différence des schismes et des conciles de l'Église. Edited by Jennifer Britnell. Geneva: Droz, 1997.

Lorris, Guillaume, and Jean de Meun. Le Roman de la Rose. Edited by Armand Strubel. Paris: LGF, 1992.

Lucian of Samosata. "How to Write History." In *Lucian*, vol. 6. Translated by K. Kilburn. LCL 430, 1–73. London: William Heinemann, 1959.

———. "Philosophies for Sale." In *Lucian*, vol. 2. Translated by A. M. Harmon. LCL 54, 449–511. London: William Heinemann, 1953.

———. "To One Who Said, 'You're a Prometheus in Words.'" In *Lucian*, vol. 6. Translated by K. Kilburn. LCL 430, 418–27. London: William Heinemann, 1959.

———. "A True Story." In *Lucian*, vol. 1. Translated by A. M. Harmon. LCL 14, 249–357. London: William Heinemann, 1953.

Lucretius. On the Nature of Things. Translated by W. H. D. Rouse. Revised by Martin F. Smith. LCL 181. Cambridge: Harvard University Press, 1992.

Macrobius. Saturnalia. Vol. 1. Translated by Robert A. Kaster. LCL 510. Cambridge: Harvard University Press, 2011.

Mantuan. Adulescentia: The Eclogues of Mantuan. Edited and translated by Lee Piepho. New York: Garland, 1989.

Marcourt, Antoine. Le Livre des Marchans d'Antoine Marcourt: Une satire anticléricale au service de la Réforme. Edited by Geneviève Gross. Paris: Champion, 2016.

Marot, Clément. L'Adolescence clémentine. Edited by Frank Lestringant. Paris: Gallimard, 1987.

———. Œuvres complètes. Edited by Claude Mayer. 5 vols. London: Athlone Press, 1958–70.

———. Œuvres complètes. Edited by François Rigolot. 2 vols. Paris: Garnier, 2007–9.

———. Œuvres poétiques complètes. Edited by Gérard Defaux. 2 vols. Paris: Bordas, 1990–93.

———. Recueil inédit offert au Connétable de Montmorency en mars 1538. Edited by François Rigolot. Geneva: Droz, 2010.

Montaiglon, Anatole de, ed. Recueil de poésies françoises des XVe et XVIe siècles. 13 vols. Paris: P. Jannet, 1855–78.

Montaigne, Michel de. The Complete Essays of Montaigne. Translated by Donald M. Frame. Stanford: Stanford University Press, 1958.

———. *Les Essais.* Edited by Pierre Villey. Revised by V.-L. Saulnier. Paris: PUF, 2004.
Ovid. *Heroides and Amores.* Translated by Grant Showerman. Revised by G. P. Goold. LCL 41. Cambridge: Harvard University Press, 1977.
———. *Metamorphoses.* Edited by R. J. Tarrant. Oxford: Clarendon, 2004.
Petrarch, Francesco. *Petrarch's Lyric Poems: The Rime Sparse and Other Lyrics.* Translated by Robert M. Durling. Cambridge: Harvard University Press, 1976.
Phaedrus. *Phaedri fabulae aesopiae.* Edited by John Percival Postgate. Oxford: Clarendon, 1919.
Pico della Mirandola, Giovanni. "Oration on the Dignity of Man." Translated by Elizabeth Livermore Forbes. In *The Renaissance Philosophy of Man,* edited by Ernst Cassirer, Paul Oskar Kristeller, and John Herman Randall, Jr., 213–54. Chicago: University of Chicago Press, 1948.
Plato. "Symposium." Translated by Michael Joyce. In *The Collected Dialogues of Plato,* edited by Edith Hamilton and Huntington Cairns, Bollingen Series, 526–74. Princeton: Princeton University Press, 1961.
Plautus. "Aulularia." In *Plautus, vol. 1.* Translated by Paul Nixon. LCL 60, 231–323. London: William Heinemann, 1956.
Pliny the Elder. *Natural History.* 10 vols. LCL 353. Cambridge: Harvard University Press, 1940.
Quintilian. *The Orator's Education, Books 3–5.* Edited and translated by Donald A. Russell. LCL 125. Cambridge: Harvard University Press, 2001.
Rabelais, François. *The Complete Works of François Rabelais.* Translated by Donald M. Frame. Berkeley: University of California Press, 1991.
———. *Gargantua and Pantagruel.* Translated by M. A. Screech. London: Penguin, 2006.
———. *Œuvres complètes.* Edited by Mireille Huchon. Paris: Gallimard, 1994.
Romains, Jules. *Knock, ou le Triomphe de la Médecine.* Edited by Annie Angremy. Paris: Gallimard, 1993.
Ronsard, Pierre de. *Œuvres complètes.* Edited by Jean Céard, Daniel Ménager and Michel Simonin. 2 vols. Paris: Gallimard, 1993–94.
Sébillet, Thomas. *Art poétique françoys.* Edited by Félix Gaiffe. Paris: Droz, 1932.
Tissier, André, ed. *Recueil de farces (1450–1550).* 13 vols. Geneva: Droz, 1989.
Statius. *Silvae.* Translated by D. R. Shackleton Bailey. LCL 206. Cambridge: Harvard University Press, 2003.
Virgil. *Opera.* Edited by F. A. Hirtzel. Oxford: Clarendon, 1900.

Secondary Works

Abélard, Jacques. *Les Illustrations de Gaule et singularitez de Troye de Jean Lemaire de Belges: Etude des éditions—Genèse de l'œuvre.* Geneva: Droz, 1976.
———. "Les *Illustrations de Gaule* de Jean Lemaire de Belges: Quelle Gaule? Quelle France? Quelle nation?" *Nouvelle Revue du Seizième Siècle* 13, no. 1 (1995): 7–27.

Ahmed, Ehsan. *Clément Marot: The Mirror of the Prince.* Charlottesville: Rookwood Press, 2005.
Alduy, Cécile. "*L'Adolescence* de Marot mise en recueil: ordre du livre, fiction d'auteur." *L'Information littéraire* 58, no. 3 (2006): 10–18.
Antonioli, Roland. *Rabelais et la médecine. ER* 12. Geneva: Droz, 1976.
Armstrong, Adrian. "Is This an Ex-Parrot? The Printed Afterlife of Jean Lemaire de Belges' *Epîtres de l'Amant Vert*." *Journal de la Renaissance* 5 (2007): 323–36.
———. "Paratexte et autorité(s) chez les Grands Rhétoriqueurs." In Bessire, *L'Écrivain éditeur*, 61–89.
———. "Prosimètre et savoir." In *Le prosimètre à la Renaissance*, 125–42. Paris: Éditions Rue d'Ulm, 2005.
———. "Songe, vision, savoir: l'onirique et l'épistémique chez Molinet et Lemaire de Belges." *Zeitschrift für romanische Philologie* 123, no. 1 (2007): 50–68.
———. *Technique and Technology: Script, Print, and Poetics in France, 1470–1550.* Oxford: Clarendon, 2000.
———. "Yearning and Learning: Spaces of Desire in Jean Lemaire de Belges' *Concorde des deux langages* (1511)." In *The Erotics of Consolation: Desire and Distance in the Late Middle Ages*, edited by Catherine E. Léglu and Stephen J. Milner, 79–94. New York: Palgrave, 2008.
Armstrong, Adrian, and Sarah Kay. *Knowing Poetry: Verse in Medieval France from the "Rose" to the "Rhétoriqueurs."* Ithaca: Cornell University Press, 2011.
Armstrong, Elizabeth. *Before Copyright: The French Book-Privilege System, 1498–1526.* Cambridge: Cambridge University Press, 1990.
Bakhtin, Mikhail. *Rabelais and His World.* Translated by Hélène Iswolsky. Bloomington: Indiana University Press, 1984.
Baudrier, H.-L. *Bibliographie lyonnaise.* 12 vols. Lyon: Librairie ancienne d'Auguste Brun, 1895–1921.
Baudrillard, Jean. *Le système des objets.* Paris: Gallimard, 1968.
Bauer, Franck. "Ballades clémentines: L'ordre du sens." In Vignes, *En relisant L'Adolescence Clémentine*, 137–152.
Baumgartner, Frederic J. *Louis XII.* New York: St. Martin's, 1994.
Bauschatz, Cathleen M. "'Une description du jeu de paulme soubz obscures parolles': The Portrayal of Reading in *Pantagruel* and *Gargantua*." *ER* 22 (1988): 57–76.
———. "From 'estudier et profiter' to 'instruire et plaire': Didacticism in Rabelais's *Pantagruel* and *Gargantua*." *Modern Language Studies* 19, no. 1 (Winter 1989): 37–49.
Beard, Jennifer J. "Letters from the Elysian Fields: A Group of Poems for Louis XII." *BHR* 31 (1969): 27–38.
Becker, Philipp August. *Jean Lemaire: Der erste humanistische Dichter Frankreichs.* Strasbourg: Karl J. Trübner, 1893.
Béné, Charles A. "Erasme et le Chapitre VIII du premier *Pantagruel*." *Paedagogica historica* 1, no. 1 (1961): 39–66.
Berger, John. *Ways of Seeing.* London: BBC and Penguin, 1977.

Bergweiler, Ulrike. *Die Allegorie im Werk von Jean Lemaire de Belges*. Geneva: Droz, 1976.
Berrong, Richard M. "Les *Illustrations de Gaule et singularitez de Troye*: Jean Lemaire de Belges' Ambivalent View of 'Eloquence.'" *Studi Francesi* 78 (Sept.–Dec. 1982): 399–407.
Berthon, Guillaume. "Clément Marot et la tentation biographique." *Cahiers parisiens* 4 (2008): 541–51.
———. *L'Intention du poète: Clément Marot "autheur"*. Paris: Garnier, 2014.
———. "'L'intention du Poète': Du pupitre à la presse, Clément Marot *autheur*." PhD diss., Université Paris-Sorbonne, 2010.
Bertin, Annie. "Les couleurs dans *L'Adolescence clémentine*." In Dauphiné and Mironneau, *À propos de* L'Adolescence clémentine, 41–55.
Bessire, François, ed. *L'Écrivain éditeur*. Vol. 1. Geneva: Droz, 2001.
Blum, Claude. "'L'ordre de mes livres': Les *Ballades* dans *L'Adolescence clémentine* de Marot." In *Désirs et plaisirs du livre: Hommage à Robert Kopp*, edited by Regina Bollhalder Mayer, Olivier Millet and André Vanoncini, 69–80. Paris: Champion, 2004.
Booth, Wayne C. *The Rhetoric of Fiction*. 2nd ed. Chicago: University of Chicago Press, 1983.
Brault, Gerard J. "Ung abysme de science." *BHR* 28 (1966): 615–32.
Britnell, Jennifer. "La mort de Jean Lemaire de Belges, l'édition de 1514 du *Traité des schismes et des conciles*, et les impertinences d'un éditeur." *BHR* 56, no. 1 (1994): 127–33.
Brown, Cynthia J. "Jean Lemaire's *La concorde des deux langages*: The Merging of Politics, Language and Poetry." *Fifteenth Century Studies* 3 (1980): 29–39.
———. *Poets, Patrons and Printers: Crisis of Authority in Late Medieval France*. Ithaca: Cornell University Press, 1995.
———. *The Shaping of History and Poetry in Late Medieval France: Propaganda and Artistic Expression in the Works of the Rhétoriqueurs*. Birmingham: Summa, 1985.
Burke, Kenneth. "Literature as Equipment for Living." In *The Philosophy of Literary Form*, 293–304. Baton Rouge: Louisiana State University Press, 1941.
Butterworth, Emily. *The Unbridled Tongue: Babble and Gossip in Renaissance France*. Oxford: Oxford University Press, 2016.
Campangne, Hervé. *Mythologie et rhétorique aux XVe et XVIe siècles en France*. Paris: Champion, 1996.
Carron, Jean-Claude, ed. *François Rabelais: Critical Assessments*. Baltimore: Johns Hopkins University Press, 1995.
Catach, Nina. *L'Orthographe française à l'époque de la Renaissance*. Geneva: Droz, 1968.
Cathélat, Bernard. *Publicité et société*. Paris: Payot, 1987.
Cave, Terence. "'Je pareillement . . .': Instances de la première personne chez Rabelais." In *Rabelais: Actes de la journée d'étude du 20 octobre 1995*. Cahiers Textuel 34/44, no. 15, 9–18. Paris: Equipe Tradition antique et modernités de l'UFR "Sciences des textes et documents," 1996.

---. *Pré-Histoires II: Langues étrangères et troubles économiques au XVIe siècle*. Geneva: Droz, 2001.

Cave, Terence, Michel Jeanneret, and François Rigolot. "Sur la prétendue transparence de Rabelais." *Revue d'Histoire Littéraire de la France* 86, no. 4 (Jul.–Aug. 1986): 709–16.

Cerquiglini-Toulet, Jacqueline. "Clément Marot et la critique littéraire et textuelle: Du bien renommé au mal imprimé Villon." In Defaux and Simonin, *"Prince des poëtes françois,"* 157–64.

Chang, Leah L. *Into Print: The Production of Female Authorship in Early Modern France*. Newark: University of Delaware Press, 2009.

Chartier, Roger. *L'ordre des livres: Lecteurs, auteurs, bibliothèques en Europe entre XIVe et XVIIIe siècle*. Aix-en-Provence: Alinéa, 1992.

Chiron, Pascale. "L'édition des *Œuvres* de Villon annotée par Clément Marot, ou comment l'autorité vient au texte." *Littératures classiques* 64 (Spring 2008): 33–51.

Chiron, Pascale, and Grantley McDonald. "The Testament of Jean Lemaire, 1524." *BHR* 71, no. 3 (2009): 527–33.

Christie, Richard Copley. *Étienne Dolet: The Martyr of the Renaissance*. London: MacMillan, 1880.

Claivaz, David. *Ce que j'ay oublié d'y mettre: Essai sur l'invention poétique dans les coq-à-l'âne de Clément Marot*. Fribourg: Éditions Universitaires, 2000.

Colard, Jean-Max. "L'apparition du paratexte." In *L'inscription du regard: Moyen Âge, Renaissance*, edited by Michèle Gally and Michel Jourde, 315–36. Fontenay-aux-Roses: ENS éditions, 1995.

---. "L'écriture comme 'passetemps.'" In Perrier, *Clément Marot*, 81–92.

Coleman, Dorothy. *Rabelais: A Critical Study in Prose Fiction*. Cambridge: Cambridge University Press, 1981.

Conley, Tom. "Un tombeau de mélanges: Les 'Epistres de l'amant vert' dans le livre imprimé des *Illustrations de Gaule et singularitez de Troie* (1512–1513)." In *Ouvrages miscellanées et théories de la connaissance à la Renaissance*, edited by Dominique de Courcelles, 79–101. Paris: Ecole Nationale des Chartes, 2003.

Cooper, Richard. "L'authenticité du *Cinquiesme Livre*: État présent de la question." In *Le Cinquiesme Livre: Actes du colloque internationale de Rome (16–19 octobre 1998)*, edited by Franco Giacone, 9–22. Geneva: Droz, 2001.

---. *Litterae in tempore belli: études sur les relations littéraires italo-françaises pendant les guerres d'Italie*. Geneva: Droz, 1997.

Cornilliat, François. "'Comme ung aultre Ilïon': Échec poétique et Renaissance lyonnaise dans *La concorde des deux langages*." In Defaux, *Lyon et l'illustration*, 363–90.

---. "On Words and Meaning in Rabelais Criticism." *ER* 35 (1998): 7–28.

---. *Or ne mens: Couleurs de l'Éloge et du Blâme chez les "Grands Rhétoriqueurs."* Paris: Champion, 1994.

---. *Sujet caduc, noble sujet: La poésie de la Renaissance et le choix de ses arguments*. Geneva: Droz, 2009.

Cotgrave, Randle. *A Dictionarie of the French and English Tongues*. Columbia: University of South Carolina Press, 1950.

Cottrell, Robert D. "Allegories of Desire in Lemaire's *Concorde des deux langages*." *French Forum* 23, no. 3 (Sept. 1998): 261–300.

Cowell, Andrew. "Advertising, Rhetoric, and Literature: A Medieval Response to Contemporary Theory." *Poetics Today* 22, no. 4 (Winter 2001): 795–827.

Cowling, David. *Building the Text: Architecture as Metaphor in Late Medieval and Early Modern France*. Oxford: Clarendon, 1998.

Crescenzo, Richard. "L'antique, l'ancien et le nouveau dans le *Temple de Cupido*." In Dauphiné and Mironneau, *À propos de L'Adolescence clémentine*, 73–87.

Dagron, Tristan. "Silènes et statues platoniciennes, à propos du prologue du *Gargantua*." In Simonin, *Rabelais pour le XXIe siècle*, 79–90.

Dauphiné, James, and Paul Mironneau, eds. *Clément Marot: À propos de L'Adolescence clémentine. Actes des quatrièmes Journées du Centre Jacques de Laprade tenues au Musée national du château de Pau les 29 et 30 novembre 1996*. Biarritz: J & D Editions, 1996.

Dauvois, Nathalie. "Portrait du jeune poète en berger: Adolescence et bucolique." In Vignes, *En relisant L'Adolescence Clémentine*, 11–22.

Davis, Natalie Zemon. *The Gift in Sixteenth-Century France*. Madison: University of Wisconsin Press, 2000.

———. *Society and Culture in Early Modern France*. Stanford: Stanford University Press, 1975.

Dealy, Ross. *The Stoic Origins of Erasmus' Philosophy of Christ*. Toronto: University of Toronto Press, 2017.

Defaux, Gérard. "Les deux amours de Clément Marot." *Rivista di Letterature moderne e comparate* 46, no. 1 (Jan.–Mar. 1993): 1–30.

———. "D'un problème l'autre: herméneutique de l'*altior sensus* et *captatio lectoris* dans le prologue de *Gargantua*." *Revue d'Histoire Littéraire de la France* 85, no. 2 (Mar.–Apr. 1985): 195–216.

———. "Un 'extraict de haulte mythologie' humaniste: Pantagruel, *Picus redivivus*,'" *ER* 14 (1977): 219–64.

———, ed. *La génération Marot: Poètes français et néo-latins (1515–1550). Actes du Colloque international de Baltimore, 5–7 décembre 1996*. Paris: Champion, 1997.

———, ed. *Lyon et l'illustration de la langue française à la Renaissance*. Lyon: ENS Éditions, 2003.

———. "Marot et 'Ferme Amour': Essai de mise au point." In *Anteros: Actes du colloque de Madison (Wisconsin) mars 1994*, edited by Ullrich Langer and Jan Miernowski, 137–67. Orléans: Paradigme, 1994.

———. "Marot et ses éditions lyonnaises: Étienne Dolet, Sébastien Gryphe et François Juste." *Revue d'Histoire Littéraire de la France* 93, no. 6 (1993): 819–49.

———. *Marot, Rabelais, Montaigne: L'écriture comme présence*. Paris: Champion, 1987.

———. *Pantagruel et les Sophistes: Contribution à l'histoire de l'humanisme chrétien au XVIe siècle*. The Hague: M. Nijhoff, 1973.

———. *Le Poète en son jardin: Étude sur Clément Marot et* L'Adolescence clémentine. Paris: Champion, 1996.

———. *Rabelais agonistes: du rieur au prophète*. Geneva: Droz, 1997.

———. "Rhétorique, silence et liberté dans l'œuvre de Marot: Essai d'explication d'un style." *BHR* 46, no. 2 (1984): 299–322.

———. "Sur la prétendue pluralité du Prologue de *Gargantua*: Réponse d'un positiviste naïf à trois 'illustres et treschevaleureux champions.'" *Revue d'Histoire Littéraire de la France* 86, no. 4 (Jul.–Aug. 1986): 716–22.

———. "Trois cas d'écrivains éditeurs dans la première moitié du XVIe siècle: Marot, Rabelais, Dolet." In Bessire, *L'Écrivain éditeur*, 91–118.

———. "'Vivre je veulx pour l'honneur de la France': Marot, Tory, Rabelais et le cas Étienne Dolet." In Defaux, *Lyon et l'illustration*, 417–49.

Defaux, Gérard, and Michel Simonin, eds. *Clément Marot, "Prince des poëtes françois," 1496–1996: Actes du Colloque international de Cahors en Quercy, 21–25 mai 1996*. Paris: Champion, 1997.

Delègue, Yves. *Le Royaume d'exil: Le sujet de la littérature en quête d'auteur*. Paris: Obsidiane, 1991.

Demerson, Guy. *Humanisme et facétie: Quinze études sur Rabelais*. Caen: Paradigme, 1994.

Demetz, Peter, Thomas Greene, and Lowry Nelson, Jr., eds. *The Disciplines of Criticism: Essays in Literary Theory, Interpretation, and History*. New Haven: Yale University Press, 1968.

Desan, Philippe. *L'imaginaire économique de la Renaissance*. Mont-de-Marsan: Editions Interuniversitaires, 1993.

Doutrepont, Georges. *Jean Lemaire de Belges et la Renaissance*. Brussels: Lamertin, 1934.

Dupèbe, Jean. "Un ami de Clément Marot, le médecin Michel Amy." In *Cité des hommes, Cité de Dieu: Travaux sur la littérature de la Renaissance en l'honneur de Daniel Ménager*, edited by Jean Céard et al., 189–96. Geneva: Droz, 2003.

Duport, Danièle. "'De pensée joyeuse' ou *Le Temple de Cupido* de Clément Marot." In *Nature et Paysages: L'émergence d'une nouvelle subjectivité à la Renaissance*, edited by Dominique de Courcelles, 141–49. Paris: École Nationale des Chartes, 2006.

Duru, Audrey. "Les *Essais poétiques*: Emplois et sens du mot *essai(s)* dans les titres de recueils poétiques à la fin du XVIe siècle et au début du XVIIe siècle." In *Le lexique métalittéraire français (XVIe–XVIIe siècles)*, edited by Michel Jourde and Jean-Charles Monferran, 123–45. Geneva: Droz, 2006.

Duval, Edwin. "*L'Adolescence clémentine* et l'œuvre de Clément Marot." *Etudes françaises* 38, no. 3 (2002): 11–24.

———. *The Design of Rabelais's* Pantagruel. New Haven: Yale University Press, 1991.

———. *The Design of Rabelais's* Tiers livre de Pantagruel. *ER* 34. Geneva: Droz, 1997.

———. "Interpretation and the 'doctrine absconce' of Rabelais's prologue to *Gargantua.*" *ER* 18 (1985): 1–17.

———. "Marot, Marguerite, et le chant du cœur: Formes lyriques et formes de l'intériorité." In Defaux and Simonin, *"Prince des poëtes françois,"* 559–71.

———. "The Medieval Curriculum, The Scholastic University, and Gargantua's Program of Studies (*Pantagruel*, 8)." In Raymond C. La Charité, *Rabelais's Incomparable Book*, 30–44.

Ehrhart, Margaret J. *The Judgment of the Trojan Prince Paris in Medieval Literature.* Philadelphia: University of Pennsylvania Press, 1987.

Eisenstein, Elizabeth. *Divine Art, Infernal Machine: The Reception of Printing in the West from First Impressions to the Sense of an Ending.* Philadelphia: University of Pennsylvania Press, 2011.

———. *The Printing Press as an Agent of Change: Communications and Cultural Transformations in Early Modern Europe.* Vol. 1. Cambridge: Cambridge University Press, 1979.

Febvre, Lucien. *Le problème de l'incroyance au XVIe siècle: La religion de Rabelais.* Paris: Albin Michel, 1968.

Febvre, Lucien, and Henri-Jean Martin. *L'apparition du livre.* Paris: Albin Michel, 1971.

Fenoaltea, Doranne. "Doing It with Mirrors: Architecture and Textual Construction in Jean Lemaire's *La concorde des deux langages.*" In *Lapidary Inscriptions: Renaissance Essays for Donald A. Stone*, edited by Barbara C. Bowen and Jerry C. Nash, 21–32. Lexington: French Forum, 1991.

Ford, Philip, and Gillian Jondorf, eds. *Humanism and Letters in the Age of François Ier: Proceedings of the Fourth Cambridge French Renaissance Colloquium, 19–21 September 1994.* Cambridge: Cambridge French Colloquia, 1996.

Francis, Scott. "Marguerite Nicodémite? *Adiaphora* and Intention in *Heptaméron* 30, 65, and 72." *Renaissance and Reformation/Renaissance et Réforme* 39, no. 3 (Summer 2016): 5–31.

Françon, Marcel. *Autour de la lettre de Gargantua à Pantagruel.* Rochecorbon: Gay, 1957.

Gadoffre, Gilbert. *La Révolution culturelle dans la France des humanistes: Guillaume Budé et François Ier.* Geneva: Droz, 1997.

Gaignebet, Claude. *A plus hault sens: L'Ésotérisme spirituel et charnel de Rabelais.* 2 vols. Paris: Maisonneuve et Larose, 1986.

Galland-Hallyn, Perrine. "Marot, Macrin, Bourbon: 'Muse naïve' et 'tendre style.'" In Defaux, *La génération Marot*, 211–40.

Gatinot, Gérard. "*Knock* (ou le triomphe ... de la publicité)." *L'Humanité*, Feb. 8, 1960.

Gawande, Atul. "Overkill." *New Yorker*, May 11, 2015.

Genette, Gérard. *Figures III.* Paris: Seuil, 1972.

———. *Introduction à l'architexte.* Paris: Seuil, 1979.

———. *Palimpsestes: La littérature au second degré.* Paris: Seuil, 1982.

———. *Seuils.* Paris: Seuil, 1987.

Geonget, Stéphan. *La notion de perplexité à la Renaissance.* Geneva: Droz, 2006.

Gilman, Peter, and Abraham C. Keller. "The 'Grosses Mesles.'" *ER* 29 (1993): 105–26.

———. "Rabelais, the 'Grandes Chronicques,' and Jean Lemaire de Belges." *ER* 29 (1993): 93–103.

———. "Who is Pantagruel?" *ER* 22 (1988): 77–100.

Glauser, Alfred. *Le faux Rabelais, ou De l'inauthenticité du Cinquième Livre*. Paris: Nizet, 1975.

Gorris Camos, Rosanna, and Alexandre Vanautgaerden, eds. *L'Auteur à la Renaissance: L'altro que è in noi*. Turnhout: Brepols, 2009.

Goyet, Francis. "Sur l'ordre de *L'Adolescence clémentine*." In Defaux and Simonin, "*Prince des poëtes françois*," 593–613.

Gray, Floyd. "Rabelais's First Readers." In Raymond C. La Charité, *Rabelais's Incomparable Book*, 15–29.

———. *La Renaissance des mots*. Paris: Champion, 2008.

Green, Lawrence D. and James J. Murphy. *Renaissance Rhetoric Short-Title Catalogue, 1460–1700*. Aldershot: Ashgate, 2003.

Greenblatt, Stephen. *Renaissance Self-Fashioning: From More to Shakespeare*. 2nd ed. Chicago: University of Chicago Press, 2005.

Greene, Thomas. "The Flexibility of the Self in Renaissance Literature." In Demetz, Greene, and Nelson, Jr., *Disciplines of Criticism*, 241–64.

Griffin, Robert. "*La concorde des deux languages*: Discordia concors." In Smith and McFarlane, *Literature and the Arts*, 54–81.

———. "Cosmic Metaphor in *La concorde des deux langages*." In *Pre-Pléiade Poetry*, edited by Jerry C. Nash, 15–30. Lexington: French Forum, 1985.

———. *Clément Marot and the Inflections of Poetic Voice*. Berkeley: University of California Press, 1974.

Gültlingen, Sybille von. *Répertoire bibliographique des livres imprimés en France au seizième siècle*. 12 vols. to date. Baden-Baden and Bouxwiller: Valentin Koerner, 1992–.

Guy, Henry. *Histoire de la poésie française au XVIe siècle. Tome I: L'école des Rhétoriqueurs*. Paris: Champion, 1968.

Hämel, Adalbert. "Clément Marot und François Juste." *Zeitschrift für französische Sprache und Literatur* 50 (1927): 131–34.

Hardison, O. B. *The Enduring Monument: A Study of the Idea of Praise in Renaissance Literary Theory and Practice*. Chapel Hill: University of North Carolina Press, 1962.

Hayes, E. Bruce. "A Decade of Silence: Rabelais's Return to Writing in a More Dangerous World." *ER* 46 (2008): 101–13.

———. *Rabelais's Radical Farce: Late Medieval Comic Theater and Its Function in Rabelais*. Aldershot: Ashgate, 2010.

Heitsch, Dorothea. *Writing as Medication in Early Modern France*. Heidelberg: Universitätsverlag Winter, 2017.

Helgeson, James. "'Ce que j'entends par ces symboles pythagoricques': Rabelais on Meaning and Intention." *ER* 42 (2003): 75–100.

———. *The Lying Mirror: The First-Person Stance and Sixteenth-Century Writing*. Geneva: Droz, 2012.

Hirsch, Rudolf. *Printing, Selling and Reading, 1450–1550*. Wiesbaden: Harrassowitz, 1967.

Hobbins, Daniel. *Authorship and Publicity Before Print: Jean Gerson and the Transformation of Late Medieval Learning*. Philadelphia: University of Pennsylvania Press, 2009.

Hochner, Nicole. "Un héros liminaire: Gaston de Foix." In *Voir Gaston de Foix (1512–2012): Métamorphoses européennes d'un héros paradoxal*, edited by Joana Barreto, Gabriele Quaranta and Colette Nativel, 67–81. Paris: Publications de la Sorbonne, 2015.

———. *Louis XII: Les dérèglements de l'image royale (1498–1515)*. Seyssel: Champ Vallon, 2006.

Hoffmann, George. "About Being about the Renaissance: Bestsellers and Booksellers." *Journal of Medieval and Renaissance Studies* 22, no. 1 (Winter 1992): 75–88.

Huchon, Mireille. *Louise Labé: Une créature de papier*. Geneva: Droz, 2006.

———. *Rabelais*. Paris: Gallimard, 2011.

———. *Rabelais grammairien: De l'histoire du texte aux problèmes d'authenticité*. Geneva: Droz, 1981.

Hudson, Robert J. "Marot vs. Sagon: Heresy and the Gallic School, 1537." In *Representations of Heresy in French Art and Literature*, edited by Gabriella Scarlatta and Lidia Radi, 159–87. Toronto: University of Toronto Press, 2017.

Huguet, Edmond. *Dictionnaire de la langue française du seizième siècle*. 7 vols. Paris: Champion, 1925–67.

Imbs, Paul. "Jean Lemaire de Belges: La Concorde des deux langages." *Bulletin de la Faculté des Lettres de l'Université de Strasbourg* 26, no. 6 (Apr. 1948): 182–87.

Iser, Wolfgang. *The Act of Reading: A Theory of Aesthetic Response*. Baltimore: Johns Hopkins University Press, 1978.

———. *The Implied Reader: Patterns of Communication in Prose Fiction from Bunyan to Beckett*. Baltimore: Johns Hopkins University Press, 1974.

Jardine, Lisa. *Erasmus, Man of Letters: The Construction of Charisma in Print*. Princeton: Princeton University Press, 1993.

Jeanneret, Michel. "Banquets poétiques et métaphores alimentaires." In *Ronsard en son IVe centenaire*, vol. 2, edited by Yvonne Bellenger et al, 73–80. Geneva: Droz, 1989.

———. "La Lecture en question: Sur quelques prologues comiques du seizième siècle." *French Forum* 14, no. 3 (Sept. 1989): 279–89.

———. *Perpetuum mobile: Métamorphoses des corps et des œuvres de Vinci à Montaigne*. Paris: Macula, 1997.

———. "Signs Gone Wild: The Dismantling of Allegory." In Caron, *Critical Assessments*, 57–70.

Jodogne, Pierre. *Jean Lemaire de Belges: Ecrivain franco-bourgignon*. Brussels: Académie Royale de Belgique, 1972.

———. "Les 'rhétoriqueurs' et l'humanisme: problème d'histoire littéraire." In *Humanism in France at the end of the Middle Ages and in the early Renaissance*, edited by A. H. T. Levi, 150–75. Manchester: Manchester University Press, 1970.

Joseph, George. *Clément Marot*. Boston: Twayne, 1985.
Joukovsky, Françoise. *La gloire dans la poésie française et néolatine du 16ᵉ siècle*. Geneva: Droz, 1969.
Kaiser, Walter. *Praisers of Folly*. Cambridge: Harvard University Press, 1963.
Kammerbeek, Jan, Jr. "Le concept du 'lecteur idéal.'" *Neophilologus* 61, no. 1 (Jan. 1977): 2–7.
Karaberopoulos, Demetrios, Marianna Karamanou, and George Androutsos. "The Theriac in Antiquity." *The Lancet* 379, no. 9830 (May 26, 2012): 1942–43.
Kem, Judy. *Jean Lemaire de Belges's Les Illustrations de Gaule et singularitez de Troye: The Trojan Legend in the Late Middle Ages and Early Renaissance*. New York: Peter Lang, 1994.
Kemp, William. "Marguerite of Navarre, Clément Marot, and the Augereau editions of the *Miroir de l'âme pécheresse* (Paris, 1533)." *Journal of the Early Book Society* 2 (1999): 113–56.
Kennedy, William J. "Petrarchan Audiences and Print Technology." *Journal of Medieval and Renaissance Studies* 14, no. 1 (Spring 1984): 1–20.
Kline, Michael B. *Rabelais and the Age of Printing*. ER 4. Geneva: Droz, 1963.
Knecht, R. J. *Renaissance Warrior and Patron: The Reign of Francis I*. Cambridge: Cambridge University Press, 1994.
Kritzman, Lawrence. "The Rhetoric of Dissimulation in *La première epistre de l'Amant Vert*." *Journal of Medieval and Renaissance Studies* 10, no. 1 (Spring 1980): 23–39.
La Charité, Claude. "La prosopopée chez Rabelais." In *Savoirs et fins de la représentation sous l'Ancien Régime*, edited by Annie Cloutier, Catherine Dubeau, and Pierre-Marc Gendron, 9–19. Quebec: Les Presses de L'Université Laval, 2005.
La Charité, Raymond C. "Du *Pantagruel* au *Quart Livre*: Projet narratif et lecteurs." In Simonin, *Rabelais pour le XXIe siècle*, 361–74.
———. "Lecteurs et lectures dans le prologue du *Gargantua*." *French Forum* 10, no. 3 (Sept. 1985): 261–70.
———. "Rabelais and the Silenic Text: The Prologue to *Gargantua*." In Raymond C. La Charité, *Rabelais's Incomparable Book*, 72–86.
———, ed. *Rabelais's Incomparable Book*. Lexington: French Forum, 1986.
Lacroix, Paul (Le Bibliophile Jacob). "François Juste: Libraire et Imprimeur à Lyon." *Bulletin du Bibliophile* (1869): 632–41.
LaGuardia, David P. *Intertextual Masculinity in French Renaissance Literature*. Aldershot: Ashgate, 2008.
Lebègue, Raymond. "Rabelais, the Last of French Erasmians." *Journal of the Warburg and Courtauld Institutes* 12 (1949): 91–100.
LeBlanc, Yvonne. "Death and Remembrance: The Immortality of the Word and the *Epîtres de l'Amant Vert*." *Medieval Perspectives* 8 (1993): 112–20.
———. *"Va Lettre Va": The French Verse Epistle (1400–1550)*. Birmingham: Summa, 1995.
Le Cadet, Nicolas. "'Beuveurs tresillustres et vous verolez tresprecieux': Rabelais et les anagnostes." *Revue d'Histoire Littéraire de la France* 115, no. 2 (2015): 261–82.

———. "Le *topos* lucianesque des 'histoires vraies' et la poétique du *Quart Livre*," *Réforme Humanisme Renaissance* 74 (Jun. 2012): 7–24.
Lecointe, Jean. *L'Idéal et la différence: La perception de la personnalité littéraire à la Renaissance*. Geneva: Droz, 1993.
Lestringant, Frank. *Clément Marot: De L'Adolescence à L'Enfer*. Padua: Unipress, 1998.
———. "L'Insulaire de Rabelais ou la fiction en archipel: Pour une lecture topographique du *Quart Livre*." *ER* 21 (1988): 268–73.
Leushuis, Reinier. "Fertilizing the French Vernacular: Procreation, Warfare and Authorship in Jean de Meun, Jean Lemaire de Belges, and Rabelais." In *Sexuality in the Middle Ages and Early Modern Times*, edited by Albrecht Classen, 783–810. Berlin: Walter de Gruyter, 2008.
Lewis, Charlton T. and Charles Short. *A Latin Dictionary Founded on Andrews' Edition of Freund's Latin Dictionary*. Oxford: Clarendon, 1975.
Losse, Deborah N. *Rhetoric at Play: Rabelais and Satirical Eulogy*. Bern: Peter Lang, 1980.
———. *Sampling the Book: Renaissance Prologues and the French Conteurs*. Lewisburg: Bucknell University Press, 1994.
Mayer, C. A. *Bibliographie des Œuvres de Clément Marot*. 2 vols. Geneva: Droz, 1954.
———. *Bibliographie des éditions de Clément Marot publiées au XVIe siècle*. Paris: Nizet, 1975.
———. *Clément Marot*. Paris: Nizet, 1972.
Mayer, C. A., and C. M. Douglas. "Rabelais poète." *BHR* 24 (1962): 42–46.
McFarlane, I. D. "Clément Marot and the World of Neo-Latin Poetry." In Smith and McFarlane, *Literature and the Arts*, 103–30.
McGrady, Deborah. *Controlling Readers: Guillaume de Machaut and His Late Medieval Audience*. Toronto: University of Toronto Press, 2006.
———. "Printing the Patron's Pleasure for Profit: The Case of the *Epîtres de l'Amant Vert*." *Journal of the Early Book Society* 2 (1999): 89–112.
McKinley, Mary B. "Parrots and Poets: Writing Alterities in Scève and Lemaire de Belges." In *Self and Other in Sixteenth-century France: Proceedings of the Seventh Cambridge French Renaissance Colloquium, 7–9 July 2001*, edited by Kathryn Banks and Philip Ford, 1–14. Cambridge: Cambridge French Colloquia, 2004.
Melançon, Robert. "La personne de Marot." In Defaux and Simonin, *"Prince des poëtes françois,"* 515–29.
Ménager, Daniel. "*La Concorde des deux langages*: Vers et prose chez Jean Lemaire de Belges." In *Prose et prosateurs de la Renaissance: Mélanges offerts à M. le Professeur Robert Aulotte*, 15–25. Paris: SEDES, 1988.
Menini, Romain. *Rabelais altérateur: "Græciser en François."* Paris: Classiques Garnier, 2014.
———. *Rabelais et l'intertexte platonicien*. ER 47. Geneva: Droz, 2009.
Mérigot, Léo. "Rabelais et l'alchimie." *Les Cahiers d'Hermès* 1 (1947): 50–64.
Meyer, Urs. *Poetik der Werbung*. Berlin: Erich Schmidt, 2010.
Miernowski, Jan. "Literature and Metaphysics: Rabelais and the Poetics of Misunderstanding." *ER* 35 (1998): 131–51.

Milhe-Poutington, Gérard. "Rabelais, Érasme, et le pourceau." *ER* 39 (2000): 39–57.

Monferran, Jean-Charles. "Va, mon Livre: Quelques jalons pour une histoire de la destination." *Nouvelle Revue du XVIᵉ Siècle* 21, no. 1 (Jan. 2003): 121–51.

Moreau, Brigitte. *Inventaire chronologique des éditions parisiennes du XVIᵉ siècle, d'après les manuscrits de Philippe Renouard*. 5 vols. to date. Paris: Imprimerie municipale, Service des travaux historiques de la ville de Paris, 1972–.

Moss, Ann. "Fabulous Narrations in the *Concorde des deux langages* of Jean Lemaire de Belges." In *Philosophical Fictions and the French Renaissance*, edited by Neil Kenny, 17–28. London: The Warburg Institute, 1991.

———. *Poetry and Fable: Studies in Mythological Narrative in Sixteenth-Century France*. Cambridge: Cambridge University Press, 1984.

Munn, Kathleen M. *A Contribution to the Study of Jean Lemaire de Belges*. Scottdale: Mennonite Publishing House, 1936.

Nelson, Lowry, Jr. "The Fictive Reader and Literary Self-Reflexiveness." In Demetz, Greene, and Nelson, Jr., *Disciplines of Criticism*, 173–91.

Noirot, Corinne. *"Entre deux airs": Style simple et ethos poétique chez Clément Marot et Joachim Du Bellay (1515–1560)*. Quebec: Les Presses de l'Université Laval, 2011.

Perona, Blandine. *Prosopopée et persona à la Renaissance*. Paris: Garnier, 2013.

Pernety, Dom Antoine-Joseph. *Dictionnaire mytho-hermétique*. Paris: Denoël, 1972.

Perrier, Simone, ed. *Clément Marot, L'Adolescence clémentine: Actes de la journée d'étude du 8 novembre 1996*. Cahiers Textuel 16. Paris: Université Paris-Diderot, 1997.

Persels, Jeffery C. "'Straitened in the bowels,' or Concerning the Rabelaisian Trope of Defecation." *ER* 31 (1996): 101–12.

Pettegree, Andrew. *The Book in the Renaissance*. New Haven: Yale University Press, 2010.

Plan, P.-P. *Bibliographie rabelaisienne: Les éditions de Rabelais de 1532 à 1711*. Paris: Imprimerie Nationale, 1904.

Pons, Jacques. "Recherches sur les 'Fanfreluches antidotées' (suite)." *Bulletin de l'association des amis de Rabelais et de La Devinière* 6, no. 8 (1999): 471–84.

Pouey-Mounou, Anne-Pascale. *Panurge comme lard en pois: Paradoxe, scandale et propriété dans le Tiers Livre*. ER 53. Geneva: Droz, 2013.

Preisig, Florian. *Clément Marot et les métamorphoses de l'auteur à l'aube de la Renaissance*. Geneva: Droz, 2004.

Presbrey, Frank. *The History and Development of Advertising*. New York: Doubleday, 1929.

Prince, Gerald. "Introduction à l'étude du narrataire." *Poétique* 14 (1973): 178–96.

———. "Reader." *Handbook of Narratology*. 2nd ed. Edited by Peter Hühn, Jan Christoph Meister, John Pier, and Wolf Schmid. Berlin: De Gruyter, 2014.

Quilliet, Bernard. *Louis XII, Père du Peuple*. Paris: Fayard, 1986.

Rajchenbach-Teller, Elise. *"Mais devant tous est le Lyon marchant": Construction littéraire d'un milieu éditorial et livres de poésie française à Lyon (1536–1551)*. Geneva: Droz, 2016.

Randall, Michael. "The Flamboyant Design of Jean Lemaire de Belges' *La Concorde des deux langages*." *L'Esprit Créateur* 28, no. 2 (Summer 1988): 13–24.

Rawles, Stephen, and M. A. Screech. *A New Rabelais Bibliography*. ER 20. Geneva: Droz, 1987.

Raynaud de Lage, Guy. "*Natura* et *Genius*, chez Jean de Meung et chez Jean Lemaire de Belges." *Le Moyen Âge* 58 (1952): 125–43.

Réach-Ngô, Anne. "De l'espace du livre à l'espace de l'œuvre: la consécration du fait littéraire à la Renaissance." In *Le livre et ses espaces*, edited by Alain Milon and Marc Perelman, 63–84. Paris: Presses Universitaires de Paris 10, 2007.

———. *L'Écriture éditoriale à la Renaissance: Genèse et promotion du récit sentimental français (1530–1560)*. Geneva: Droz, 2013.

The Reader in the Text: Essays on Audience and Interpretation. Edited by Susan R. Suleiman and Inge Crosman. Princeton: Princeton University Press, 1980.

Reeser, Todd. *Moderating Masculinity in Early Modern Culture*. Chapel Hill: North Carolina Studies in the Romance Languages and Literatures, 2006.

Regosin, Richard. "Opening Discourse." In Caron, *Critical Assessments*, 133–47.

Remer, Gary. *Humanism and the Rhetoric of Toleration*. University Park: The Pennsylvania State University Press, 1996.

Renner, Bernd. "Changes in Renaissance Epistemology: The Dialogism of Rabelais's Prologues." In *Charting Change in France around 1540*, edited by Marian Rothstein, 186–212. Selinsgrove: Susquehanna University Press, 2006.

———. "'Clément devise dedans Venise': Marot's Satirical Poetry in Exile." In *Multicultural Europe and Cultural Exchange in the Middle Ages and Renaissance*, edited by James P. Helfers, 139–54. Turnhout: Brepols, 2005.

———. *Difficile est saturam non scribere: L'herméneutique de la satire rabelaisienne*. ER 45. Geneva: Droz, 2007.

———. "'Ni l'un ni l'autre et tous les deux à la fois': Le paradoxe ménippéen inversé dans le *Tiers Livre* de Rabelais." *Romanic Review* 97, no. 2 (2006): 153–68.

Renouard, Philippe. *Répertoire des imprimeurs parisiens, libraires, fondeurs de caractères et correcteurs d'imprimerie depuis l'introduction de l'Imprimerie à Paris (1470) jusqu'à la fin du seizième siècle*. Paris: Minard, 1965.

Rigolot, François. "Authorial Authority in the Early Age of Printing: Clément Marot (1496–1544)." *Princeton University Library Chronicle* 70, no. 1 (Autumn 2008): 35–48.

———. "Clément Marot et l'émergence de la conscience littéraire à la Renaissance." In Defaux, *La génération Marot*, 21–34.

———. "D'un libraire, l'autre: Marot, de Tory à Dolet via Montmorency." In *Les poètes français de la Renaissance et leurs "libraires": Actes du Colloque international de l'Université d'Orléans (5–7 juin 2013)*, edited by Denis Bjaï and François Rouget, 311–35. Geneva: Droz, 2015.

———. "Hybridity, Exemplarity, and Dialogism in a Historical Perspective: Rabelais's Dialogue on Dialogue with Lucian." In *Der Dialog im Diskursfeld seiner Zeit: Von der Antike bis zur Aufklärung*, edited by Klaus W. Hempfer and Anita Traninger, 205–17. Stuttgart: Franz Steiner, 2010.

———. "Jean Lemaire de Belges: Concorde ou discorde des deux langages?" *Journal of Medieval and Renaissance Studies* 3 (1973): 165–75.
———. *Les langages de Rabelais*. 2nd ed. Geneva: Droz, 1996.
———. *Poésie et Renaissance*. Paris: Seuil, 2002.
———. "Prolégomènes à une étude du statut de l'appareil liminaire des textes littéraires." *L'Esprit Créateur* 27, no. 3 (Fall 1987): 7–18.
———. "Rhétoriqueurs." *Dictionnaire des lettres françaises: Le XVIe siècle*. Ed. Michel Simonin. Paris: LGF, 2001.
———. *Le Texte de la Renaissance: Des Rhétoriqueurs à Montaigne*. Geneva: Droz, 1982.
———. "Vraisemblance et Narrativité dans le *Pantagruel*." *L'Esprit Créateur* 21, no. 1 (Spring 1981): 53–68.
Rommel, Bettina. *Rabelais zwischen Mündlichkeit und Schriftlichkeit: Gargantua, Literatur als Lebensführung*. Tübingen: Niemeyer, 1997.
Rosenthal, Olivia. "L'auteur devant son œuvre: l'exemple de Jean Lemaire de Belges." *Nouvelle Revue du Seizième Siècle* 17, no. 2 (1999): 181–93.
———. "L'œuvre et ses éditeurs au début du XVIe siècle." In *L'Autre de l'œuvre*, edited by Yoshikazu Nakaji, 23–37. Paris: Presses Universitaires de Vincennes, 2007.
Rothstein, Marian. "Jean Lemaire de Belges' *Illustrations de Gaule et Singularitez de Troye*: Politics and Unity." *BHR* 52, no. 3 (1990): 593–609.
Sainéan, Lazar. *La langue de Rabelais*. Geneva: Slatkine Reprints, 1976.
Scheller, Robert W. "Gallia Cisalpina: Louis XII and Italy, 1499–1508." *Simiolus* 15, no. 1 (1985): 5–60.
Schneider, Lars. *Medienvielfalt und Medienwechsel in Rabelais' Lyon*. Münster: LIT, 2008.
Schwartz, Jerome. "Rhetorical Tensions in the Liminary Texts of Rabelais's *Quart Livre*." *ER* 17 (1983): 21–36.
Scollen-Jimack, Christine. "Clément Marot: Protestant Humanist, or Court Jester?" *Renaissance Studies* 1, no. 2 (June 1989): 134–46.
———. "Marot and Deschamps: The Rhetoric of Misfortune." *French Studies* 42 (Jan. 1988): 21–32.
Screech, M. A. *Rabelais*. London: Duckworth, 1979.
Sherman, Michael. "Political Propaganda and Renaissance Culture: French Reactions to the League of Cambrai, 1509–10." *The Sixteenth Century Journal* 8, no. 2 (1977): 97–128.
———. "The Selling of Louis XII: Propaganda and Popular Culture in Renaissance France, 1499–1514." PhD diss., University of Chicago, 1974.
Simonin, Michel, ed. *Rabelais pour le XXIe siècle: Actes du colloque du Centre d'études supérieures de la Renaissance (Chinon-Tours, 1994)*. Geneva: Droz, 1998.
Skenazi, Cynthia. *Le poète architecte en France: Constructions d'un imaginaire monarchique*. Paris: Champion, 2003.
Smith, Paul J. "Le prologue du *Pantagruel*: Une lecture." *Neophilologus* 68, no. 2 (Apr. 1984): 161–69.
Smith, Pauline M. "Clément Marot and the French Language." In Smith and McFarlane, *Literature and the Arts*, 163–93.

———. "Clément Marot and Humanism." In Ford and Jondorf, *Humanism and Letters*, 133–50.

Smith, Pauline M., and I. D. McFarlane, eds. *Literature and the Arts in the Reign of Francis I: Essays Presented to C. A. Mayer*. Lexington: French Forum, 1985.

Soubeille, Georges. "Amitiés de Salmon Macrin parmi les poètes de langue vernaculaire." In *Neo-Latin and the Vernacular in Renaissance France*, edited by Grahame Castor and Terence Cave, 98–112. Oxford: Clarendon, 1984.

Spitzer, Leo. "Ancora sul prologo al primo libro del *Gargantua* di Rabelais." *Studi Francesi* 9, no. 3 (1965): 423–34.

———. "Rabelais et les 'rabelaisants.'" *Studi Francesi* 4 (1960): 401–23.

Stephens, Walter. *Giants in Those Days: Folklore, Ancient History, and Nationalism*. Lincoln: University of Nebraska Press, 1989.

Stone, Donald. "Some Observations on the Text and Possible Meanings of Lemaire de Belges' *La Concorde des deux langages*." *BHR* 55, no. 1 (1993): 65–76.

Szabari, Antónia. "Rabelais *Parrhesiastes*: The Rhetoric of Insult and Rabelais's Cynical Mask." *MLN* 120 Supplement (2005): S84–S123.

Tetel, Marcel. "Rabelais et Lucien: De deux rhétoriques." In Raymond C. La Charité, *Rabelais's Incomparable Book*, 127–38.

Thornton, Sara. *Advertising, Subjectivity and the Nineteenth-Century Novel*. Basingstoke: Palgrave Macmillan, 2009.

Totelin, Laurence. "Mithridates' Antidote: A Pharmacological Ghost." *Early Science and Medicine* 9 (2004): 1–19.

Tournon, André. "*Ce sont coups d'essai*: L'ironie poétique." In Perrier, *Clément Marot*, 117–29.

———. "Le pantagruélisme, mode de lecture du *Tiers Livre*." *Littératures* 33 (Autumn 1995): 5–16.

———. "Le Paradoxe ménippéen dans l'œuvre de Rabelais." *ER* 21 (1988): 309–17.

Vecce, Carlo. "La 'mort de l'auteur' à la Renaissance." In Gorris Camos and Vanautgaerden, *L'Auteur à la Renaissance*, 83–99.

Verkamp, Bernard. *The Indifferent Mean: Adiaphorism in the English Reformation to 1554*. Athens: Ohio University Press, 1977.

Vestergaard, Torben and Schrøder, Kim. *The Language of Advertising*. Oxford: Blackwell, 1985.

Veyrin-Forrer, Jeanne. "Les Œuvres de Clément Marot: Questions bibliographiques." In Ford and Jondorf, *Humanism and Letters*, 151–70.

———. "Les premières éditions collectives de Clément Marot publiées à Lyon." In Defaux and Simonin, *"Prince des poëtes françois,"* 699–711.

Vigliano, Tristan. "Pour en finir avec le prologue de *Gargantua*." *@nalyses* 3.3 (Fall 2008), https://uottawa.scholarsportal.info/ojs/index.php/revue-analyses/article/view/704/605.

Vignes, Jean. "'En belle forme de livre': La composition de *L'Adolescence clémentine*," *Op. cit.* 7 (Nov. 1996): 79–86.

———, ed. *En relisant* L'Adolescence Clémentine: *Actes de la journée d'étude du 24 no-*

vembre 2006 organisée par Marie-Madeleine Fragonard, Pascal Debailly et Jean Vignes. Cahiers Textuel 30. Paris: Université Paris-Diderot, 2007.

Villey, Pierre. *Tableau chronologique des publications de Marot*. Paris: Champion, 1921.

———. "A propos d'une édition de Marot." *Revue du seizième siècle* 15 (1928): 156–60, 388–89.

Walsby, Malcolm. "La voix de l'auteur? Autorité et identité dans les imprimés français au XVIe siècle." In Gorris Camos and Vanautgaerden, *L'Auteur à la Renaissance*, 65–81.

Weems, Erica. "Charity and Interpretation in the *Heptaméron* and the *Tiers Livre*." PhD diss., Columbia University, 2013.

Wicke, Jennifer. *Advertising Fictions: Literature, Advertisement, and Social Reading*. New York: Columbia University Press, 1988.

Williams, Raymond. "Advertising: The Magic System." In *The Cultural Studies Reader*, edited by Simon During, 320–36. New York: Routledge, 1993.

Williamson, Judith. *Decoding Advertisements: Ideology and Meaning in Advertising*. London: Marion Boyars, 1978.

Wilson-Chevalier, Kathleen. "Feminising the Warrior at Francis I's Fontainebleau." In *Masculinities in Sixteenth-Century France: Proceedings of the Eighth Cambridge French Renaissance Colloquium, 5–7 July 2003*, edited by Philip Ford and Paul White, 23–59. Cambridge: Cambridge French Colloquia, 2006.

Wolff, Erwin. "Der intendierte Leser." *Poetica* 4, no. 2 (1971): 141–66.

Index

Adages (Erasmus), 156, 199n36; "Ad amussim exigere" [To demand a precise equivalent], 220n29; "Ad unguem facere" [To do something to the fingernail], 220n29; "Asinus ad lyram" [An ass to the lyre], 176, 180; "Culicem colant" [Straining at a gnat], 230n21; "Festina lente" [Make haste slowly], 8–9; "Momo satisfacere" [Satisfying Momus], 123, 220n27; "Monstrari digito" [To be pointed at], 151; "Proteo mutabilior" [As many shapes as Proteus], 83; "Sileni Alcibiadis" [Sileni of Alcibiades], 159; "Stelli signare, obelo notare" [To mark with stars, to brand with an obelus], 121; "Surdaster cum surdastro litigabat, judex autem erat utroque surdior" [Two deaf men had a legal dispute, but the judge was deafer than either of them], 225n35; "Thesaurus carbones erant" [The treasure consisted of coals], 2

Adam, 44

adiaphora, 32

Adolescence clementine, L' (Marot), 14–15, 84, 112, 117, 139; "Au Roy pour avoir esté dérobé," 96; "Ballades," 98; "Chansons," 98; compared to "arres" [down payment], 90, 107; compared to "coups d'essay," 84, 114, 158, 211n14; "Complainctes et epitaphes," 97, 98; "Déploration de Florimond Robertet," 86, 87, 97, 104; "Epistre de Maguelonne," 84, 86, 96, 117–18; "Epistres," 95, 97, 98; etymology of "adolescence," 86–87; horticultural metaphors in, 89–90, 94–98, 105, 116–17, 128, 132; Latin epigraphs, 90–91; order of works in, 87, 93–99, 215n54; "Oroison contemplative devant le Crucifix," 97–98, 132; as "passetemps," 89; preface, 84, 86, 89–90, 126, 128, 169; "Petite epistre au Roy," 134; "Premiere eglogue de Virgile," 88, 93–95, 96, 128, 214n47; *princeps* edition, 85, 86–87, 99, 103, 117; rivalry with Mantuan's *Adulescentia*, 87–89; "Le Temple de Cupido," 84, 86, 91, 96–98, 101, 107, 115, 214n50, 215n53; unauthorized editions, 99–110, 117, 118–22, 128, 215n61, 219nn21–22, 220–21nn31–32

advertising, 5–10, 12, 15, 135, 160, 165–66, 185–88; etymology of, 5; false freedom of, 78, 140, 184; history of, 5–6, 185. *See also* prestige advertising; publicity

Aeneas, 42

Affair of the Placards, 86, 106, 108, 110, 121–22, 167

agape, 96, 165, 173

Agnadello, Battle of, 59

Akakia, Martin, 215–16nn61–62

Albumasar, 155

Alcofrybas Nasier, Rabelais as, 146–49, 158–62, 165–66, 176

Alduy, Cécile, 215n54

Alexander the Great, 1, 58, 59, 207n16

alexandrine, 57–59, 62

Alexandrinus, Johannes, 178

allegorical reading, 14, 69–71, 180

Amboise, Michel d', 87

Amy, Michel, 102

Anaxagoras, 153, 154

257

Andromache, 55
Anne of Brittany, 13, 20, 48; grave illness in March 1512, 56–57; patronage of Lemaire, 13, 20, 22, 43; portrayed as Juno by Lemaire, 37–38; subject or dedicatee of Lemaire's works, 53, 58
Annius of Viterbo, 23
antidote, 142, 145; first attested occurrence in French in *Pantagruel*, 146; in Rabelais, 149, 157–58, 162, 165–66, 177
Antisthenes, 159
Antonioli, Roland, 140
Apollo, 36, 89, 126
Argonautica (Apollonius of Rhodes), 148
Aristarchus of Samothrace, 120–21
Aristotle, 7, 26; *Nicomachean Ethics*, 28; *Rhetoric*, 7, 8, 11, 158, 170, 199n29
Armstrong, Adrian, 37, 54, 76, 201n61
Arnoullet, Olivier, 84, 85–86, 89, 103. See also *Opuscules*
Artemidorus, 153
Athena. See Pallas
Augereau, Antoine, 103, 104, 118, 215n59
Augustus, 178
Auton, Jean d', 54, 201n57, 207n5, 207n7
Avicenna, 155

Bacchus, 96
Badius, Josse, 87
Bakhtin, Mikhail, 141
Baland, Étienne, 34, 204n31, 206n1
Barat, François, 45–46
Barthes, Roland, 2
Baudrillard, Jean, 12
Bauschatz, Cathleen, 140, 161
Beaumarchais, Pierre-Augustin Caron de, 143
Béda, Noël, 105, 108, 110, 122, 153, 216n70, 219n24
Bede, the Venerable, 153
Bembo, Pietro, 219n18
Bérault, Nicolas, 90, 91, 94
Berger, John, 12
Berthon, Guillaume, 14–15, 86, 100, 106, 132, 134, 135

Bissipat, Guillaume de, 53, 60. See also "Plaincte sur le trespas de messire Guillaume de Byssipat"; recueil-*Epistre*
Blaubloom, Louis. See Cyaneus
Boccaccio, Giovanni, 23; *Genealogy of the Pagan Gods*, 27, 28, 31, 41, 64, 74
Boethius, 28
Booth, Wayne, 11
Bouchet, Jean, 83, 201n57
Bourbon, Nicolas, 112, 114, 115, 117, 123–24, 126; *Nugae*, 124
Bourdieu, Pierre, 201n61
Braillon, Louis, 216n62
Brant, Sebastian, 83
Brault, Gerard, 150–51
Brisset, Pierre, 90–91, 213n37
Brown, Cynthia, 20, 53, 54, 61, 83
Budé, Guillaume, 90
Burgundy, 20, 22, 34; Burgundian poets, 57; ducal court of, 20, 58
Burke, Kenneth, 188
Byblis, 96

Calcagnini, Celio, 110
Calvin, Jean: *De scandalis*, 177; *Institutes of the Christian Religion*, 167
Canossa, Paolo. See Paradis, Paul
captatio benevolentiae [securing good will], 7–11, 56, 64, 77, 134, 149–50, 158, 173–77, 178; role of persona in, 8
Castiglione, Baldassare, 2, 78
Catach, Nina, 100
Cave, Terence, 149
Celsus, 142, 146
Cerberus, 160
Ceres, 124
Cerquiglini-Toulet, Jacqueline, 210n4
Champier, Symphorien, 24
Chang, Leah, 8
Charlemagne, 58
Charles d'Orléans, 46
Charles V (Holy Roman Emperor), 20, 25, 27, 29, 44, 64, 163, 205n45
Chartier, Roger, 4
Chastelain, Georges, 20, 201n57

INDEX

Châtillon, Odet de, 178
Chaucer, Geoffrey, 142
Cicero, 7, 158; *De inventione*, 170; *De oratore*, 171; *Orator*, 7–8. See also *Rhetorica ad Herennium*
Cinquiesme Livre (Rabelais), 140; authenticity of, 222n1; Fredon friar, 181; prologue, 180–81
Claivaz, David, 134
Claude of France, 20
Claude of Lorraine, 102
Clementine Recognitions (Niceta), 27
Colin, Jacques, 2–4, 221n33
Colonne, Guido delle, 24
Concorde des deux langages, La (Lemaire), 13, 22, 24, 34, 37, 60, 96, 215n53; *acteur*'s similarities with the Amant Vert, 73–74; association of *acteur* with Lemaire's authorial persona, 52, 73–77; Belacueil and Dangier as models of reception, 71–72; exemplarity misappropriated by Genius in, 66, 73; extension of the Judgment of Paris, 52, 61, 74; Genius as allusion to the sale of indulgences, 208n28; Genius as foil of Lemaire's authorial persona, 63–70, 73, 77; Labeur Historien, Repos, and Guerdon, 75–76; Lyon in, 63, 70, 73, 74; Paris compared to youth in Temple of Venus, 67; published in recueil-*Epistre*, 53–54; relationship between Mercury and Genius in, 64; Temple of Minerva, 58, 61, 62, 68, 74–76, 229n10; Temple of Venus, 24, 61, 62–68, 73; varying scholarly interpretations of, 61. See also Genius
Conley, Tom, 21
Constance School. See Jauss, H. R.; Iser, Wolfgang
contrafacta, 131, 221n37
contrepèteries, 174
coq-à-l'âne, 110, 162
Coquillart, Guillaume, 201n57
Cornilliat, François, 24, 61, 215n53
Council of Clermont, 23
Council of Pisa, 20, 22, 23
Council of Trent, 181

Cowell, Andrew, 5
Crenne, Hélisenne de, 211n11
Cretin, Guillaume, 44, 53, 60–61, 81, 201n57, 207n17
cris de Paris, 141, 223n8
Crusades, 23, 54
Ctesias, 148
Cupid, 26
Cyaneus, 112

danse macabre, 107
Dante Alighieri, 47, 62
Dares Phrygius, 24
Dauvois, Nathalie, 87–88
Davis, Natalie Zemon, 4
Defaux, Gérard, 14, 82, 87, 105, 131, 150–51, 210n3, 219n24, 221n33
Delègue, Yves, 135
Demerson, Guy, 11
Demosthenes, 151
Desan, Philippe, 9, 121, 219n19
Des Périers, Bonaventure, 177
Dictys Cretensis, 24
Dido, 42, 96
Diogenes the Cynic, 159, 170, 175
Disciple de Pantagruel. See *Navigations de Panurge*
Dolet, Étienne, 2, 85, 197n6; burnt at the stake, 167; first printer and dedicatee of Marot's *Œuvres* (1538), 82, 123–30; printer's mark, 124–26; piracy of Rabelais, 168–69, 228n5
Doutrepont, Georges, 23
Du Bellay, Guillaume, 167, 178
Du Bellay, Jean, 167, 178
Du Bellay, Joachim, 21, 213n38
Du Moulin, Antoine, 49
Du Pré, Galliot, 44, 49
Duru, Audrey, 211n14
Duval, Edwin, 99, 106, 215n53

Ehrhart, Margaret, 28
Eisenstein, Elizabeth, 5, 135, 199n36
Epictetus, 159
Epicurus, 30, 43

Epistolae Obscurorum Virorum, 154, 225n38

Epistre du Roy a Hector de Troye, et aucunes aultres oeuvres assez dignes de veoir (Lemaire). See recueil-*Epistre*

Épîtres de l'Amant Vert, Les (Lemaire): Amant Vert an extension of Lemaire's authorial persona, 47–52, 57; bold humor of, 47; Margaret of Austria's quatrain to Lemaire attached to, 49–50, 206n3; Mercury guides Amant Vert through afterlife, 47, 51; narrated by Margaret of Austria's pet parrot, 47; printed with Book One of *Illustrations*, 21–22, 46–47, 48; published by Janot in *Le Triumphe de l'Amant Vert*, 46

Erasmus, Desiderius, 87, 90, 167, 198n14, 219n18; *Apophtegmata* 156; *De interdicto esu carnium*, 231n40; *De pueris instituendis*, 11, 157, 160; *Novum Instrumentum*, 156, 226n45; *Paraclesis*, 156–57, 226n45; *Querela pacis*, 60; Rabelais's admiration for, 156, 183. See also *Adages*

Estissac, Geoffroy d', 104

Eve, 44

exemplarity, 21, 55; linked to masculinity and Pallas in Lemaire, 26, 42, 45, 56, 68–69; misappropriated by Genius, 66, 73

Fabri, Pierre, 7, 8, 161

farce, 15, 107, 142–46; *Chambrière à louer à tout faire*, 143; *Ditz de Maistre Aliborum qui de tout se mesle*, 143–44, 145, 146, 147; *Maistre Hambrelin, serviteur de Maistre Aliborum, cousin germain de Pacolet*, 144, 146; *Le pardonneur, le triacleur, et la tavernière*, 145–46, 147, 155, 160, 179; Rabelais's use of farces and *sotties*, 144, 146–50, 152, 154, 155, 158–59, 179; *Recueil du British Museum*, 143; *Recueil Trepperel*, 144; *Sottie de Maître Pierre Doribus*, 144, 147, 149, 159; *Tout-Ménage*, 147; *Varlet à louër à tout faire*, 143; *Watelet de tous mestiers*, 143

Ficino, Marsilio, 25, 68, 155; two Venuses, 25, 68

Foix, Françoise de, 221n42

Foix, Gaston de 22, 53, 57–60, 62; epitaph in recueil-*Epistre*, 53, 57–60, 62

Fournier, Humbert, 24

Frame, Donald, 141, 147

France: French youth corrupted in the Temple of Venus, 65–70; in Lemaire, 22, 34, 37, 54, 55, 56–57, 62; royal court of, 13, 39, 53, 99

Francis I, 25–26, 44, 45, 133, 167, 229n10; appointment of *lecteurs royaux* in Hebrew, 119; banishment of Béda, 105–6, 122

Francus, 55

Frappier, Jean, 49

Froben, Johann, 198n14

Fulgentius, 27–28, 41, 64, 74

gabelle, 167

Gadoffre, Gilbert, 26

Galen, 26; *De antidotis*, 142, 146; *De theriaca*, 142, 146

Galland-Hallyn, Perrine, 94

Gargantua (Rabelais), 2; Alcofrybas's discovery of the manuscript, 161–62; "Aux lecteurs," 158, 164; "Enigme en prophetie," 164–65; "Fanfreluches antidotées," 162–65, 227n68; Gargantua's education under Ponocrates, 141, 143; Gargantua's games, 147; interpretative controversy, 140, 180, 222n2; prologue, 158–62, 165, 171, 176, 180, 211n14

Gatinot, Gérard, 187

Gaul, 24, 33–34, 37, 39–40, 42, 43, 52; etymological associations of, 65

Genius (mythology), 34, 64

Geonget, Stéphan, 183

Gilman, Peter, and Abraham Keller, 182

Girault, Ambroise, 22

Giudacerio, Agazio, 119

Gréban, Simon, 153

Greenblatt, Stephen, 11–12, 226n50

Greimas, A. J., 12

Grévin, Jacques, 142; *Deux livres des venins*, 142–43, 146

Griffin, Robert, 115

Gringore, Pierre, 53, 85, 201n57

INDEX

Gryphe, Sébastien, 82, 85, 123, 127, 129, 220n28
Guicciardini, Francesco, 40
Guy, Henri, 19, 65

Ham, 33, 37
Harsy, Denis de, 120–21, 218–19nn18–19
Hayes, E. Bruce, 152
Hector, 31, 54–55, 58
Hecuba, gives birth to Paris, 21, 55
Heitsch, Dorothea, 146
Helen of Troy, 25, 31, 96; feminization of Paris, 29–31, 33, 62–63
Henri II, 167
Henry VIII, 22
Hercules, 21, 36
Héricault, Charles d', 201n57
Hermes Trismegistus, 155, 225–26n41; association with Hermeticism and *prisca theologia*, 155
Hermeticism. *See* Hermes Trismegistus
Herodotus, 148
Héroët, Antoine, 85, 228n5
Hesiod, 51, 229n10
Hippocrates, 26, 178, 179
Hipponax, 153, 154
Hirsch, Rudolf, 4
Hochner, Nicole, 58
Hoffmann, George, 200n41
Hofmannstahl, Hugo von, 200n44
Holy League, 22, 57
Homer, 114, 121; *Iliad*, 63; *Odyssey*, 51, 148
Horace, 34, 37, 101, 219n18; *Ars poetica*, 89, 114, 115, 124, 126; *Epistles*, 114–15; *Satires*, 220n29
Housman, A. E., 139
Huchon, Mireille, 24, 83, 216n69, 222n1
Hugo, Victor, 14
humanism, 7, 11, 90, 121, 162; connection with evangelical Christianity, 7, 12, 19, 84, 134; influence on Sartrean existentialism, 201n56; self-fashioning and humanistic philosophy, 11, 150–66

Iambulus, 148
iatrosophism, 177, 181, 182, 185, 187

ideal reader, 10–11, 12, 14, 15, 135; conceptual similarities with *captatio benevolentiae*, 10–11; distinct from Iser's implied reader, 10; in Lemaire, 21, 24, 42–44, 48, 56, 71, 77–78, 85, 183; in Marot, 85, 91–93, 123–24, 129; *pantagruélisme* as, 165, 173, 178; in Rabelais, 140–41, 149–58, 158–66, 173
Illustrations de Gaule et Singularitez de Troye, Les (Lemaire), 13, 21, 54, 56, 58, 62, 66, 68, 120; allegorical reading of, 70–71; historical context of, 22–24; Lemaire's writing of, 42; mirror for princes and men, 25–34, 76; *princeps* edition of, 34–44; Rabelais's possible parody of, 182–83; subsequent editions of, 44–46. *See also* Ham; Judgment of Paris; Juno; masculinity; Mercury; Noah; Pallas; Paris (Trojan prince); Troy; Venus
Index Librorum Prohibitorum, 21
indiciaire, 20, 48, 57, 74
Innocents, 145, 160
Iris, 28
Iser, Wolfgang, 10
Ismail I (Shah of Persia), 23
Italian Wars, 19, 22, 40, 52, 53–60, 167, 170, 183; role of Venice, 19. *See also* Charles V; Francis I; Julius II; Louis XII
Italy: associated with Venus by Lemaire, 14, 24, 33, 52, 62–63; influence of Italian letters in France, 13–14, 23–24, 34, 70, 183; in Lemaire, 23, 33, 55, 62

James IV of Scotland, 22
Janot, Denis, 46, 219n19, 219n21
Jason, 96
Jauss, H. R., 10
Jeanneret, Michel, 11
Jodogne, Pierre, 23, 33
Joukovsky, Françoise, 214n42
Jouvet, Louis, 185
Joyce, James, 200n44
Judgment of Paris, 14, 21, 24, 34, 41; Lemaire writing the *Illustrations* compared to, 42; model for reading Lemaire, 43, 76–77, 78;

Julius II (*continued*)
  mythological association with free will and self-fashioning, 25–28, 67, 78. *See also* Juno; Pallas; Paris (Trojan Prince); Venus
Julia the Elder, 178
Julius II, 20, 57; conflict with Louis XII, 13, 20, 22, 23, 53–55, 60; contrasted with Urban II by Lemaire, 23; Lemaire's criticism and satire of, 53, 54, 62, 71, 182
Juno, 25, 29–30, 41, 43; Anne of Brittany portrayed as by Lemaire, 37–38; mythological association with active life and wealth or power, 27–28, 56; vituperation of Paris in *Illustrations*, 68, 69. *See also* Judgment of Paris
Jupiter, 27, 36
Juste, François, 2–5, 8, 9; editions of Marot, 103–6, 110, 121–22, 216n71; editions of Rabelais, 155, 156, 158, 162–63, 171, 226n51
Juvenal, 219n18

Kabbalah, 150, 152, 156
Kem, Judy, 25, 68
Kennedy, William, 10
Knock, ou le triomphe de la médicine (Romains), 185–88

Labé, Louise, 83
La Charité, Raymond, 227n53
Lacroix, Paul, 103
Lactantius, 87
LaGuardia, David, 26
La Vigne, André de, 201n57
La Vigne, Pierre de. *See* Lavinius, Petrus
Lavinius, Petrus, 34, 37, 39–41
League of Cambrai, 19
Lebègue, Raymond, 156
LeBlanc, Yvonne, 50
Le Cadet, Nicolas, 152
Le Duchat, Jacob, 165
Lefèvre d'Étaples, Jacques, 167
Lefranc, Abel, 222n2
Lemaire de Belges, Jean, 13, 19, 140, 175, 188, 201n57; "A la louenge des princes et princesses qui ayment la science historialle," 55–56, 68; authorial persona of, 21, 24, 34, 36, 46, 47–52, 60–61, 77–78, 81–82, 183; *Chroniques annales*, 23; coat of arms, 34–39, 41, 45; *La Concorde du genre humain*, 19, 36, 37, 43; death, 205n50; "Le dyalogue de Vertu militaire et de Jeunesse françoise," 68–69; exemplarity linked to masculinity and Pallas by, 26, 42, 45, 56, 68–69; "Histoire, que faiz-tu?," 55–56, 68; ideal readership in, 21, 24, 42–44, 48, 56, 71, 77–78, 85, 183; importance of gratitude to, 43–44, 71–72, 128, 174; Italy in work of, 23, 33, 55, 62; *La Légende des Vénitiens*, 19–20, 23, 39; motto ("De peu assez"), 35, 44; *Pronosticque historial de la felicite future de l'an mil cincq cens et douze*, 58–59; Rabelais's depictions of, 182–83; self-fashioning in, 24, 25, 27, 56, 67, 70–71; *Le Temple d'Honneur et de Vertus*, 45, 62; *Le Traicté des schismes et des conciles de l'Eglise*, 20, 39, 62, 71. *See also Concorde des deux langages, La*; *Épîtres de l'Amant Vert, Les*; *Illustrations de Gaule et Singularitez de Troye, Les*; Judgment of Paris; Juno; Pallas; Paris (Trojan prince); Venus
Lent, 172, 180; medical opposition to, 181, 231n40; upheld by Council of Trent, 181
Leo X, 22
Le Pen, Marine, 224n17
Le Rouge, François, 53, 54
Lestringant, Frank, 229n10
Leushuis, Reinier, 66
Louise of Savoy, 101
Louis of Luxembourg, 76
Louis XII, 24, 25–26, 39, 47, 183; conflict with Julius II, 13, 20, 22, 23, 53–55, 60; death, 44; subject or dedicatee of Lemaire's works, 56–57, 58–59, 76–77
Lucan, 219n18
Lucian of Samosata, 1, 168; *How to Write History*, 170; *Icaromenippus*, 183; "Philosophies for Sale," 231n30, 231n39; "The Rooster," 231n39; "To One Who Said, 'You're a Prometheus in Words,'" 1, 171; *True History*, 148–49

INDEX

Lucretius, 43
Luther, Martin, 198n14
Lyon, 24, 34, 39, 46; in the *Concorde des deux langages*, 63, 70, 73, 74; Petrarch's influence on literary culture of, 24; print culture of, 83, 85–86, 103, 122, 226n44

Macault, Antoine, 112, 113–14
Machiavelli, Niccolò, 29
Macon, Gustave, 221n42
Macrin, Salmon, 112–13, 114–15, 117
Macrobius, 178
Macron, Emmanuel, 224n17
Maecenas, 101
Mantuan (Baptista Spagnuoli Mantuanus), 87–89, 91, 94, 116, 213n34, 218n18; as Christian successor of Virgil, 87, 94
manuscript culture, 13, 20, 199n37
Manutius, Aldus, 8, 199n36
Marcourt, Antoine, 221n36
Marguerite de Navarre, 99, 103–4; *Heptaméron*, 133; *Miroir de l'âme pécheresse*, 103, 118
Margaret of Austria, 13, 19–20, 23; patronage of and disputes with Lemaire, 13, 20, 22, 43, 76, 77, 209n40; quatrain to Lemaire attached to *Épîtres de l'Amant Vert*, 49–50, 206n63; subject or dedicatee of Lemaire's works, 19, 25, 41, 47, 51
Marnef, Geoffroy de, 53, 206n1
Marot, Clément, 13–15, 19, 139–40, 144, 168, 188; adaptability of, 132, 134–35, 210n3; authorial personae of, 82–85, 105, 110, 128–29, 132–35; bout with the plague, 96, 102–4, 106, 118–19, 130; career trajectory according to different editions, 84–85, 93–99, 100–110, 117–19; as *dépourvu*, 216n74; Dolet as first printer and dedicatee of Marot's *Œuvres* (1538), 82, 123–30; claim to authority over publication of his works, 87, 91–92, 116–17; editor of Jean Marot and Villon, 82–83, 111, 210n4; evangelical leanings, 14, 82, 83, 91, 99, 103–10, 119, 130–35, 183; exile in Ferrara and Venice, 110, 121–22, 220n31; as French Virgil, 83, 94, 101, 114, 213n36; Juste's editions of, 103–6, 110, 121–22, 216n71; ideal readership in, 85, 91–93, 123–24, 129; Anne de Montmorency, presentation manuscript for, 111, 115–17, 217n78, 221n42; motto ("La mort n'y mord"), 104, 121, 216n67; Paris in work of, 109; popularity of, 83–84; Psalm translations, 14, 98, 118, 130, 218n16; royal poet of Francis I, 14, 83, 99, 101, 104, 108, 110, 119, 139; self-fashioning in, 83. See also *Adolescence clementine, L'*; *Œuvres*; *Opuscules*; *Suite de l'Adolescence clementine*
Marot, Jean, 82, 130–31, 201n57
Mars, 26, 62, 66, 73, 164
Marsyas, 176
masculinity, 14, 25–26, 29, 31, 68, 182–83; exemplarity linked to in Lemaire, 26, 42, 45, 56, 68–69
Maximilian I, 13, 22
Mayer, Claude, 83–84, 222n2
McGrady, Deborah, 36, 48
Melanchthon, Philip, 7
Menini, Romain, 15, 149, 231n30, 231n39
Menippean paradox, 183
Mephitis, 146
Mercury, 34, 156, 179, 226n43; association with Hermes Trismegistus, 155; attributes, 31, 37; in Boccaccio and Fulgentius, 31, 41, 64; god of commerce, 64; god of eloquence and rhetoric, 31, 32, 33, 41; narrator of prologues in *Illustrations*, 25, 37, 41–42, 47; guides Amant Vert through afterlife, 47, 51; relationship with Genius in *Concorde des deux langages*, 64
Merovingians, 21
Meschinot, Jean, 85, 201n57
Meun, Jean de. See *Roman de la Rose*
Midas, 175–76
Middle Ages, 13, 185, 199n37
Minerva. See Pallas
Minos, 51
mithridate (*metridal*). See treacle
Mithridates VI of Pontus, 139, 142
Molière (Jean-Baptiste Poquelin), 174
Molinet, Jean, 20, 47, 60, 201n57

264 INDEX

Momus, 123–24
Montaigne, Michel de, 15, 137, 159
Montmorency, Anne de, 111; Marot's presentation manuscript for, 111, 115–17, 217n78, 221n42
Muses, 60, 101, 176; Clio (muse of history), 73, 74

Navigations de Panurge, 168, 228n3
Nelson, Lowry, 11
Nicander, 142
Noah, 21, 33
Noirot, Corinne, 213n36
Nourry, Claude, 155

Ockhegem, Johannes, 60
Oenone, 25, 62
Œuvres (Marot), 14–15, 85, 108, 113, 215n61; dedicatory epistle to Dolet, 127–30, 169; basis for Defaux's edition of Marot's complete works, 82, 220n26; "Chants divers," 131–32; "Cimetiere," 133–35; definitive edition by scholarly consensus, 122; "Epigrammes," 129; "Epistres," 124–25, 130–31; Latin epigraphs, 123, 126; "Marot à son livre," 125–26; order of works in, 123, 129; "Oroisons," 130, 132; preface, 127–30
Opuscules (Marot), 84, 85–86, 87, 89, 91, 212n16
Ottoman Empire, 23, 54, 58, 66
Ovid, 163; Alcofrybas Nasier's name an allusion to, 155; *Amores*, 50, 73; *Heroides*, 47

Pallas, 25, 30, 36–37, 41; associated with France and historical exemplarity by Lemaire, 14, 34, 42, 47, 52, 62; attributes, 31–32; exemplarity linked to in Lemaire, 26, 42, 45, 56, 68–69; masculinizing effects of, 14, 29, 31, 68–69; mythological association with contemplative life, prudence, and virtue, 14, 28–29, 56, 60; Temple of Minerva in *Concorde des deux langages*, 58, 61, 62, 68, 74–76, 229n10; tutelage of Paris, 25, 27, 30–31, 37, 58, 59. See also Judgment of Paris

Pandora, 1, 145
Pantagruel (Rabelais), 15, 140, 171–72; Baisecul and Humevesne, 151–52, 154; Écolier limousin, 152–53, 154, 169; Epistemon's descent into Hell, 182, 229n8; Gargantua's letter to Pantagruel, 150–51, 154–55; Library of Saint-Victor, 153–54; Pantagruel's association with thirst, 15, 153, 201n62; Panurge, 146–47; Giovanni Pico della Mirandola, Pantagruel's similarities to, 150–52; prologue, 147–50, 157, 158, 159, 165, 171, 176–77, 182; Thaumaste, 152–57, 161, 165
pantagruélisme, 165, 171–72; as ideal readership, 165, 173, 178
Paradis, Paul, 119
paratext, 8, 9, 10, 15, 20; Genette's distinction between *péritexte* and *épitexte*, 200n40
Paris (city): *cris de Paris*, 141, 223n8; in Marot, 109; Parlement of Paris, 86; print culture of, 83; in Villon, 82
Paris (Trojan prince), 21, 55; birth of, 26, 56; feminization by Venus and Helen, 29–31, 33, 62–63; similarities with the Amant Vert, 48; similarities with youth in Temple of Venus, 67; virtuous youth under Pallas's tutelage, 25, 27, 30–31, 37, 58, 59. See also Judgment of Paris
Peletier du Mans, Jacques, 21
perplexity, 183
Perréal, Jean, 24, 47–48
Persius, 161
persona: authorial, 8–9, 12–15, 132, 135, 182, 188; editorial or printerly, 8–9, 12, 13, 15, 83, 99–100, 112–15, 120–21, 124–25, 128; etymology, 8; of Lemaire, 21, 24, 34, 36, 46, 47–52, 60–61, 77–78, 81–82, 183; of Marot, 82–85, 105, 110, 128–29, 132–35; of Rabelais, 141, 159, 166, 167–68, 169–77, 177–84; role in rhetorical *captatio benevolentiae*, 8. See also prestige advertising; publicity
Petit, Jean, 87
Petrarch, Francesco, 13, 40, 73, 218n18; *Canzoniere*, 89–90; influence on Lyonnais

literary culture, 24; Lemaire associates with Italy, 14, 24, 33, 52, 62–63; *Trionfi*, 49
Petronius, 133
Phaedrus, 36–37, 41, 45, 204n35
pharmakon, 141, 146
philautia, 157
Philibert II of Savoy, 43
Philip of Macedon, 175
Philistion, 153, 154
Pico della Mirandola, Giovanni, 14, 150; *Apologia*, 152; *Oration on the Dignity of Man*, 11, 83, 150; Pantagruel's similarities to, 150–52
Pius II, 23
Plato, 141, 161; *Symposium*, 159
Plautus, 174
Pléiade, 21
Pliny the Elder, 49, 50–51, 142
Plotinus, 153
Poggio Bracciolini, Gian Francesco, 7, 162, 198n26
Poseidon, 123
Pouey-Mounou, Anne-Pascale, 231n40
Preisig, Florian, 90, 91, 213n40
prestige advertising, 6–8, 12; *captatio benevolentiae* [securing good will], 7–11, 56, 64, 77, 134, 149–50, 158, 173–77, 178; in Lemaire, 40; in Marot, 84, 115, 120, 121, 126, 128, 133; in Rabelais, 140, 171, 173. *See also* advertising; persona; publicity
Priam, 58
Priapeia, 133
Priapus, 96, 133
print culture, 12, 20, 156; anxiety of reception inherent to, 2, 9; authors at odds with printers, 81, 120–21, 127–29, 220n31; commercial risk and cost of printing, 3–4; of Lyon, 83, 85–86, 103, 122, 226n44; of Paris, 83; print runs as gauge of success, 198n14; wider audience afforded by, 82–83
prisca theologia. *See* Hermes Trismegistus
Proclus, 153
Prometheus, 1
prosopopoeia, 176, 179
Ptolemy I Soter, 1, 171, 197n2

publicity, 6–7, 84, 140; *captatio benevolentiae* [securing good will], 7–11, 56, 64, 77, 134, 149–50, 158, 173–77, 178. *See also* advertising; persona
putto, 33, 204n30
Pythagoras, 231n39

Qansou Ghoury (Mamluk sultan), 23
Quart Livre (Rabelais), 140, 168; Dindenault, 149; 1548 prologue, 177–79, 180–81; 1552 preface to Odet de Châtillon, 178; 1552 prologue, 179; Quaresmeprenant, 181
Quintilian, 7, 198n26, 219n18

Rabelais, François, 13, 15, 19, 103, 128, 188; as Alcofrybas Nasier, 146–49, 158–62, 165–66, 176; antidote in, 149, 157–58, 162, 165–66, 177; authorial personae of, 141, 159, 166, 167–68, 169–77, 177–84; author of poems signed "F.R." in unauthorized Marot editions, 104, 216n69; "Calloïer des Isles Hieres" in the *Tiers Livre*, 169, 229n10; change in circumstances between *Gargantua* and *Tiers Livre*, 167; *Chroniques gargantuines* (apocryphal), 147, 155, 156, 157, 159; editorial work with Juste, 105–6, 139, 168, 216n69; evangelical leanings, 156–58, 163–64, 167, 181, 183; farces and *sotties*, use of, 144, 146–50, 152, 154, 155, 158–59, 179; French Lucian, 1, 152; *Geste Pantagruéline*, 15, 139–40, 149, 165–66, 168, 177, 182–83, 222n2; *Grands annales*, 168–69, 228n5; ideal readership in, 140–41, 149–58, 158–66, 173; medical persona starting with the *Tiers Livre*, 140, 158, 166, 169–84, 185; *Pantagrueline Prognostication*, 168; self-fashioning in, 140, 150–58, 158–66, 180, 182–84; unauthorized editions, 168–70. *See also Cinquiesme Livre*; *Gargantua*; *Pantagruel*; *pantagruélisme*; *Quart Livre*; *Tiers Livre*
Rajchenbach-Teller, Elise, 46
Ravenna, Battle of, 22, 57
Réach-Ngô, Anne, 211n11
reception theory, 10

recueil-*Epistre* (Lemaire), 22, 24, 45; capitals in, 72; companion piece and advertisement for the *Illustrations*, 54, 55, 120; copy printed on vellum, 72, 209n38; "Epistre du Roy à Hector de Troye," 53, 54–55, 58, 60, 66, 207n5; epitaph of Gaston de Foix, 53, 57–60, 62; historical context of, 53–54; "Plaincte sur le trespas de messire Guillaume de Byssipat" (Crétin), 53, 60–61; "24 coupletz de la valitude et convalescence de la Royne," 53, 56–57. See also *Concorde des deux langages, La*

Reformation, 7, 32, 108, 110; role of Pauline Christianity in, 7, 96, 173, 216n67

Renaissance, 11–12, 13, 15, 19, 185, 188. See also humanism

Renée of France, 110

Renner, Bernd, 110, 140, 175, 183

rhetoric, 7–11, 15, 140, 141, 185, 188; epideictic, 34, 65; *exordium*, 170; first and second, 21, 33–34, 70; *insinuatio*, 170–71, 173, 177; *inventio*, 7, 82, 134; *praesumptio*, 77. See also *captatio benevolentiae*

Rhetorica ad Herennium (pseudo-Cicero), 7, 8, 149, 170, 174

Rhétoriqueurs, 13, 19–20, 29, 65, 75, 85, 183, 201n57, 214n42

Riccio, Michele, 13, 24

Richier, Jean, 34

Rigolot, François, 14, 83, 107, 131, 133, 148, 164, 188, 215n59

rimes équivoquées, 134

Riolan, Jean, 231n40

Robertet, Jean, 201n57

Roffet, Pierre, 86, 99, 103, 104, 106, 112, 120

Rohan, François de, 39

Roman de la Rose (Lorris and Meun), 63–64, 71, 75, 96

Rondelet, Guillaume, 231n40

Ronsard, Pierre de, 15, 21, 174–75, 217n5, 223n13

Roussel, Gérard, 216n70

Rutebeuf, 142

Sagon, François, 110, 144, 217n77

Sainéan, Lazar, 223n8

Saint-Gelais, Mellin de, 82

Saint-Gelais, Octavien de, 85, 201n57

Salel, Hugues, 171

Sappho, 83

Sartre, Jean-Paul, 12, 201n56

Scève, Maurice, 103

Schneider, Lars, 226n44

scholasticism, 152–53, 154, 173

Schwartz, Jerome, 170

Screech, M. A., 162

Sébillet, Thomas, 94, 164–65

self-fashioning, 11–12, 15, 185, 187–88; authorial persona subject to, 83; false freedom of, 78; in Lemaire, 24, 25, 27, 56, 67, 70–71; in Marot, 83; in Rabelais, 140, 150–58, 158–66, 180, 182–84; similarities with modern advertising, 12. See also humanism

Seneca, 218n18

Seyssel, Claude de, 213n40

Shakespeare, William, 77

Sherman, Michael, 20

Silenus, 159, 162

Sirens, 33

Sisyphus, 175

Socrates, 159–60

Sorbonne, 86, 108, 122, 146, 172, 175, 220n31

sottie. See farce

Soubeille, Georges, 114

Spitzer, Leo, 222n2

Statius, 50

Suite de l'Adolescence clementine (Marot), 14, 85, 103, 111; "Le Cimetiere, autrement les epitaphes," 120, 214n51; "Elegies," 115, 117–18; "Epistre à Monseigneur le Grant Maistre de Montmorency," 115–17, 126; "Epistres," 117, 218n9; Latin epigraphs, 112–15, 124, 126; "Menu," 117, 120, 218n10; *princeps* edition, 112–18; unauthorized editions, 118–22, 133, 220n31, 221n33

Suleiman, Susan, 10

Talmud, 150

Tantalus, 201n62

terza rima, 62, 68, 73

Tetzel, Johann, 208n28

theriac. *See* treacle

thériacleur (treacle-seller), in literature, 141–46. *See also* treacle

Thucydides, 213n40

Tiers Livre (Rabelais), 1–3, 140–41, 166, 181–83, 220n27; Nazdecabre, 147; prologue, 170–77, 231n37; Raminagrobis, 183

Tory, Geoffroy, 86, 90–91, 99–100, 112, 215n59; *Champ Fleury*, 90, 92–93, 100, 161, 214n42

Tournes, Jean de, 46

Tournon, André, 165

Tours, Pierre de, 168, 228n5

translatio studii, 50, 55, 63, 114

treacle, 141–42; in Rabelais, 141, 146–49, 150, 158, 166, 170, 177, 183; synonymous with mithridate (*metridal*), 142; *thériacleur* (treacle-seller) in literature, 141–46. *See also* antidote

Trojan War. *See* Troy

Troy, 14, 21, 23, 26, 54; House of, 21; Lyon as new Troy in the *Concorde des deux langages*, 63; myth of French as descendants of Trojans, 21, 59, 65, 175; Trojan War, 14, 23. *See also* Hector; Helen of Troy; Judgment of Paris; Paris (Trojan prince); Priam

Turks. *See* Ottoman Empire

Valéry, Paul, 200n44

varietas, 91, 134

Vatable, François, 119

Venice, 19; Lemaire's criticism of, 19, 23; role in the Italian Wars, 19

Venus, 1–2, 26–27, 41, 42, 56; Amant Vert's devotion to, 48, 51; associated with Italy and Petrarchism by Lemaire, 14, 24, 33, 52, 62–63; feminizing effects on Paris, 29–31, 62–63; Ficino's two Venuses, 25, 68; mythological association with life of pleasure, 14, 27; rhetorical skill of, 21, 32–33, 55, 69–70; Temple of, in *Concorde des deux langages*, 24, 61, 62–68, 73. *See also* Judgment of Paris

Vérard, Antoine, 83

vers senés, 65–66

Vestergaard, Torben, and Kim Schrøder, 6, 12, 160

Vigliano, Tristan, 230n23

Villey, Pierre, 219n19

Villon, François, 82–83, 111

Virgil, 114; *Aeneid*, 42, 47, 51, 99; *Eclogues*, 93–95; Mantuan as Christian successor of, 87, 94; Marot as French Virgil, 83, 94, 101, 114, 213n36

Vulcan, 124

Vuyard, Pierre, 102, 103, 105

Waldensians, 167

Wars of Religion, 167

Wechel, Chrestien, 169

Williams, Raymond, 5–6; history of advertising, 5–6, 185

Williamson, Judith, 12

Xerxes, 182, 229n8

www.ingramcontent.com/pod-product-compliance
Lightning Source LLC
Chambersburg PA
CBHW030436300426
44112CB00009B/1030